MW01225545

Edited by
Rand Morimoto

Microsoft® Windows

Vista®

Management and Administration

SAMS | 800 East 96th Street, Indianapolis, Indiana 46240 USA

ISBN-13: 978-0-672-32961-6
ISBN-10: 0-672-32961-1

Library of Congress Cataloging-in-Publication Data:

Abbate, Andrew.

  Microsoft Windows Vista : management and administration / Andrew Abbate, James Walker, Scott Chimner ; Edited by Rand Morimoto.

     p. cm.

   ISBN 0-672-32961-1

  1. Microsoft Windows (Computer file) 2. Microsoft Windows Vista (Computer file) 3. Operating systems (Computers) I. Walker, James. II. Chimner, Scott. III. Morimoto, Rand. IV. Title.

QA76.76.063.M524768 2007

005.4'46—dc22

                                                2007041863

Printed in the United States of America

First Printing November 2007

Trademarks

All terms mentioned in this book that are known to be trademarks or service marks have been appropriately capitalized. Sams Publishing cannot attest to the accuracy of this information. Use of a term in this book should not be regarded as affecting the validity of any trademark or service mark.

Warning and Disclaimer

Bulk Sales

Sams Publishing offers excellent discounts on this book when ordered in quantity for bulk purchases or special sales. For more information, please contact

   U.S. Corporate and Government Sales
   1-800-382-3419
   corpsales@pearsontechgroup.com

For sales outside of the U.S., please contact

   International Sales
   international@pearsoned.com

Editor-in-Chief
Karen Gettman

Acquisitions Editor
Neil Rowe

Development Editor
Mark Renfrow

Managing Editor
Gina Kanouse

Project Editor
Betsy Harris

Copy Editor
Barbara Hacha

Indexer
Erika Millen

Proofreader
Water Crest Publishing

Technical Editor
Todd Meister

Publishing Coordinator
Cindy Teeters

Book Designer
Gary Adair

Compositor
Nonie Ratcliff

Contents at a Glance

Table of Contents

About the Authors

Andrew Abbate has been in the IT and consulting world for well over 15 years. His experiences in messaging, security, PKI, operational practices, and project management have granted him a unique perspective on how IT works from a "big picture" perspective. Coauthor of half a dozen books on Microsoft technologies and security, Andrew continues to work with San Francisco Bay area companies to improve their infrastructures and enable them to provide services to their users to improve productivity and security.

James Walker, MCSE, CPM, BSME, has been in the information technology industry for more than 20 years and has been a contributing author, technical editor, and technical reviewer for a number of books involving security, electronic messaging, network operating systems, and data communications. He has worked with computers in one form or another since the late 1970s and was an early adopter of Windows since version 1.0 was released in the middle 1980s. As VP Support for Pandora Networks in Sunnyvale, CA, James is involved in the technology selection, design, planning, implementation and migration, and troubleshooting of VoIP telephony, collaboration, and presence IT projects for Fortune 500 companies. After years of supporting Microsoft-based technologies, James uses his experiences as an author, primary technical editor, and contributing author for a number of Sams Publishing technology books, including *Teach Yourself Exchange Server 2003 in 10 Minutes*, *Microsoft Windows Server 2003 Unleashed*, *Microsoft Exchange Server 2003 Unleashed*, *Microsoft Windows Server 2003 Insider Solutions*, and *Microsoft Exchange Server 2003 Delta Guide*, and Addison-Wesley technology books, including *Exchange 2003 Distilled*.

Scott Chimner, CISSP, MCSE, MCSA, TCSE 2, A+, has been in the computer industry for more than 12 years, with a 7-year concentration on information security. Scott's experience ranges from large-scale ethernet cable drops and deploying networked Point-of-Sale (POS) systems for retail stores, to securely migrating offices to Microsoft solutions such as Active Directory and Exchange. Prior to joining CCO as a consultant, Scott administered several networks for a worldwide environmental engineering company and later filled the role of webmaster for a nationwide investment firm. Scott is a seasoned expert in security operations with extensive experience in system hardening, incident response, and managing network defenses. Scott has designed and implemented anti-malware, antivirus, and host intrusion prevention, and anti-spam and email filtering solutions. Scott is an ISSA member and has served as a contributing writer for books on Microsoft Exchange 2007 and Windows Server 2008.

Dedication

I dedicate this book to my parents. A long time ago they gave me a piece of advice that has always stuck with me: "Pick a job you love, because if you love what you do—you'll be good at it. If you're good at it, success will follow."

—Andrew Abbate

I would like to dedicate this book to Anne, my beautiful wife, and to Malcolm and Nellie, my exceptional parents. Thank you for your loving support and guidance throughout this project!

—James Walker

I dedicate this, my first book, to my wife, Heather, and my son, Reese, who always selflessly support and encourage me to succeed, regardless of all the "crazy projects" I continue to undertake.

—Scott G. Chimner

Acknowledgments

Andrew Abbate:

Although I've coauthored books before, this is the first one where I was on the hook for the other coauthors. As such, I'd like to acknowledge James and Scott, my coauthors, for their exceptional efforts in getting this one done. They were both a joy to work with and a wealth of knowledge. I can't thank them enough for being involved in this one.

I'd also like to thank all the great folks at Sams/Pearson for their efforts. I've worked with them in the past and hope to continue to work with them in the future. They allow us "techie" guys to do the techie side of things and they massage it into something that's beautifully organized and exceptionally well presented. Thanks again!

I also can't get away without thanking friends and family for being supportive of me all those times I had to pass on plans in order to "work on the book." Thanks for being there and not giving me too hard a time about it.

James Walker:

Although my name is highlighted on the front of the book, many people worked very hard in getting this book published. Without the monumental efforts of the entire editorial and production team at Sams, this book would not have come together as nicely as it has. THANK YOU for your hard work and support to get this book finished. All books projects should run this smoothly. It was truly a pleasure working with you.

A special thanks to Neil Rowe for providing me the opportunity to write this book; looking forward to many more book projects!

Thanks again to Anne, my wife, for gently pushing me when I didn't feel like writing. Without her support, I would still be writing!

A special thanks to Scott Chimner and Andrew Abbate, my coauthors, for their patience and persistence and "not so gentle" pushing while writing this book project. Their extra eyes and ears made a big difference to the technical content written in this book!

An extra thanks to Scott Chimner for keeping me awake on many a late night when writing! Or was it vice versa?

Finally, thanks to my extended network of family, friends, and peers. Your enthusiasm and encouragement was astounding and provided energy to keep me plugging away. A special thanks to Joe Piette, MCSE and certified Microsoft and Cisco instructor, for reviewing technical topics and asking key questions regarding the book content.

Scott G. Chimner:

First, thank you to Rand Morimoto for always enthusiastically pushing that "can do" attitude and for being a pillar of support in so many ways! Many thanks to Chris, Rich, Martha, and the gang at CCO who are excellent to work with and always there to lend a hand! Thank you to Anne and Jim Walker for being awesome friends and for all the late night Vista brainstorming sessions! Huge thanks to Andrew for choosing me to coauthor this text, for your patience, humor, and for being a terrific mentor!

Thank you to Neil Rowe for this wonderful opportunity and to everyone else at Sam's Publishing for all the hard work that goes into making these books successful! I look forward to working with you on many more!

Last, a special thank you to all my family and extended family: Mom, Grandma, Sarah, Bones, Dad, Amy, Mike, Bonnie, Pete, Samantha, and everyone else back in Michigan for everything you do and for pretending to be interested in all of this "computer stuff." You make trips back home seem like we never left.

We Want to Hear from You!

As the reader of this book, *you* are our most important critic and commentator. We value your opinion and want to know what we're doing right, what we could do better, what areas you'd like to see us publish in, and any other words of wisdom you're willing to pass our way.

You can email or write me directly to let me know what you did or didn't like about this book—as well as what we can do to make our books stronger.

Please note that I cannot help you with technical problems related to the topic of this book, and that due to the high volume of mail I receive, I might not be able to reply to every message.

When you write, please be sure to include this book's title and author as well as your name and phone number or email address. I will carefully review your comments and share them with the authors and editors who worked on the book.

E-mail: feedback@samspublishing.com

Mail: Neil Rowe
           Senior Acquisitions Editor
           Sams Publishing
           800 East 96th Street
           Indianapolis, IN 46240 USA

Reader Services

Visit our website and register this book at
www.informit.com/title/9780672329616 for convenient access to any
updates, downloads, or errata that might be available for this book.

Introduction

Over the years, we've written numerous books on applications, operating systems, messaging systems, and security products. All that time we were intimately aware of the fact that there was a lack of focus on how the desktop operating system was involved in these other items. As such, when we were approached with the idea of a Microsoft Vista book that was focused on management and administration, we immediately found our outlet for sharing concepts of how the desktop was involved in the larger Information Technology picture.

Vista brought with it a lot of controversy over where it was drawing the line between security and user convenience. Early adopters often let the lack of third-party driver support overshadow the breakthroughs that Vista was bringing with it. IT workers were understandably concerned about how existing systems would interact with Vista and how they would fold Vista into their existing compliance and security rules.

This book is intended to help those IT personnel integrate Vista into their existing environment as well as help those who are starting from scratch and want to begin with the "latest, greatest" operating system from our friends in Redmond.

This book is organized so that topics can easily be looked up and a complete set of instructions found for implementing or understanding a particular function. Each chapter is meant to stand on its own but will often reference another chapter for further information on a particular topic.

It is the wish of the authors that readers gather not only a basic set of how-to instructions but that they additionally receive advice and recommendations based on the experiences of using and deploying Vista in real production environments.

The book is organized into seven parts, with each part containing related chapters:

Part I: Windows Vista Health Check

- **Chapter 1, "Windows Vista Technology Primer"**—This chapter is an introductory chapter to Windows Vista and covers the basic functions of Vista, such as what's new and different compared to Windows XP, the different versions of Vista (Home, Business, Enterprise, Ultimate), features that are focused toward business productivity, features that are focused toward home entertainment, and so on.

- **Chapter 2, "Getting to Understand Your Windows Vista System"**—This chapter provides a step-by-step guide on how to do an assessment on a Windows Vista system relative to which version of Vista is installed, performance metrics on how the system is operating, configuration settings on key components such as auto update and firewall functions, how to determine the User Account Control setting for the user, and so on. The goal of this chapter is to provide the reader with the ability to assess a system configuration (that is, creating a baseline understanding) so that functionality can be added or modified to meet the needs of the user and/or organization. This chapter also covers the Windows Shell options (classic versus Vista), the ability to restrict configurations, force prompting, and control functions such as item sharing, PC to PC sharing, and folder redirection.

- **Chapter 3, "Understanding Windows Vista Performance Optimization"**—This chapter provides an in-depth view on assessing the characteristics of a system relative to performance, such as how much memory the system has and how much disk space is in the system. It provides recommendations on how to tune, optimize, or even assess a user's needs so that an appropriate system can be purchased to meet the requirements of the user. This includes doing a system requirements assessment on the applications, tasks, and functions of a user's applications to determine appropriate configuration needs. Also included is the assessment of where 64-bit Windows comes into play regarding a user's requirements.

Part II: Security for Windows Vista Systems

- **Chapter 4, "Securing a Windows Vista System"**—This chapter focuses on basic Windows Vista security, such as password protection, Internet Explorer protected mode hardening, Windows Defender,

Windows Firewall, Windows malicious software removal tool, and so on. Also included in this chapter are topics on Device Installation Control and Network Access Protection.

■ **Chapter 5, "Patching and Keeping Windows Vista Up-to-Date"**— This chapter focuses on the basics of patching and keeping a Windows Vista system up-to-date, such as the use of auto updates as well as internal and network-based patching and updating options that turn passive (pull) updates into a more active (push) update process.

■ **Chapter 6, "Using User Account Control to Establish System Security"**—This chapter covers the new User Account Control (UAC) privileges, what rights the Standard, Standard with Admin Password, Admin Approval with Restricted Elevation, and Admin Approval roles provide, how to configure different UAC levels, how to apply UAC to different users, and how to delegate privileges to administrators to temporarily elevate user rights.

■ **Chapter 7, "Implementing BitLocker Drive Encryption to Improve Data Privacy"**—This chapter focuses on BitLocker and the capability to encrypt the content of a system's hard drive. This topic covers the installation, configuration, best practice management, and recovery of lost keys for the operation of BitLocker. Also covered are the capability to do automated key backup to Active Directory, Group Policy integration to support BitLocker, and the capability to wipe keys and repurpose systems.

Part III: Windows Vista Mobility

■ **Chapter 8, "Configuring and Using Offline Files"**—This chapter focuses on offline files and the capability for a user to configure files for offline access, the proper synchronization of files, how offline files work with server shares, personal shares, encrypted content, and DFS replicated content, as well as how to manage offline files and folders. This chapter also addresses the uniform namespace found with the "ghosting" functionality of cached files and cache encryption.

■ **Chapter 9, "Configuring Mobile Functionality in Windows Vista"**—This chapter covers the basic functions of mobility for a Windows Vista system, such as configuring basic wireless access settings, mobile to mobile device sync, basic VPN settings, and so on.

■ **Chapter 10, "Creating a Secured Mobile Communications Configuration"**—This chapter covers the setup and installation of mobility functions on a Windows Vista system, such as configuration of PEAP-TLS, WPA2, 802.1x, EAP-TLS, L2TP, IPSec, and other secured communications for mobile systems. Also covered are the setup of Radius servers, wireless group policies, and user and computer authentication for secured communications.

Part IV: Backup and Recovery of Information

- **Chapter 11, "Using Shadow Copy to Recover Lost or Damaged Files"**—This chapter focuses on the configuration, use, and recovery of files using the Shadow Copy function. This includes creating snapshots of data, sharing folder content, and recovering files.

- **Chapter 12, "Backing Up and Recovering Windows Vista Information"**—This chapter focuses on the basic backup and restore function built in to Windows Vista, using the basic Windows Backup utility. Covered in this chapter are Volume Shadow Copy Service, backup to optical media (UDFS), and the use of the Windows Recovery Environment for offline repair or restore.

- **Chapter 13, "Using the Complete PC Backup Utility"**—This chapter expands on the backup function of Windows Vista and covers the Complete PC backup and restore options for block-level backup to local and remote devices for better administrative control of data for centralized backup and remote restores. This chapter covers Windows Recovery Environment (Windows RE), and the use of the VHD format.

- **Chapter 14, "Microsoft Vista System Restore"**—This chapter focuses on the System Restore capability of Windows Vista that allows for the full rollback of an entire system. This includes incremental recovery of data from block level increments and picking restore points for recovery.

Part V: Managing Vista

- **Chapter 15, "Setting Up Users and Computers in Windows Vista"**—This chapter focuses on the best practices, tips, and tricks at configuring users, user accounts, computer settings, and basic day-to-day administration of Windows Vista.

- **Chapter 16, "Establishing Printer Management in Windows Vista"**—This chapter focuses on Printer Management in Windows Vista, such as the capability to deploy printers to machines and users using policies, per-machine shared use configurations, per-user configurations where printers follow users, rollout of trusted printer drivers, preventing and allowing the installation of trusted printer devices only, and the delegation of printer installation rights.

■ **Chapter 17, "Troubleshooting Windows Vista"**—This chapter focuses on common issues that can occur with Vista and how to troubleshoot them. It will introduce the new tools available in Vista to troubleshoot problems with the operating system itself.

■ **Chapter 18, "Using Internet Explorer 7"**—This chapter focuses on the new features of Internet Explorer 7 and will help administrators prepare their users for the transition from older versions of Internet Explorer to the current version.

Part VI: Deploying Vista

■ **Chapter 19, "Creating Windows Vista Images"**—This chapter will focus on the new image-creation tools for Vista.

■ **Chapter 20, "Imaging Tools and Processes"**—This chapter demonstrates ways to deploy Vista in an automated fashion. This includes systems that will be recycled as well as "net new" machines.

■ **Chapter 21, "Deploying Windows Vista in an Automated Fashion"**—This chapter demonstrates how to properly upgrade an existing XP system to Vista and shows the pros and cons of upgrading versus replacing.

Part VII: Windows Vista in an Active Directory Environment

■ **Chapter 22, "Understanding Group Policy Basics to Manage Windows Vista Systems"**—This chapter focuses on the basic group policies new in Windows Vista, including device installation and usage, Internet Explorer policies that are now exposed to GPOs, IPSec and firewall policies, UAC, Defender, Remote Assist, Terminal Services, globalization support, shell, tablet, and other GPO options. This chapter covers not only what the policies are but how a network administrator sets policies at the Active Directory level and applies policies to Windows Vista devices.

■ **Chapter 23, "Expanding on the Use of Group Policies to Better Manage Windows Vista Systems"**—This chapter goes beyond the basics of group policies and addresses the new search and filter functionality, use of Group Policy templates, use of WMI for expanded policy support, and so on.

The real-world experience we have had in working with Microsoft Vista and our commitment to writing this book based on the combined years of field experience in early adopter environments allows us to bring you information that we genuinely hope will benefit you in planning for and implementing Microsoft Vista in your environments.

Conventions Used in This Book

Code lines, commands, statements, and any other code-related terms appear in a monospace typeface. Placeholders (which stand for what you should actually type) appear in italic monospace. When a line of code is too long to fit on one line of text, we wrap it to the next line and precede the continuation with a code-continuation arrow. For example:

```
SYSTEMINFO [/S system [/U username [/P [password]]]]
➥[/FO format] [/NH]
```

This book uses several extra elements:

Note

Notes give extra information on the current topic.

Tip

Tips offer advice or describe an additional way of accomplishing something.

Caution

Cautions signal you to be careful of potential problems and give you information on how to avoid or fix them.

PART I

Windows Vista Health Check

IN THIS PART

CHAPTER 1

Windows Vista Technology Primer

Introduction to Windows Vista

Microsoft Windows Vista is the most significant rollout of the Windows operating system since Windows 95. Windows Vista is different from previous versions of Windows from login to logout. The new operating system with its subsystem and driver model enhancements is a major improvement over its predecessor, Windows XP, in terms of Vista's stability and usability for future Windows versions. The revolutionary architecture of Windows Vista changes the way users work with and manage data on their computers. Key architecture changes include changes to user account controls and privileges, preinstallation and preboot environments, and modularization and disk imaging. All these modifications are meant to improve the user experience in regard to usability, such as finding documents, email messages, applications, or configuration settings. Security is also enhanced with improvements to User Account Control to help prevent installation of prohibited applications and system protection against spyware and malware, with improved versions of Windows Defender and Windows Firewall.

Understanding Windows Vista Versions

Microsoft Windows Vista is the latest release of the Windows operating system and is designed to dramatically improve the computing experience of every kind of PC user—from people at home who use their PCs for simple web browsing, to business people who must organize and act on large volumes of data, to engineers and designers who routinely perform complex mathematical analysis. To meet the specific needs of the broad range of users, Microsoft will deliver five editions of Windows Vista. Each edition is geared toward the needs of a specific type of person. The five editions of Windows Vista available are the following:

- **Windows Vista Home Basic**—A budget version of Windows Vista meant for home users with basic computing needs. This version includes a basic set of entertainment features but does not include the capability to join a domain.

- **Windows Vista Home Premium**—An enhanced version of Windows Vista meant for home users with elevated computing needs. This version includes an enhanced set of entertainment features but does not include the capability to join a domain.

- **Windows Vista Business**—A basic version of Windows Vista for business users. This version includes a basic set of management tools and the capability to join a domain.

- **Windows Vista Enterprise**—An enhanced version of Windows Vista for business users. This version includes an advanced set of management features and the capability to join a domain.

- **Windows Vista Ultimate**—An enhanced version of Windows Vista that contains all the advanced infrastructure features of a business-focused operating system, all the management and efficiency features of a mobility-focused operating system, and all the digital entertainment features of a consumer-focused operating system. This version also allows joining a domain.

Note

Windows Vista Starter, a budget version of Windows Vista, is meant for emerging markets and is designed for first-time PC users. Windows Vista Starter is easy to learn and includes help features tailored to beginner users. Windows Vista Starter is not currently scheduled to be available in the United States, Canada, the European Union, Australia, New Zealand, or other high-income markets as defined by the World Bank. Features and functions for Windows Vista Starter Edition are not covered in the scope of this book.

Understanding Windows User Experience (UX)

Windows Vista introduces a breakthrough user experience and is designed to help users feel confident in their ability to view, find, and organize information and to control their computing experience.

The visual style of Windows Vista helps streamline the computing experience by refining common window elements so users can better focus on the content on the screen rather than on how to access it. The desktop experience is more informative, intuitive, and helpful. New tools bring better clarity to the information on the computer, allowing users to see what their files contain without opening them, find applications and files instantly, navigate efficiently among open windows, and use wizards and dialog boxes with added confidence.

Windows Vista provides the following four levels of user experience:

- **Windows Classic**—Provides a Windows 2000 look and feel, yet preserves the functionality of Windows Vista. This level of user experience is available on any version of Windows Vista and requires just the core Windows Vista system requirements.

- **Windows Vista Basic**—Provides the basic user experience for entry-level desktop systems (see Figure 1.1). The interface is upgraded when compared to earlier version of Windows. The Start menu allows instant search capability and easy access to programs; live icons reveal their contents, preview panes, reading panes, new wizards, diagrams, and dialog boxes. This level of user experience is available on any version of Windows Vista and requires just the core Windows Vista system requirements.

- **Windows Standard**—Provides improved performance and reliability to the basic user experience. This experience level is perfect for mid-level computers equipped with graphics hardware that supports the Windows Driver Display Model (WDDM). The Standard experience uses the WDDM graphics technology to enable smoother window handling, enhanced stability, and a reduction in display glitches while refreshing. This level of experience can be used with any version of Windows Vista, except for the Starter version, and requires the same level of hardware as Windows Aero.

- **Windows Aero**—Provides the highest level of visual design and enhanced dynamic effects to the Standard user experience (see Figure 1.2). These new enhancements allow the user to experience user interface essentials such as transparent glass, live taskbar icons and thumbnails, the Windows Flip 3D, and Flip views. The Windows Aero user experience includes additional benefits, such as improved productivity (real-time thumbnail previews, new 3D task switching, interface scaling), enhanced visual quality (fast and effective window redrawing), and visual aesthetics (translucent window frames and taskbar, enhanced transitional effects). Windows Aero is available only in Home Premium, Business, Enterprise, and Ultimate versions of Windows Vista.

FIGURE 1.1
Viewing the Windows Vista Basic graphical user interface.

FIGURE 1.2
Viewing the Windows Vista Aero graphical user interface.

As noted previously, each level of user experience builds on the features of the previous version and is dependent on the Windows Vista version and the computer's hardware.

Understanding Windows Vista Hardware Requirements

As with previous versions of Windows, Windows Vista has more stringent hardware requirements to maximize the user experience and provide added functionality. However, unlike previous versions of Windows, hardware requirements vary for the different releases of Windows Vista. In some cases, actual hardware requirements will vary, depending on system configuration and on the programs and the features that are installed. Before purchasing and installing Windows Vista, be sure to determine whether the company computers meet the requirements for processing power in megahertz (MHz) or gigahertz (GHz), graphical display memory in megabytes (MB), and physical memory in megabytes (MB). The next sections discuss minimum and recommended hardware specifications.

Minimum Hardware Specifications

The following list describes the recommended minimum hardware requirements for basic functionality of the different editions of Windows Vista. Actual hardware requirements will vary, depending on system configuration and on the programs and the features that you install. If you install Windows Vista over a network, additional hard disk space may be required. Computer systems that meet the minimum hardware specifications can run all versions of Windows Vista's core features, such as innovations in organizing and finding information, security, and reliability.

The minimum hardware specifications for Microsoft Vista Home Basic are as follows:

- 800 megahertz (MHz) 32-bit (x86) processor or 800MHz 64-bit (x64) processor
- 512 megabytes (MB) of system memory
- DirectX 9-class graphics card
- 32MB of graphics memory
- 20 gigabyte (GB) hard disk that has 15GB of free hard disk space
- Internal or external DVD drive

- Internet access capability
- Audio output capability

The minimum hardware specifications for Microsoft Vista Home Premium, Microsoft Vista Business, Microsoft Vista Enterprise, and Microsoft Vista Ultimate are

- 1 gigahertz (GHz) 32-bit (x86) processor or 1GHz 64-bit (x64) processor
- 1GB of system memory
- Windows Aero-capable graphics card
- 128MB of graphics memory that supports DirectX 9 or later
- 40GB hard disk with 15GB of free hard disk space (temporary file storage during the install or upgrade)
- Internal or external DVD drive
- Internet access capability
- Audio output capability

Note

A Windows Aero-capable graphics card must meet specific hardware specifications. Be sure that the video card meets the following requirements:

- Windows Display Driver Model (WDDM) driver support
- DirectX 9-class graphics processor unit (GPU) that supports the following:
  - Pixel Shader 2.0 and 32 bits per pixel
  - Passes the Windows Aero acceptance test in the Windows Driver Kit

---

Administrators who are unsure if their computers are Vista compatible can run the Windows Vista Upgrade Advisor on individual machines to learn which version of Windows Vista can successfully be installed on the computer. This software tool will scan a computer and create a report of all known system, device, and program compatibility issues and recommend ways to resolve the issues. In addition, Upgrade Advisor will report if the hardware is not sufficient to run any version of Windows Vista. The Upgrade Advisor can be downloaded at www.microsoft.com/windowsvista/getready/upgradeadvisor/default.mspx.

Recommended Hardware Specifications

As with prior versions of Windows, Microsoft provides a different set of hardware specifications that are needed to experience all the features and functions available in Windows Vista. The following list describes the recommended hardware requirements from Microsoft for enhanced functionality of the different editions of Windows Vista. Actual hardware requirements will vary, depending on system configuration and on the programs and the features that you install. If you install Windows Vista over a network, additional hard disk space may be required.

Computer systems that meet the recommended hardware will be capable of running all versions of Windows Vista core features, such as innovations in organizing and finding information, security, and reliability. These systems will also provide an even better Windows Vista experience with the Windows Aero graphical user interface, such as translucent, glasslike interface elements, live taskbar thumbnails, and Windows Flip 3D.

The recommended hardware specifications for Microsoft Vista Home Premium, Microsoft Vista Business, Microsoft Vista Enterprise, and Microsoft Vista Ultimate are

- 1 gigahertz (GHz) 32-bit (x86) processor or 1GHz 64-bit (x64) processor
- 1GB of system memory
- Windows Aero-capable graphics card
- 128MB of graphics memory that supports DirectX 9 or later
- 40GB hard disk with 15GB of free hard disk space (temporary file storage during the install or upgrade)
- Internal or external DVD drive
- Internet access capability
- Audio output capability

Note

A Windows Aero-capable graphics card must meet specific hardware specifications. Be sure that the video card meets the following requirements:

- Windows Display Driver Model (WDDM) driver support
- DirectX 9-class graphics processor unit (GPU) that supports the following:
  - Pixel Shader 2.0 and 32 bits per pixel
  - Passes the Windows Aero acceptance test in the Windows Driver Kit

---

Tip

The Windows Vista experience is really based on the amount of hardware available to the Vista OS. If you want the best user experience in Windows Vista, make sure your hardware is the best it can be. To do so, consider the following alternative hardware specifications:

- 2.5GHz Intel-compatible "P4 generation" processor or better (which includes the newer, lower-clocked Core Solos and Duos)
- 2GB of system memory (RAM)
- A Windows Aero-capable graphics card with 256MB of graphics memory that supports DirectX 9 or later
- 200GB hard disk with a drive speed of 7200RPM or greater

Understanding Productivity Features

The Windows Vista user experience depends on the performance level of the system hardware. Aside from the hardware requirements, there are common features within Windows Vista that are available in all versions of Windows, whereas other features are targeted only to business users or to consumer users. This section looks at the OS function and features common to all users of Windows Vista. The following sections will explore features and functions targeted at business users and consumer users.

Users expect a lot from their computers. Their computers are used for accessing, searching, and sharing information from a variety of sources. Where sharing and communication of information between systems was once localized, delivery of information is now worldwide, instantly, at a user's fingertips. The prevalence of communication has made information sharing risky as well. By design, Windows Vista is ready to deliver a new user experience that is informative, intuitive, helpful, and secure. Following is a brief look at some of the features that combine to create a breakthrough computer experience for Windows Vista users:

- **User Experience**—Windows Vista provides a streamlined user interface with refined common window features that allow the user to focus on using the information on the screen rather than trying to retrieve it.

- **Security**—New security features, such as User Account Control, Windows Defender for spyware and malware protection, Automatic Updates, and the new Windows Security Center for the latest security patches, set a new standard for PC security.

- **Search and Organization**—New controls such as the Enhanced Column Headers and the Instant Search box make it easy to search, organize, and manage large amounts of onscreen data.

- **Internet Explorer 7**—The new IE7 Protected Mode feature, along with tabbed browsing, live previews, and shrink-to-fit printing, makes finding and delivering information easy, safe, and secure.

- **Sidebar and Gadgets**—The Windows Sidebar boosts personal productivity by providing instant access to gadgets and easy-to-use, customizable miniapplications offering easily accessible tools and information.

- **Performance**—New features such as Windows SuperFetch (memory management), Windows ReadyBoost (performance boost via flash drives), and Windows ReadyDrive (utilizing hybrid hard drives integrated with flash drives) helps productivity by improving battery life, system performance, and reliability.

- **Windows Backup**—New features such as Windows Backup and Previous Versions provide protection against data loss from user error, hardware failure, or software-related issues.

- **Networking**—New features such as Network Center and Network Map provide computer-to-network connectivity information in a graphical representation. If a PC on the network loses Internet connectivity, Network Diagnostics can determine the cause of the problem and provide a potential solution.

- **Windows SideShow**—The new Windows Vista SideShow platform enables hardware manufacturers to build auxiliary displays in a wide range of peripheral devices, such as keyboards, LCD display casings, remote controls, and cell phones. This feature saves users time and battery life by providing quick access to key information such as appointments, emails, or notes—without turning on the laptop.

- **Speech Recognition**—A new feature in Windows Vista enables users to interact with the computer using their voices. Using voice commands, users can start and stop applications, control the Vista operating system, or dictate documents and email.

- **Help and Feedback**—Windows Vista itself detects, diagnoses, and helps you respond to common problems. Also, when necessary, Windows Vista provides centralized support tools, such as Remote Assistance, to quickly diagnose and resolve issues.

■ **Windows Update**—An improved version of Windows Update automatically keeps the computer up-to-date and more secure by providing software updates to the Vista operating system.

Exploring Business User Features

Some of the new technologies in Windows Vista are targeted at addressing issues that impact organizations, helping users to be more productive and drive business success. Windows Vista will help users collaborate and communicate more effectively by easily connecting them to corporate resources, to the Internet, and to each other, regardless of their physical locations. In addition, Windows Vista will also help businesses lower costs, improve system security, and comply with regulatory requirements. The new and improved business user features are the following:

■ **Security**—Windows Vista includes key security features such as User Account Control to prevent unauthorized application installations, Windows Service Hardening to prevent file system and Registry changes, Brower Security with Internet Explorer 7 Protected Mode, Windows Firewall to control rogue programs, and Network Access Protection, which prevents systems that do not meet internal system health policies from connecting and infecting other systems with malware.

■ **Mobile PCs**—Mobile computing has never been easier than with Windows Vista. New power-management features provide greater control over power options and system battery life. The Windows Mobility Center, discussed in Chapter 9, "Configuring Mobile Functionality in Windows Vista," contains key mobile computing-related settings in one easy-to-locate place. The new Windows Vista Sync Center provides one place where users can manage data synchronization for multiple PCs, between network servers and PCs, and with externally connected devices.

■ **Sharing and Collaboration**—Windows Vista helps you more easily share files, folders, and computers. A new Sharing Wizard helps users specify other users to share information with. Formerly Windows Collaboration, Windows Meeting Space allows groups to instantly and securely form a shared, common session for up to 10 people. The capability to share files, programs, or something as simple as a desktop, anytime or anywhere, makes group collaboration a snap.

- **Faxing and Scanning**—New enhancements in Windows Fax and Scan provide complete document-handling and communications capabilities. Integrated with improved scanning capability, Windows Fax and Scan supports scanning of documents from both local or network-connected scanners and multifunction print/scan/fax devices.

- **Built-in Diagnostics**—Although Windows Vista is more reliable than Windows XP, system problems may still occur. To reduce the frequency and impact of disruptions, Windows Vista can self-diagnose a number of common problems, including failing hard disks, memory problems, and networking issues. Built-in Diagnostics provides automatic diagnosis and correction for common error conditions and helps to protect data when failures occur. For example, the Built-in Diagnostics feature in Windows Vista will warn users of impending hard drive failures and provide advice for corrective action before data is lost. In the worst case, a new Startup Repair technology provides step-by-step diagnostics to guide users through recovery and minimize data loss if a computer will not start up.

- **Data Protection**—With increasingly mobile workforces, companies' sensitive data is at risk if a laptop is lost or stolen. Windows Vista includes both software and hardware solutions for protecting against data loss and unauthorized access. Encrypting File System provides user-level file and folder encryption to protect data. BitLocker Drive encryption, new to Windows Vista, is a hardware-enabled data protection that encrypts the entire Windows file system and prevents data from being compromised on lost or stolen PCs. Additionally, Windows Vista includes the capability to restrict the use of removable storage devices such as Universal Serial Bus (USB) flash drives with corporate computers.

Exploring Consumer User Features

Windows Vista delivers better personal productivity and digital entertainment for consumer PCs through its improved reliability, security, and performance. Windows Vista helps home users accomplish tasks faster, with a rich new interface and new ways to organize and find the information stored on their PCs. Windows Vista includes the tools and entertainment features necessary to incorporate a family PC as an integral part of the home entertainment experience.

■ **Family Safety Settings**—Windows Vista makes it simple for parents to control their children's experiences at the computer. With the new Family Safety Settings, parents can limit computer time, access to certain programs and games, and restrict content viewed or downloaded from the Web. Parents can also view reports that detail their children's computer activities.

■ **Windows Mail**—Windows Mail is the latest version of its "free" email client. It is the successor to Outlook Express and builds on the foundation of Outlook Express. Windows Mail adds an assortment of new features designed to make the email experience more productive and fun, while helping reduce risks and annoyances such as phishing and junk email.

■ **Windows Calendar**—Windows Calendar is a flexible, easy-to-use calendar built directly into the Windows Vista operating system. It allows users flexibility in coordinating and scheduling events with peers, family, or friends. Windows Calendar includes all the features needed to manage personal schedules, such as personal task lists, task notifications, and appointment reminders.

■ **Windows Photo Gallery**—Windows Photo Gallery provides home users with the tools needed to organize, find, and view family photos and home videos. Home users can save, edit, print, and share photos with peers, family, and friends. Providing a complete solution for photo and video management, Windows Vista facilitates transferring photo data from camera to PC with a simple import process.

■ **Windows Media Player**—The latest version of Windows Media Player is incorporated into Windows Vista. Windows Media Player 11 is an easy way to enjoy, organize, and manage digital information such as videos, music, and pictures on the PC.

■ **Windows Movie Maker**—With the latest Windows Vista edition of Windows Movie Maker, home users can easily import, edit, and organize all their digital home videos. With new tools, such as new effects and transitions and improved graphics performance, home users can manage and edit their home videos like professionals.

■ **Windows Media Center**—Windows Media Center in Windows Vista makes it easier than ever for home users to find, play, and manage their digital photos and home movies on their PC or TV. Optimized for the latest in widescreen and high definition display technology, Windows

Media Center using Windows Media Extenders (included in Xbox 360) systems can display digital entertainment on up to five additional displays.

■ **Gaming**—Consumer gaming has never been so convenient. Windows Vista contains enhancements that make managing, accessing, and playing games easy. The Games folder is located directly on the Start menu, and thumbnail graphics display game information, such as publisher, developer, version owned, the last time the game was played, game release, rating, and genre. Another nice feature is support for the universal controller so that home users can use the same controller for their Xbox 360 and their PC.

■ **Windows Easy Transfer**—Using a data transfer wizard, Windows Vista makes transferring personal data easy. Windows Easy Transfer helps home users transfer important data such as files and folders, email messages and settings, contacts, photos, music, and more. Transfer media choices are plentiful and home users can use an Easy Transfer cable, home network, or removable storage devices such as USB drives, CDs, or DVDs.

Running Windows Vista

After Windows Vista is installed on their computers, users can begin to take full advantage of the new technologies and productivity enhancements incorporated into the operating system. Computers running Windows Vista can be part of a workgroup (an associated network of independently managed computers) or of a domain (a group of computers collectively managed by domain controllers and Windows servers). Some aspects of Windows Vista may be different depending on whether a computer is a member of a workgroup or a domain.

Logging On to a Windows Vista System

When the computer is a member of a workgroup, Windows Vista displays a logon screen at startup. If more than one standard user or administrator account has been created, all will be listed on the Log On screen. Logging on is a simple three-step process:

1. Click the account name with which to log on.

2. If the account is password protected, type the account password.

3. Click the arrow button to log on.

When the computer is a member of a domain, Windows Vista displays a blank startup screen after initializing the Vista operating system. Logging on involves a few more steps than a workgroup logon. The logon process is as follows:

1. Press Ctrl+Alt+Del to display the Log On screen. By default, Windows Vista will display the last account to log on to the computer. The user account format will be shown as computer\username or as domain\username.

2. To log on to this account, type the password and then click the arrow.

3. If this is not the account to log on with, click the Switch User button, press Ctrl+Alt+Del, and then click Other User. There are a few more options depending on the type of account being used. If the account is in the default domain, type the username and password. If the account is in a different domain, specify the domain and account name in the format domain*username*; that is, companyabc.com\airjimi. If logging on to the local machine is desired, use .*username*; that is, .\airjimi.

By design, Windows Vista stores user profile date in %SystemDrive%\Users \%UserName% (C:\Users\Airjimi). Within each user profile folder, there are individual folders called personal folders for each person who logs on to the system. Each personal folder contains several additional folders. The folders are as follows:

- **Contacts**—This folder is the default location for storing the user's contacts and contact groups.

- **Desktop**—This folder is the default location for storing the user's desktop.

- **Documents**—This folder is the default location for storing the user's document files.

- **Downloads**—This folder is the default location for storing information downloaded from the Internet.

- **Favorites**—This folder is the default location for storing the user's web browser favorites.

- **Links**—This folder is the default location for storing the user's web browser links.

- **Music**—This folder is the default location for storing the user's music files.

- **Pictures**—This folder is the default location for storing the user's picture files.

- **Searches**—This folder is the default location for storing the user's saved searches.

- **Videos**—This folder is the default location for storing the user's video files.

Using the Welcome Center

The Welcome Center provides new users of Windows Vista easy access to configuration tasks such as viewing computer details, transferring files and settings, managing user accounts, setting up devices, and personalizing Windows. As shown in Figure 1.3, the Welcome Center also contains a variety of offers and other downloads available from Microsoft. Some of the offers are free and some need to be paid for.

FIGURE 1.3
Exploring the Windows Vista Welcome Center window.

The Welcome Center layout isn't designed just for novice users but also for users new to Windows Vista. It provides a one-stop area for users without any in-depth knowledge and encompasses most of the configuration choices that users of Vista might require when working with Windows Vista, whether they are new users or experts.

By default, when users log on, Windows Vista displays the Welcome Center. If displaying the Welcome Center is not desired, the feature can be disabled by deselecting the Run at Startup option in the bottom-left side of the screen. The Welcome Center can be reopened as necessary by using the following steps:

1. Click the Start button and then select Control Panel.

2. In Control Panel, click the System and Maintenance link.

3. Click the Welcome Center link.

If you are using the Classic view of the Control Panel, the Welcome Center can be reopened by using the following steps:

1. Click the Start button and then select Control Panel.

2. In Control Panel, if necessary, scroll down and locate the Welcome Center icon.

3. Double-click the Welcome Center icon.

Exploring Vista Product Keys and Activation

Although volume licensed versions of Windows Vista might not require activation or product keys, retail versions of Windows Vista will require both activation and product keys. Users can check the activation status with Windows Vista Welcome Center by checking the Activation Status contained in the View Computer Details screen. If the operating system has not been activated, the operating system can be activated by clicking Show More Details and then scrolling down in the View Basic Information About Your Computer screen and selecting the option Activate Windows Now under Windows Activation.

Microsoft changed its policy in regard to product-key entry and modification. Windows Vista product keys, contrary to previous versions of Windows, provide additional flexibility in accommodating different licensing plans and can be changed as needed. Changing the product key is fairly easy with the following steps:

1. Open the System window in the Welcome Center by clicking Show More Details.

2. In the System window, click Change Product Key, located under Windows Activation.

3. Enter the new product key in the Windows Activation screen and then click Next.

Exploring Basics of User Account Control

Microsoft introduced User Account Control (UAC) in Windows Vista as an answer to user-community complaints about computer security. UAC helps prevent unauthorized changes to the computer by programs such as viruses, spyware, and malware. This feature enhances computer security by ensuring complete separation of standard user and administrator user accounts. By definition, a standard user is an account that allows most software and system changes that do not affect other users or threaten computer security. In contrast, administrator accounts have complete access to the computer and its underlying operating system to make any changes as required.

> **Note**
>
> In this version of Windows, the user groups have been simplified and the Power Users present in the Windows XP group no longer exist. If a user upgrades from Windows XP to Windows Vista and has folders or files that were set up with specific rights for Power Users in Windows XP, the folders and files can still be used as in Windows XP.

If a user is logged in as standard user or administrator, a security prompt will be displayed by default (dependent on Group Policy settings and account type) if an application is run that requires administrator privileges. When a user is logged on using a standard user account, the user is asked to provide a password for an administrator account. If the user is logged in to a workgroup, local computer administrator accounts are listed by name. The user must select an account and type the associated password and then click Submit.

In a domain environment, administrator accounts for users who have logged on to the computer are listed. Typically, these accounts are either local administrator accounts or domain administrator accounts. The user must select an account and type the associated password and then click Submit. In addition, the user has the option of choosing an administrator account other than those listed. The user does this by clicking on Use Another Account, then typing in the account name and password and clicking Submit.

If the user is logged in as an administrator account, a confirmation dialog box will appear, as shown in Figure 1.4. The user must click Continue to allow the task to be completed or Cancel to stop the task from being executed.

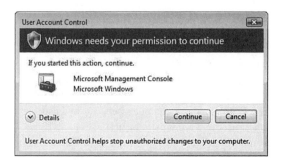

FIGURE 1.4
Using User Account Control to confirm program installation.

Applications can also be run with an elevation of privileges. Elevation of privileges allows a standard application to be run with administrator account rights. After performing the following steps, a user can run applications using elevated privileges:

1. Right-click the application shortcut or menu icon and then select Run as Administrator.

2. When the User Account Control prompt appears, select Continue to allow the task to be completed or Cancel to stop the task from being executed.

Tip

Elevation of privileges also applies when using the command prompt. When trying to run an administrative utility or task requiring administrator privileges via command line, an error will occur if the user does not have the administrator rights and permissions. Be sure to use the Run as Administrator option to avoid seeing an error message.

Powering Down Windows Vista Systems

Typically, when a user turns off a computer running Windows Vista, the system enters sleep state rather than shutting down and turning off completely; the system saves all work, turns off the display, and puts the system into sleep mode. Sleep mode is a low-power-consumption mode where the system state is saved into memory and the computer disk drives and cooling fans turn off. By clicking the Power button on the Start Menu, most computers can be put into sleep mode. Waking up the computer can be accomplished by pressing any key on the keyboard or by pressing the power button on the computer itself.

Startup, Sleep, and Shutdown Performance

In Windows Vista, users can switch their computers between different powered states of low-power consumption and high-power consumption. Users can easily place their computers in a lower power sleep mode using the Power button on the Windows Start menu. In addition, if properly configured, the computer can be placed in sleep mode by pressing the computer's external power button. Sleep, a new power state in Windows Vista, combines the benefits of the standby (fast startup) and hibernation (data protection) features previously available in Windows XP. In sleep mode, the state of the operating system is saved in the computer's memory and although the hard drive and system fans are shutdown, the system can quickly be powered back up to a working state.

Some computers cannot be put into sleep mode because of the system hardware, system state, or applied power-saving configurations. If the system hardware doesn't support sleep mode, the system is completely powered off. If a computer has just completed installing new software updates requiring a restart or a new program has been installed, the system will also not go into sleep mode. In addition, if power options have been reconfigured and have set the Power button to use the Shut Down action, the computer cannot use sleep mode, and turning off the computer shuts it down completely.

With the new GUI enhancements in Windows Vista, it is easy to determine how the Power button works (see Figure 1.5). Windows Vista displays two different views for the Power button. If the Power button displays an amber icon with a circle with a vertical line through the top, pressing the Power button will turn the system off and put the system in a low-power-consumption state so the working session can be resumed quickly. If the Power button displays a red icon with a circle and a vertical line through the middle of it, pressing the power button will turn the system off completely.

FIGURE 1.5
Viewing the Power button.

Summary

Windows Vista is the next-generation client operating system from Microsoft, with significant advances in usability, security, performance, and productivity. The visually enhanced user experience is different from previous versions of Windows from login to logout. The new operating system with its subsystem and driver model enhancements is a major improvement over its predecessor, Windows XP, in terms of Vista's stability and usability for future Windows versions. Revolutionary architecture improvements such as user account controls and privileges, preinstallation and preboot environments, and modularization and disk imaging change the way users work with and manage data on their computers. These modifications are meant to improve the user experience with regard to usability, such as finding documents, email messages, applications, or configuration settings. Security is also enhanced with improvements to the User Account Control to help prevent installation of rogue applications and provide system protection against malware with improved versions of Windows Defender and Windows Firewall.

CHAPTER 2

Getting to Understand Your Windows Vista System

Getting Around in Windows Vista

Getting around in Windows Vista is relatively easy, especially for anyone who has been using a previous version of a Microsoft Windows operating system. The look and feel of Windows Vista is similar to that of Windows XP, but some noticeable changes have been made in Windows Vista to the Explorer interface, desktop, Start menu, Internet Explorer, and where things are located. Some items in Windows Vista are now hidden or disabled by default, where they weren't in previous releases of Windows. A few of the more predominant changes in the navigation structure of Windows Vista when compared to previous versions of Windows are the nonexpanding start menu and submenus, the addition of the Windows Sidebar on the desktop, and some restructuring of menu bars and toolbars. Users will find the category-based organization of settings, applications, and tools along with the suggestive links that appear on the left side of certain windows convenient and extremely helpful. Getting around in Windows Vista is effortless, and the countless ways to customize things and easy access to information about the new features is impressive.

Using the Start Menu

As mentioned in the previous chapter, the Start menu in Windows Vista is similar to that of XP, but Microsoft has incorporated some nice changes into Windows Vista's Start menu, providing more flexible customization and ease of use. In Windows Vista, the

Start button no longer contains the word "Start" and the graphical icon has been replaced by a circle shaped button with the Windows logo inside. The new Windows Vista Start button, as shown in Figure 2.1, is sometimes referred to on the Internet as an orb, although Microsoft officially refers to it as the Start button. Regardless, the Start menu still serves the same purpose as in previous versions of Windows.

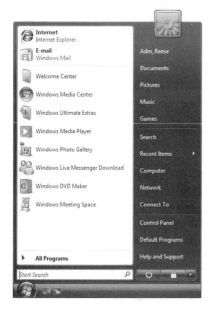

FIGURE 2.1
The Windows Vista Start menu.

Changes to the Start menu in Windows Vista include the following:

■ The All Programs menu expands within the same area instead of left to right.

■ A field to enter a search query immediately without launching a new window.

■ Graphical representations of links in the right column appear at the top when hovered over.

■ The Run command has been removed.

Customizing the Start menu is easy in Windows Vista. Simply right-click the Start button and select Properties. The Taskbar and Start Menu Properties window will appear with the Start menu tab selected, allowing you to choose between the Windows Vista Start menu or Classic Start menu, which is similar to that of Windows 2000.

Clicking the Customize button next to the chosen Start menu style will launch the Customize Start Menu window, as shown in Figure 2.2. From here you can select which items to display in the Start menu, how links launch their target menu or program, how many recent programs to display (10 by default), whether to display links to the default email and Internet applications, and whether program icons should be large or small.

FIGURE 2.2
Customizing the Windows Vista Start menu.

Note

As mentioned previously, the Run command is no longer included on the Start menu by default in Windows Vista; however, it can be quickly reenabled in the Customize Start Menu window. Administrators and advanced users prefer the convenience of the Run dialog allowing quick access to

programs by entering short commands like **cmd** or **eventvwr**. The search
menu in the Start menu also acts like the old Run Dialog box in previous
versions of Windows. For example, clicking the Start button and entering
eventvwr launches the Event Viewer, just as if it had been entered in the
Run dialog of previous versions of Windows.

Using the Taskbar

Like the Start menu, the taskbar in Windows Vista is similar to that of
Windows XP. The taskbar in Windows Vista is composed of three areas in
addition to housing the Start button. Right-clicking the taskbar and selecting
Properties launches the Taskbar and Start Menu Properties window with the
Taskbar tab selected. All taskbar appearance options are enabled by default,
except for the Auto-hide feature. The different options for customizing the
taskbar are outlined in the following list:

- **Auto-hide the Taskbar**—This minimizes the taskbar, hiding it when
  not in use. This option is disabled by default.

- **Lock the Taskbar**—This prevents the taskbar from being moved or
  resized.

- **Keep the Taskbar on Top of Other Windows**—This setting ensures
  that the taskbar is always displayed at the bottom of the desktop, with
  open applications above it.

- **Group Similar Taskbar Buttons**—This setting groups similar buttons
  based on the application.

- **Show Quick Launch**—The Quick Launch bar allows instant access to
  the desktop, Internet Explorer, and switching between windows (Flip
  3D if Windows Aero is enabled). These items are displayed as small
  icons immediately to the right of the Start button.

- **Show Windows Previews (thumbnails)**—This feature displays a
  thumbnail image of the open application immediately above it when
  hovered over in the taskbar. If the system isn't capable of running
  Windows Aero, this feature will be disabled.

Note

The Show Windows Previews (thumbnails) option is enabled only if the
system supports the Windows Aero experience; otherwise, this feature is
turned off and a standard text description appears above programs in the
taskbar. Windows Aero is covered in the "Navigating the Desktop" section
of this chapter.

Tip

Items can be added to the Quick Launch bar a couple of different ways: for example, right-clicking on the item and selecting Add to Quick Launch or dragging and dropping the program icon to the Quick Launch area of the taskbar. The Quick Launch folder is a hidden folder located in the `C:\Users\%username%\AppData\Roaming\Microsoft\Internet Explorer\Quick Launch` folder, where *%username%* represents the username of an account on the computer.

The Notification area of the taskbar, also known as the system tray, includes the clock, volume, network, and power icons. By default, inactive icons will hide when not in use. The Notification area can be customized by right-clicking the taskbar, selecting Properties, and then the Notification area tab.

Additional toolbars can be added to the taskbar two ways: by selecting the Toolbars tab in the taskbar and Start Menu Properties window or by right-clicking the taskbar and selecting the Toolbars menu. By default, Windows Vista includes the following toolbars:

- **Address**—Adds the Internet Explorer address bar to the taskbar.

- **Windows Media Player**—Adds the Windows Media Player icon to the Quick Launch bar and allows Windows Media Player to run in mini-mode when the application is minimized.

- **Links**—Adds the user's Internet Explorer Links menu to the taskbar.

- **Tablet PC Input panel**—Activates the Tablet PC Input panel, allowing users to write on the screen, converting that handwriting into text; this feature is commonly used on Tablet PCs, although it can be used without one.

- **Desktop**—Adds a toolbar that displays links to the items on the logged on user's desktop.

- **Quick Launch**—Adds the Quick Launch items to the toolbar. This toolbar is activated by default.

Tip

A new toolbar can be created only by right-clicking on the taskbar, selecting Toolbars, New Toolbar. A new toolbar cannot be created in the Toolbars tab of the Taskbar and Start Menu Properties window.

Right-clicking the Windows Vista taskbar also gives access to the Task Manager and ability to stack, cascade, or tile windows when they are open.

Navigating the Desktop

The desktop in Windows Vista, shown in Figure 2.3, also includes some impressive new features and enhancements. By default, the desktop is nice and clean, containing only one icon—the Recycle bin—and the new Windows Vista Sidebar. Right-clicking anywhere on the desktop displays a quick menu providing access to options for how desktop icons are displayed and sorted and a menu to create new icons or shortcuts to files and folders. The last item in this menu is the Personalize option, which provides access to further customize the desktop.

FIGURE 2.3
The Windows Vista desktop.

Appearance and Personalization

As previously mentioned, the desktop can be customized by right-clicking it and selecting Personalize at the bottom. This launches the Personalize Appearance and Sounds options page, which can also be accessed through the Control Panel's Appearance and Personalization category heading link.

In the Personalize Appearance and Sounds category, users can change the color and appearance of Windows, choose a different background or screensaver, or select a theme incorporating a collection of these settings.

Windows Aero

As covered in the previous chapter, Windows Aero provides an enhanced visual experience to the end user and incorporates the latest in user interface design technologies. Microsoft created the Desktop Window Manager, featuring a specific composition engine that changes the way computers render images to the display. The Desktop Window Manager is the driving force behind Windows Aero and the Windows Vista user interface. Windows Aero, as also outlined in the previous chapter, requires specific hardware to run. If the hardware of the system meets these requirements, Windows Aero will be enabled by default. If the system does not meet the requirements Windows Aero will be disabled.

Windows Aero includes the following components:

- **Transparent glass**—Makes window frames and certain icons semi-transparent.

- **Live taskbar icons and thumbnails**—Icons and thumbnails that display the actual content in real-time. Placing the mouse cursor over an icon in the system tray now displays graphics, some animation, and detailed information about the program. Placing the mouse cursor over a button in the taskbar for a running program displays a "live" thumbnail image of the application. If the application contains dynamic content, the thumbnail image will change with it. Selecting the thumbnail view within a window displays the actual contents of the file in the thumbnail image.

- **Windows Flip 3D**—Displays running programs in a 3D view when the user presses the Windows and Tab key simultaneously or clicks the Switch Between Windows button in the Quick Launch area of the taskbar. Pressing the Alt and Tab keys simultaneously moves between windows. Alternatively, the arrow keys can also be used. An example of Windows Flip 3D in action is shown in Figure 2.4.

- **Windows Flip**—Pressing the Alt and Tab keys simultaneously launches Windows Flip, which contains live thumbnails just like with the taskbar. An example of Windows Flip in action is shown in Figure 2.5.

FIGURE 2.4
Windows Aero Flip 3D with live thumbnails.

FIGURE 2.5
Windows Flip with Live thumbnails.

- **Enhanced transitional effects**—Windows appear to fade and fall in or away when opened or closed. Menus, alerts, and pop-up windows also fade away and transition in or out in an animated manner.

Windows Aero also delivers enhancements to animations, such as the progress indicator, option buttons, dialog boxes, alerts, fonts, icons, menus and more. Through delivering a better user interface, Windows Aero truly makes the computing experience more enjoyable and easier to interact with. Those in search of even more information on how Windows Aero works and what it provides Windows Vista can refer to the MSDN article on Aero Aesthetics at msdn2.microsoft.com/en-us/library/aa511291.aspx.

Tip

If you want to experience Windows Aero over a Remote Desktop connection, both computers must have the Terminal Services Client 6.0 installed (included with Windows Vista and Windows Server 2008), the remote system (host) must be configured to accept remote connections, both systems must support the Windows Aero experience and have it activated, and the terminal session must be in at least 800×600 resolution with 32-bit color. At the time of writing, Windows Aero could be experienced only over a Remote Desktop connection with the Enterprise and Ultimate editions of Windows Vista.

Windows Aero, although quite enjoyable, consumes enough system resources that Microsoft added the capability for Windows Vista to automatically disable it under certain conditions; for example, when a laptop is running off the battery and Windows Vista is in "Power Saver" mode, when a program that is incompatible with Aero is launched, or if too many programs are running, making the system low on resources. This allows your Windows Vista system to perform smoothly overall, adding enhancements such as Aero when appropriate. Windows Aero features can also be enabled or disabled by following a set of steps:

1. Click the Start button and then click Control Panel.
2. Click Appearance and Personalization.
3. Click Personalization. Alternatively, you can right-click the desktop and select Personalize.
4. Click Window Color and Appearance.

    4a. If Windows Aero is currently enabled and you wish to disable it, click Open Classic Appearance Properties for More Color Options at the bottom of the Windows Color and Appearance screen, shown in Figure 2.6. When the Appearance Settings window shown in Figure 2.7 appears, select the Windows Vista Basic color scheme from the list.

Note

The Windows Color and Appearance screen is displayed only if Windows Aero is currently enabled on the computer.

    4b. If Windows Aero is currently disabled and you wish to enable it, select the Windows Aero color scheme from the list in the Appearance Settings window, shown in Figure 2.7.

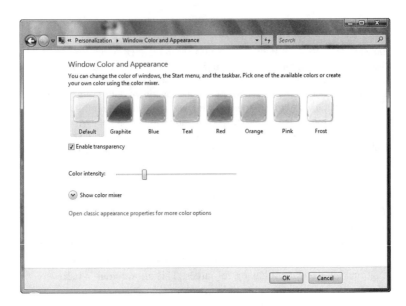

FIGURE 2.6
The Window Color Appearance screen.

FIGURE 2.7
Windows Color Schemes in the Appearance Settings window.

To enable or disable the Aero Transparency effect, follow these steps:

1. Click the Start button and then click Control Panel.

2. Click Appearance and Personalization.

3. Click Personalization. Alternatively, you can right-click the desktop and select Personalize.

4. Click Window Color and Appearance.

5. Check or uncheck the Enable Transparency option to activate or deactivate it, as shown previously in Figure 2.6.

Note

The Aero Transparency effect is only available if Windows Aero is enabled on the computer.

In addition, some Windows Aero features can be configured in the Visual Effects tab of the Performance Options window, shown in Figure 2.8. To access the Performance Options window, open the System Properties window by clicking the Start button, right-clicking the Computer link in the right column, selecting Properties, clicking the Change Settings link, clicking the Advanced tab, and clicking the Settings button in the Performance section.

The Windows Vista Sidebar and Gadgets

Another impressive new feature of Windows Vista is the Sidebar and Gadgets. By default, the Sidebar is enabled on the right side of the screen and includes the following gadgets: clock, slide show, and news headlines from MSNBC. Gadgets are small applications that provide quick access to information, tools, and Internet feeds. Gadgets can be easily added and customized, and the Sidebar is flexible with its configuration options. Gadgets don't have to live on the Sidebar; they can be disconnected and moved to another location on the desktop if needed.

You can activate the Sidebar in three ways:

- Press the Windows key and spacebar simultaneously.

- Right-click the Sidebar icon in the system tray and select Open or Bring Gadgets to Front.

- Click Start and type `sidebar` into the Start Search field and press Enter.

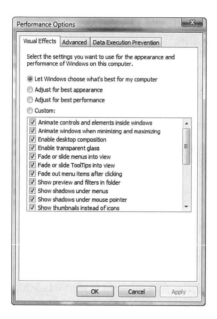

FIGURE 2.8
Windows Vista visual effects.

You can access the Sidebar Properties in three ways:

- Right-click the Sidebar and select Properties.
- Click the Start button, open the Control Panel, click Appearance and Personalization, and click Windows Sidebar Properties.
- Right-click the Sidebar icon in the system tray and select Properties.

To add gadgets to the Sidebar, right-click the Sidebar and select Add Gadgets. A window displaying a list of available gadgets appears. From here you can select a new gadget, search for gadgets, or get more gadgets online (http://vista.gallery.microsoft.com/). Windows Vista includes the following gadgets:

- Calendar
- Clock (enabled by default)
- Contacts
- CPU Meter
- Currency Converter

- Feed Headlines (enabled by default)
- Notes
- Picture Puzzle
- Slide Show (enabled by default)
- Stocks
- Weather

You can keep the Sidebar or detached gadgets on top of other windows in three ways:

- Right-click the Sidebar and select Properties.
- Select Sidebar Is Always on Top of Other Windows and click Apply.
- To keep a detached gadget on top of other windows, right-click the gadget and select Always on Top.

Tip

If the Sidebar or gadgets are configured to always be on top of other windows, consider changing the opacity of the gadgets so they are barely visible, but legible. To accomplish this, right-click an existing gadget, select Opacity, and choose a percentage. Placing a mouse over a gadget changes it to full color.

Exploring the Welcome Center

This Welcome Center launches each time you log on to Windows Vista, until you disable it from automatically starting. The Welcome Center is a great place to start for new users and administrators. The Welcome Center can always be accessed in the Control Panel under the System and Maintenance category. Upon launch, the Welcome Center provides a basic summary about your computer, such as the version of Windows Vista, processor speed, memory, video adapter model, and computer name, with a link on the right to obtain more details.

Below the computer summary pane are two categories containing several helpful links to get started. The first category, Getting Started with Windows, lists the most commonly used items when configuring and exploring Windows Vista for the first time. From here you can view computer details, transfer files and settings from another computer, add new user accounts, set up a connection to the Internet, and find out what's new in Windows Vista and what extra add-ons are available.

The second category, Offers from Microsoft, contains links to the Windows Live, Windows Marketplace, and Microsoft Security websites.

Exploring the Control Panel

Accessing the Control Panel can be done by clicking the Start button and selecting, you guessed it, Control Panel. The Control Panel in Windows Vista, unlike previous versions of Windows, is organized by category rather than just containing links to each necessary item for configuring Windows. Users can always switch to the original view by selecting Classic View on the left. The Classic View is always nice to have around when you want to jump right to a specific item.

Windows Vista Control Panel contains the following categories:

- **System and Maintenance**—View system information, configure backups, restore files, configure power options, set indexing parameters, view problems and solutions, check performance, configure hardware, and access administrative tools.

- **User Accounts and Family Safety**—Manage user accounts, set parental controls, and configure Microsoft's new CardSpace online community service.

- **Security**—Configure automatic updating, the Windows Firewall, Windows Defender Anti-Spyware software, Internet options, and BitLocker drive encryption (select versions).

- **Appearance and Personalization**—Personalize user interface items such as the desktop and theme, configure the taskbar and Start menu, folder options, fonts, and Windows Sidebar.

- **Network and Internet**—Configure network connections, devices and sharing, Internet options, offline files, People Near Me for online meetings, and synchronize with other devices, computers, and network folders.

- **Clock, Language, and Region**—Configure the date and time, add additional clocks for other time zones, and configure language and keyboard layouts.

- **Hardware and Sound**—Configure computer hardware and audio options.

- **Ease of Access**—Configure accessibility options for making Windows Vista easier to use, such as increasing the font size for easier reading and configuring speech recognition options.

- **Programs**—Change or uninstall programs, configure Windows features, set older applications to run in compatibility mode, configure default programs, configure a second display monitor with Windows Sideshow, and buy software online.

- **Additional Options**—Control Panel items that do not specify a category to reside under appear in this section.

- **Mobile PC**—Specifically for laptops, the Mobile PC category focuses on mobility items such as connecting to a projector, setting power options, configuring Tablet PC options, and synchronization with other devices, computers, and networks.

Using Windows Explorer

Windows Explorer has also changed a bit in Windows Vista. Explorer, not to be confused with Internet Explorer, can be accessed by clicking the Start button, entering **Explorer** into the Start Search field, and selecting Windows Explorer from the search results or by clicking the Start button, clicking All Programs, Accessories, and selecting Windows Explorer.

Windows Explorer has two menus: Organize and Views. The Organize menu includes the common commands Cut, Copy, Paste, Undo, Select All, Layout, and folder and search options. The columns in the right pane contain the capability to further sort and organize files and folders by clicking the arrow to the right of the column name and choosing the criteria for sorting the contents of the folder.

The Address Bar includes another handy new feature: displaying the sub-categories of items listed in the Address Bar, as shown in Figure 2.9. For example, if a user is in the Security category of the Control Panel, the user could click the arrow immediately to the right of Control Panel in the Address field to display a list of all items available in the Control Panel.

The standard menu is no longer displayed by default in Windows Explorer and some applications; however, it can be quickly accessed by pressing the Alt key. To enable the classic Windows menu, follow these steps:

1. In Windows Explorer, press the Alt key.
2. Select the Tools menu and Folder Options.

3. Click the View tab.

4. In the Files and Folders section under Advanced Settings, check the box Always Show Menus.

5. Click Apply or OK.

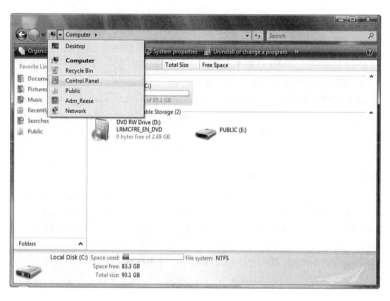

FIGURE 2.9
Windows Vista drop-down navigation menu.

Windows Vista also provides an alternative to using the Shift or Ctrl keys to select multiple items by including check boxes next to them. This feature, although very handy, is not enabled by default. To enable the use of check boxes for selecting items for an action such as copy or move, follow these steps:

1. In Windows Explorer, press the Alt key.

2. Select the Tools menu and Folder Options.

3. Click the View tab.

4. In the Files and Folders section under Advanced Settings, scroll down and check the box Use Check Boxes to Select Items, as shown in Figure 2.10.

5. Click Apply or OK.

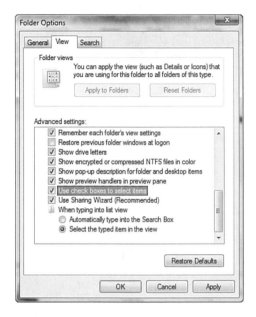

FIGURE 2.10
Enabling use of check boxes to select items in Folder Options.

6. A check box now appears in the Name column of a folder, as shown in Figure 2.11.

Searching for Files, Folders, and Other Items

The searching and indexing function of Windows Vista has changed dramatically from previous Windows releases—for the better. One major change is how information is retrieved. In previous versions of Windows, and practically any search engine for that matter, you enter a phrase or keyword to search for and then launch the query. Not so in Windows Vista. In Windows Vista, as soon as you begin typing, the Search engine begins looking for any matches, displaying them in real-time as the search parameters change. This allows for much faster retrieval of items such as documents and programs. By default, Windows Vista searches "everywhere," meaning it returns results for anything from anywhere it can (besides the Internet). For example, if you searched for **Admin**, the search results could display an email message, link to Administrative Tools, a Windows Vista user account, picture, document, and more.

FIGURE 2.11
Using check boxes to select multiple items.

Searching for items can be accomplished from virtually anywhere. As mentioned previously, the search field is available at the bottom of the Start menu and in almost every other open window. When performing a search in the Start menu, the results are displayed in the left column. In other windows, they are usually displayed on the bottom.

Users can also assign keywords to files and folders, allowing them to appear in a future search that looks in a specific category—another very useful search feature and example of grouping things together in Windows Vista by category.

The Search menu in the Start menu can also act like the old Run dialog box in previous versions of Windows. For example, clicking the Start button and entering **eventvwr** launches the Event Viewer, just as if it had been entered in the Run dialog of previous versions of Windows.

Another great feature added to the Search capabilities of Windows Vista is the capability to save search results. In Windows Vista, this is referred to as a Search folder. Search folders that contains previously returned results from a search query are stored in the user's Searches folder.

To save search results, follow these steps:

1. Perform a search.

Note

Search queries and results entered in the Windows Start Menu can only be saved after the search has run and clicking on the See All Results link, which invokes the main search window.

---

2. When the search has finished and the results have appeared, click the Save Search button.

3. If desired, add a tag to the Search folder being saved.

4. Give the file (search results) a name. (The contents are saved with an extension of .search-ms.)

The Command Prompt and Windows PowerShell

Administrators will be happy to learn that the good old command prompt still exists in Window Vista. The command prompt provides a method of accomplishing tasks without using Windows. The command prompt comes in handy when a quick task needs to be accomplished, such as mapping a network drive or restarting a service. Launching the command prompt can be quickly done by clicking the Start button and entering `cmd` or `Command Prompt` into the Start Search field, similar to entering `cmd` into the Run dialog in previous versions of Windows. The command prompt is also available in the Start menu under All Programs, Accessories.

Note

Some commands that can be run in the command prompt may require elevated privileges. In those instances, the command prompt should be launched using the Run as Administrator option, available by right-clicking the command prompt icon.

Windows PowerShell, shown in Figure 2.12 is a command interface similar to that of the command prompt; however, Windows PowerShell runs only on specific versions of Microsoft Windows and includes support for automating tasks and scripts, editing the Registry, and more. Windows PowerShell was conceived and created by Microsoft specifically for advanced users and system administrators. Windows PowerShell includes more than 129 ready-to-use commands and allows administrators to create their own.

Windows PowerShell 1.0 for Windows Vista can be downloaded from the System Tools section of the Microsoft download center at www.microsoft.com/downloads/.

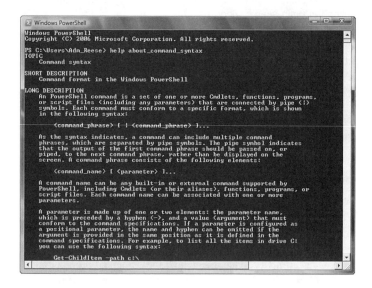

FIGURE 2.12
Windows PowerShell 1.0.

Note

More information about Windows PowerShell can be obtained from the Windows PowerShell website or blog available at the www.microsoft.com/powershell and http://blogs.msdn.com/powershell websites, respectively.

Note

Windows PowerShell 1.0 installs and runs only on nonbeta versions of the Business, Enterprise, and Ultimate editions of Windows Vista. Windows PowerShell 1.0 also requires the 2.0 version of Microsoft .NET Framework, which is included in Windows Vista.

Tip

For security reasons, a policy embedded in Windows PowerShell prevents scripts from executing inside Windows PowerShell. To enable the capability to launch scripts from within Windows PowerShell, use the Set-ExecutionPolicy command in a Windows PowerShell session. After choosing an execution policy, enter the **Set-ExecutionPolicy** cmdlet to set it. For example, type **Set-ExecutionPolicy Unrestricted** to allow all digitally signed and unsigned scripts to run. Be aware that allowing PowerShell to run unsigned script reduces the overall security of the computer. Different execution policies exist; one must be selected and set that corresponds with the script you are attempting to run. For more information about each execution policy, type **get-help about_signing** into a Windows PowerShell prompt.

Understanding Key Components of Windows Vista

Certain components of an operating system are key to system administration. Windows Vista eases the pain of system administration by providing quick access to administrative tools and flexibility in how the operating system functions and is secured. System administrators can customize Windows Vista, troubleshoot issues, configure settings, and enhance security—all relatively easily. Knowing where the different key components of Windows Vista are located and how they work is essential for day-to-day administration and troubleshooting.

Configuring Default Programs

A default program is defined by associating specific file or media type(s) to always launch in a particular application. For example, JPG picture files can be configured to always open in Windows Photo Gallery, or they could be configured to launch in a different application, such as Internet Explorer. Files can of course still be read by multiple applications. To access the Default Programs category, click the Start button and select Default Programs on the right column. The Default Programs category can also be accessed within the Control Panel under the Programs category.

The Default Programs options in Windows Vista allow configuration for the following:

- **Set your default programs**—Choose which programs Windows should use by default. For example, a preferred web page editor could be specified here.

- **Associate a file type or protocol with a program**—Select which application should launch when a specific file type is accessed.

- **Change AutoPlay settings**—Specifies what should automatically happen when specific media containing specific content is inserted into the computer. For example, DVDs can automatically start in Windows Media Player when inserted into a DVD drive. Autoplay can be disabled altogether by unchecking the Use AutoPlay for All Media and Devices option at the top of the AutoPlay window.

- **Set Program Access and Computer Defaults**—Allows a default program such as a web browser or email application to be specified for everyone who uses the computer.

Configuring Advanced System Settings

Advanced system settings in Windows Vista include configuration options related to system performance, user profiles, and Windows Vista startup and recovery. Advanced system settings are configured under the Advanced tab of the System Properties window. To access the System Properties window, click the Start button, right-click the computer link in the right column, select Properties, and click the Advanced tab. Alternatively, Advanced system settings can be reached through the Control Panel, System and Maintenance, System category, Advanced system settings link on the left.

The Advanced System Settings tab has three sections; Performance, User Profiles, and Startup and Recovery. The Performance section contains settings for visual effects such as enabling the Windows Aero transparent glass effect, advanced settings such as allocating processor resources and virtual memory, and enabling or disabling Data Execution Prevention, which helps protect data from malicious code. The User Profiles section provides settings for local and roaming user profiles. The Startup and Recovery section includes settings for startup options, such as the amount of time to display a list of available operating systems and actions to take during a system failure, such as writing events to log files and creating a memory dump.

Using Administrative Tools in Windows Vista

The collection of administrative tools in Windows Vista shown in Figure 2.13 has changed from those in Windows XP. By default, Administrative Tools is not available on the Start menu. To include Administrative Tools on the Start menu, right-click the Start button, select Properties, click the Customize button, scroll to the bottom, and select either Display on the All Programs Menu or Display on the All Programs Menu and the Start Menu. After the Administrative Tools item has been added, click Start and enter **Administrative Tools** in the Start Search field or click the Start button, select All Programs, and click the Administrative Tools folder to access the different tools available.

FIGURE 2.13
Windows Vista Administrative Tools.

Listed next, along with brief descriptions, are the administrative tools available in Windows Vista:

- **Computer Management**—Use this tool to manage the local or remote computers and perform tasks such as configuring services, maintaining drives, scheduling tasks, viewing events, viewing shared folders, managing accounts and groups, and checking the system's reliability and performance metrics.

- **Data Sources (ODBC)**—Open Database Connectivity (ODBC) is used to manage connections to databases and transfer data between databases.

- **Event Viewer**—Event Viewer is used to monitor and review system events. In Windows Vista, the Event Viewer has been given a face lift, providing more robust filtering options and many more logs than in previous versions of Windows.

- **iSCSI Initiator**—Internet Small Computer System Interface (iSCSI) establishes advanced connections to networked storage devices, commonly used with a storage area network (SAN).

- **Local Security Policy**—Similar to a Group Policy in Active Directory, the Local Security Policy can set parameters for user accounts such as password expiration, auditing, security options, and more. Windows Vista security is covered in depth in Chapter 4, "Securing a Windows Vista System."

- **Memory Diagnostics**—Used to check system memory for problems. Windows Vista system performance is covered in detail in Chapter 3, "Understanding Windows Vista Performance Optimization."

- **Print Management**—Manage local and network printers. Print management is covered in detail in Chapter 16, "Establishing Printer Management in Windows Vista."

- **Reliability and Performance Monitor**—Provides an overview and troubleshooting for system stability. Windows Vista system performance is covered in Chapter 3.

- **Services**—View, configure, and troubleshoot services running on the system.

- **System Configuration**—Configure how Windows Vista should start up, which services and applications should load, and determine access to commonly used administrative tools.

- **Task Scheduler**—Schedule tasks to run on the local computer or a remote one.

- **Windows Firewall with Advanced Security**—Configure, troubleshoot, and monitor the Windows Firewall. Windows Firewall can be configured on the local computer or a remote one. Additional information about Windows Firewall can be found in the next section and in Chapter 4.

Understanding Security Options for Windows Vista

Windows Vista includes a myriad of enhancements regarding security. Windows Vista includes the programs and tools to secure a computer from malicious code such as viruses, spyware, and phishing attempts for personal information through email and the Internet. Furthermore, automatic updating has been enhanced, drive encryption has been added, and more.

Configuring Windows Firewall with Advanced Security

By default, the Windows Firewall is enabled in Windows Vista. The Windows Firewall in Windows Vista can be configured locally or remotely. In the Windows Firewall with Advanced Security, program security components can be monitored, and inbound and outbound firewall rules can be managed along with several other items. Windows Firewall is up and running after Windows Vista is installed, which helps ensure that the system is protected as soon as it is built. Detailed information on Windows Firewall can be found in Chapter 4.

Configuring Windows Update

Updating Windows Vista is easy, and keeping Windows Vista automatically updated is even easier through scheduled updating. Windows Update is flexible with its options of providing information about updates before they are installed or even downloaded to the computer.

By default, automatic updating is not enabled on the computer; however, the Security Center brings this to attention because updating Windows and essential software is part of an overall security strategy.

Windows Update not only downloads and installs patches for security vulnerabilities, it can also keep other security products from Microsoft up-to-date, such as the Windows Defender Anti-Spyware program and Forefront Client Anti-Virus program, and provide updated hardware drivers and other updates for Microsoft Office and Windows Vista Extras.

Windows Update can be configured through the Windows Update link under the Security category in the Control Panel or through the Windows Security Center under the Automatic Updating link.

Windows Update and patch management are covered extensively in Chapter 5, "Patching and Keeping Windows Vista Up-to-Date."

Configuring Windows Defender

Windows Defender is a real-time and on-demand antispyware scanning program. Windows Defender works in real-time to notify the user when a malicious program is attempting to install itself or make unwanted system changes. By default, Windows Defender is up and running in Windows Vista;

however, Automatic Updating should be configured to keep the definition files used for detection current.

Window Defender can be configured through the Windows Security Center or by clicking Windows Defender in the Security category of the Control Panel. In the Windows Defender program, you can view the status of scans, run or schedule a scan, and configure additional options. Windows Defender is discussed further in Chapter 4.

Configuring Internet Explorer 7 Security Options

To ensure a safe Internet browsing experience, certain security settings should be in place and configured properly. For example, the new antiphishing filter and parental controls in Internet Explorer 7 and Windows Vista will help block websites that attempt to extract personal information from a user and ensure that parents have control over what their children can access online. Configuring Internet Explorer 7's security options can greatly help reduce exposure to malicious code, online scams, identity theft, and unacceptable content.

Security settings for Internet Explorer 7 can be found under the Internet Options category in the Control Panel. Clicking the Security Settings link launches the Internet Explorer 7 Internet Properties window with the Security tab selected. From here you can configure the different zones: Internet, Local Intranet, Trusted sites, and Restricted sites. The Privacy, Content, and Advanced tabs also contain security settings for Internet Explorer 7. For example, to configure Parental Controls, click the Content tab; to configure items such as certificates and SSL, click the Advanced tab.

For more information about Securing Windows Vista, see Chapter 4. For more information about Internet Explorer 7, see Chapter 18, "Using Internet Explorer 7."

Configuring BitLocker

BitLocker, introduced in Chapter 1, "Windows Vista Technology Primer," is a drive encryption program that works under Windows Vista Enterprise and Ultimate editions. BitLocker encrypts all data stored on a volume, and the information used to encrypt or decrypt data is stored either in an embedded microchip called a Trusted Platform Module (TPM) or on a USB drive if the computer does not have a TPM. Specific hard drive configurations and updated BIOS may be necessary to configure BitLocker properly. BitLocker is covered in Chapter 7, "Implementing BitLocker Drive Encryption to

Improve Data Privacy." BitLocker can be found in the Control Panel under the Security category. Clicking the BitLocker Drive Encryption link launches the BitLocker configuration advising of necessary steps to get BitLocker working.

Understanding Networking Components

The Network and Sharing Center in Windows Vista contains everything an administrator or user needs to manage network adapters, connections, troubleshoot connectivity, and configure sharing and security. The Network and Sharing Center is located in the Control Panel under the Network and Internet category. Launching the Network and Sharing Center provides a diagram of the computer's network configuration, an overview of any connections that are currently active, and a summary of the network Sharing and Discovery settings.

Network Discovery is disabled by default in Windows Vista, as is file sharing, Public Folder sharing, and Media sharing. Network shares can still be established to resources on the computer as long as the user making the connection has a valid account and password.

From within the Network and Sharing Center, an administrator can quickly view other networked computers and devices, establish network connections, manage wireless devices, set up a network, and diagnose and repair problems.

Managing Network Connections

Network connections are managed in the Network Connections folder, located in the Network and Sharing Center in the Control Panel. The Network Connections folder contains the network adapters and any active connections made to them. From here you can enable and disable a connection, obtain a connection's status, diagnose and repair problems, bridge connections between networks, and perform other advanced tasks.

To set up a network or connection to another network, follow these steps:

1. Click the Start button, click Control Panel, click Network and Internet, click Network and Sharing Center, and then click the Set Up a Connection or Network link under Tasks on the left side of the screen.

2. From here you can create a connection to the Internet, set up wireless access, create a Virtual Private Network (VPN) connection, and create dial-up connections.

3. Select the task you want to perform and click Next.

4. A message will appear, stating whether the connection was created successfully and providing additional information if it was not.

Connecting to the Internet

Connecting to the Internet couldn't be easier in Windows Vista. After a network adapter has been configured, usually automatically during the Windows Vista installation, a connection to the Internet can be created. After a connection to the Internet has been established, additional Internet options may need to be configured in Internet Explorer 7, such as the use of a proxy server. For more information about Internet Explorer 7, refer to Chapter 18.

To set up an Internet connection, follow these steps:

1. Click the Start button, click Control Panel, click Network and Internet, click Network and Sharing Center, and then click the Set Up a Connection or Network link under Tasks on the left side of the screen.

2. From here select Connect to the Internet and click Next.

3. Select the connection type—Wireless, Broadband, or Dial-Up—and click Next.

4. If Wireless, select a network to connect to; if Broadband or Dial-Up was selected, provide the information required by the ISP and click Next.

5. A message will appear, stating whether the connection was created successfully and providing additional information if it was not.

Sharing Resources

In addition to creating and managing network connections, the Network and Connection Center also houses the configuration settings necessary to share resources on a Windows Vista computer. As previously mentioned, file, folder, and resource sharing is disabled by default in Windows Vista, unless the user making the connection has a valid account and password and knows what resource to connect to.

To set up Resource Sharing, follow these steps:

1. Click the Start button, Control Panel, Network and Internet, and then click Network and Sharing Center.

2. In the Sharing and Discovery section, shown at the bottom of Figure 2.14, turn on the type of item you want to share: files and folders, the Windows Vista Public Folder or Printers, and click Apply.

3. Acknowledge the Security warning.

4. Find the resource such as a folder or printer, right-click it, and select Share.

5. Choose with whom you want to share the resource, give it a name, and click Share.

Tip

To share a printer, both File Sharing and Printer Sharing must be turned on and the printer must be shared.

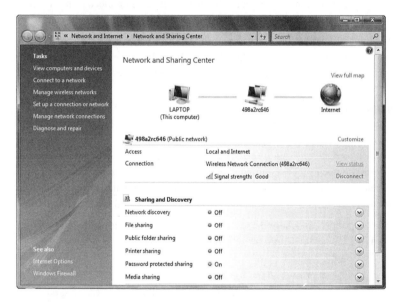

FIGURE 2.14
Windows Vista Sharing and Discovery (the bottom section) in the Network and Sharing Center.

Managing Hardware in Windows Vista

Managing and configuring hardware in Windows Vista is also easier. Windows Vista automatically detects and configures most computer hardware. In the event a piece of computer hardware needs to be added, removed, or configured manually, it can be done in the Hardware and Sound category listing found in the Control Panel. In most cases, Windows Vista does not require manual addition, removal, and configuration of hardware. Some components, however, may require additional steps to get them working.

Adding and Removing Hardware

As mentioned previously, adding hardware is usually as simple as powering down the computer (if necessary), adding the component, and powering the computer back on. In some cases, a Windows Vista compatible driver may be needed from the manufacturer. The Add New Hardware Wizard is still available under the Control Panel's classic view in the event a piece of hardware needs to be added manually along with a driver from the manufacturer.

The Hardware and Sound category in the Control Panel contains configuration options for Printers, AutoPlay, Sound, Mouse and Keyboard, video displays and adapters, Tablet PCs, and a quick link to the Device Manager.

Understanding Power Options

Power Options in Windows Vista have been enhanced and include a few default power plans to choose from for laptops: Balanced, Power Saver, and High Performance. In addition, administrators can configure what the power buttons do when pressed and what closing the lid of a laptop accomplishes; you can create a customized power plan and choose when the computer saves on energy by turning off the display, going to sleep, or hibernating.

Power Options, especially those focused around laptops, are covered in more detail in Chapter 9, "Configuring Mobile Functionality in Windows Vista."

Configuring Windows Vista for Mobility

Windows Vista takes mobility to a new level for those who rely on laptops. As mentioned previously, new power plans help balance performance with up time. The Windows Mobility Center provides easy access to things that commonly change when users travel with a laptop. The Windows Mobility Center includes the capability to quickly control the volume, check batteries, configure wireless settings, connect to external displays and projectors, and configure synchronization.

Windows Vista Mobility is covered extensively in Part III of this book.

Accessibility Options in the Ease of Access Center

The Ease of Access Center located immediately in the Control Panel contains tools that make certain things in Windows Vista easier to interact with. For example, someone who wears glasses may benefit from a larger font size, different resolution or color scheme, whereas someone who has a hard time hearing may benefit from having text displayed on the screen when a sound launches, much like closed captioning on television. Tools are available immediately at the top and a brief description of each is outlined below. Administrators will find the different task-based configuration changes easy to use for dealing with scenarios such as blindness or corrective vision, hearing impairments, deafness, and other physical limitations.

The Ease of Access Center is located in the Control Panel and contains the following tools:

- **Magnifier**—Turns the mouse into a magnifying glass that displays the highlighted content twice as large (by default) at the top of the screen.

- **Narrator**—This tool reads aloud what is on the screen where the user is navigating at the time or for a window that is open.

- **Onscreen Keyboard**—Places a keyboard on the screen that can be used with a Tablet PC or mouse.

- **High Contrast Colors**—Makes fonts and text more apparent and easier to read by placing Windows Vista in a high contrast environment (minimal graphics, white on black text). Press Alt+Shift+PrntScreen to activate or deactivate.

Configuring Backups

A back up and restore plan is a task on every system administrator's list, and Windows Vista makes it easy for administrators and users to implement one. Windows Vista includes the Backup and Restore Center, which is located in the Control Panel under the System and Maintenance category. The Backup and Restore Center provides quick access to backing up and scheduling backups of files, folders, or the entire computer, and restoring files from a backup, creating restore points, and repairing Windows.

Backup and Recovery in Windows Vista is covered in the chapters in Part IV of this book.

Working with User Accounts

User Accounts in Windows Vista have changed, primarily because of security reasons, new tools, and sharing enhancements. Some of these changes are necessary to support future Microsoft Windows Server operating systems, such as Windows Server 2008, SharePoint Server, and more. User accounts, by default, run with fewer privileges than in previous versions of Windows. For example, a user account in Windows Vista that belongs to the Administrators group isn't functioning with totally unrestricted access. Administrators will be prompted, like other users, when system changes are made, security settings are modified, or when something is being installed. This level of protection is delivered by User Account Control. Windows Easy Transfer is a program that transfers user accounts, files, and settings from other computers. Windows Easy Transfer is discussed next.

User Account Control

User Account Control (UAC) was established to provide a framework in which user accounts can exist and function while preventing undesired and, in most cases, malicious changes to a computer. UAC is another security layer in Windows Vista that helps combat spyware, adware, and viruses. UAC can also prevent unintentional changes and mistakes from happening by displaying a request for permission from the operating system to continue. For advanced system administrators, UAC can be disabled, and exceptions can be made. To get started with UAC, click the User Accounts and Family Safety link in the Control Panel. UAC is covered thoroughly in Chapter 6, "Using User Account Control to Establish System Security."

Using Windows Easy Transfer

Windows Easy Transfer is used to move user accounts, files, and settings from a computer to a Windows Vista system. To access Windows Easy Transfer, click the Start button, Accessories, System Tools, and then click Windows Easy Transfer. The Windows Easy transfer window appears, as shown in Figure 2.15. Windows Easy Transfer can obtain files from another computer through different means, such as directly with a cable, over a network, or from removable media. Not all Windows Easy Transfer methods are available for all Windows Operating Systems, and some settings won't be transferred based on the operating system version.

FIGURE 2.15
Windows Easy Transfer.

Note

The Windows Easy Transfer Program will launch in full screen mode, and the desktop will be unavailable during the process.

Windows Easy Transfer transfers the following:

- Everything in the user's folder such as Documents, Pictures, and everything in the Shared Documents folder,

- Email account settings, contacts, and messages.

- Program settings.

- User accounts and settings such as desktop themes, screensavers, accessibility options, and more.

- Internet Favorites, cookies, and other settings.

- Other files and folders specified during the transfer process.

Windows Easy Transfer works with the following versions of Microsoft Windows:

- **Windows Vista**
- **Windows XP**—Except Starter Edition.
- **Windows 2000**—Files and folders only, program and system settings will not be transferred.

Windows Easy Transfer must also be running on the source computer in order to use it. Windows Easy Transfer can be used with a USB cable, network connection, USB jump drive, CD, DVD, or external hard drive.

Checking System Performance

System performance has improved immensely in Windows Vista and so have the features and programs. Performance monitoring and troubleshooting is a part of any system administrator's routine, and the tools in Windows Vista make it easier. The Task Manager, Memory Diagnostics Tool, and Reliability and Performance Monitor are essential tools an administrator should know how to use. Each of these tools is described next. Computers running Windows Vista are now assigned an overall score known as a *base score*, which is calculated by weighing the processor speed, memory, graphics, and hard disk specifications. Each category is given a score from 1.0–5.9, and the system is assigned an overall base score, also ranging from 1.0–5.9. System performance in Windows Vista is covered extensively in Chapter 3.

Using Task Manager

The Task Manager provides a quick overview of running applications, processes, services, performance, networking utilization, and connected users. The interface of the Task Manager is virtually unchanged from the version in Windows XP, and you can jump to the new Reliability and Performance Monitor under the Performance tab, shown in Figure 2.16.

To launch Task Manager, right-click the taskbar or press Ctrl+Alt+Del and select Start Task Manager.

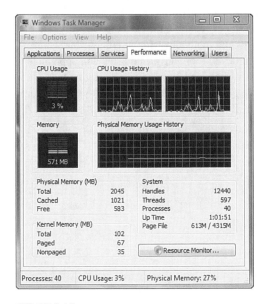

FIGURE 2.16
Windows Task Manager.

Using the Memory Diagnostics Tool

The Windows Memory Diagnostics tool checks the system memory for any problems or bad memory sectors. The Windows Memory Diagnostics tool must run at system startup before the Vista operating system finishes loading. The Memory Diagnostics tool can be launched by typing **Memory Diagnostics** into the Start Search field under the Start button.

Using the Reliability and Performance Monitor

The Reliability and Performance Monitor in Windows Vista replaced the Performance Monitor in Windows XP. The Reliability and Performance Monitor looks similar to the Task Manager and highlights components that are critical to system performance.

Summary

As we've seen in this chapter, although Vista may at first appear to be a very new and very daunting interface, it's actually quite easy to navigate. Microsoft has done an excellent job of reducing the learning curve by retaining many of the common features and methods of finding things that were present in earlier versions of Windows. More advanced users will appreciate the improvements in areas such as search and system customization that will allow them to improve their own productivity. Don't be afraid to explore your Vista system and try out the new functions.

CHAPTER 3

Understanding Windows Vista Performance Optimization

Assessing System Performance

As with previous versions of Windows operating systems, new and improved technology in Windows Vista makes computer systems more responsive in performing everyday tasks. Improved startup and sleep performance features help both desktop and mobile PCs get up and running more quickly. Because Windows Vista manages both memory and input/output devices more efficiently, computer performance is more consistent and responsive to end user applications.

Windows Vista incorporates a new approach to address performance issues and offers a Performance Information and Tools Control Panel applet that helps users easily understand their computers' performance characteristics and manage and troubleshoot performance issues. Because some Windows Vista features and third-party applications will work only if the computer meets certain hardware requirements, a new Windows Experience Index scale helps users understand how their computer measures up and whether those features and applications will work on their machines.

Windows Vista is also designed to take advantage of the latest hardware to improve system performance. Windows ReadyBoost uses flash memory to boost performance without the need for additional RAM. Windows ReadyDrive takes advantage of new hybrid hard disk technology to improve reliability, battery life, and performance. Windows SuperFetch helps make the computer consistently responsive to user applications by making better use of the computer's RAM. Last, self-tuning and diagnostics make Windows Vista easier for users and administrators to manage performance effectively.

A comprehensive list of key performance features is shown in Table 3.1.

Table 3.1   **Windows Key Performance Features**

Feature	Description
Fast shutdown	Provides quick response to the user's request to sleep, shut down, or restart, eliminating the confusion caused by delays or a lack of responsiveness and providing a consistent and reliable "off" experience.
Low-priority I/O	Windows Vista differentiates between high-priority, low-priority, and critical I/O, as well as deadlines for I/O requests. Windows Vista also background processes to run with lower I/O priority than user processes, for greater system and application responsiveness.
Performance self-tuning and diagnostics	Automatically detects and self-corrects problematic performance. Provides instrumentation and services that support user-driven and tool-driven diagnoses of performance problems, such as media glitches, slow application or system startup, and network-related delays.
Reliable power-state transitions	User-initiated transitions to sleep or shut down via a laptop lid closure or the improved shutdown interface significantly increase reliability and prevent unexpected system wakeup and overheating while in a briefcase.
Sleep, fast startup	As the default "power off" setting in Windows Vista, Sleep provides consistent and reliable power transitions using a simple usage model, two-to-three-second resume times, and nonvolatile protection of end-user data.
Windows Experience Index	A numeric rating system that helps users understand the performance capabilities of their Windows Vista-based PC and suggests software that will provide the best user experience with their computers.
Windows ReadyBoost	Windows Vista can use available memory on a memory device, such as a USB flash drive, as extra memory cache to provide more consistent and responsive performance.

Table 3.1   **continued**

Feature	Description
Windows ReadyDrive	Windows Vista takes advantage of the additional capabilities of hybrid hard disk drives by proactively managing the nonvolatile cache that is integral to these hybrid devices. Windows ReadyDrive helps provide performance, battery life, and reliability advantages over standard drives.
Windows SuperFetch	Intelligent memory management lets users access their data more quickly. SuperFetch makes the computer consistently responsive to user applications by making better use of the computer's RAM and optimizes memory based on usage patterns over time.
Windows System Assessment Tools	A new set of tools in Windows Vista that runs tests on the processor, memory, hard disk, general graphics and gaming graphics and converts results into the Windows Experience Index ratings.

Exploring Control Panel

The Control Panel in Windows Vista contains most of the tools used to manage computers. The new Programs category heading, which uses the typical Windows Explorer framework (Navigation pane, Instant Search, and the like), provides users with a real-time account of installed applications on the desktop. Programs and Features replaces the Add or Remove Programs control and presents installed application information in a clear, understandable format. As a result of extensive usability testing, many of the accessories in the Windows Vista Control Panel have been redesigned and integrated into the Explorer framework, making them more consistent and accessible.

To help organizations with asset management, the Programs application interface also displays licensed applications that are available for installation by users. A user can use Instant Search to quickly find a specific application among a long list of applications that are available within the organization.

Control Panel is accessed in Windows Vista by clicking the Start button on the taskbar and then clicking Control Panel.

The redesigned Control Panel also exploits the Windows Explorer framework. It contains two views to help users efficiently manage system settings. The default view, shown in Figure 3.1, is a more advanced version of the category and task-based view first introduced in Windows XP. In addition to categories, the new view lists specific tasks, such as adjust screen resolution, to help the average user find the right control. Instant Search lets users type common word search terms, which results in matching tasks being displayed.

FIGURE 3.1
Accessing Windows Vista category-based Control Panel.

The second view, shown in Figure 3.2, is the classic, standard view, similar to the Control Panel introduced in Windows 2000 and earlier versions of the Windows operating system. In this view, Instant Search works as well.

Unlike the Classic Panel, which lists each utility individually, Category Control Panel is a console window that displays 10 categories of utilities (11 categories if the computer being used is a laptop). Each category included a top-level link. Beneath the top-level link are frequently performed tasks for the category. When the top-level category link is clicked, Control Panel displays a list of utilities for that category. Each utility has a link that opens the utility and under this link are several of the most frequently performed tasks for the utility.

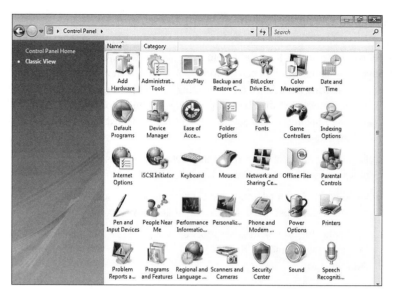

FIGURE 3.2
Accessing Windows Vista Classic View Control Panel.

Checking Windows Vista System Info

Computer users want a computer that performs consistently day in and day
out. Nothing is more aggravating to a computer user than a computer that
works well at the beginning of the day, when the applications launch quickly
and everything works well, and then sometime in the afternoon, the computer
becomes sluggish. The next morning, applications are slower to launch.
Fortunately, Windows Vista includes tools and instrumentation for managing,
diagnosing, and troubleshooting system performance problems. The built-in
performance diagnostics in Windows Vista detect and self-correct many
performance issues. Performance diagnostics provide instrumentation and
services for both administrator-driven and tool-driven diagnoses of common
problems, such as glitchy media playback, slow application startup, slow
startup of the operating system, or network-related delays. Built-in performance diagnostic tools also track how long it takes to execute common
activities; they analyze performance declines and display results in the
Performance Center, where users can then take action to remedy the problem.
Performance issues are also written to the system event log, where they can
be monitored by administrators.

Using the Computer Management Console

The Computer Management system console is designed to handle core administration tasks on local or remote computer systems. Using Computer Management, administrators can perform tasks, such as monitoring system events, configuring hard disks, and managing system performance. The console can be started in different ways. Many administrators place a shortcut on the Start menu for easy access. This is accomplished by performing the following steps:

1. Right-click the Start button and then select Properties to display the taskbar and Start Menu Properties dialog box.

2. On the Start Menu tab, click the Customize button. Scroll down the options in the Customize Start Menu dialog box.

3. To display the Administrative Tools option, select Display on the All Programs Menu and the Start Menu option under System Administrative Tools.

4. Click OK to finish.

The Computer Management console can now be started by clicking Start, Administrative Tools, and Computer Management.

For those administrators who prefer a simple Start menu, the Computer Management console can be started as follows:

1. Click Start and then click Control Panel.

2. In Control Panel, click the System and Maintenance link.

3. Click Administrative Tools and then double-click Computer Management.

As Figure 3.3 shows, the main window has a multiple pane display similar to Windows Explorer. The left pane is used for navigation and tool selection. The far-right pane is the Action pane, similar to the shortcut menu, which is displayed when right-clicking an item. The Action pane can be opened or closed using the Show\Hide button located on the console toolbar.

In the Computer Management console, tools are divided up into three broad categories: System Tools, Storage, and Services and Applications. Within each of these categories, a variety of tools are available:

■ **Task Scheduler**—View and manage scheduled tasks used to automate common tasks and processes such as diagnostics testing.

- **Event Viewer**—View and manage event logs on the selected computer. Event logs record events that take place on the computers and are useful for troubleshooting configuration issues and other system issues.

- **Local Users and Groups**—Manage local users and groups on the currently selected computer.

- **Performance Diagnostics**—Provides reporting and monitoring tools useful for assessing a computer's current performance and for tracking performance over time.

- **Device Manager**—A central location for checking device status, updating of device drivers, and troubleshooting device problems.

- **Disk Management**—Manage hard drives, drive partitions, and volume sets.

- **Services**—View and manage services running on a computer.

- **Windows Management Instrumentation Control**—Configure and control the Windows Management Instrumentation Service, which gathers system information, monitors system health, and manages system components.

FIGURE 3.3
Using the Computer Management console to manage computers and resources.

Checking Basic System Information

Administrators use the System console to view and manage system properties. To access the System console, use the following steps:

1. Click Start and then click Control Panel.

2. In Control Panel, click the System and Maintenance link.

3. Click System.

The System console shows four areas of information, including links for completing common tasks and a system overview. As shown in Figure 3.4, the four areas of information in the System console are the following:

- **Windows Edition**—Displays the operating system edition and version.

- **System**—Lists the Windows Experience Index rating, processor type and speed, system memory (RAM), and type of operating system installed. The type of operating system will be shown as 32 bit or 64 bit.

- **Computer Name, Domain, and Workgroup Settings**—Lists the computer name, computer description, workgroup, and domain details. To change any of the information, click Change Settings and then edit information as needed in the System Properties dialog box.

- **Windows Activation**—Shows whether the installed operating system has been activated. The activation process is started by clicking the provided link. The product key may also be changed to allow different licensing schemes for corporate users.

Link to additional system tools such as Device Manager, Remote Settings, System Protection, and Advanced System Settings are located in the left pane for quick access by administrators.

Checking Advanced System Information

Administrators often will want to view detailed system information or check computer performance on remote computers. Advanced system information is available via System Information (MSinfo32.exe). System Information is easily started by clicking Start, typing msinfo32 into the Search box and then pressing Enter. As shown in Figure 3.5, by selecting System Summary, System Information displays summaries of configuration information.

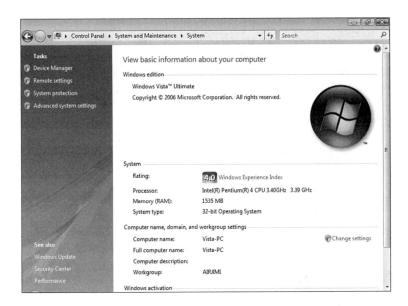

FIGURE 3.4
Using the System console to view system information and manage system settings.

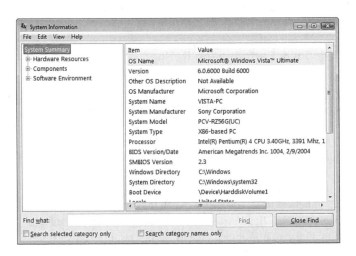

FIGURE 3.5
Using Advanced System Information to troubleshoot system performance.

System Information provides detailed information on hardware resources, components, and the software environment of the Windows Vista operating system. Administrators can use this information to be sure that hardware resources (interrupt requests, Direct Memory Access, memory, PnP devices), components (audio and video codecs, input devices, USB ports) and the software environment (drivers, environment variables, running tasks, services, programs group, and startup programs) are all working properly and are not conflicting with one another, causing less-than-optimal system performance.

To view the system configuration information of a remote computer, use the following steps:

1. Start System Information. In the View menu, select Remote Computer to display the Remote Computer dialog box.

2. In the Remote Computer dialog box, select Remote Computer on the Network.

3. Type the name of the remote computer into the space provided and then click OK.

Note

Remember, the account used must have the appropriate administrative rights and permissions for the local machine or for the domain.

Checking Windows Performance Rating

With Windows Vista, Microsoft introduces the Windows Experience Index (WEI) aimed at helping users understand the performance capabilities of their computers. The performance capabilities of a computer are directly tied to the processor, memory, graphics card, and storage specifications; typically, the higher the hardware specifications the better. The Windows Experience Index is a simple numeric system that rates how well the computer will run the performance-oriented features in Windows Vista, such as the new Aero user interface, multiple monitors, high definition TV, and personal video recording. The numerical rating also helps match the correct software to the capability of the computer. If a system has a low rating, Windows Vista will recommend disabling certain features, such as Aero glass, to improve system performance.

The Windows Experience Index rating is first determined during the installation of Windows Vista. The rating is computed by running a set of capability tests on five hardware component subsystems: Processor, Memory, Graphics, Gaming Graphics, and Primary Hard Disk. Each test results in a capability score between 1 and 5.9. A computer is given an overall test result called a base score, which is determined by the lowest of the five scores. The rating system is useful when buying or upgrading a computer or when purchasing software, because administrators will have a better idea how a computer will perform or what piece of hardware will be most beneficial when upgraded. To correctly match software to specific rating scores and help users purchase the proper software for their system rating, Microsoft is working with software companies to include the recommended WEI rating on software packaging.

A computer's performance rating is important in determining which operating system features are supported. If the computer has not been rated for performance, an administrator can click System, Score This Computer to begin the rating process. After a computer has been rated, administrators can click Update My Score on the Performance Information and Tools page, as shown in Figure 3.6.

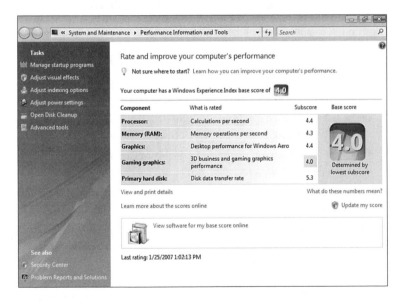

FIGURE 3.6
Using the Performance Information and Tools console page to view or rate a system's performance.

The Performance Information and Tools console displays the computer's overall rating index and lists the installed hardware and associated rating as follows:

- **Processor**—Rates the number of calculations per second
- **Memory**—Rates memory operations per second
- **Graphics**—Rates desktop performance for Windows Aero
- **Gaming Graphics**—Rates 3D business and gaming graphics
- **Primary Hard Disk**—Rates disk data transfer rate

Administrators can also view and print system details, view software that matches the base score, and learn about ways to improve the computer's performance from the Performance Information and Tools console.

Tip

System factors such a low disk space on the primary drive can affect the performance rating. When installing new hardware or resolving a computer problem that affects the computer rating, be sure to click Update My Score to update the computer's rating performance rating.

Windows Vista also includes a way to view current performance issues. Performance issues can be viewed by following these steps:

1. In the left pane of the Performance Information and Tools console, click Problem Reports and Solutions located in the See Also section.
2. Under the Tasks section, click See Problems to Check. This will display a report of all detected problems.
3. Click View Details for an issue to see a detailed description of the problem, as shown in Figure 3.7.
4. Click OK to return to the detected problem report. Select the check box for an issue and then click Check for Solutions to see potential solutions to the problem.

Administrators can remove the list of problems after all the problems are resolved. To do so, use the following steps:

1. Click Start and then click Control Panel.
2. In Control Panel, click the System and Maintenance category link.

3. Click the Problem Reports and Solutions.

4. In the Problem Reports and Solutions console, click Clear Solution and Problem History in Tasks section in the left pane.

5. Confirm the action by clicking Clear All.

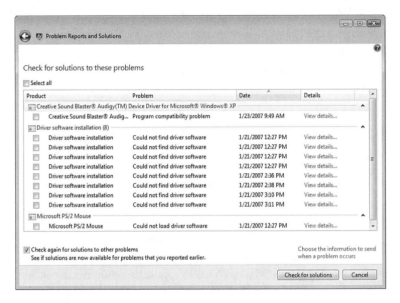

FIGURE 3.7
Viewing performance issues in Windows Vista.

Configuring Windows Vista Performance Settings

In addition to improvements in transition settings such as startup, sleep, and shutdown functions, Windows Vista is designed to take advantage of the latest hardware to improve system performance; performance management in Windows Vista has never been easier. Performance configuration settings for the Windows graphical user interface performance, application performance, virtual memory, and data execution prevention are all available to administrators. New features such as Windows ReadyBoost, Windows ReadyDrive, and Windows SuperFetch provide enhanced technology to improve reliability, battery life, and performance. Finally, state-of-the-art self-tuning and diagnostics make it much easier for users and administrators to keep Windows Vista running like new.

The Windows Vista graphical user interface contains many new graphical enhancements. These enhancements include visual effects for toolbars, the taskbar, menus, and windows. Other enhancements also include the Windows Flip and Windows Flip3D features of the Aero interface.

Administrators can tweak the performance of Windows by performing the following steps:

1. Click Start and then click Control Panel.

2. Click the System and Maintenance category heading link in Control Panel.

3. Click System and then in the Computer Name, Domain, and Workgroup settings section, click Change Settings (or click Advanced System Settings in the left pane).

4. Click the Advanced tab in the System Properties Dialog box and then click Settings in the Performance panel.

5. By default, the Visual Effects tab is displayed. The following options are available for managing the Windows graphical interface:

   - **Let Windows Choose What's Best for My Computer**—This option allows Windows Vista to choose the performance options based on the hardware setup and configuration. On a new computer with high-level hardware, this option may look similar to the Adjust for Best Appearance option.

   - **Adjust for Best Appearance**—This option optimizes and enables Windows Vista for all visual effects. Graphical interface enhancements such as menu and taskbar transitions and shadows, smooth edges of screen fonts, and smooth list box scrolling are enabled with this option.

   - **Adjust for Best Performance**—This option optimizes Windows Vista for the best performance by turning off hardware-intensive visual effects such as menu shadows, windows animations, and smooth font edges. This option reserves a basic set of visual effects.

6. When you're finished modifying visual effects, click OK twice to apply changes and close any open dialog boxes.

Configuring Application Performance

Application Performance in Windows Vista is related to scheduling of processor-related activities. Processor scheduling determines how responsive a running application is in comparison to services that run in the background. Windows Vista allows administrators to actively choose how processor resources are allocated. Administrators can adjust processor resources and control application performance using the following steps:

1. Click Start and then click Control Panel.

2. Click the System and Maintenance category heading link in Control Panel.

3. Click System and then in the Computer Name, Domain, and Workgroup settings section, click Change Settings (or click Advanced System Settings in the left pane).

4. Click the Advanced tab in the System Properties dialog box and then click Settings in the Performance panel.

5. Click the Advanced tab in the Performance Options dialog box.

6. The Processor Scheduling panel has two options:

   ■ **Programs**—This option gives applications the best share of system resources and enhances system response time. Typically this is the best option in Windows Vista.

   ■ **Background Services**—This option gives background services, like print servers, a better response time than active applications. Typically, this option is used with server systems not being used as Windows Vista Workstations.

7. Click OK twice to finish.

Configuring Virtual Memory

If a computer lacks the memory needed to run a program or operation, Windows Vista uses virtual memory to compensate. Virtual memory combines the computer's RAM with temporary space on the hard disk. When RAM runs low, virtual memory moves data from RAM to a space called a paging file. Moving data to and from the paging file frees up RAM to complete its work.

The more RAM the computer has, the faster the programs will generally run. If a lack of RAM is slowing the computer, it is tempting to increase virtual memory to compensate. However, a computer can read data from RAM much more quickly than from a hard disk, so adding RAM is always a better solution.

Administrators can manually configure the virtual memory by performing the following steps:

1. Click Start and then click Control Panel.

2. Click the System and Maintenance category heading link in Control Panel.

3. Click System and then in the Computer Name, Domain, and Workgroup settings section, click Change Settings (or click Advanced System Settings in the left pane).

4. Click the Advanced tab in the System Properties Dialog box and then click Settings in the Performance panel.

5. Click the Advanced tab in the Performance Options dialog box and then click Change to display the Virtual Memory dialog box. The following configuration information will be shown: Drive Size and Paging File Size, Paging File Size for Each Drive, and Total Paging File Size for All Drives.

6. Windows Vista manages the paging file size automatically by default. To manually configure the virtual memory, deselect the Automatically Manage Paging File Size for All Drives check box.

7. Select the volume to work with in the Drive list box.

8. Select Custom Size and then enter an Initial Size and a Maximum Size.

9. Click Set to save the changes. Repeat steps 7–9 to configure additional volumes.

10. Click OK. If prompted, confirm the action to overwrite the current PAGEFILE.SYS. If the current pagefile is being changed, the operating system will display a prompt explaining that a system restart is needed. Click OK to clear the message.

11. Click OK three times to close the open dialog boxes. When the System Utility is closed, a prompt will appear, asking whether to restart the system now or restart the system later. Click Restart Now.

You can allow Windows Vista to automatically manage virtual memory by using the following steps:

1. Click Start and then click Control Panel.

2. Click the System and Maintenance category heading link in Control Panel.

3. Click System and then in the Computer Name, Domain, and Workgroup settings section, click Change Settings (or click Advanced System Settings in the left pane).

4. Click the Advanced tab in the System Properties dialog box and then click Settings in the Performance panel.

5. Click the Advanced tab in the Performance Options dialog box and then click Change to display the Virtual Memory dialog box.

6. Enable the Automatically Manage Page File Size for All Drives check box.

7. Click OK three times to finish and close the open dialog boxes.

Tip

Windows Vista is much better at handling virtual memory than previous Windows versions were. Typically, Windows Vista allocates virtual memory at least as large as the computer's physical memory, which helps prevent pagefile fragmentation and poor system performance. To maximize the performance of the Windows Vista virtually memory, manually set the pagefile size to at least two to two and one-half times the size of the physical memory in the computer by setting the initial and maximum size to equal values. This creates a consistently sized paging file and if disk space is available, allows the pagefile to be written as a contiguous file.

Configuring Data Execution Prevention

Data Execution Prevention (DEP) is a memory protection technology and instructs the system's processor to mark all memory locations in applications as nonexecutable unless the location explicitly contains executable code. As seen in previous version of Windows operating systems, buffer overflow exploits have proved very harmful to Windows in the past several years. A buffer overflow occurs when an area of memory (a buffer) expects to have a maximum amount of data but is given more and doesn't handle it correctly. The MSBlaster worm was this type of exploit. The MSBlaster worm took advantage of email clients that were designed to handle attachments with a maximum of 255 characters in the filename. When an email client received an attachment with a 256-character filename, a buffer overflow occurred. The adjacent memory space was overwritten and malicious code ended up being executed. Because DEP prevents malicious code from being run from a memory area marked as containing nonexecutable code, it may have prevented the spread of the MSBlaster worm.

The 32-bit Windows Vista versions utilize a less effective, software-based version of DEP. Not all 32-bit processors contain built-in hardware support for DEP, but the 32-bit editions of Windows Vista will support DEP 32-bit processors that do contain hardware support for Data Execution Prevention.

The 64-bit editions of Windows Vista support the 64-bit processor's DEP feature to help protect computers against buffer overflow attacks. In conjunction with the No Execute (NX) technologies in AMD and Intel x64 microprocessors, Windows Vista x64 versions also provide support for hardware-backed Data Execution Protection, which helps to prevent the buffer overflows used in electronic attacks.

Note

Another unique x64 feature, PatchGuard, also known as Kernel Patch Protection, prevents malicious software from patching the Windows Vista kernel. PatchGuard works by preventing kernel-mode drivers from extending or replacing other kernel services and preventing third-party software from patching the kernel. Kernel Patch Protection does not prevent all viruses, root kits, spyware, or other malware from attacking the operating system. It provides an additional layer of security and helps prevent one method of attacking the system: patching kernel structures and code to manipulate kernel functionality. Protecting the integrity of the kernel is a fundamental step in protecting the entire system from malicious attacks and from inadvertent reliability problems that result from patching.

Administrators can check whether a computer supports DEP and then configure DEP by completing the following steps:

1. Click Start and then click Control Panel.

2. Click the System and Maintenance category heading link in Control Panel.

3. Click System and then in the Computer Name, Domain, and Work-group settings section, click Change Settings (or click Advanced System Settings in the left pane).

4. Click the Advanced tab in the System Properties dialog box and then click Settings in the Performance panel.

5. Click the Data Execution Prevention tab in the Performance Options dialog box, as shown in Figure 3.8. This tab indicates whether DEP is supported on the computer.

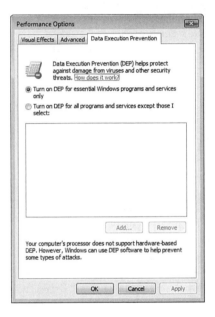

FIGURE 3.8
Configuring Data Execution Prevention in Windows Vista.

6. If the computer supports execution protection and is configured correctly, administrators can configure DEP using the following options:

   ■ **Turn on DEP for Essential Windows Programs and Service Only**—This option is the default selection and enables DEP for the OS services, applications, and components.

■ **Turn on DEP for All Programs Except Those I Select**—This option configures DEP and allows administrators to configure specific programs that should run without execution protection. This setting allows execution protection for all running programs except for those excluded here.

7. Click OK two times to finish and exit open dialog boxes.

Tip

Applications must be able to mark memory with the Execute permission. If applications cannot, they will not be compatible with DEP and the NX processor feature. To handle problematic memory-related applications, administrators should configure the applications as exceptions in DEP rather than completely disabling DEP. This will retain the memory protection benefits of DEP and allow selective disabling of noncompliant programs with the NX.

Understanding Hard Disk Performance and Using ReadyBoost, ReadyDrive, and SuperFetch

Taking advantage of leading-edge advances in technology and hardware, Windows Vista can scale its feature set and performance set to the hardware available. If a Windows Driver Display Model graphics card is installed, Windows Vista will display the Aero interface. If a compliant graphics card is not available, Windows Vista will operate but not show the Aero interface. Windows Vista handles performance features in a similar fashion. When the right hardware is available, Windows Vista unlocks some of the most innovative performance features: Windows ReadyBoost, Windows ReadyDrive, and SuperFetch.

Windows ReadyBoost helps alleviate the performance impact due to reading and writing the computer's system cache. With Windows ReadyBoost, administrators can use nonvolatile flash memory devices such as universal serial bus (USB) 2.0 flash drives, Secure Digital (SD) cards, or Compact Flash cards to improve performance without having to add additional system memory. To use Windows ReadyBoost, the removable flash device must have at least 256MB free and have fast enough read/write performance. It also must provide at least 2.5MB/sec throughput for random 4KB reads and 1.75MB/sec for random 512KB writes. The 256 MB or larger flash memory device serves as an additional memory cache that the computer can access much more quickly than it can access data on the hard drive. Windows Vista automatically checks to see whether the flash drive's performance is fast enough to work with Windows ReadyBoost. If so, administrators can choose to allocate part of a USB drive's memory to speed up performance and use the remainder to store files. Windows ReadyBoost technology is both reliable and secure using optimizing algorithms for maximizing the life cycle of the device and encrypting data stored (and keyed to the original computer) on the device in case it's lost or stolen.

Administrators can enable ReadyBoost using a USB 2.0 device by completing the following steps:

1. Insert a USB flash device into a USB 2.0 or later computer port. Windows Vista analyzes the speed of the flash memory on the device. If the device performs sufficiently, the computer memory can be extended onto the device.

2. An Autoplay dialog box will appear automatically. Select the Speed Up My System Using Windows ReadyBoost option. If the flash device will be used only for Windows ReadyBoost, select the Always Do This for Software and Games check box.

3. When the Speed Up My System Using Windows ReadyBoost is clicked, the computer's memory is extended to the flash device.

4. In the Properties dialog box, select the button for Use This Device. Accept the default value for Space to Reserve for System Speed or set another value.

5. Click OK to finish.

If a flash drive had previously been inserted and declined for use for Windows ReadyBoost, administrators can make it ready for Windows ReadyBoost using the following steps:

1. Click Start and then Computer.

2. Right-click the appropriate flash device in the Devices with Removable Storage list and then select Properties.

3. Select Use this Device on the ReadyBoost tab and then click OK.

> **Tip**
>
> Windows Vista comes with a service called ReadyBoost that is started auto-matically. If this service is stopped or disabled, Windows Vista will not prompt for whether to use this drive as a ReadyBoost drive when a USB flash drive is inserted. If this occurs, reenable the Windows ReadyBoost service with the following steps:
>
> 1. Click the Start button and then type **services.msc** into the Search field and press the Enter key.
> 2. Scroll down to and double-click the ReadyBoost service.
> 3. Change the Startup Type drop-down menu to Automatic.
> 4. Click the Start button to activate the service.
> 5. Click OK to finish and then close the Services console.
>
> The ReadyBoost service is now active and any inserted flash drive will be prompted for use with Windows ReadyBoost.

Windows ReadyDrive is a new feature in Windows Vista that enables PCs equipped with a hybrid hard disk. Hybrid hard disks are disks that add flash memory to a standard mobile computer hard drive. This combination provides better performance, more reliability, and improved battery life with mobile computers.

Using the flash buffer on the hybrid hard disk to cache disk reads and writes, a computer outfitted with a hybrid hard disk can actually read and write from the hard disk without needing to start up and spin the disk, thus saving battery power on the machine and reducing drive wear or drive damage when temporarily transporting the system from one location to another.

Like Windows ReadyBoost, the flash memory on the hybrid hard disk is used by Windows ReadyDrive to increase application performance. In addition, Windows ReadyDrive can improve startup and hibernate resume time because key information for the startup and resume process is written to the flash for quicker access. When starting or waking up the computer, this information is read from the flash drive.

Administrators do not need to enable Windows ReadyDrive. Windows ReadyDrive is automatically enabled on mobile computers employing hybrid drives.

Windows SuperFetch improves system performance and responsiveness by modifying the method in which user processes and background processes are used. In previous versions of Windows, users' processes and background processes had the same memory-use prioritization scheme and were loaded into memory simultaneously, causing performance lags and memory contention. Windows Vista corrects this problem by ensuring that background process are unloaded from memory after they are run and when user process data is reloading into memory.

Windows SuperFetch optimizes memory usage based on how the user is using the computer. Windows SuperFetch does this by prioritizing the current user's processes over background tasks, optimizing memory for users after running background tasks by repopulating memory to the state prior to running the background task and tracking the usage of user applications and anticipating user application needs. Windows SuperFetch also takes advantage of input and output queues to improve read and write times for user processes and improve the computer's responsiveness.

Windows SuperFetch is available on all versions of Windows Vista and runs as a service named SuperFetch using the Local System account. Windows SuperFetch also utilizes the SvcHost.exe program and runs in a network restricted mode so that it can access only the local computer. Last, Windows SuperFetch uses prefetch data to help start applications quicker and writes the prefetch data to the %SystemRoot%\prefetch folder.

Reducing Disk Space Usage with Disk Cleanup

Administrators should monitor disk usage on all system drives. As drives begin to fill up, drive performance and operating system performance suffers as the systems runs low on virtual memory and temporary file storage space. Using Drive Cleanup, administrators can remove unnecessary files, compress old files, and increase available disk space. Administrators reduce unnecessary files by using the following steps:

1. Click Start, Programs or All Programs, Accessories, System Tools. Then highlight and select Disk Cleanup.

2. Choose whether to clean up the current user's files or files from all users on the computer. If cleaning files from all users on the computer, administrator privileges are required.

3. If the computer has multiple drives, the Drive Selection dialog box is displayed. Use the drop-down list to select the drives to clean up and then click OK. Disk Cleanup scans the drive looking for temporary files, Recycle Bin files, system files, and other items that are no longer needed. It also looks for files that can be compressed for saving disk space. The bigger the disk, the longer Disk Cleanup search will take.

4. After Disk Cleanup completes, it presents a list of files that are candidates for deletion and/or compression. The report will look similar to the one shown in Figure 3.9 and may contain the following items:

- **Downloaded Program Files**—Contains downloaded program files, such as Java Applets and Active X controls, for the Internet browser.

- **Temporary Internet Files**—Contains web pages stored on the disk for quick viewing.

- **Hibernation File Cleaner**—Contains information about the state of the computer as it enters hibernation. This file can be removed if the user is not using hibernation. Removing the file will disable hibernation.

- **Previous Windows Installation(s)**—Contains files from a previous Windows installation. After any existing user data is backed up or saved, this option can be selected to free up disk space.

- **Recycle Bin**—Contains files that have been deleted from the computer but not yet purged from the disk. Emptying the Recycle Bin permanently removes the files from the computer.

- **System Error Memory Dump Files**—Contains system error dump files.

- **Temporary File**—Contains data stored in the TEMP folder. These files are primarily temporary data files created by applications and are usually deleted by the application upon close.

5. Use the check boxes in the Files to Delete list to choose files to be removed. Click OK. When prompted to confirm the permanent deletion, click Delete Files.

Defragging a Disk

Whenever files are added to or removed from a drive, disk fragmentation can occur. When a drive is fragmented, large files cannot be written to a single contiguous space on the drive and must be written to several small noncontiguous areas on a disk, which increases disk read and write time.

Infrequent disk defragmentation leads to an inefficient layout of files on the hard disk, which can slow computer performance. Windows Vista includes a new disk defragmenter that runs in the background and when needed automatically defragments the hard disk.

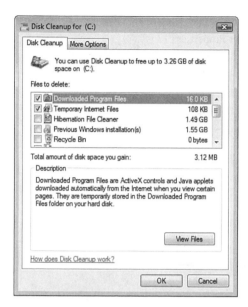

FIGURE 3.9
Using Disk Cleanup to free up disk space.

The Windows Vista version of Disk Defragmenter includes two major improvements over previous Windows versions. First, the application sports a vastly simplified user interface that does away with the colorful disk layout view, which you could literally watch as your hard disk was graphically defragged. Second, Disk Defragmenter can be automatically scheduled to run. This is important because disk defragging is one of those mundane chores that most administrators or users really don't have time to perform. It is, however, something that should happen regularly to keep computer performance up to par.

The new disk defragmenter also no longer needs to complete in a single session—it can defragment incrementally, whenever the computer is idle. Because disk defragmentation is one of the processes that takes advantage of low-priority I/O, a hard disk can be defragmented in the background without hurting the responsiveness of running applications.

By default, Windows Vista runs Disk Defragmenter automatically at 1:00 a.m. every Wednesday. Administrators can modify or cancel the defragmentation schedule by completing the following steps:

1. Click Start and then click Computer. Under Hard Disk Drives, right-click a drive and then select Properties.

2. Click Defragment Now on the Tools tab to display the Disk Defragmenter dialog box shown in Figure 3.10.

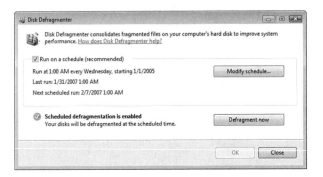

FIGURE 3.10
Modifying automatic scheduling in Windows Vista Disk Defragmenter.

3. To cancel scheduled defragmentation, deselect the Run On a Schedule option and click OK twice, skipping any remaining steps.

4. To modify the automated scheduling, click Modify Schedule. Use the Modify Schedule dialog box to set a new defragmentation schedule.

5. Click OK three times to finish saving the new settings and exit.

Tip

Disk defragmentation can take several hours to complete and is dependent on the size of the disk. Be sure to schedule automated disk defragmentation outside of normal business hours. If needed, click Cancel Defragmentation at any time to stop the defragmentation process.

Administrators can also manually defragment a disk by performing the following steps:

1. Click Start and then click Computer. Under Hard Disk Drives, right-click a drive and then select Properties.

2. Click Defragment Now on the Tools tab to display the Disk Defragmenter dialog box.

3. In the Disk Defragmenter Dialog box, click Defragment Now.

Checking for Disk Errors

Administrators should periodically check disk integrity using the Check Disk Utility. Check disk scrubs disks and corrects errors related to bad sectors, lost clusters, cross-linked files, and directory errors on FAT16, FAT32, and NTFS drives. Check Disk can be run through a graphical interface or from a command line.

To run Check Disk interactively from within Windows Vista using Windows Explorer, administrators should perform the following steps:

1. Click Start and then click Computer. Under Hard Drives, right-click a drive and then select Properties.

2. Select the Tools tab and then click Check Now. The Check Disk dialog box appears.

3. To run in read-only mode and check for errors without repairing them, click Start without selecting either of the check boxes in the Check Disk dialog box.

4. To check for errors and attempt to repair them, select one or both of the following check box options and then click Start.

    ■ **Automatically Fix File System Errors**—Repair errors without scanning the volume for bad sectors.

    ■ **Scan for and Attempt Recovery of Bad Sectors**—Repair errors, locate bad sectors, and recover readable information.

5. Click OK when Check Disk finishes analyzing and repairing the disk.

> ### Note
>
> If one or more of the files on the hard disk are open, the following message is displayed: The disk check could not be performed because the disk check utility needs exclusive access to some Windows files on the disk. These files can be accessed by restarting Windows. Do you want to schedule the disk check to occur the next time you restart the computer?
>
> Click Yes and the scheduled the disk check will occur on the next system restart.

The Check Disk utility can also be run from the command line with elevated privileges. When the command chkdsk C: is run, check disk analyzes the disk and returns a status message displaying any errors found. This check is good for finding errors but will not repair errors that are found. To find and repair disk errors on a drive C, use this command:

```
chkdsk C: /f
```

Check disk analyzes the disk and repairs any errors found (as long as the disk is not in use). If the disk is in use, Check Disk displays a prompt that asks whether the disk can be checked at the next system restart. Clicking Yes will schedule Check Disk to run after a system restart.

The complete command-line syntax for Check Disk is as follows:

```
chkdsk [volume:][[Path] FileName]
➥[/f] [/v] [/r] [/x] [/i] [/c] [/l[:size]] [/b]
```

The command-line options and switches for Check Disk are the following:

volume :—Specifies the drive letter (followed by a colon), mount point, or volume name.

[Path] FileName:—Specifies the location and name of a file or set of files to check for fragmentation.

/**f**—Fixes errors on the disk. The disk must be locked. If chkdsk cannot lock the drive, a message appears that asks if you want to check the drive the next time you restart the computer.

/**v**—Displays the name of each file in every directory as the disk is checked.

/**r**—Locates bad sectors and recovers readable information.

/**x**—Use with NTFS only. Forces the volume to dismount first, if necessary. /x also includes the functionality of /f.

/**i**—Use with NTFS only. Performs a minimum check of index entries, reducing check disk running time.

/**c**—Use with NTFS only. Skips the checking of cycles within the folder structure.

/**l**[:size]—Use with NTFS only. Sets the log file size.

/**b**—NTFS only: Re-evaluates bad clusters on the volume (implies /R).

/**?**—Displays help at the command prompt.

Summary

As with previous versions of Windows operating systems, new and improved technology in Windows Vista makes computer systems more responsive in performing everyday tasks. Improved start-up and sleep performance features help both desktop and mobile PCs get up and running more quickly. Because Windows Vista manages both memory and input/output devices more efficiently, computer performance is more consistent and responsive to end user applications. Windows Vista incorporates a new approach to address performance issues and offers a Performance Information and Tools Control Panel and a new Windows Experience Index scale that helps users easily understand their computers' performance characteristics and manage and troubleshoot performance issues. Windows Vista is also designed to take advantage of the latest hardware to improve system performance. Windows ReadyBoost uses flash memory to boost performance without the need for additional RAM. Windows ReadyDrive takes advantage of new hybrid hard disk technology to improve reliability, battery life, and performance. Windows SuperFetch helps make the computer consistently responsive to user applications by making better use of the computer's RAM. Last, self-tuning and diagnostics make Windows Vista easier for users and administrators to manage performance effectively.

PART II

Security for Windows Vista Systems

IN THIS PART

CHAPTER 4

Securing a Windows Vista System

Understanding Windows Security

Under development and testing for five years, Windows Vista is the most secure operating system ever produced by Microsoft. In the era of the Trustworthy Computing Initiative, Windows Vista looks to lock down desktop security, improve the user experience, and prevent malware, spyware, and viruses from invading the new operating system. Unlike previous versions of Windows, Windows Vista introduces several security enhancements that create a solid defense against operating system exploits, computer security breaches, user permission violations, and other malicious activities.

Not available in previous versions of Windows, Windows Vista introduces several new security features aimed at eliminating the threat of hackers and mitigating malware threats. Some of the new features are the following:

- **User Account Control (UAC)**—Discourages users from running as administrator and requires confirmation for potential system damaging actions.

- **Internet Explorer Protected Mode**—Operates with reduced rights and permissions to protect against surreptitious program installations, program communications, or any hostile program that attempts to alter system settings or files.

- **Windows Defender**—Blocks malicious programs from striking the operating system using built-in malware scanners

- **BitLocker Drive Encryption**—Protects hard drive data using encryption in case the computer is stolen.

- **Windows Firewall**—Screens incoming and outgoing network connections for suspicious activities and threats caused by malware, phishing attempts, or DDoS attempts.

- **PatchGuard (64-Bit Security Enhancement)**—Allows only digitally signed device drivers to be installed. This feature ensures kernel level code is from a known source and has not been maliciously altered (rootkit installation).

Moreover, Microsoft listened to the user community and the professional IT community in regard to operating security by adding operating system improvements designed to mitigate application vulnerabilities. A group of new technologies, which includes Data Redirection and Address Space Layout Randomization (ASLR), has also been introduced to protect the operating system and obscure memory space, preventing hackers from exploiting operating system bugs. By using virtual file areas unique to each user, Data Redirection prevents malicious applications from writing to core system areas and causing system-crippling issues that could bring down a system. ASLR, initiated during the boot process, loads system code into a different location of memory. This prevents well-known attacks that use explicit code from calling a system function from a known memory location.

As administrators know, security settings are critical for maintaining the system integrity of Windows systems. In Windows Vista, Microsoft makes it easy to evaluate and manage the status of security features using Windows Security Center. Windows Security Center is the central location for checking security configuration and accessing security features contained in Windows Defender, Windows Update, Windows Firewall, and third-party antivirus products.

Configuring Windows Security Center

Windows Security Center is designed to be the central location for managing system security. Using Windows Security Center, administrators can determine the status of security features and get recommendations for quickly resolving security issues. If the computer is at security risk, the administrator can access Windows Security Center by clicking the Windows Security Center icon (the red shield with an X or a yellow shield with an exclamation mark) in the notification area of the system tray. If no alert is present, administrators can access Windows Security Center by typing **wscui.cpl** at the

Search box or using the following steps:

1. Click Start and then click Control Panel.

2. In Control Panel, click Security.

3. Click Security Center to display Windows Security Center, as shown in Figure 4.1.

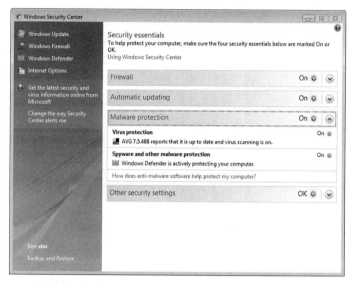

FIGURE 4.1
Viewing Windows Vista security settings via Windows Security Center in Windows Vista.

The status section, located in the right pane of Windows Security Center, displays information about the security settings of the computer. If everything is okay for the individual firewall, updates, malware, and other security settings, a green bar with the work ON will be displayed. A yellow or red bar will be displayed with error status wording like OFF, Out of Date, Check Settings, Not Automatic, or Not Monitored. Beneath the bar, explanatory text and buttons are displayed to allow for the problems to be corrected. Windows Security Center can be configured so that it will not alert the user.

The left pane in Windows Security Center includes several links for the following:

■ **Windows Update**—Opens the Windows Update utility in Control Panel.

- **Windows Defender**—Opens Windows Defender if the feature is turned on.

- **Windows Firewall**—Opens Windows Firewall.

- **Internet Options**—Opens the Internet Properties dialog box with the Security tab displayed.

Windows Security Center is designed to work with third-party firewall, anti-spyware, and antivirus programs, as well as those programs incorporated in Windows Vista, such as Windows Defender and Windows Firewall, and other Microsoft products such as Windows Live OneCare.

Although the same set of security tools are available in both workgroups and domain environment, the default behavior in each setting is different. In workgroups, individual users can manage security settings, and Windows Security Center displays the current status of security features. In a domain environment, the core functionality of Windows Security Center is turned off by default. Windows Security Center doesn't display the current status of security features, no Windows Security Center icon appears in the notification area, Windows Security Center does not monitor the computer's security status, and Windows Security Center settings can be accessed only by using the provided links in the left panel.

Tip

If the computer is joined to a domain, administrators can allow users to manage and view the status of security features. By making a group policy change, administrators can enable Windows Security Center for a domain-based computer and use it just as if the computer is not joined to a domain by performing the following steps:

1. In the Search box, type `gpedit.msc` to open the Group Policy Object Editor. To do so, administrative privileges are required.

2. In Group Policy Object Editor, open `Computer Configuration\ Administrative Templates\Windows Components\Security Center`.

3. Double-click the Turn On Security Center (Domain PCs Only) policy.

4. Select Enable and then click OK.

5. Restart the computer to have the policy take effect and enable access to the Windows Security Center.

Firewall

Windows Security Center provides administrators with options to help manage and track the status of Windows Firewall. Windows Security Center shows the status of the computer's firewall. The firewall protects the computer against incoming threats and attacks from LAN computers and remote systems. As in Windows XP Service Pack 2, Windows Vista comes with Windows Firewall and Windows Firewall with Advanced Security installed and enabled for all connections by default.

Administrators can manipulate the Windows Firewall settings within Windows Security Center. If the firewall is disabled, administrators can enable the firewall by clicking the Windows Firewall option in the left pane, clicking the radio button next to the On (recommended) option on the General tab, and then clicking OK. When enabled, Windows Firewall blocks all incoming connections that do not have an exception rule configured and will display a notification when a program is blocked.

Windows Firewall will also check for existing installed firewalls. If Windows Firewall fails to detect a previously installed firewall, administrators can tell Windows Security Center that they will monitor the firewall status themselves. If more than one firewall wall product is detected, Windows Security Center will allow only one product to operate at the same time so that operational conflicts are avoided.

Automatic Updating

Automatic Updating provides the status of programs that are updated by Windows Update. Windows Security Center verifies that Automatic Updates is enabled and using the default recommended settings. If the Windows Automatic Updates service is not running or if settings differ from Microsoft's recommended settings, the user will receive an alert notification and will be provided with a way to enable Automatic Updates in Windows Security Center.

Malware Protection

Malware protection software prevents a computer from being affected by malicious programs such as viruses, spyware, and other operating system-compromising programs. The most common programs for malware protection are antispyware programs and antivirus programs.

Because Windows Vista does not ship with its own antivirus application, Windows Security Center verifies the installation of third-party antivirus solutions. Windows Security Center reports whether real-time scanning is enabled and whether the virus signature files are up-to-date. If any of these conditions are not met, the user receives an alert notification and is prompted with a way to resolve the problem.

Other Security Settings

Security settings that are associated with Internet Explorer are monitored by Windows Security Center and alerts are generated for the user whenever those security settings are lower than the recommended levels, putting the computer at risk. Windows Security Center provides a Restore Settings button that the user can click to have Windows Security Center automatically fix the settings, or the user can go to the Control Panel to fix the settings manually.

To help ensure a safe and secure computing experience and environment, the User Account Control (UAC) service and policy must not be disabled or degraded. Window Security Center monitors the status of UAC and notifies the user if User Account Control settings have been modified from default values. Windows Security Center provides a button to restore User Account Control to the default recommended settings, if needed.

Caution

Many users become accustomed to repetitive warnings, and confirmation screens are displayed time and time again. It is natural to want to click through them without reading them or eventually to disable the feature altogether; User Account Control is no different! Disabling UAC can be performed, but is not recommended. User Account Control is much more than an annoying confirmation screen and performs the following critical functions:

- Allows administrators to run with a standard access token
- Allows Internet Explorer 7 to run in a low privilege Protected mode
- Prevents rogue applications from performing a task that can cause systemwide damage and/or failure

Recommended advice? Leave User Account Control enabled for the safest and securest computing environment and system protection. Instead of blowing past the Confirmation dialog box, stop, read the info, think, and then click to continue or cancel the requested action.

Understanding Password Protection

Password protection is the most popular method of authentication and is the first line of defense against intruders. Requiring passwords goes a long way toward securing a computer. However, this type of single-factor authentication has many limitations. A short, easy-to-remember password can easily be determined by a hacker; complex passwords are difficult to remember and are often written down by users on sticky notes and posted on their computer monitors. If a password is not set for a user account and that user account has administrator privileges, intruders have unfettered access to all folders, files, and configuration settings on the computer.

Windows Vista introduces a revised architecture for adding alternative authentication methods. The redesigned Win logon process allows independent software vendors and organizations to implement their own authentication methods (biometrics, tokens, or smart card) by writing credential providers. The credential provider model allows multiple providers to function side by side and is much simpler than replacing the Graphical Identification and Authorization (GINA) method, which involves a dynamic link library (DLL) file that is part of the Windows operating system. In Windows, GINA is loaded early in the boot process and handles the user identification and authorization logon process.

The inventory tracking and management of credentials (passwords and certificates) and hardware (smart cards that hold credentials) challenges many organizations. Tools created to aid in management and tracking are often lacking usability and completeness. Because Microsoft heard the IT community on this issue, Windows Vista includes new tools to help support credentials management for roaming users. The new tools include the new Digital Identity Management Service certificate enrollment process and a self-service personal identification number reset tool for easier smart cards deployment and management. Additionally, small businesses and consumers can now employ tools to back up and restore the credentials stored in the Stored User Names and Passwords key ring.

Administrators should advise users to create complex passwords. Because an easily guessed password is of little protection value, users should not use their names, their spouse's or pet's name, or any other easily guessed word. Users should also not use a random word, one that can be guessed using a brute force/dictionary type of hacking tool. By observing the following guidelines, administrators can help users create passwords that will take a reasonable amount of time for attackers to hack. The following are key guidelines to creating secure passwords:

- Use random sequences, interspersed punctuation marks (,.;), special characters (!#$%^), and numbers with words (for example, V!5T4 R()ck5).

- Mix capitalization (uppercase and lowercase) of letter, space characters, numbers, and punctuation.

- Use eight characters at a minimum for short passwords. Better yet, create a pass phrase. Passwords or pass phrases can contain a maximum of 127 characters, including spaces and punctuation.

- Avoid using the user's name or user account name in the password.

Tip

Want to create a complex but easier to remember password? Start with something easy to remember like a hobby or a little-known fact about the user. For example, I like Seattle-based musicians, so my little-known fact leads me to choose **I'm A Hendrix Fan** as my password. I change a few letters, misspell a word or two, and then I have **I'm 4 H3ndr!x F4n**. It is long and complex, uses four types of characters, is easy to remember, and I won't be tempted to write it down on a sticky located near the computer.

For users of Windows Vista Business, Enterprise, or Ultimate edition, administrators can set password policies using the Local Security Policy console. Here, administrators can change policies such as minimum and maximum password age, password complexity, and minimum password length. Administrators can configure password policies by typing `secpol.msc` at the command prompt or by using the following steps:

1. Click Start and then Control Panel.

2. Click the System and Maintenance category link and then Administrative Tools.

3. In the Administrative Tools console, click the Local Security Policy located in the right pane to display the Local Security Policy management interface.

4. To see the password policies, click the Account Policies node and then the Password Policy node.

Administrators can now set the appropriate password polices and provide the additional security for the organization.

Understanding Internet Explorer Protected Mode

Available only to users running Internet Explorer 7 in Windows Vista, Internet Explorer Protected Mode will provide new levels of security and data protection for Windows users. Using a web browser exposes a computer to a lot of security risks. By mistyping a URL or unintentionally clicking a link in an email, users can be redirected to a malicious website containing malicious scripting or downloadable code that adversely affects the computer. Protected mode, which runs in all Internet Explorer 7 security zones except the Trusted Zone, is designed to defend against "elevation of privilege" attacks and takes advantage of Windows Vista security enhancements such as User Account Control (UAC). Protected mode severely limits the privileges available to programs.

In Protected mode, Internet Explorer 7 runs as a low-privilege process as defined by the Mandatory Integrity Control (MIC) feature (for more information on MIC, check this link athttp://blogs.technet.com/steriley/archive/2006/07/21/442870.aspx). Because MIC limits the privileges of Internet Explorer 7, Internet Explorer 7 is unable to modify system files and/or the Registry that requires a higher privilege. All communications occur via a broker process that mediates between the Internet Explorer browser and the operating system. The broker process is initiated only when the user clicks the Internet Explorer menus and screens. The highly restrictive broker process prohibits workarounds from bypassing Protected mode. Any scripted actions or automatic processes will be prevented from downloading data or affecting the system. If a user action requires a higher-level access level, such as an ActiveX installation or saving a file, the broker process kicks in. Typically, this action is displayed to the user as the UAC dialog box asking for confirmation to continue.

Protected mode might prevent a website or program from working properly. If all attempts to work around the application or website compatibility fail, Protected mode can be disabled. Administrators can disable Protected mode using the following steps:

1. From within Internet Explorer 7, click Tools, and then click Internet Options.

2. Click the Security tab and clear the Enable Protected Mode check box.

3. Click OK to continue and save the changes. Windows will display a warning box as shown in Figure 4.2. Click OK to Continue.

FIGURE 4.2
Warning displayed when disabling Protected mode in Internet Explorer 7.

When Protected mode is disabled, users will see a warning message in the Information Bar when visiting any web page. User can reenable Protected mode by clicking the Information Bar and then clicking Open Security Settings. Select the Enable Protected Mode check box and then click OK. To make the changes take effect, Internet Explorer 7 must be closed and reopened.

Caution

Disabling Protected mode in Internet Explorer 7 is not recommended. If Protected mode must be disabled for any reason, it is recommended that Protected mode is reenabled immediately after the activity conflicting with it is completed. If a particular website is conflicting with Protected mode *and* it is known to be a safe site, administrators can add this site to the Trusted Zone where Protected mode is not in effect. Again, use this option with caution; it enables a wide range of potentially risky behaviors.

Managing Windows Firewall

Windows Vista ships with a two-way stateful packet inspection (SPI) packet-filtering firewall called Windows Firewall. Windows Firewall is enabled by default for all connections on the computer and begins protecting the computer as soon as it boots. By default, Windows Firewall blocks all incoming traffic except traffic that is in response to a packet sent by the computer or unsolicited traffic that is allowed by a firewall exception rule. All outgoing traffic is allowed by default unless the traffic matches a configured exception rule. Compared to the firewall that is included in Windows XP, Windows Firewall is a much improved firewall for protecting the computer against unsolicited attacks by hackers. The new improvements in Windows Firewall include support for both incoming and outgoing traffic monitoring, an advanced security console for improved configuration flexibility, firewall exceptions for items such as Active Directory accounts or groups, and the capability of being configured for three different profiles—a public network profile, a private network profile, and a domain profile. Using Windows Firewall with Advanced Security, administrators can view and manage the applicable profile.

Typically, administrators will manage Windows Firewall using one of the following tools:

- **Windows Firewall**—This Control Panel application is the simplest tool. Administrators can configure routine tasks such as allowing or blocking incoming programs.

- **Windows Firewall with Advanced Security**—This is a snap-in and predefined console for the Microsoft Management console, which allows more detailed configuration options for rules, exceptions, and profiles.

- **Group Policy Object Editor (GPOE)**—Available only in Business, Enterprise, and Ultimate editions, GPOE incorporates a number of policies for managing Windows Firewall; they are found in `Computer Configuration\Administrative Templates\Network\Network Connections\Windows Firewall`. GPOE also incorporates the Windows Firewall with the Advanced Security snap-in, which is located in `Computer Configuration\Windows Settings\Security Settings\Windows Firewall With Advanced Security`.

Note

Administrators who like batch files or scripts can also configure Windows Firewall settings via the Command Prompt window. Using the NETSH utility, administrators can configure Windows Firewall settings using the Firewall and Advfirewall contexts. Type **NETSH /?** for additional help with these commands.

Configuring Windows Firewall

By default, Windows Firewall is enabled for all network connections on the computer. All modem, hard-wired network connections, wireless network connections, and FireWire (IEEE 1394) connections are protected by Windows Firewall. Using the Windows Firewall interface, administrators can enable and disable the firewall, enable program exceptions, configure TCP and UDP port and services exceptions, and reset Windows Firewall to default settings. For computers that are part of a domain, administrators can use group policies to set specific system conditions. Using the policies under the `Computer Configuration\Administrative Templates\Network\Network Connections\Windows Firewall\Domain Profile`, administrators can control the way a system behaves when connected to a Microsoft Active Directory directory service domain. Similarly, administrators can use the policies under the `Computer Configuration\Administrative Templates\ Network\Network Connections\Windows Firewall\Standard Profile`. Administrators can control the way a system behaves when the system is disconnected from an Active Directory domain, such as when a laptop user is traveling from the office to remote office sites.

Enabling and Disabling Windows Firewall

Administrators can enable or disable Windows Firewall on all connections or on a per connection basis. To do so, click Windows Firewall from within Windows Security Center and then click Change Settings to display the Windows Firewall dialog box show in Figure 4.3.

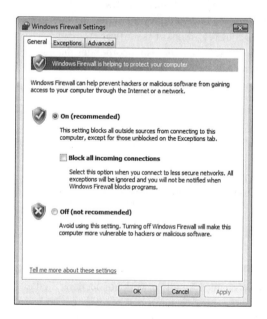

FIGURE 4.3
Enabling or disabling Windows Firewall using the General tab.

Using the General tab, administrators can choose to enable or disable the firewall. By selecting On to enable Windows Firewall, all outside sources are prevented from connecting to the computer except for the unblocked connections configured on the Exceptions tab. In this configuration, users are notified of any programs that are blocked, and users have the option to keep blocking, allow the program, or be prompted again later. Enabling the additional option, Block All Incoming Connections, ignores connections configured on the Exception tab and blocks all incoming connections. This option does not provide user notification. This setting is the preferred setting when the computer is used in a nonsecure environment outside the office environment. By selecting Off to disable Windows Firewall, administrators can turn the firewall completely off. This configuration leaves the system open to outside attack because the firewall is turned off for all network connections.

Administrators can also enable and disable Windows Firewall on a per connection basis using the following steps:

1. In Windows Security Center, click Windows Firewall. Note the network location you are configuring and then click Change Settings.

2. In the Windows Firewall dialog box, make sure that the firewall is set to On and then select the Advanced tab. If prompted, confirm the action by clicking Continue.

3. In the Network Connection Settings section, each of the configured network connections is listed. Clear the check box for a connection to disable Windows Firewall for that connection. Select the check box to enable Windows Firewall for a connection.

4. Click OK when finished enabling or disabling Windows Firewall connections.

Configuring Program Exceptions in Windows Firewall

Administrators can configure exceptions in Windows Firewall for programs and services such as network discovery, file and printer sharing, antivirus utilities, or remote desktop functionality. In a domain environment, only Core Networking is enabled by default. Standard exceptions, however, can be allowed or disallowed fairly easily by administrators. To enable an exception, administrators can select the check box for the exception. To disable an exception, administrators can deselect the check box for the exception.

Administrators can add programs as exceptions if computers need to communicate remotely with a program or connect to a program over a specific port.

To configure a program exception, administrators can perform the following steps:

1. In Windows Security Center, click Windows Firewall. Note the network location you are configuring and then click Change Settings. If prompted, click Continue to confirm the action and continue on to display the Windows Firewall dialog box.

2. In the Windows Firewall dialog box, select the Exceptions tab and then click Add Program. In the Add a Program dialog box, select the program from the program list or click Browse to find the program on the computer.

3. By default, any local computer or Internet computer can access the program remotely. To restrict access, administrators can click Change Scope. On the Change Scope dialog box, administrators can choose to allow any computer (including those on the Internet), allow only computers on the same subnet to access the program, or enter a custom list of IP addresses that can remotely communicate with the program.

4. Click OK three times to finish and close the dialog boxes.

Configuring TCP and UDP Port Exceptions in Windows Firewall

Administrators can also configure port exceptions in Windows Firewall. TCP and UDP ports can be opened to allow remote access to a computer by configuring the port as an exception. Administrators can do this by completing the following steps:

1. In Windows Security Center, click Windows Firewall. Note the network location you are configuring and then click Change Settings. If prompted, click Continue to confirm the action and continue on to display the Windows Firewall dialog box.

2. In the Windows Firewall dialog box, select the Exceptions tab and then click Add Port. In the Name field of the Add a Port dialog box, type a descriptive name for the port and then type a number for the port, such as 8080, in the Port Number field.

3. Select a TCP or UDP port by selecting the appropriate button.

4. By default, any computer, including those on the Internet, will have access to the computer. To restrict access, administrators can click Change Scope, change the access permissions, and then click OK.

5. Click OK two times to close the open dialog boxes.

Configuring Advanced Security in Windows Firewall

Windows Firewall with Advanced Security is a core component of Windows Vista. Although it is available in all versions of Windows Vista, the Windows Firewall with Advanced Security console, which allows the granular control over configuration changes, is included only in the Business, Enterprise, and Ultimate editions of Windows Vista. Administrators who want to work with more advanced Windows Firewall settings can do so in the Windows Firewall with Advanced Security console. Administrators can access the Windows Firewall using a preconfigured management console, using a MMC snap-in, command-line interface, or using Group Policy settings. Each of the options has the following advantage or disadvantage:

- **Windows Firewall with Advanced Security Management console—** If Administrative Tools have previously been added to the All Programs menu, this preconfigured management tool is found on the Administrative Tools menu by clicking Start, All Programs, Administrative Tools, Windows Firewall with Advanced Security. The console can also be started by typing **wf.msc** in the Search box. The disadvantage to this tool is that it can be used only to configure the local computer.

- **A MMC snap-in—**A snap-in can be added to any Microsoft Management console. The advantage of using the snap-in is that administrators can use the snap-in to configure firewall settings on remote computers without using a remote desktop connection.

- **Command-line interface—**Administrators can use the NETSH Advfirewall, such as `netsh advfirewall firewall show rule name=all`, context to configure both basic and advanced firewall settings. The disadvantage to this method is that this setting will not work with Windows XP Service Pack 2 or Windows Server 2003 Service Pack 1 systems.

- **Group Policy—**Administrators can use group policies settings found under `Computer Configuration/Windows Settings/Security Settings/Windows Firewall with Advanced Security`. This setting will not work with Windows XP Service Pack 2 or Windows Server 2003 Service Pack 1 systems. The advantage of using Group Policy is that the policy for Windows Firewall with Advanced Security is applied to all computers processing the Group Policy object.

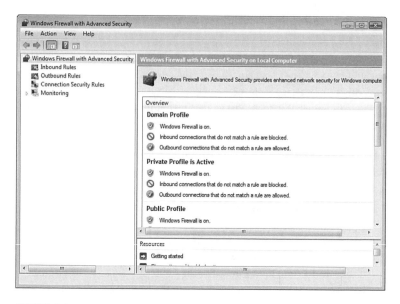

FIGURE 4.4
Using Windows Firewall with Advanced Security to configure advanced firewall settings.

As shown in Figure 4.4, the Windows Firewall with Advanced Security console provides administrators with an overview of the state of the firewall for each profile—domain, private, or public. The console tree pane contains nodes for Inbound Rules, Outbound Rules, Connection Security Rules, and Monitoring. The Inbound Rules node lists all inbound traffic rules and displays a summary of the configurations. The Outbound Rules node lists all outbound traffic rules and displays configuration information of the rules. The Connection Security Rules node lists all protected traffic and displays summary configuration information. The Monitoring node provides a summary of the individual firewall profiles. By default, the active firewall profile is expanded and the name displays the word "Active" in the name field.

Configuration of the Advanced Firewall is more complicated than configuration of the basic Windows Firewall. Administrators will want to think and plan how they want to configure the profile properties, inbound and outbound traffic exceptions, port assignments, and define connection security rules.

Each firewall profile has its own settings for allowing or denying connections, notifications, logging, and firewall state. Administrators can configure these settings by using the following steps:

1. Select the Windows Firewall with Advanced Security node in Windows Firewall with Advanced Security. Scroll down and click Windows Firewall Properties.

2. Select the profile to work with—domain, private, or public. Select On (Recommended), and then configure the default inbound and outbound connection setting. Select the appropriate setting (Block, Block All, or Allow) for inbound and outbound connections.

3. To configure profile behavior, click Customize on the Settings panel and then use the provided options to configure the firewall profile behavior.

4. To enable logging, click Customize on the Logging panel and then set the Log Dropped Packets and Log Successful Connections to Yes. The log file path is `C:\Windows\system32\LogFiles\Firewall\ pfirewall.log.`Click OK to continue.

5. To configure IP Security settings and determine how secure connections are established, click Customize on the IPSec Settings tab. Use the options provided to configure the security, integrity and encryption, and the authentication setting for IPSec and then click OK to continue.

Administrators can also create and manage inbound rules from within Windows Firewall with Advanced Security. To view currently enabled rules, double-click the Enabled column to prioritize the rules with the Enabled rules listed first. To create and enable a new inbound rule, administrator can use the following steps:

1. Select the Inbound Rules node in Windows Firewall with Advanced Security.

2. Under Actions, click New Rule to start the New Inbound Rule Wizard and then follow the wizard prompts to configure the inbound rule. Click Finish to close the Inbound Rule Wizard.

3. Enable the new inbound rule by right-clicking and selecting Enable Rule.

Modify an existing rule by performing the following steps:

1. Select the Inbound Rules node in Windows Firewall with Advanced Security.

2. Double-click the rule to modify and change options as necessary.

3. If required, enable the modified inbound rule by right-clicking and selecting Enable Rule.

Administrators can also create and manage outbound rules from within Windows Firewall with Advanced Security. To view currently enabled rules, double-click the Enabled column to prioritize the rules with the Enabled rules listed first. To create and enable a new outbound rule, administrator can use the following steps:

1. Select the Outbound Rules node in Windows Firewall with Advanced Security.

2. Under Actions, click New Rule to start the New Outbound Rule Wizard and then follow the wizard prompts to configure the outbound rule. Click Finish to close the Outbound Rule Wizard.

3. Enable the new inbound rule by right-clicking and selecting Enable Rule.

Modify an existing outbound rule by performing the following steps:

1. Select the Outbound Rules node in Windows Firewall with Advanced Security.

2. Double-click the outbound rule to modify and change options as necessary.

3. If required, enable the modified outbound rule by right-clicking and selecting Enable Rule.

Administrators can also create and manage Connection Security Rules within Windows Firewall with Advanced Security. IPSec provides rules for securing IP traffic. By default, no IPSec rules are defined in Windows Firewall with Advanced Security. Administrators can create a new connection security rule using the following steps:

1. Select and then right-click the Connection Security Rules node in Windows Firewall with Advanced Security. Click New Rule to start the Connection Security Rule Wizard.

2. Specify the type of connection security rule to create on the Rule Type page and then click Next. Connection Types are as follows:

   - **Isolation**—This rule restricts connections based on authentication status such as health status (Network Access Protection (NAP)) or domain membership.

   - **Authentication Exemption**—This rule specifies an authentication exception for computers that are not required to authenticate or secure their connection traffic.

- **Server to Server**—This rules defines how authentication is used for server-to-server traffic.

- **Tunnel**—This rule creates a secure connection between computers, such as gateway computers, which send IP traffic over the Internet.

- **Custom**—This option manually creates a rule with custom authentication behavior.

3. After the configuration is complete, click Finish to create and enable the rule.

Administrators can modify a connection security rule by right-clicking the rule, selecting Properties, and then modifying the settings of the rule. To disable a connection security rule, Administrators can right-click the connection security rule and then select Disable Rule.

Restoring Default Windows Firewall Configurations

Sometimes the configuration and state of Windows Firewall becomes unstable, and the behavior of Windows Firewall may become erratic. If this situation occurs, administrators can restore the default secure configuration of Windows Firewall and then reconfigure the program and port settings as needed for the computer.

Administrators can restore the default settings of Windows Firewall using the following steps:

1. In Windows Security Center, click Windows Firewall. Note the network location you are configuring and then click Change Settings. If prompted, click Continue to confirm the action and continue on to display the Windows Firewall dialog box.

2. In the Windows Firewall dialog box, select the Advanced tab.

3. Click the Restore Defaults button. When prompted, confirm the action by clicking Yes.

4. When the restore is complete, click OK.

Managing Windows Defender

Spyware is any technology that aids in gathering information about a person or organization without their knowledge. On the Internet, spyware is programming that is put in someone's computer and that secretly gathers personal information about the user, the user's web-browsing habits, and system information and transmits the info to advertisers or other suspicious parties. Spyware can get into a computer as a software virus or as the result of installing a new program. Spyware usually gets on a computer by deceitfully requesting permission to do one thing but then doing another or injected itself using known web programs exploits.

In Windows Vista, Windows Defender is there to work without interrupting the user. Windows Defender works in the background to intercept and quarantine or delete the malicious program. Using characteristics of the spyware's signature, Windows Defender blocks and defends against malicious software installation and possible compromising actions. Definition files containing information about spyware signatures are stored and updated to keep up with the latest and greatest spyware programs and activities. Windows Defender's automatic update feature makes periodic update checks to ensure that the spyware signatures are kept updated and current.

Working with Windows Defender

Administrators can open Windows Defender in Windows Vista by clicking the Windows Defender link in the left pane in Windows Security Center. As shown in Figure 4.5, the Windows Defender home page displays an overview of the current status. The computer status will be indicated as normal if the software definitions are up-to-date and all systems are operating normally. If the system definitions are out-of-date or if harmful malware has been detected, a warning status is displayed.

The current status of Windows Defender is located in the bottom half of the home page. It displays the following information:

- **Last Scan**—The date, time, and type of the last performed scan
- **Scan Schedule**—The set schedule for automatic scans
- **Real-Time Protection**—The ON or OFF status of the real time protection
- **Definition Version**—The version, date, and time of the most recent spyware definitions

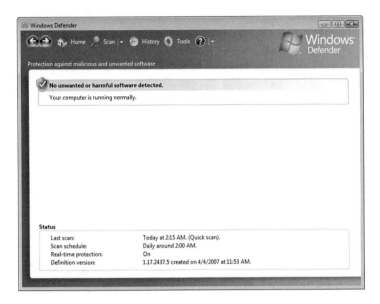

FIGURE 4.5
Viewing the Windows Defender application in Windows Vista.

The configuration settings of Windows Defender can be modified by administrators to run different program configurations. Administrators can customize the scanning options of Windows Defender using the following steps:

1. In Windows Defender, click Tools, and then click Options.

2. On the Options page, shown in Figure 4.6, the following options can be used to customize Windows Defender:

   ■ **Automatic Scanning**—This option is used to set and maintain the automatic scanning and updating options. To automatically scan for malware, select Automatically Scan My Computer and then configure the scan frequency, time of scan, and type of scan. To automatically search for definition updates before spyware scanning, select Check for Updated Definitions Before Scanning. To apply default actions to detected or quarantined programs, select Apply Default Actions to Items Detected During a Scan.

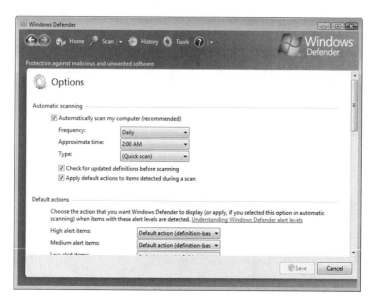

FIGURE 4.6
Configuring program settings in Windows Defender using the Options page.

- **Default Actions**—This option is used as the default action to take based on the alert level of a detected spyware program. Spyware with a high alert level is the most dangerous type of software and has the most potential for damaging a computer. The default applied action is to either ignore the program, quarantine the program, always allow the program, or remove the program.

- **Real-Time Protection**—This option is used to initiate and configure real-time protection. Real-Time Protection runs in the background, monitoring for spyware looking to run or install itself. Administrators can turn on and turn off real-time protection using the check boxes and also can choose which security agents to run. Administrators can also configure whether Windows Defender should provide notifications regarding real-time protection.

- **Advanced Options**—This option is used to configure advanced spyware scanning features such as rule-based detection (heuristics) and scanning within archive files. Rule-based detection is important for detecting hidden spyware, new spyware, and maliciously performing software.

- **Administrator Options**—This option is used to enable and disable Windows Defender, determine who can and cannot perform scans, and choose actions to perform on detected software. By default, users do not have permissions to run Windows Defender. Administrators must enable the Allow Everyone to Use Windows Defender option by selecting the check box.

3. Click Save to save any modifications made to the configuration.

Note

Windows Defender is a great antispyware utility for the Small Office Home Office (SOHO) market. For domain-based networks, typically installed in medium to large enterprises, administrators should look at Microsoft's enterprise client security solution called Microsoft Forefront Client Security. Microsoft Forefront Client Security delivers three key features:

- **Unified Protection**—Provides unified protection from viruses, spyware, and other threats so businesses are better protected.

- **Simplified Administration**—Provides quick and efficient administration through centralized management.

- **Visibility and Control**—Produces a summary of results and security reports, giving administrators visibility and control over malware threats.

For hands-on experience with Microsoft Forefront Client Security, download the public beta at www.microsoft.com/technet/prodtechnol/beta/betacentral.mspx. Additional Microsoft Forefront information can be found at www.microsoft.com/forefront/default.mspx.

Scanning for Spyware and Malware

Other than real-time protection, scanning for spyware and malware is the primary detection and prevention method in Windows Defender. When scanning, Windows Defender checks detected applications against a database of spyware definition files. The database is frequently updated via Windows Update, so the most current definition files are available. The database contains information such as filenames and version numbers, a description of the threat, and a recommended course of action for the offending program.

Using Windows Defender in both real-time protection mode and automatic scanning mode enhances a system's security. If the computer is not turned on when the automatic scan is supposed to occur, or spyware is suspected to reside on the computer, a quick scan, full scan, or custom scan should be initiated in Windows Defender.

Windows Defender Quick Scan option checks the places on the computer's hard disk that spyware is most likely to infect, such as memory, system Registry, and the file system. It does not perform a complete search for spyware. Administrators can run a quick scan using the following steps:

1. Open Windows Defender by clicking Start, All Programs, and then clicking Windows Defender.

2. On the Windows Defender toolbar, click Scan.

Windows Defender Full Scan option thoroughly checks all areas of the memory, system Registry, and the file system on the computer's hard disk and all currently running programs. A full scan puts an additional load on the computer, causing the computer to run slowly until the scan is complete. If administrators suspect that spyware has infected the computer, they should run a full scan. Administrators can run a full scan using the following steps:

1. Open Windows Defender by clicking Start, All Programs, and then clicking Windows Defender.

2. On the Windows Defender toolbar, click the down arrow next to Scan, and then click Full Scan.

The Windows Defender Custom Scan option thoroughly checks all areas of the memory and system Registry, but only checks areas of the file system on the computer's hard disk that are specified by the administrator. The system is as intensive as the Full Scan option but can take less time depending on the file system areas selected for testing. Administrators can run a custom scan using the following steps:

1. Open Windows Defender by clicking Start, All Programs, and then clicking Windows Defender.

2. On the Windows Defender toolbar, click the down arrow next to Scan, and then click Custom Scan.

3. Click Scan Selected Drives and Folders and then click Select.

4. Select the files or folders that you want to scan.

5. Click OK and then Scan Now to start the custom scan.

By default, Windows Defender is set to automatically remove dangerous, malicious programs. Programs that are not dangerous but are suspect programs are put in quarantine. The computer user receives a notification that suspect programs have been detected and Windows Defender provides the user an option to quarantine the program or allow it to run.

Quarantined items are moved to a different folder and are prevented from running so that no system problems are created. Administrators can view and manage quarantined items by clicking Tools on the Windows Defender toolbar and then clicking Quarantined Items. On the Quarantined Items page, items are listed name, alert level, and date stamp. Administrators can manage quarantined items using the following options:

- Permanently remove all quarantined programs by clicking Remove All.

- Permanently remove a specific program by selecting the program and then clicking Remove.

- Restore a specific program by selecting the program and then clicking Restore.

Programs that are allowed to run on the computer are also tracked by Windows Defender. Administrators can manage and view allowed items by clicking Tools on the Windows Defender toolbar and then selecting Allowed Items. On the Allowed Items page, allowed items are listed by name, alert level, and a recommendation on the action to take with the program. Sometimes programs are allowed accidentally and need to be removed by the administrator from the allowed items list. Administrators can remove a program from the allowed items list by selecting the program and then selecting Remove from List. From here on, Windows Defender will monitor and track the activities of the program and alert the user if any malicious activity is detected.

Updating Windows Defender

If the database spyware definitions are out-of-date, Windows Defender cannot effectively do its job of protecting the computer. Before every automatic scan, Windows Defender checks for updated spyware definitions. As long as the computer has Internet access or access to an update server on the LAN, Windows Defender is able to update the spyware definitions. Manual updates of the definition files can also be performed. To manually update the definition files, administrators can follow these steps from within Windows Defender:

1. On the Windows Defender toolbar, click the Help Options arrow located next to the Help button (the blue question mark).

2. On the drop-down menu, select Check for Updates. If prompted, confirm that you want to perform the action.

3. Windows Defender will begin looking for new updates and will pop up a notification balloon to inform the user whether new definitions are available.

Managing Windows Malicious Software Removal Tool

The Microsoft Windows Malicious Software Removal Tool (MSRT) checks Windows Vista (Home Basic and Premium, Business, Enterprise, and Ultimate) computers for infections by specific, prevalent malicious software such as Blaster, Sobig, Doomjuice, and Mydoom. MSRT also helps remove any infection found. When the detection and removal process is complete, the tool displays a report describing the outcome, including which, if any, malicious software was detected and removed. A record of detected programs and actions taken is kept in the MRt.logfile. The log file is typically located in the %windir%\debug folder on the computer, where %windir% refers to the location of the Windows folder.

As part of its security strategy, on the second Tuesday of each month Microsoft releases an updated version of this tool. The tool is downloadable from Microsoft Update, Windows Update, or the Microsoft Download Center. Administrators who need to perform scans on multiple computers should download the executable version of the program available at the Download Center. The version of MSRT delivered by Microsoft Update and Windows Update runs silently in the background and then reports if an infection is found.

The MSRT is not a replacement for antivirus software. Be sure that current antivirus software is running on the computer at all times to protect the computer from other malicious software. The tool provides post-infection removal of malicious software and can only remove malicious software from an already-infected computer. In contrast, antivirus products block malicious software from running on a computer, preventing any potential system damage from occurring.

For more information about the Windows Malicious Software Removal Tool, read the Microsoft Knowledge Base article 890830 located at support. microsoft.com/kb/890830/.

Working with Windows Malicious Software Removal Tool

Administrators will find this tool fairly easy to use. When downloading from the Web, administrators will be presented with a few options to do one of the following:

- To start the installation immediately, click Run.

- To save the download to the computer for installation at a later time, click Save.

- To cancel the installation, click Cancel.

Most administrators will save the file to the system for use at a later time or to use on multiple computers. After the tool is downloaded, administrators can perform a quick, extended, or custom scan.

Selecting a Quick Scan or a Full Scan

The MSRT tool can be run only with administrative permissions. If a user with administrator privileges attempts to run the MSRT tool, the user will be prompted with a User Account Control dialog box requesting an administrative password. If an administrative password is not supplied, the programs will not run, and the user must select Cancel to close the program. As shown in Figure 4.7, administrators can select Quick Scan, Full Scan, or Customized Scan.

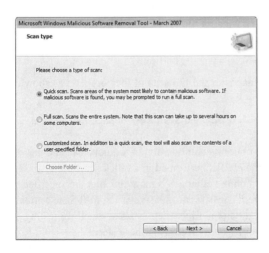

FIGURE 4.7
Selecting a scan in the Windows Malicious Software Removal Tool.

Using a Quick Scan

The MSRT Quick Scan option checks the places on the computer's hard disk that malicious software is most likely to infect, such as memory, the system Registry, and the file system. It does not perform a complete search for spyware but may prompt the user to perform a full scan if suspicious software is detected. Administrators can run a quick scan using the following steps:

1. Run the MSRT software. If prompted, confirm the requested action by selecting Continue. Click Next on the Windows Malicious Software Removal Tool Welcome page.

2. Select Quick Scan on the Scan Type dialog box.

3. Click Next to continue and start the quick scan of the computer.

4. When the scan is finished, review the Scan Results page information.

Using a Full Scan

The MSRT Full Scan (also known as an Extended Scan) option thoroughly checks all areas of the memory, system Registry, and the file system on the computer's hard disk. A full scan puts an additional load on the computer, causing the computer to run slowly until the scan is complete. If administrators suspect that malicious software has invaded the computer, they should run a full scan. Administrators can run a full scan using the following steps:

1. Run the MSRT software. If prompted, confirm the requested action by selecting Continue. Click Next on the Windows Malicious Software Removal Tool Welcome page.

2. Select Full Scan on the Scan Type dialog box.

3. Click Next to continue and start the full scan of the computer as shown in Figure 4.8.

4. When the scan is finished, review the Scan Results page information.

The MSRT Customized Scan option, a combination of a quick scan and an extended scan, performs all the checks performed in a quick scan and also checks areas of the file system on the computer's hard disk that are specified by the administrator. The system check is as intensive as the Full Scan option but can take less time depending on the file system areas selected for testing. Administrators can run a custom scan by following these steps:

1. Run the MSRT software. If prompted, confirm the requested action by selecting Continue. Click Next on the Windows Malicious Software Removal Tool Welcome page.

2. Select Customized Scan on the Scan Type dialog box and then click Choose Folder.

3. In the Browse for Folder dialog box, select the file areas to scan and then click OK.

4. Click Next to continue and start the quick scan of the computer.

5. When the scan is finished, review the Scan Results page information.

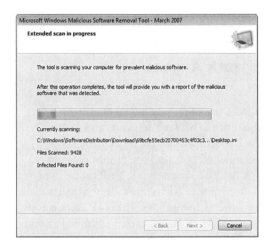

FIGURE 4.8
Viewing an in-progress extended scan in the Windows Malicious Software Removal Tool.

Reporting Results

When the scan is finished, the Microsoft Windows Malicious Software Removal Tool shows the results of the system scan. The software will report any malicious software that was detected and removed from the system. Administrators can view detailed results of the scan by clicking the View Detailed Results of the Scan link on the Scan Results page and viewing the scan results.

Working with Antivirus Software

The Microsoft Windows Malicious Software Removal Tool is not a replacement for antivirus software. Periodic scanning with the MSRT or any other online scanning tool is not a substitute for antivirus software and does not provide continuous protection against virus infections. MSRT complements antivirus software and will work alongside third-party antivirus products. As an alternative to MSRT and third-party antivirus products, Microsoft offers an online Windows Live OneCare Safety scanner at http://onecare.live.com/site/en-US/center/howsafe.htm?s_cid=mscom_msrt. The Windows Live OneCare scanner, which uses an ActiveX control, must be run using Internet Explorer. If an alternative browser attempts to run the safety scanner, an error page will be displayed that provides hints on how to run the online scanner successfully.

Understanding Network Access Protection (NAP)

Windows Vista includes an agent that can provide information about a client's health state and configuration to network access servers or peers. With Network Access Protection (NAP), clients that lack current security updates, lack virus signatures, or fail other system health specifications are not allowed to communicate on the local area network. NAP can be used to protect the local area network from remote access clients as well as local area network clients using wired or wireless connections. The NAP agent reports Windows Vista client health status, such as having current operating system updates, up-to-date virus signatures, or up-to-date spyware definitions installed, to a server-based NAP enforcement service. A NAP infrastructure, included with the future release of Windows Server 2008, determines whether to allow or deny the client access to your private network or to a restricted network. See www.microsoft.com/technet/network/nap/default.mspx for more information.

Exploring Usage of NAP

NAP is designed to help administrators maintain the health of the computers on a network. In doing so, the network's overall health integrity is maintained. Compliant computers that meet health policy requirements are allowed unrestricted network access. Noncompliant computers, those that do not meet policy requirements, are allowed restricted access to the network until they are brought into compliance and deemed safe for unrestricted access. It is important to remember that NAP does not prevent an authorized user with a compliant computer from uploading a malicious program to the network or performing other suspicious activities.

For a successful NAP implementation, administrators must gain a basic understanding of how NAP works. To do so, administrators should grasp three important areas in regard to NAP functionality:

- **Health Policy Validation**—As a user attempts a network connection, the computer's health state is validated against the defined health policies set by the administrator. Administrators can then choose what to do if a computer is not compliant by setting up different environments:

  - **Monitoring-Only Environment**—All authorized computers are granted access and the compliance of each computer is logged.

  - **Restricted Access Environment**—Health policy compliant computers are allowed unlimited access to the network, but health policy or NAP noncompliant computers are allowed access limited to a restricted network.

In both environments, computers that are compatible with NAP can automatically become compliant, and administrators can define exceptions to the validation process.

- **Health Policy Compliance**—Administrators can help ensure compliance with health policies by choosing to automatically update noncompliant computers with the missing requirements through management software such as Microsoft Systems Management Server. Administrators can then choose what to do if a computer is not compliant by setting up different environments:

  - **Monitoring-Only Environment**—All computers will have access to the network even before they are updated with required software or configuration modifications.

  - **Restricted Access Environment**—Computers that do not comply with health policies have limited access until the software and configuration updates are completed.

In both environments, computers that are compatible with NAP can automatically become compliant, and the administrator can define policy exceptions.

- **Limited Access**—Administrators can protect network assets by limiting the access of computers that do not comply with health policy requirements. Network access limits can be time based or resource based. Administrators have flexibility here in how they work with limited access systems:

- If an administrator configures health policies to enforce an update of the computer's resources, the limited access will last only until the computer is brought into compliance.

- If an administrator does not configure health policies to force an update of the computer's resources, limited access will last for the duration of the network connection.

Understanding Components of Network Access Protection

NAP depends on a bunch of different system components in order to maintain integrity of the network. Each component plays a key role in how computers are allowed full access or restricted access, how computers are forced or not forced to update resources, and how computers are allowed access to network resources or restricted access to network resources. By design, NAP allows administrators the flexibility to configure NAP so that it fits their individual network environment preferences and requirements.

NAP provides limited access enforcement components for the Internet Protocol security (IPSec), IEEE 802.1X authenticated network connections, virtual private networks (VPNs), and Dynamic Host Configuration Protocol (DHCP) technologies. The enforcement technologies can be used together or separately to limit noncompliant computers. Network Policy Server (NPS) acts as a health policy server for all of these technologies. NPS is the replacement for Internet Authentication Service (IAS) in Windows Server 2003 and in Windows Server 2008.

NAP requires servers to run Windows Server 2008 and requires clients to run Windows Vista or Windows Server 2008. Microsoft is currently beta testing an update for clients running Windows XP with Service Pack 2 (SP2).

NAP consists of client components, server components, remediation servers, and policy servers. Administrators can configure some or all of the following components when they implement NAP:

- Client components for NAP:

    - **NAP Agent**—Client software that coordinates information between the various system health agents and NAP enforcement clients.

    - **System Health Agent (SHA)**—Client software that integrates with the NAP Agent to provide system policy checks and to indicate system health.

- Server components for NAP:

    - **NAP Administration Server**—A component of a Network Policy Server that coordinates the output from all the system health validators and determines whether NAP Enforcement Server components should enforce the health policy configuration and limit the access of a client.

    - **System Health Validator (SHV)**—Server software that validates whether the Statement of Health (SoH) submitted by an SHA complies with the required health state. A System Health Validator runs on the NPS server and act as the coordinator for all SHV output. A Statement of Health Response (SoHR) is issued by the SHV to indicate compliance or noncompliance with the required health state and remediation instructions.

    - **Health Policy**—Specifies the required conditions for unlimited network access and is configured on the NPS server. A network can have more than one health policy; 802.1X Enforcement and IPSec Enforcement might use different health policies.

    - **Accounts Database**—Stores user accounts, computer accounts, and network access properties necessary for authenticated network access. Active Directory functions as the accounts database for Windows Server "Longhorn" domains.

    - **Health Registration Authority (HRA)**—A computer running Windows Server 2008 and Internet Information Services (IIS). This computer obtains health certificates from a certificate authority (CA) for compliant computers. A health certificate can be used instead of Statements of Health, proving that a client computer is compliant with system health requirements.

    - **Remediation Server**—Servers, services, or other network resources that noncompliant computers can access on the restricted network. These server resources could be a spyware definition file server, an antivirus signature file server, or a Windows update server. The SHA will communicate directly with a remediation server or will use installed client software.

    - **Policy Server**—The SHA communicates with policy servers to validate the Statement of Health from a corresponding SHA.

Shown in Figure 4.9, an example NAP deployment is configured for DHCP, IPSec, VPN, and 802.1X enforcement. The Network Policy Server (NPS) is installed on a separate server and acts as the health policy server. In this configuration, the network is set up for health policy validation and compliance and limited access for computers that are not in compliance.

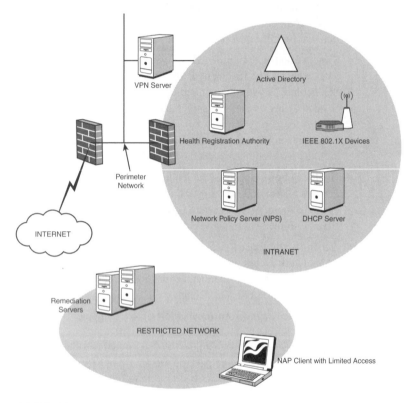

FIGURE 4.9
Example NAP network deployment.

When obtaining a health certificate, making an 802.1X or VPN connection to the network, or leasing or renewing an IP address from the DHCP server, each computer is classified in one of the two following ways:

- Computers that meet the health policy requirements are classified as compliant and are allowed unlimited access to the network.

- Computers that do not meet the network health policy requirements are classified as noncompliant and have their access limited to the restricted network until they meet the requirements. System Health Agents automatically update the noncompliant computers with the software required for unlimited access.

The example network in Figure 4.9 also contains a restricted network that can be defined logically or physically. Administrators can place specific restrictions on limited access computers using IP filters to define which remediation servers the computers can communicate.

Summary

Windows Vista is the most secure operating system ever produced by Microsoft. Windows Vista looks to lock down desktop security, improve the user experience, and prevent malware, spyware, and viruses from invading the new operating system. Unlike previous versions of Windows, Windows Vista introduces several security enhancements that create a solid defense against operating system exploits, computer security breaches, user permission violations, and other malicious activities. Windows Vista introduces several new security features aimed at eliminating the threat of hackers and mitigating malware threats, such as Internet Explorer Protected Mode, Windows Defender, and Windows Firewall. Network Access Protection is a new platform to limit the access of connecting computers until they are compliant with system health requirements, and it provides an infrastructure where administrators can create their own health polices and requirements for maintaining the integrity of the network.

CHAPTER 5

Patching and Keeping Windows Vista Up-to-Date

Understanding Automatic Updating and Patch Management

Patch management is a crucial part of any business's network processes and procedures, and home computers and home networks are no exception. Technically, patch management encompasses all systems and devices on a network, not just Windows PCs. Routers, servers, mobile phones, applications, and almost every computer device today has some sort of updating process. These updates usually address some sort of security vulnerability, such as a buffer overflow or remote code execution. Organizations and home users need to ensure that systems are patched on a timely basis, thus reducing the window of time in which a vulnerability could be exploited. Patch management complements other security initiatives such as malware and virus defense, and in turn, those defenses can also help identify patch management issues.

Organizations that have large install bases, a great number of laptops, customized applications, and specific uptime requirements have some additional obstacles to overcome that a home network usually doesn't. Those obstacles include being able to test updates before they are released, monitoring deployment of the updates, and rolling back updates, if needed. Developing an efficient and effective patch management process greatly reduces the level of exposure to old and new threats and assures availability of the company's network resources. Home networks should also include a strategy for reviewing and installing security updates as they become available.

Windows Vista's updating mechanisms and patch management support have improved greatly from previous versions of Windows. With Automatic Updating, systems can check for, obtain, and install updates for numerous components and programs in Windows Vista. In fact, Microsoft's overall approach to addressing and resolving security vulnerabilities has come a long way from 2001 when the Code Red and Nimda worms saturated the Internet by exploiting vulnerability in unpatched Windows 2000 servers running Internet Information Services (IIS). The worms moved from system to system, hooking themselves into memory, the Registry, and system files. Affected systems had to be patched, had to have antivirus software updated or installed, and the system had to be scanned to remove the malicious code, all of which required resources and downtime to accomplish. Systems that were properly patched and that were running current antivirus software were not impacted. In fact, in this particular case, if systems had the security update installed, they were protected; unfortunately, those systems were in the minority.

Windows Vista includes enhanced alerting, automatic updating mechanisms, integration with Windows Software Update Services (WSUS), and Microsoft's Network Access Protection (NAP). This helps administrators place secured systems on the network. For administrators, the Microsoft Baseline Security Analyzer and Enterprise Scanning programs help with troubleshooting and identifying vulnerable systems after deployment, as will WSUS. With Windows Vista, companies and home networks can effortlessly deploy security updates without a major impact on day-to-day computing.

Since Code Red and Nimda struck in 2001, Microsoft has drastically reduced the window of time systems and networks are left vulnerable, but administrators and home users must be proactive in their patch management practices to help ensure success. Microsoft has a Security Guidance for Patch Management website at the TechNet Security Center, www.microsoft.com/technet/security/guidance/patchmanagement.mspx, which contains case studies, guides, and links to other related information.

Note

When running the Windows Vista setup installation, before Windows Vista is installed you are asked if you would like to go online and obtain updates such as security patches and hardware divers so that they are included during the installation. Before the Windows Vista installation finishes, you are also prompted on how Automatic Updates should be configured.

Using the Security Center

The Security Center, found in the Security category of the Control Panel, was introduced in Chapter 2, "Getting to Understand Your Windows Vista System." The Security Center, as the name implies, is the central status console for all critical security-related items in Windows Vista, including Automatic Updating. The Security Center contains four categories: Firewall, Automatic Updating, Malware Protection, and Other Security Settings. Figure 5.1 shows the Automatic Updating component in the Windows Vista Security Center.

Windows Vista Security and the Security Center are covered throughout Part II of this book, "Security for Windows Vista Systems."

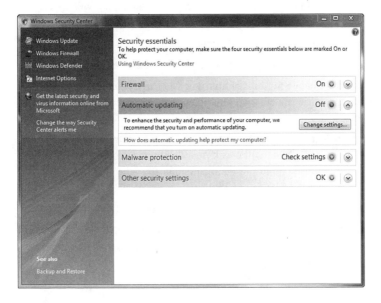

FIGURE 5.1
Automatic Updating status shown in the Windows Vista Security Center.

Note

Visit the Microsoft TechNet Security Center at www.microsoft.com/ technet/security/default.mspx to sign up for security bulletins, technical details on updates, documentation on patch management, tools for administrators, and more.

Configuring Automatic Updating

Automatic Updating, as mentioned previously, is an integral part of patch
management and lowering the overall risk that a system will be compromised. In addition, other Microsoft products, such as Microsoft Office,
Windows Defender, and Forefront, can be updated along with security
updates and nonsecurity-related items. Assuring Automatic Updating is
configured and scheduled properly will keep applications as well as Windows
Vista current. The Automatic Updating section in the Security Center
displays the status of Automatic Updating and how it is configured. If
Automatic Updating is not configured, or is configured for anything besides
downloading and installing updates automatically, a yellow shield icon
appears in the system tray. Clicking this icon will launch the Security Center.
If Automatic Updating is disabled altogether, a red shield icon will appear in
the system tray. Figure 5.2 shows the Windows Update options.

To enable Automatic Updating, follow these steps:

1. Click Automatic Updating on the right side in the Security Center.

2. Click the Change Settings button. The Choose an Automatic Updating
   Option window appears, presenting options for scheduling automatic
   updates:

   ■ **Select Install Updates Automatically (recommended)**—
   Windows Vista will check periodically for updates, and then
   download and install them automatically. The default for this
   setting is every day at 3:00 a.m.

   ■ **Let Me Choose**—Select from these options:

      ■ Install Updates Automatically (recommended)

         ■ Select a day of the week or Every Day (default) from the
         drop-down list

         ■ Select a time from the drop down-list

      ■ Download updates but let me choose whether to install them

      ■ Check for updates but let me choose whether to download and
      install them

      ■ Never check for updates (not recommended)

■ **Optional**—The option Include Recommended Updates When Downloading, Installing, or Notifying Me About Updates under the Recommended Updates section includes updates for other products such as hardware drivers, antivirus and antimalware definitions, games, applications, extras, and so on. This option is enabled by default. Unchecking the checkbox prevents updating of extra products.

■ **Optional**—The Use Microsoft Update under the Update Service section upgrades the computer to the latest version of Microsoft's online updating service, Microsoft Update. Microsoft Update replaces the Windows Update online service from Microsoft because it includes the technology necessary to update multiple components, not just Windows. After the system is upgraded to this service, the option is no longer be present. This option is enabled by default. Unchecking the check box prevents upgrading to Microsoft Update.

FIGURE 5.2
Windows Update settings.

> **Note**
>
> These options can also be configured in Group Policy and when preparing a Windows Vista image. Imaging Windows Vista is covered in Part VI of this book, "Deploying Vista," and Group Policy is covered in brief later in the Windows Software Update Services (WSUS) section of this chapter and is the focus of Part VII, "Windows Vista in an Active Directory Environment."

After Automatic Updating has been enabled, the status in the Security Center switches to reflect that it is running, which no longer triggers an icon in the system tray. When the Windows Update client has finished downloading and installing updates, a pop-up message appears in the system tray stating that the updates have been installed successfully. Clicking the message balloon opens a list of installed updates.

> **Note**
>
> Windows Update uses the Background Intelligence Transfer Service (BITS) version 2.0. BITS 2.0 is a bandwidth-aware service that transfers files in the background without negatively impacting running applications or consuming all available bandwidth. BITS prevents network congestion and ensures that systems obtain updates regardless of their connection speed.

Checking for Updates

Checking for security updates and other available updates can be accomplished manually or automatically. Automatic updating is the easiest to implement and support, but manual updating and update review is essential to administrative duties. To stay informed on the latest security bulletins and upcoming patch releases, administrators should subscribe to Microsoft's Technical Security Bulletin Notification service at www.microsoft.com/technet/security/bulletin/notify.mspx. After registering, a security bulletin summary will arrive monthly from Microsoft@newsletters.microsoft.com with the subject "Microsoft Security Bulletin for (month)." These messages are digitally signed and contain a summary of all security updates being released, sorted by criticality. The summary contains a list of the bulletins by criticality (critical, important, moderate, or low), their title, bulletin number, respective Knowledgebase ID, what products are affected, and what the impact is, such as Remote Code Execution or a Buffer Overflow.

> **Note**
>
> Microsoft releases security bulletins on the second calendar Tuesday of each month, unless a virus, worm, or other malicious activity is actively exploiting the vulnerability, in which case the bulletin may be released sooner, depending on the impact of the threat. For a comprehensive breakdown of what a detailed security bulletin contains, visit www.microsoft.com/technet/security/bulletin/revsbwp.mspx.

The Microsoft website also contains an update catalog, security bulletin search, and download catalog to find any updates related to Microsoft products. Microsoft categorizes the different types of updates by classification.

The updating component in Windows Vista supports the following:

- **Connectors**—Code that contains connection information between programs.

- **Critical Updates**—Addresses critical software issues that are not security related.

- **Development Kits**—Development software.

- **Drivers**—Computer hardware drivers.

- **Feature Packs**—Product enhancements that will usually be included in the next full product release, but are now available as a standalone application—for example, the Terminal Services client.

- **Guidance**—Documentation, scripts, and supporting documentation for Microsoft products.

- **Security Updates**—Patches that address security-related issues and vulnerabilities.

- **Service Packs**—Packaged collection of all security- and nonsecurity-related updates and hot fixes, and in some cases, changes to program features and mechanisms.

- **Tools**—Programs or utilities used to accomplish administrative tasks.

- **Update Rollups**—Packaged collection usually by category, such as security, Internet Explorer, and so on.

- **Updates**—Nonsecurity and noncritical patches for Windows and programs.

> **Note**
>
> For a complete list of terminology developed by Microsoft around updates and downloads, see Knowledgebase article 824684 at support.microsoft.com/?kbid=824684.

> **Note**
>
> Microsoft Update or Windows Update? Microsoft Update is the new updating architecture that is replacing Windows Update. Microsoft Update is designed to provide updates for all products through one mechanism: Automatic Updating. Some examples are Microsoft Office, Microsoft Exchange, and SQL. Updates are retrieved by criticality for all products configured on the system to obtain them. Microsoft Update supports Windows 2003 Server SP1, Windows 2000 SP4, Windows Vista, and Windows XP SP2. For more information, visit update.microsoft.com/

The new Microsoft Update website stores updates for the following products:

- Windows 2000 or later
- Exchange Server 2000 or later
- SQL Server 2000 or later
- Office 2003 or later
- Microsoft ISA Server 2004 or later
- Microsoft Data Protection Manager
- Microsoft Forefront
- Windows Live
- Windows Defender

Manual Updating

Automation is a wonderful thing, but sometimes the best way to accomplish, understand, or troubleshoot something is by walking through the manual process. Understanding manual updating processes can also benefit in scenarios such as disaster recovery and virus and malware removal. Windows Vista can be manually updated in several ways:

- Clicking the first link under the security category Check for Updates
- Launching the Microsoft Update site update.microsoft.com/ in a web browser

- Searching for a specific item or security bulletin on the Microsoft website, downloading, and then installing it

Windows Update can check for updates and notify before downloading and installing them or download them first, but notify before installing. This is similar to the first two methods mentioned previously, with the main differences being the mechanism for delivery and whether updates are downloaded before being notified about installation. Figure 5.3 shows the list of available updates that can be downloaded immediately, later, or hidden to prevent installation.

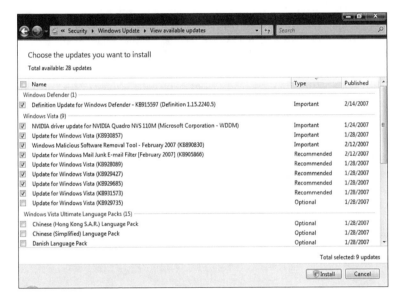

FIGURE 5.3
List of available updates.

Automatic Updating
Automatic Updating will run on the schedule you configure; however, the same steps for manual updating can be invoked if necessary. For example, administrators may need to deploy an update immediately after being alerted of new exploit or viral code that targets a known vulnerability in Windows 2003 servers, or a different update that fixes a known issue. In situations like these, it may be necessary to circumvent Automatic Updating or change the Automatic Updating schedule to have the update deployed sooner.

Note

Companies that use Windows Software Update Services (WSUS) and Group Policy will have a much easier time handling scenarios like this and will also be able to report on the success of the deployment. WSUS and Group Policy are covered in brief later in this chapter, and Group Policy is the focus of Part VII.

Downloading and Installing Updates

Downloading and installing updates, as stated previously, is considered a manual update procedure. As also discussed earlier, the Windows Update component in Windows Vista can automatically notify you when downloads are available, or download them first and then notify you. In addition, updates can be retrieved directly from Microsoft's website and downloaded for later use. After an update or updates have been installed, a restart may be required and on reboot Windows Vista will display the message Configuring updates before anyone is allowed to log on.

You can find Security Updates at the Security Bulletin search page located at the Microsoft TechNet Security Center (www.microsoft.com/technet/security/current.aspx). This search page provides a configurable search engine for finding security updates by product, technology, or Knowledge Base (KB) number and also provides a list of all security bulletins in reverse chronological order. There is also a link to report security vulnerabilities to Microsoft.

The Microsoft Download Center at www.microsoft.com/downloads/ contains an extensive catalog of other downloadable items such as software, patches, utilities, tools, and more.

Note

It is recommended that systems are backed up prior to installing any updates, especially business critical systems. In the event an update unintentionally causes issues, the system can be rolled back to its previous state. This is particularly useful if the update can't be removed through standard means.

Hiding Updates

Hiding updates can be beneficial when you don't want to be prompted about the update being available or have it appear in the list of available updates when selecting which ones to download. This usually applies when the update shouldn't be installed if it is known to cause issues or simply isn't needed or wanted. To hide an update, right-click the update in the View Available Updates window and select Hide. A security prompt will appear, requesting acknowledgment of the change. The updates will be moved to the Restore Hidden Updates window and will no longer appear in the View Available Updates page, nor will they generate a prompt that they are available for installation. Figure 5.4 shows the Hide Update option for a Windows Vista update.

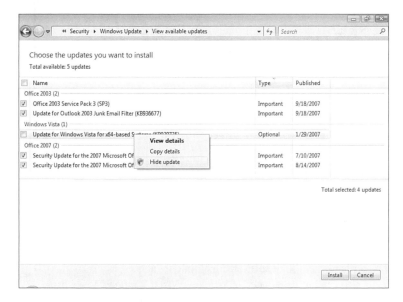

FIGURE 5.4
Hiding available updates.

Restoring Hidden Updates

Restoring hidden updates is as simple as hiding them. In the Control Panel, select Windows Update under the Security category and click Restore Hidden Updates on the left side. The Restore Hidden Updates window will appear. Check the update(s) you want to restore and click the Restore button at the bottom. The update(s) can now be installed. Figure 5.5 shows the Restore Hidden Update button located at the bottom for revealing updates that were previously hidden.

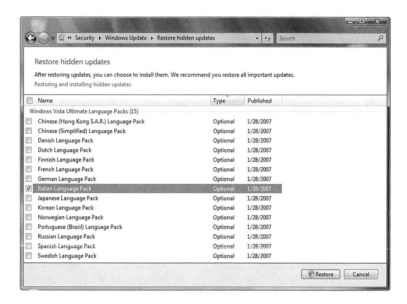

FIGURE 5.5
Restore hidden updates.

Automatically Updating Hardware and Other Optional Components

Computer hardware, other software, and optional nonsecurity-related components also need to be updated in Windows Vista. Windows Vista, as mentioned earlier, has built-in support for the new updating structure through Microsoft Update, http://update.microsoft.com/. Microsoft Update, which is replacing Windows Update, provides support for Windows Vista systems to obtain updates for other applications such as Microsoft Office, hardware drivers, and optional Windows Vista components and extras. In addition, this new updating structure form Microsoft delivers definition updates for Windows Defender's Anti-Malware engine, Microsoft Forefront Client Antivirus protection, and Anti-Spam definitions for Windows Mail and Outlook.

For Windows Update to obtain updates for these applications and nonsecurity-focused items, the Include Recommended Updates when downloading, installing, or notifying me about updates check box must be selected (checked by default) in the Change Settings page of Windows Update.

Figure 5.6 shows the option for including recommended updates in the Recommended Updates results when Windows Vista checks the Microsoft website for new updates. If this option is not selected, only security bulletins are downloaded.

FIGURE 5.6
The Recommended Updates option of Windows Update.

Reviewing Update History

The update history of a system can be reviewed at any time, and there are a few different locations to find information about an installed update. In the Security category of the Control Panel, select Windows Update and click View update history on the left. This will display the history of all installed updates. Right-click an update and select View Details to learn more about the update.

For more detailed information on what the Windows Update client is doing, the Event Viewer stores an event log under Applications and Services Logs, Microsoft, Windows, WindowsUpdateClient, Operational. In addition, the WindowsUpdate.log text file located in the C:\Windows directory also contains detailed information about the Windows Update program. Although these last two items are used more for troubleshooting and are covered again at the end of this chapter, they also contain the times and dates of update activity, including when updates were installed. Figure 5.7 shows the Windows Update event log in the Windows Vista event viewer.

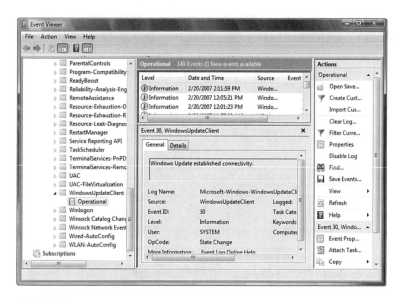

FIGURE 5.7
Operational log for WindowsUpdateClient in Event Viewer.

Integration with Network Access Protection (NAP)

Microsoft's Network Access Protection (NAP) is built in to Windows Vista and Windows Server 2008. NAP identifies systems that do not meet certain security requirements and isolates those systems from the rest of the network until they can meet the security requirements set by the company. NAP uses System Health Agents (locally running agent) and System Health Validates (things to check) to report on the status of a system and ensure that it meets the necessary requirements to see the rest of the network. The requirements are defined in a Health Policy, which contains a summary of all requirements that must be met. If the requirements are not met, the system can be isolated and given a web page where they can fix the problem or contact support personnel. NAP is especially useful with IPSec, VPN, and 802.11x connections. NAP can prevent DHCP from assigning leases to noncompliant systems and check for an active firewall, installed and up-to-date antivirus software, installed and up-to-date antispyware programs, and—the focal point of this chapter—that Automatic Updates is enabled. NAP can also direct noncompliant systems to an internal Windows Software Update Services (WSUS) server to retrieve updates.

Not only can NAP check to see if Automatic Updates are enabled, but NAP can also quarantine a system based on certain updates that are missing. For example, a company may require that all moderate security updates and higher should be installed by a specific date after release. Configuring NAP to enforce this would result in quarantining any system that is missing moderate, important, and critical severity level updates.

NAP is another robust component of the Windows Operating System family that can assist with patch management and overall protection of the network; however, NAP is beyond the scope of this book and requires several components to function correctly. Because of the integration with NAP, companies that deploy Windows Vista and Windows Server 2008 will have a much easier time enforcing system compliance in regard to patch management. For more information about NAP, visit www.microsoft.com/technet/network/nap/default.mspx. For more information about Windows Server 2008, visit www.microsoft.com/windowsserver2008/default.mspx.

Integration with Windows Software Update Services (WSUS) and Group Policy

Windows Software Update Services (WSUS) runs on Windows Server operating systems and allows companies to retrieve updates from a server within the network and control what updates get deployed and when. Administrators can use Group Policy to direct internal systems to the WSUS server for updates. This type of configuration eliminates the need for systems to go directly to Microsoft for updates and gives corporations granular control of which updates must be deployed. Figure 5.8 shows the Windows Group Policy editor and options for Windows Update available through Group Policy in an Active Directory domain. Figure 5.9 shows the configurable path for the internal Windows Software Update Services server.

Administrators have complete control over which updates are approved for distribution, which eases the burden of end users having to keep systems up-to-date and also helps avoid potential problems because the updates could be tested or piloted before approval. Updates can be approved, removed, or ignored. If the update is approved or designated to be removed, a deadline for the task can also be specified. If other WSUS servers exist in the network, they can obtain copies of updates from a single WSUS server, provided that server is configured to obtain updates from Microsoft.

Note

WSUS version 3.0 or later is required to support Windows Vista clients. At the time of writing, WSUS 3.0 was in the beta-2 release phase.

To configure a Group Policy to direct systems to an internal WSUS server for updates, follow these steps:

1. Open the Group Policy Object Editor by right-clicking the domain in Active Directory, selecting Properties, and switching to the Group Policy tab.

2. Create a New Group Policy or edit an existing one.

3. Click Computer Configuration.

4. Click Administrative Templates.

5. Click Windows Components.

6. Click Windows Update.

7. Double-click Specify Intranet Microsoft Update Service Location.

8. Click Enable and enter the http address of the internal WSUS server and statistics server.

9. Click Apply or OK.

10. Link the Group Policy to the appropriate computer, site, domain, or Organizational Unit.

Several components can be configured in Group Policy to support Automatic Updating, such as the frequency that systems should check for updates, how to handle system restarts, and so on. Windows Software Update Services (WSUS) is beyond the scope of this book and requires several components to function correctly; however, a basic understanding of its integration with Windows Vista is necessary if administrators plan to obtain updates internally.

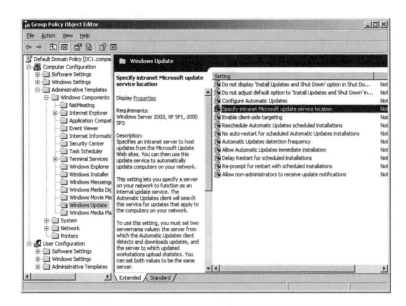

FIGURE 5.8
Group Policy configuration options for Windows Update.

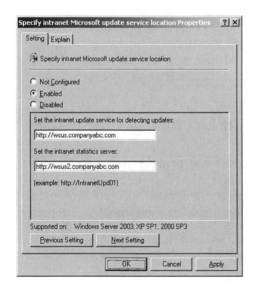

FIGURE 5.9
Specifying an intranet server in Group Policy for Microsoft updates.

Companies that deploy WSUS will have better flexibility managing
Automatic Updating on Windows Vista systems and assuring that necessary
updates are deployed in a timely fashion. WSUS also includes canned reports
and monitoring tools to report on update deployments and assist with troubleshooting. For more information about WSUS, visit www.microsoft.com/
windowsserversystem/updateservices/default.mspx. For more information
about Group Policy and Windows Vista, refer to Part VII of this book.

Troubleshooting and Rolling Back Updates

A lot of security updates can't be removed because they hook directly into
the Operating System. Some, however, can be removed, and optional updates
can, of course, always be removed. On mission-critical systems, a backup
should be performed before the updates are loaded so the system can be
rolled back to its original state. This level of preparation usually isn't necessary for home networks. Security updates address system vulnerability and
shouldn't be removed unless they are creating apparent system issues.

Troubleshooting and rolling back updates is usually pretty straightforward,
but there are some differences depending on what the update does and how it
was installed. More often than not, updates pose no problems, and when they
do, simply removing them (when applicable) through the Programs category
in the Control Panel usually does the job. In some cases, more extensive troubleshooting of an update or the Windows Update program itself is necessary.
Several components can cause Windows Update to fail: for example, the
incorrect date and time on the local machine, services aren't running or aren't
configured correctly, low disk space, Internet Explorer is misconfigured,
and more.

Troubleshooting Windows Update When Updating Directly from Microsoft

If the Windows Update program isn't working or the system isn't obtaining
and installing updates, there may be a problem with the computer's configuration, Group Policy, or something else. If a computer can't retrieve updates
automatically from the Internet, basic troubleshooting should be performed
like the ones listed next:

Note

Click the red X next to the failed update in the Review Your Update History
page to reveal the error code associated with the failed update.

- Is the computer connected to the Internet (Windows Update error 8024001F)? Is Automatic Updating turned on and configured? Is the system receiving a valid IP address, properly forwarding DNS requests, and is the Microsoft Update website accessible?

- Are the appropriate services running and configured to run automatically (for example, Windows Update, BITS, Windows Time Server, Windows Event Log)?

- Ensure that the computer's date and time are correct (Windows Update error 800b0101).

- Check the Event Viewer for any Windows Vista system or application errors as well as the event log for Windows Update located in the Event Viewer under Applications and Services Logs, Microsoft, Windows, WindowsUpdateClient, Operational.

- Check the `WindowsUpdate.log` text file in the `C:\Windows` directory for any errors or technical details that may help with troubleshooting. Detailed information about reading and digesting the contents of this file can be found at support.microsoft.com/kb/902093/en-us.

- Ensure that the computer has enough free space (Windows Update error 80070070).

- Ensure that Internet Explorer is configured to automatically detect LAN settings (Windows Update error 8024402C).

- Ensure that the files used for the update aren't corrupt or missing (Windows Update error 80070003). To rectify this issue, stop the Windows Update service, delete all files in the `C:\Windows\SoftwareDistribution\DataStore` and `C:\Windows\SoftwareDistribution\Download` folders, start the Windows Update service, and check for updates again.

- Ensure that the Hosts file located in `C:\Windows\System32\Drivers\etc\` doesn't contain a static IP address for a Windows Update server (Windows Update error 80072ee7). If it does, open the hosts file with Notepad, remove the entry, or place a # sign next to both the hostname and IP address of the Windows Update server, and check for updates again. Alternatively, you can delete the entry. For example:

  # 10.2.19.231 http://wsus.companyabc.com

- Check that the applicable Microsoft Update sites, listed here, are added to the trusted sites list in Internet Explorer or a firewall (Windows

Update error 80072ee2). This applies only if the Windows Firewall, which contains these entries by default, has been disabled.

- http://*.update.microsoft.com and http://update.microsoft.com
- https://*.update.microsoft.com
- http://download.windowsupdate.com
- http://download.windowsupdate.microsoft.com
- http://update.microsoft.com/microsoftupdate/v6/default.aspx

- If an update is removed and then reinstalled, the update hasn't been hidden and Automatic Updates is configured to automatically install them, even if they have been removed.

- If a hardware device is no longer working, the driver may need to be rolled back. To accomplish this, click the Rollback Driver button under the Driver tab of the Hardware's Properties page in Device Manager.

- If an update no longer appears in the Available Updates window, or if it had previously been hidden and then restored, but no longer appears, the update has been replaced by a more recent release. Windows Update will not offer the previous version anymore.

Troubleshooting Windows Update When Updating from an Internal Windows Software Update Services (WSUS) Server

If the computer is set to update from an internal source but can't, the following troubleshooting steps can help pinpoint the problem:

- Ensure that the computer is properly receiving Group Policy and check with an Active Directory administrator to ensure that the computer is set to receive the policy and the proper configuration. Running gpupdate /force in the command prompt on the local machine will ensure that the latest Group Policies are loaded and applied.

- Ensure that the system is configured to query DNS and the entry for the WSUS server is valid.

- Ensure that the Hosts file located in `C:\Windows\System32\Drivers\etc\` doesn't contain a static IP address for a Windows Update server (Windows Update error 80072ee7). If it does, open the hosts file with Notepad, remove the entry, or place a # sign next to both the hostname and IP address of the Windows Update server and check for updates again: for example, # 10.2.19.231 wsus.companyabc.com or delete the entry altogether.

- If an update is removed and then reinstalled, Group Policy is in effect and the updated is required in WSUS. Contact the WSUS administrator.

- Ensure that the WSUS server is up and functioning, that its date and time are correct, and that there are updates to retrieve.

- If a hardware device is no longer working, the driver may need to be rolled back. To accomplish this, configure WSUS to uninstall the update and have the computer refresh its policy by running gpupdate /force in a command prompt.

If problems still persist, more extensive troubleshooting with Windows Vista, Windows Update, WSUS, Active Directory, or the network may be required. If all troubleshooting efforts have been exhausted, consider opening a support ticket with Microsoft or researching other issues and resolutions on the Microsoft support website at http://support.microsoft.com.

Windows Update Troubleshooting Tools

In addition to WSUS and common troubleshooting techniques, an administrator can use a couple of other tools in regard to Windows Update—the Enterprise Scan Tool and the Microsoft Baseline Security Analyzer.

The Enterprise Scan Tool

The Enterprise Scan Tool is released every month when new updates are posted (second calendar Tuesday). The Enterprise Scan Tool looks for installations of that month's releases only and displays the results in XML as shown in Figure 5.10. A version of the Enterprise Scan Tool is also available for integration with Microsoft Systems Management Server (SMS). For detailed information and instructions on the Enterprise Scan Tool and to obtain the latest version, visit support.microsoft.com/kb/894193.

The Microsoft Baseline Security Analyzer (MBSA)

The Microsoft Baseline Security Analyzer (MBSA) is a security tool that provides a scanning mechanism for one or more systems to determine the overall status of common security items. For example, the MBSA will identify administrative vulnerabilities and weaknesses, weak passwords, IIS and SQL vulnerabilities, and security updates. The security update section allows you to specify whether to use an internal update source (for example, WSUS) or the Microsoft Update site only. MBSA is a comprehensive tool for administrators. To cover the MBSA in its entirety is outside the scope of this book. For additional information, the website for the MBSA program is located at www.microsoft.com/technet/security/tools/mbsahome.mspx. Figure 5.11 shows the security update results of a scanned Windows Vista system.

FIGURE 5.10
Enterprise Scan Tool results.

Note

Only MBSA 2.1 will run on Windows Vista. At the time of writing, MBSA 2.1 was in its first beta release with a scheduled release time-frame of Q3 2007. The second beta release will include online remote scanning of Windows Vista systems, enhanced 64-bit support, and checks to include new Windows Vista security features.

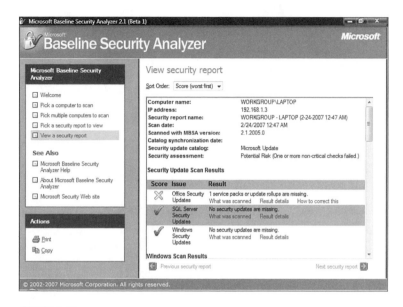

FIGURE 5.11
Microsoft Baseline Security Analyzer results.

Summary

Patch management and keeping Windows Vista systems up-to-date are
important security measures to integrate into system maintenance. When
configured properly, Windows Update can keep Windows Vista systems
current and protected from the latest security vulnerabilities, especially those
with known exploits, commonly built in to malicious software. If systems
aren't kept current with security patches and other updates, the system can be
vulnerable to attack, which could even result in a breach of security that can
impact other systems on the network. This chapter focused on providing
guidance for addressing patch management and Windows Vista utilizing the
latest tools available to administrators from Microsoft.

CHAPTER 6

Using User Account Control to Establish System Security

Introduction to User Account Control (UAC)

Another, and possibly the most significant, security improvement in Vista is the introduction of User Account Control (UAC). UAC addresses the questions: "Do you know this program and do you trust it?" and "System changes are about to be made, should this be allowed?" along with requesting the appropriate level of rights to take action. UAC was designed as another defense mechanism for preventing malware and virus infections along with unauthorized or unintentional system changes. It accomplished this by providing two levels of access: standard user and administrator in Admin Approval Mode. UAC also separates the local System account from Administrator accounts. Whereas the administrator invokes the change or system task, the local System account actually does the "work."

UAC essentially disables the ability to directly invoke certain tasks such as installing software and making system and security changes for all user accounts, including those in the Administrators group. Instead, Windows Vista injects a pop-up alert requesting "consent or credentials" and locks down the rest of the desktop. When attempts to modify the system or carry out certain routines are made, the logged on user will be prompted for authorization to do so. If the account is a standard user account, a password and/or account with administrative privileges on the local system must be given to complete the task. Accounts that are members of the Administrators group won't have to provide a password because they are running in Admin Approval mode; however, their rights must still be elevated first, which is accomplished by acknowledging the security prompt that appears. The Windows Vista development team at Microsoft named this approach the "Right Privilege at the Right Time." Windows Vista also retained fast user switching, originally introduced in Windows XP, so users and administrators have the flexibility they need from an operating system.

UAC eliminated the need for accounts to be members of the Power Users group found in previous versions of Windows. Common tasks such as checking email and browsing the Internet don't require administrative privileges; therefore any account in Windows Vista is running in a standardized, less privileged role until an escalated level of access is truly needed, including administrators.

Proper deployment and administration of UAC will reduce an organization's overall exposure and risk level to malicious code and unauthorized system changes. Although UAC assists in defending against malicious code and unauthorized system changes, other defense mechanisms should also be in place, such as a firewall, virus and malware scanners, and up-to-date security patches. Users should be educated on the impact of UAC and how to understand and acknowledge the different alerts and prompts it generates; it is a best practice that all accounts used for everyday business be standard user accounts, which reduces the overall exposure level to malicious software.

Note

It is important to note that accounts in the Administrators group can elevate their privileges much easier than standard users because they do not have to provide additional credentials. This can increase the potential for mistakes, virus infections, and so forth because alerts and warnings are more likely to be ignored or disabled altogether. For the most effective level of security, it is a best practice that all users log on to Windows with a standard user account. If necessary, like with IT staff, users can log on with an administrator account when performing administrative tasks or elevate privileges under their regular account. This configuration helps prevent security incidents and delivers accountability for system changes, especially in Enterprise environments.

Ultimately, in an Active Directory environment, System Administrators have total control of these items and more by leveraging Group Policy. For example, administrators can preapprove hardware drivers and websites for end users who may need to install certain things such as printers, wireless cards, and ActiveX controls for online applications. This level of flexibility gives administrators the control they need while minimizing the impact on a user's day-to-day routine. When elevated privileges are required or the feature is blocked (delivered through Group Policy), the Windows Security shield icon appears next to the setting, as shown next to several items of the User Accounts and Family Safety section in Figure 6.1. Clicking the setting will invoke the Windows Needs Your Permission to Continue window, shown in Figure 6.2. If the logged on account is not a member of the local Administrators group, the user is prompted to provide alternate credentials to complete the task. The Windows Needs Your Permission to Continue window, shown in Figure 6.2, provides the ability to choose an account with elevated privileges.

FIGURE 6.1
The Windows Security shield icon denoting which items in the User Accounts and Family Safety category of the Control Panel are protected by User Account Control.

FIGURE 6.2
The Windows Needs Your Permission to Continue prompt generated by User Account Control under an account without local Administrative privileges.

In previous versions of Windows, some tasks and settings required an administrator account to interact with. In some cases, this resulted in users being placed in the local administrators account when they only needed access to a particular task, such as adjusting how Windows handled power management. Microsoft reviewed the items in previous releases of Windows that ran under administrator credentials and deemed some to be safe for standard users in Windows Vista. In certain cases, additional configuration through Group Policy may be necessary. Group Policy and User Account Control are covered briefly at the end of this chapter. Part VII of this book covers Group Policy and Windows Vista.

Following are some of the tasks that no longer need administrator credentials in Windows Vista:

- Creating and configuring Virtual Private Network connections
- Changing power management settings such as system standby and hibernation

Following are some of the tasks that require administrative privileges in Windows Vista:

- Making changes in the Local Security Policy Editor
- Configuring the Windows Firewall and Remote Desktop Settings

---

Note

Chapter 15, "Setting Up Users and Computers in Windows Vista," covers creation and management of User Accounts and Groups.

Windows Vista analyzes the behavior of installation programs using heuristic technology, similar to that found in antivirus and anti-malware programs. Heuristics allows a computer or program to educate itself on the behavior of another program or installation routine and make decisions based on the observed behavior. Because one of the primary objectives of UAC is to prevent installation of malicious or unauthorized programs, Windows Vista carefully monitors programs that request elevated privileges or that attempt to write to the Registry or system files and directories. The same applies to programs that run an update or uninstallation routine. Microsoft has labeled this functionality Installer Detection Technology. Installer Detection Technology requires UAC to function properly.

Note

References to the Local Security Policy Editor and Active Directory Group Policy are made throughout this chapter. These items are available and supported only for the Business, Enterprise, and Ultimate editions of Windows Vista.

Enabling and Disabling User Account Control Components

Some UAC items can be enabled or disabled; however, to totally disable UAC all the features must be turned off and everything applicable would need to always run in Elevated Privilege mode, which is not recommended and far from a good security practice. However, in some circumstances, administrators may want to disable or change the behavior of certain UAC functions, such as running a custom-created in-house application without the need for elevation of rights or disabling Admin Approval mode for accounts in the Administrators group.

UAC can be configured through two means: Local Security Policy and Group Policy in Windows Server (code named Longhorn). Local security policies and Group Policy specific to UAC are covered later in this chapter. Part VII of this book fully covers Group Policy and Windows Vista. The next list gives a couple of example items, along with typical scenarios for use that can be configured within the Local Security Policy editor for UAC.

UAC can be enabled or disabled by clicking the Turn User Account Control On or Off link in the User Accounts section of the User Accounts and Family Safety category in the Control Panel. When disabling UAC through the Control Panel, you will first be prompted to confirm the change and then you will be warned of the security impact that is generated from disabling UAC. The second dialog also discourages you from deactivating UAC and includes a setting to keep it enabled. To confirm that you want to disable UAC and continue, deselect the check box labeled Use User Account Control (UAC) to Help Protect Your Computer and then click OK, as shown in Figure 6.3.

FIGURE 6.3
Recommendation to leave User Account Control (UAC) enabled.

> **Note**
>
> Only the Business, Ultimate, and Enterprise Editions of Windows Vista have a Local Security Policy editor with additional User Account Control settings. All editions of Windows Vista can configure User Account Control in the Security Center located in the Control Panel.

When UAC has been disabled, the Security Center will notify you. When UAC has been disabled through the Control Panel, this has an impact only on administrators, not standard users. Disabling UAC in the Control Panel only turns off the Run All Administrators in Admin Approval Mode setting, one of nine things that can be configured in regard to UAC. To reenable UAC, click the Turn User Account Control On or Off link in the User Accounts section of the User Accounts and Family Safety category in the Control Panel.

> **Note**
>
> Disabling or enabling UAC in the Control Panel has no effect on the eight other UAC settings that are configured through the Local Security Policy or Group Policy, only the Run All Administrators in Admin Approval mode.

As previously mentioned, nine components related to UAC can be configured either through the Local Security Policy or Group Policy. Although a couple of examples are given next, all of the configurable options related to UAC that can be found in the Local Security Policy and Group Policy are covered at the end of this chapter in the section "Administering User Account Control with Security Policies." Part VII of this book covers Group Policy and Windows Vista.

Following are some of the configurable options for UAC in the Local Security Policy:

- Behavior of the elevation prompt for standard users
    - Default Setting: Prompt for credentials
- Detect application installations and prompt for elevation
    - Default setting: Enabled
- Only elevate executables that are signed and validated
    - Default setting: Disabled

Caution

Disabling the UAC policies is recommended only for troubleshooting and administrative purposes because modification of these settings reduces the overall security level of the computer and exposes the system more openly to malicious software and unauthorized changes. When a UAC component has been disabled, the Security Center will notify you. In addition, UAC shouldn't be disabled simply because an application is generating too many prompts. Instead, run the application against the Application Compatibility Toolkit discussed in the "Using the Application Compatibility Toolkit" section of this chapter, and make adjustments as necessary.

Tip

Additional guidance on UAC and overall hardening of Windows Vista systems in an Active Directory or high-risk environment can be found in the Windows Vista Security Guide, a prescriptive document for establishing security baselines. Information about the Windows Vista Security Guide and a link to download it can be found at this website: www.microsoft.com/technet/windowsvista/security/guide.mspx.

Defining User Account Roles

Noted earlier in this chapter was the removal of rights that were granted to the Power Users group included in previous releases of Windows. The Power Users group was originally designed for reasons similar to that of UAC; however, because of security architecture changes in the Windows Vista and Server 2008 operating systems, the Power Users group was no longer needed. Instead, all user accounts now run as standard users leveraging elevated privileges when needed (and with permission), unless they are specifically placed in the local Administrators group. To support legacy versions of Windows, the Power Users group is still available, however. Use Computer Management to access the Power Users group and add members to it.

To add users to the Power Users group with the Computer Management snap-in:

1. Click Start and enter `compmgmt.msc` into the Search field, press Enter when `compmgmt.msc` appears in the results pane.

2. Acknowledge the consent prompt.

3. In Computer Management, expand Local Users and Groups.

4. Click the Groups folder and double-click the Power Users group on the right side.

Note

When Windows Vista is installed for the first time the Guest and Administrator accounts exist; however, they are disabled. The first account made in Windows Vista will be a member of the local Administrators group; however, all subsequent accounts will be standard users. But the local administrator account is enabled if it was the only active account present on a Windows XP system during an upgrade to Windows Vista. The local administrator account was disabled in Windows Vista because it was a common attack target in previous Windows releases. Chapter 15 covers Windows User Account creation and management.

Tip

When you are creating Administrator accounts in Microsoft Windows or any other operating system, it is a best practice that the account name doesn't make reference to its purpose. For example, an account labeled "admin_mel7" reveals that the account most likely has administrative access, whereas an account such as "a_mel7" won't be so obvious. Organizations are encouraged to implement standards for creating administrative accounts. Chapter 15 covers Windows User Account creation and management.

Administrators

Administrator accounts have access to system tasks, settings, and security controls that standard users do not. To resolve certain issues, IT administrators had no choice but to make a standard user's account a member of the local Administrators group. This generates a security issue and makes the system more vulnerable to attack because the logged on user is always running under administrative credentials, even though the user may not need it. If a user whose account is in the local Administrators group were to run a virus- or malware-infected executable, the malicious program could do much more damage than in Windows Vista. In Windows Vista, the user would be prompted about the application and that it needs elevated privileges (even though the account exists in the local Administrators group). This presents the user with an opportunity to avoid infecting the system. The same holds true for administrator accounts running in Admin Approval mode (enabled by default). If the malware program did happen to get installed, UAC can still provide a level of protection from updates or additional installations called by the local malware program, both common tricks found in most spyware and adware programs today.

Administrator accounts should primarily be used when the person logged on will be frequently performing administrative tasks relative to computer administration, such as when software or noncritical updates need to be installed.

Administrators, however, don't have the rights to automatically launch certain things by default, either, regardless of the fact that they ultimately have the correct level of permissions to perform the task or function. Administrators, like standard users, must first consent to the elevation request prompt. This occurs because any administrator account in Windows Vista is running in Admin Approval mode (enabled by default). Admin Approval mode generates two access tokens for administrators; one with administrative privileges and one with standard user privileges. This segregates tasks that truly need administrative access to be carried out, such as changing firewall settings, from something that doesn't, such as running Microsoft Word.

When an administrator logs on, both access tokens are created and the standard access token is used to run the Windows desktop and Explorer.exe process. A *process* contains the executable code used to run a program or part of a program. Programs can use and/or create multiple processes. All applications launched thereafter will be done under a standard access token unless consent or credentials are given. The Explorer.exe process provides access tokens to all other (user initiated) processes. Applications requiring the use of the administrator's access token will generate an elevation prompt. The only exception is if the process launches a second process (known as a child), in which case the access token in use is automatically inherited. Elevation prompts are discussed in the Consent and Credential Prompts section of this chapter.

Common administrative tasks that require elevated privileges in Windows Vista are the following:

- Installing and removing software, device drivers, and Active X controls for Internet-based applications
- Installing optional Windows Updates (critical system updates can be installed under a standard user account)
- Scheduling and configuring automatic updates and other automated tasks

- Configuring security controls such as Windows Firewall and settings in the Local Security Policy
- Configuring system settings such as Remote Desktop and Virtual Memory
- Placing files in or writing to the %SYSTEM%\Windows and %SYSTEM%\Program Files directories
- Managing User Accounts and Parental Controls
- Browsing folders and files in other users' directories
- Restoring system files from a backup

Standard User Accounts

As a best practice, all accounts used for day-to-day work should be standard user accounts. This also holds true for IT administrators and support staff. Standard user accounts have changed in Windows Vista and are allowed to perform more tasks than standard user accounts in previous versions of Windows. This reduced the need for accounts to be members of the Administrators group. If elevated privileges are needed to run an application or perform a task, the items will be marked with the Windows Security shield or the user can right-click the item and select Run as Administrator. The Run as Administrator command replaced the Run As command in previous versions of Windows. Standard users operate in a safer computing environment by default because only one access token is created by the operating system. An administrative access token therefore won't be created until it is needed and proper credentials are provided. After installing Windows Vista for the first time, the first account created is an administrator account and all subsequent accounts will be created as standard users.

Common tasks that no longer require elevated privileges in Windows Vista are the following:

- Establish network, wireless, and remote desktop connections
- Configure synchronization for mobile devices (for example, laptops, personal digital assistants (PDAs), and Windows Mobile devices)
- Configure BlueTooth devices and power options for laptops
- Configure display settings
- Configure Accessibility options in the Ease of Access Center
- Change the date and time and add or change time zones (up to three different time zones can be displayed)

Built-In Accounts

A few accounts are built in to the Windows Vista operating system. Each built-in account has a specific purpose. Some are included to complete tasks and run processes that allow the operating system to function. These accounts have specific privileges to certain routines and system files. Other built-in accounts, such as the Guest and Administrator accounts, are included for different reasons. The administrator account, for example, was mentioned earlier and exists to support Vista upgrades from Windows XP (if that was the only active account in Windows XP). The Administrator account is disabled by default to prevent it from being used—inadvertently or maliciously.

Most operating system processes, however, run under the System account, a built-in account created explicitly to handle functions between the user interface, operating system, and machine. When a user launches a program, some processes are passed to the System account, which has the appropriate level of access to complete the task. The System service intercepts a process initiated under a user account that has been given consent or credentials to run under an administrative account. This is known as the Application Information Service (AIS), new to Windows Vista. The AIS creates a new process for the program that is run and uses the Administrators access token for the new process.

The only built-in account that is accessible through the User Accounts applet in the Control Panel is the Guest account, which is disabled by default. Listed below are the built-in accounts along with a brief description of their purpose. Chapter 15, "Setting Up Users and Computers in Windows Vista," covers Windows User Account creation and management.

Accounts built in to the Windows Vista Operating System:

- **Administrator**—Disabled by default, used for Windows XP upgrades, cannot log on in Safe Mode.

- **Guest**—Disabled by default, used for temporary access to the system when a user account for the person doesn't exist, can only run applications that are already installed.

- **System**—Controls interaction between the operating system, hardware, applications, and more.

- **IUSR**—Used for anonymous access to web content on Internet Information Services (IIS), member of the IIS_IUSRS group.

- **INTERACTIVE**—Used to control the interaction between the logged on user and the physical console (keyboard, mouse, monitor).

> **Note**
>
> If the computer is joined to an Active Directory Domain, the local Administrator account, which is disabled by default, is prohibited from logging on in Safe Mode. The same holds true for workgroup systems if there is at least one active account in the Administrators group.

Understanding Consent and Credential Prompts

Mentioned throughout this chapter are consent and credential prompts, which are pop-up notifications that inform the user of an action that is about to take place and either requests permission or requests credentials to carry out the request. Depending on the configuration of the local security policy or a Group Policy, the action may be denied altogether.

These prompts reduce the risk of accidental system changes, malicious software installations (sometimes in stealth mode), and unauthorized activity. Both prompts generate a window titled Windows Needs Your Permission to Continue, and depending on the group membership of the account logged on, the appropriate prompt will be displayed. The behavior of these prompts can be configured in the Local Security Policy or through a Group Policy. Local Security policies and Group Policy specific to UAC are covered later in this chapter. Part VII of this book fully covers Group Policy and Windows Vista.

The consent prompt simply asks for permission to continue, recognizing that the logged on user has the appropriate level of access to carry out the task but needs administrative access to continue. The consent prompt differs, depending on what action is being initiated. For example, installation of software will ask if the user trusts the application, whereas initiating a system change will prompt for permission to continue. Acknowledging the consent prompt will launch the program under the administrator's access token, and the prompt will not appear until the same executable is called again. Figure 6.4 shows the consent prompt asking for permission to make changes to the Windows Firewall. Figure 6.5 shows the consent prompt that is displayed when an unknown program wants access to the computer.

> **Note**
>
> Applications written for Windows Vista, specifically those that are compatible with the new UAC, do not generate the consent prompt, whereas older applications do, including some legacy Microsoft applications. Applications with the "Designed for Windows Vista" logo comply with the new UAC standard.

Note

The Cancel button is selected by default when the consent prompt appears, so permission cannot be granted accidentally by quickly pressing the Enter key, an irreversible action.

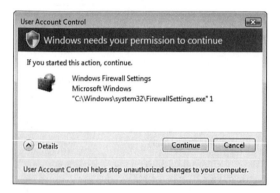

FIGURE 6.4
The Windows Needs Your Permission to Continue consent prompt generated when accessing restricted system settings.

FIGURE 6.5
The Unidentified Program Wants Access to Your Computer consent prompt.

The credentials prompt is also asking for permission to continue as with the consent prompt; however, the logged on user is not a member of the Administrators group or does not have the appropriate level of access, thus new credentials must be provided, as shown in Figure 6.6. A list of local Administrator accounts will appear in the prompt, recognizing which accounts on the system have the necessary level of rights to perform the task.

FIGURE 6.6
The Windows Needs Your Permission to Continue consent prompt generated when accessing restricted system settings under an account without administrator rights.

The consent prompt for applications is further broken down using color coding. The color coding in these prompts correlates to specific program categories: blocked, Windows Vista administration, signed by Authenticode, and unsigned or signed but not trusted.

Color codes for application consent prompts are the following:

- **Red background and red shield with exclamation point**—The application is blocked by policy or from a blocked publisher.

- **Blue and green background with standard Windows Security Shield**—Administrative application for Windows Vista, such as Computer Management.

- **Gray background and standard Windows Security Shield—** Application is Authenticode signed and trusted by the computer.

- **Yellow background and red shield icon with question mark—** Application is unsigned or signed but not yet trusted by the local computer.

Both the consent and credential prompts are launched in a Secure Desktop environment. The Secure Desktop is similar to what you would see in previous versions of Windows when the Ctrl+Alt+Del keys are pressed. When the Secure Desktop is invoked, the user must acknowledge and take action on the prompt being displayed with the rest of the desktop being unavailable. Computers that are Windows Aero compatible will see the desktop and items on it through a darkened translucent overlay, but interaction with it is still prohibited. Computers that aren't capable of running Windows Aero will also launch a Secure Desktop, but without the ability to "see it," similar to pressing Ctrl+Alt+Del in previous versions of Windows, where the desktop isn't visible and a solid color is displayed. After consent or credentials are provided, interaction with the desktop is restored.

Note

One of the main objectives of UAC is to prevent installation of malicious software; however, since the beta release of Windows Vista, malware authors have been discussing ways to forge these prompts to either trick the user into entering credentials or approving the application. The ideal target for this is the prompt denoting that the program is a Windows Administrative tool. This is a type of social engineering attack, tricking the user into believing the application is from someone they should trust. The best proven defense against malicious software is an anti-malware program such as Windows Defender, included in Windows Vista. Windows Defender provides real-time and scheduled system scanning to detect malicious code. Windows Defender is covered in Chapter 4, "Securing a Windows Vista System."

Control and modification to the consent and credential prompts is covered in the "Enabling and Disabling User Account Control Components" and "Administering User Account Control with Security Policies" sections of this chapter.

Managing Pre-Windows-Vista Applications

Applications written for versions of Microsoft Windows prior to that of Windows Vista should function, but some additional steps may be necessary to get the application to function properly or in some cases work at all. It depends on what the application needs to do to function correctly. The transition into UAC for developers will be a large task; however, the end result of conforming to UAC protects the application, the user, the system, and data. Unfortunately, this isn't quite as straightforward for applications that are written in-house to fulfill a specific need an organization has, applications that are modified, or applications that require unfettered access to system files and processes.

Microsoft took this into account when UAC was developed; ultimately, application developers will need to comply with this new standard, which in some cases will require rewriting the code and/or possibly changing the way the application functions. Organizations and individuals who have older applications but want to use them on Windows Vista have a few options other than waiting for the "next version" or an upgrade that is compatible with UAC and Windows Vista. Virtualization, the Application Compatibility Toolkit, Standard User Analyzer Tool, and repackaging of software all exist to help developers and IT Administrators offset the impact of UAC. If software vendors don't comply with UAC, the user has to question the integrity of the application and confidentiality of the user's data. These items are discussed in the next few sections.

Note

Applications that bear the "Certified for Windows Vista" logo, as shown in Figure 6.7, are deemed to be in compliance with UAC as well as written for and supported on the Windows Vista operating system. Applications bearing the "Works with Windows Vista" logo, as shown in Figure 6.8, have been tested and verified to "work" on Windows Vista. A list of these applications is available at the http://support.microsoft.com/default.aspx/kb/933305 Microsoft support website. Those wanting to obtain one of these logos for an application can find guidance at the Innovate on Windows Vista website located at www.innovateonwindowsvista.com.

FIGURE 6.7
The Certified for Windows Vista logo.

FIGURE 6.8
The Works with Windows Vista logo.

Understanding Virtualization

Windows Vista incorporates a new technology called *virtualization*, which helps protect the Registry and system files from malicious or unintentional changes. Virtualization applies to any application that is not compatible with UAC and normally required administrative access to function properly. Virtualization creates a virtual copy of the directory, Registry, and/or files that the application needs to modify. A virtual copy of these items is stored under each user's account that runs the application. This allows the application to make the changes it needs to function, without writing directly to the same areas in the operating system. This also allows undesired changes made by the application to be rolled back or halted quickly and effectively. In addition to security, virtualization was also created to ensure the application will function properly.

Caution

By design applications that are elevated, thus running under an administrative access token, will not be virtualized.

Using the Application Compatibility Toolkit

Changes in security and system architecture built in to Windows Vista no doubt impacted older applications written for Windows XP, 2000, and before. Although some older operating systems are no longer supported, or are only supported on a contractual basis, Microsoft recognized the need to provide some sort of backward compatibility when migrating to Windows Vista. In fact, Microsoft tested almost 2,000 applications to determine which ones need "help" or what common components among legacy applications generated compatibility issues—and how they could address those issues, providing solutions or workarounds when possible. In some cases, this buys the application developers time to work on an upgrade or patch that would include code compatible with Windows Vista. The introduction of UAC was one of the impacts, if not the biggest, to legacy applications.

Enterprise organizations, companies with applications written in-house, and companies supporting different versions of Microsoft Windows will benefit greatly from the Application Compatibility Toolkit. The Application Compatibility Toolkit is a comprehensive program that allows IT administrators to search for compatibility issues with UAC and other functions, in multiple applications, and store that information in a centralized location so it can be later reviewed. The Application Compatibility Toolkit includes several tools to help ascertain whether Windows Vista will allow the analyzed applications to function properly or provide direction on addressing the issue(s).

The Application Compatibility Toolkit allows administrators to obtain an inventory of applications and any issues in one central location. Analysis and prioritization of the results derived from the Application Compatibility Toolkit give administrators a birds-eye view of the impact and preparation needed when deploying and supporting Windows Vista.

The Application Compatibility Toolkit is a robust set of tools for IT administrators and application developers. The Application Compatibility Toolkit is available as a separate download in the "System Tools" part of the downloads section of the Microsoft website at www.microsoft.com/downloads/. The Application Compatibility Toolkit has several requirements for use, which are outlined next.

Note

The Application Compatibility Toolkit is not the same as the Program Compatibility Assistant or Program Compatibility Wizard included with Windows Vista. Although they share some of the same functionality and essentially the same purpose, they are very different, mainly in regard to their feature set and target audience. The Program Compatibility Assistant launches automatically when a problem is discovered with an older program and cannot be manually invoked. The Program Compatibility Assistant will provide direction on rectifying a problem with an application when one is detected. The Program Compatibility Wizard allows you to configure an application to run in a "compatibility" mode for the operating system the application was originally built for (for example, Windows XP SP2). The Program Compatibility Wizard can be run at any time.

Application Compatibility Toolkit 5.0 requirements are the following:

- Operating system—Windows Vista, Windows XP SP2, Windows 2003 Server SP1, or Windows 2000 SP4

- Database—SQL Server 2005, SQL Server 2005 Express, or SQL Server 2000

- Recommended hardware—2.8GHz Processor with 2GB of RAM

- Microsoft .NET Framework 1.1 (Windows Vista)

- Microsoft .NET Framework 2.050727 (Windows XP SP2, Windows Server 2003 SP1, Windows 2000 SP4)

Caution

The Application Compatibility Toolkit only runs on 32-bit versions of Windows Vista and requires the Microsoft .NET Framework 1.1 for Windows Vista systems (2.050727 for all others). If .NET Framework 1.1 isn't installed when the installation for the Application Compatibility Toolkit is launched, you will be prompted to download and install it. .NET Framework 1.1 can also be downloaded and installed from the .NET Framework Developer Center at msdn.microsoft.com/netframework.

Included with the Application Compatibility Toolkit are the following:

- **Application Compatibility Manager**—A central location to gather, store, sort, and generate reports for application compatibility issues. The Application Compatibility Manager reports on issues related to software, hardware, Windows updates, and specified websites.

- **Compatibility Administrator**—Shown in Figure 6.9, this is included as a proactive tool for identifying and resolving compatibility issues before deployment into a production environment. Also allows for customization of compatibility fixes and the capability to search for installed fixes.

- **Developer and Tester Tools**—Tools for application developers.

  - **Internet Explorer Compatibility Tool**—Reports on compatibility issues with websites, especially useful for online applications or those requiring extra components such as ActiveX controls.

  - **Setup Analysis Tool**—Monitors and identifies compatibility issues during the installation of a program.

  - **Standard User Analyzer Tool**—Monitors and identifies compatibility issues when a program is run under a standard user account.

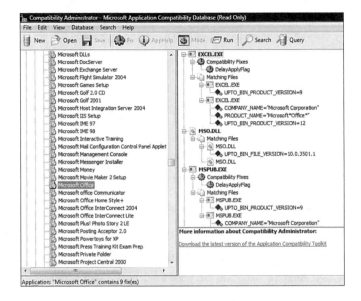

FIGURE 6.9
Details on Microsoft Office analysis in the Compatibility Administrator.

Tip

The Application Compatibility Manager can use a database connection like SQL Express or a SQL server to collect and report on the results of application analysis performed by the Application Compatibility Toolkit, especially for larger networks.

Complete configuration and administration of the Application Compatibility Toolkit is beyond the scope of this book; however, several new compatibility evaluators were included and/or upgraded to support Windows Vista and are worth mentioning.

Compatibility evaluators included to support Windows Vista:

- **Vista Compatibility Evaluator**—Lists compatibility issues with Windows Vista system files and processes.

- **User Account Control Compatibility Evaluator**—Lists compatibility issues related to permissions restricted by UAC.

- **Internet Explorer Compatibility Evaluator**—Lists compatibility issues with web applications and websites running in Internet Explorer 7.

- **Update Compatibility Evaluator**—Lists issues related to specific Windows updates.

- **Inventory Collector**—Collects application and system information to run compatibility evaluators against.

The Application Compatibility Toolkit is a valuable tool for IT administrators planning to upgrade systems to Windows Vista. The Microsoft TechNet has a website dedicated to all aspects of application compatibility, including the Application Compatibility Toolkit, at http:// technet.microsoft.com/en-us/desktopdeployment/bb414773.aspx.

Working with the Standard User Analyzer Tool

The Standard User Analyzer Tool was designed to identify issues with UAC that stem from running applications under a standard user account. The Standard User Analyzer Tool, shown in Figure 6.10, is included with the Application Compatibility Toolkit and can be located under the Start menu in the All Programs, Application Compatibility Toolkit 5.0, Developer and Tester Tools folder. As mentioned in the previous section, the Application Compatibility Toolkit is available as a separate download from the Microsoft website at www.microsoft.com/downloads/.

To analyze an application with the Standard User Analyzer Tool follow these steps:

1. Launch the Standard User Analyzer Tool shown in Figure 6.10, under Start, All Programs, Application Compatibility Toolkit 5.0, Developer and Tester Tools.

2. Click the Browse button in the Standard User Analyzer window to locate the executable file associated with the application.

3. Click the Launch button (the application will be invoked).

4. Click the Refresh Log button to populate the Standard User Analyzer Tool with the results.

5. Browse through the tabs to review any issues, or click View in the menu bar and select Detailed Information to include a summary of errors on the App Info tab, as shown in Figure 6.10.

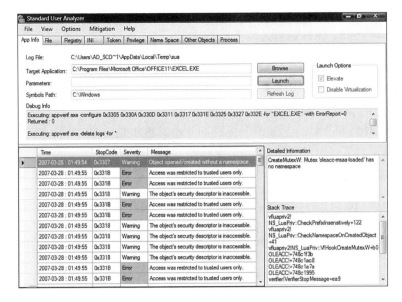

FIGURE 6.10
Analysis results of Microsoft Excel 2003 SP2 (EXCEL.EXE) in the Standard User Analyzer Tool.

Repackaging Applications

Windows Vista includes Microsoft Installer version 4.0, which is fully compliant with UAC. Repackaging of applications is often referred to as a daunting task and is usually required only in large organizations with centralized asset and application management systems. Repackaging of applications has many advantages, such as the ability to install the program silently from distributed repositories and include configuration settings. However, the process can be quite time consuming and must be tested before deployment into a production environment.

Several third-party tools are available for repackaging software, but companies utilizing Microsoft Systems Management Server (SMS) can download FLEXnet AdminStudio 7 SMS Edition for free. FLEXnet AdminStudio can repackage older applications into current Microsoft Installer packages (a single MSI file) for distribution with SMS. FLEXnet AdminStudio 7 SMS Edition and supporting documentation can be downloaded from Microsoft TechNet at www.microsoft.com/technet/prodtechnol/sms/sms2003/downloads/tools/adminstudio.mspx. Information about Microsoft Systems

Management Server 2003 can be found at www.microsoft.com/smserver/
default.mspx.

Administering User Account Control with Security Policies

Referenced throughout this chapter is the capability to control how UAC is
configured through either a local or group policy. Restricting the ability to
provide alternative credentials or escalate privileges may be necessary in
higher risk environments, whereas looser restraints might be required when
systems aren't as vulnerable to attack or don't store sensitive data. Security
policies provide an extra layer of protection by enforcing configuration for
multiple items related to UAC, whereas disabling UAC in the Control Panel
affects only the Run All Administrators in Admin Approval Mode setting.
Policies are a great way to deploy and administer a consistent UAC configuration scheme.

Caution

Windows Server 2008 is required to configure UAC through an Active
Directory Group Policy for Windows Vista systems.

Nine items related to UAC can be configured via policy. Each is listed next
along with their options and a brief description. The User Account Control
options in the Local Security Policy editor are shown in Figure 6.11.

Configurable User Account Control items in the Local Security Policy
Editor:

- Admin Approval Mode for the Built-in Administrator account

    - **Enabled**—Built-in Administrator account runs in Admin
      Approval mode (default).

    - **Disabled**—Built-in Administrator account won't be prompted
      for consent or credentials.

- Behavior of the elevation prompt for administrators in Admin
  Approval mode

    - **No Prompt**—Accounts in the Administrators group will not be
      prompted for consent or credentials.

    - **Prompt for Consent**—Invokes the prompt for consent to
      continue without requiring credentials to be entered (default).

- **Prompt for Credentials**—Invokes the prompt for credentials requiring an account and password to be entered to continue.
- Behavior of the elevation prompt for standard users
  - **No Prompt**—The prompt for credentials is not invoked and the action is not allowed. Users can log on either under a different account or use the Run as Administrator option (default).
  - **Prompt for Credentials**—Invokes the prompt for credentials requiring an Administrative account and password to be entered to continue.
- Detect application installations and prompt for elevation
  - **Enabled**—The prompt for credentials or consent will appear (default).
  - **Disabled**—The installation will fail silently and the application will not be installed.
- Only elevate executables that are signed and validated
  - **Enabled**—The program must be digitally signed to run.
  - **Disabled**—Digitally signed or unsigned code can be launched (default).
- Only elevate UIAccess applications that are installed in secure locations
  - **Enabled**—Programs will run only if they reside in the Program Files or Windows directory, because these locations are protected (default).
  - **Disabled**—Applications can be launched regardless of where they reside.
- Run all administrators in Admin Approval mode
  - **Enabled**—All user accounts (administrative and standard) will be prompted for consent or credentials when necessary (default).
  - **Disabled**—Same as clicking the Turn User Account Control On or Off link in the User Accounts section of the User Accounts and Family Safety category in the Control Panel. The Application Information Service is disabled and a restart is required. The Windows Security Center will display a warning message denoting that UAC has been disabled.

- Switch to the secure desktop when prompting for elevation
    - **Enabled**—The desktop will be locked down when a prompt for consent or credentials is displayed (default).
    - **Disabled**—Interaction with the desktop will be allowed.
- Virtualize file and Registry write failures to per-user locations
    - **Enabled**—Turns on virtualization of system files and Registry entries for legacy applications (default).
    - **Disabled**—Only UAC-compliant applications can be run and noncompliant applications will fail.

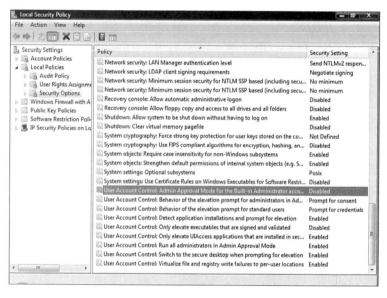

FIGURE 6.11
User Account Control Options in the Local Security Policy editor.

Local Security Policies

Local Security Policies and templates are designed for use in small networks that don't utilize Active Directory or standalone systems such as kiosks. The Local Security Policy editor can be used to configure User Account Control settings and either apply them to the local computer or export them to the Security Template (INF) file for use on multiple systems.

To modify the Local Security Policy to configure and apply user Account Control settings, follow these steps:

1. Launch the Local Security Policy Editor by clicking the Start button and entering `secpol.msc` into the Search field.

2. Click Enter when secpol is displayed in the Search Results field.

3. In the Local Security Policy editor, expand Local Policies and click Security Options.

4. On the right, scroll down to the User Account Control Settings.

5. Adjust and apply the User Account Control Settings as necessary.

6. Exit the Local Security Policy editor to apply the settings to the local system.

To create and import a security template, do the following:

1. Configure User Account Control Settings in the Local Security Policy editor as desired.

2. Highlight Security Settings in the left pane and click Action in the menu bar.

3. Select Export Policy to create an INF file that contains the new settings, or repeat step 2 and select Import Policy to load a preconfigured Security Template.

4. Exit the Local Security Policy Editor when finished.

Active Directory Group Policies

The Group Policy editor in Active Directory works exactly like the Local Security Policy editor, except it has a larger reach because the policy can be assigned to a computer, group, organizational unit, site, or domain and can be included in a larger policy that encompasses many settings. The same items in the Local Security Policy related to UAC can be configured in Group Policy; however, Local Security policies are overridden when the computer joins a domain and Group Policy is applied. Group Policy administration for Windows Vista systems in an Active Directory environment is covered in Part VII of this book.

Summary

User Account Control (UAC) provides a crucial layer of security between the user, operating system, and software. When configured properly, UAC helps protect the Windows Vista operating system from unauthorized changes and the installation and/or use of malicious and unapproved software. Not using or configuring UAC properly can leave the system vulnerable to attack or misconfiguration. The focus of this chapter was to provide guidance for the configuration and management of the different UAC options.

CHAPTER 7

Implementing BitLocker Drive Encryption to Improve Data Privacy

Introduction to BitLocker Drive Encryption

BitLocker Drive Encryption is a new hardware-enhanced feature in the Microsoft Windows Vista operating system that provides offline data protection for computers. Available in only the Enterprise and Ultimate versions of Windows Vista and in Windows Server 2008, BitLocker provides an extra layer of protection for the operating systems and data stores on the operating system drive volume. BitLocker makes sure that data is protected against offline attacks made by disabling and/or circumventing the operating system or by physically removing the drive from the system to attack the data separately. Large or small enterprises will benefit from using BitLocker Drive Encryption on any computer or mobile PC that stores sensitive information.

BitLocker Drive Encryption uses the Trusted Platform Module (TPM) to provide enhanced data and ensures boot integrity by validating the computer's boot manager integrity and boot files at startup. It guarantees that a computer's encrypted drive is in the original computer and checks that the hard disk has not been subjected to unauthorized viewing while in an offline state by encrypting the entire Windows volume. This includes system and user files as well as swap files and hibernation files. In addition, BitLocker saves measurement details related to core operating system files in TPM, creating a sort of system fingerprint. The fingerprint remains the same unless the boot system is tampered with.

BitLocker Drive Encryption provides seamless protection at system startup. Because this is transparent to the user, the user login experience is unchanged. However, if the TPM is changed or missing, or if startup information has changed, BitLocker enters recovery mode and the user needs to provide a recovery password to regain access to the data.

BitLocker Drive Encryption protects data while the system is offline because it does the following:

- Encrypts the entire Windows volume, user data and system files, the hibernation file, the page file, and temporary files.

- Provides umbrella protection for third-party applications installed on the encrypted volume.

BitLocker Drive Encryption ensures boot process integrity because it

- Locks the system so it will not boot if any monitored files are tampered with.

- Protects the system from offline software attacks against the Windows volume.

- Provides a method to check that boot file integrity is intact and has not been attacked by boot sector viruses or root kits.

BitLocker Drive Encryption also eases equipment recycling by

- Reducing the time to permanently and safely delete all data on the drive. Data on the encrypted volume can be rendered useless by simply deleting the keys that are required to access the drive.

Who Needs BitLocker Drive Encryption?

Data theft and unwanted media exposure from a lost or a stolen computing device is a growing concern among office managers, IT planners, security experts, and corporate executives. Loss of information can be damaging to the reputation and long-term survival of an organization, resulting in lost revenue, weakened competitive advantage, and reduction in customer confidence.

Recent government regulations have emerged that focus on data protection and the requirement for privacy. This legislation has a strong impact on organizational storage policies, especially for PC devices that have a relatively short life span and are often either portable or are easily lost or stolen.

The target audience for BitLocker Drive Encryption is any organization that stores valuable business data office systems or mobile PCs where the loss or disclosure of that data would have a negative impact on the organization, customers, shareholders, or personnel.

BitLocker Drive Encryption is designed to provide the data protection these organizations need while also providing for a transparent user experience that is simple to deploy and manage.

Reviewing System Requirements

BitLocker Drive Encryption is a data protection feature available in Windows Vista Enterprise and Ultimate editions and in Windows Server 2008. A computer that meets the minimum system requirements for Windows Vista Enterprise and Ultimate editions will support enabling BitLocker Drive Encryption. All other versions of Windows Vista and any previous version of Windows operating systems will not support BitLocker Drive Encryption.

Hardware

BitLocker Drive Encryption is designed to offer a seamless user experience. BitLocker Drive Encryption can be used both on computers that have compatible TPM architecture and on computers that do not have compatible TPM architecture.

If a system has TPM version 1.2, BitLocker Drive Encryption requires additional items: a properly configured TPM, properly configured disk drives, and to have BitLocker Drive Encryption enabled. It is designed for systems that have a compatible TPM microchip and BIOS. A compatible TPM is defined as a version 1.2 TPM. A compatible BIOS must support the TPM and the Static Root of Trust Measurement as defined by the Trusted Computing Group.

A summary of Windows Vista BitLocker Drive Encryption requirements for computers with TPM version 1.2 or higher is as follows:

- A TPM microchip, version 1.2, turned on.
- A Trusted Computing Group (TCG)-compliant BIOS.
- Two NTFS drive partitions, one for the system volume and one for the operating system volume. The system volume partition must be at least 1.5 gigabytes and set as the active partition.
- A BIOS setting to start up first from the hard drive, not the USB or CD drives.

Note

For any test that includes the USB flash drive, your BIOS must support reading USB flash drives at startup.

Tip

The information in this chapter applies to Windows Vista versions with BitLocker. For server-specific information, visit Microsoft at technet2. microsoft.com/WindowsVista/en/library/ba1a3800-ce29-4f09-89ef-65bce923cdb51033.mspx?mfr=true. Also visit the TPM Specifications section of the Trusted Computing Group's website (go.microsoft.com/fwlink/ ?LinkId=72757) for more information about TPM specifications.

If a computer does not have TPM version 1.2 or later, the computer must meet the following requirements to use BitLocker Drive Encryption:

- Properly configured disk drives for BitLocker Drive Encryption
- Have BitLocker Drive Encryption enabled

Unfortunately, systems that do not have a TPM that is Windows compatible, or that have no TPM at all, will not have the additional security or early boot file integrity validation. In this case, BitLocker Drive Encryption will use USB flash drive key mode, which requires a USB flash drive with a startup key. If the computer user is unable to have the startup key or is unable to provide the startup key, BitLocker Drive Encryption will enter the drive recovery mode. BitLocker Drive Encryption also will enter recovery mode if the integrity of the encrypted volumes has been tampered with or changed.

Software

BitLocker Drive Encryption is a data protection feature available in Windows Vista Enterprise and Ultimate editions and in the upcoming Windows Server 2008. A computer that meets the minimum requirements for Windows Vista Enterprise and Ultimate editions will support enabling BitLocker Drive Encryption. All other versions of Windows Vista and any previous version of Windows operating systems will not support BitLocker Drive Encryption.

Using BitLocker Drive Encryption

Most business class computers that are shipped with Windows Enterprise or Ultimate editions should have properly configured TPMs and drives. So typically, administrators will only need to enable BitLocker Drive Encryption.

If for some reason the computer does not have TPM enabled for use, administrators can initialize and enable the TPM. Administrators can start the TPM via the Trusted Platform Management console using the following steps:

1. Click Start, All Programs, Accessories, and then Run.

2. Type **tpm.msc** into the Open box and then press Enter.

3. Using the commands listed under Action, manage the computer's TPM configuration.

The console can also be used to perform the following tasks:

- Changing the owner password associated with the TPM. This may be necessary if the TPM owner password has been compromised.

- Disabling and turning off TPM if it is no longer needed.

- Canceling TPM ownership and shutting off TPM when disposing of a computer.

Partitioning a Hard Drive for Windows BitLocker Drive Encryption

BitLocker Drive Encryption requires that a computer have at least two partitions on the hard disk. The first partition is the system volume and contains the boot information in an unencrypted space. The second partition is the operating system volume which is encrypted and contains the operating system and user data. The partitions can be created before or after installing Windows Vista.

Note

In some situations, a volume can involve multiple partitions. In most situations with simple volumes, a volume and a partition are functionally equivalent. BitLocker works with volumes, a logical structure, but many disk tools are concerned with physical disk partitions. Before creating the partitions required for BitLocker Drive Encryption, make sure that any data on the disk has been backed up.

Before implementing BitLocker Drive Encryption, administrators should double-check that data is backed up and the product key for Windows Vista is available. Using the Windows Vista DVD, administrators will perform a series of steps that will create a primary partition of at least 1.5GB and set the partition as active, create a secondary partition, format both partitions, and then install Windows Vista.

Your drive letters might not correspond to those in the steps shown. For easier understanding, the operating system volume is labeled C, and the system volume is labeled S (for system volume). In this example, we also assume that the system has only one physical hard disk drive.

To partition a disk with no operating system for BitLocker, follow these steps:

1. Start the computer from the Windows Vista product media. Choose the correct installation language, time and currency format, and keyboard layout in the Install Windows screen, and then click Next.

2. In the next Install Windows screen, click System Recovery Options, located in the lower-left of the screen. In the System Recovery Options dialog box, choose your keyboard layout and then click Next.

3. In the next System Recovery Options dialog box, make sure no operating system is selected. To do this, click in the empty area of the Operating System list, below any listed entries. Then click Next.

4. In the next System Recovery Options dialog box, click Command Prompt.

5. At the command prompt, type **diskpart**, and then press Enter. Diskpart creates the partition for the operating system volume.

6. Type **select disk 0** and then type **clean** to erase the existing partition table.

7. Type **create partition primary size=1500** to set the partition you are creating as a primary partition.

8. Type **assign letter=S** to give this partition the S designator, and then type **active** to set the new partition as the active partition.

9. Type **create partition primary** to create another primary partition. Windows Vista will be installed on this larger partition. Type **assign letter=C** to give this partition the C designator.

10. Type **list volume** to see a display of all the volumes on this disk. A list is displayed showing each volume, volume numbers, letters, labels, file systems, types, sizes, status, and information. Double-check that you have two volumes and make a note of the label used for each volume.

11. Type **exit** to leave the diskpart application.

12. Type **format c: /y /q /fs:NTFS** to properly format the C volume.

13. Type **format s: /y /q /fs:NTFS** to properly format the S volume.

14. Type **exit** to leave the command prompt.

15. Close the System Recovery Options window to close the window to return to the main installation screen. *Do not* click Shut Down or Restart.

16. Click Install now and proceed with the Windows Vista installation process. Be sure to install Windows Vista on the larger operating system volume, C:.

If the system does not have a second partition already created, administrators can create a secondary partition using tools included within Windows Vista. Microsoft included the capability within Windows Vista to repartition a hard disk by using the Shrink feature in Disk Management. Administrators can shrink an existing partition or volume to create unallocated disk space for a new partition or volume using the following steps:

1. Click Start, Control Panel, System Maintenance, Administrative Tools, and then double-click the Computer Management shortcut in the right pane. If prompted, supply an administrator password or click Continue to confirm the action and proceed.

2. In the navigation pane, under Storage, click Disk Management.

3. Right-click the volume to shrink, and then click Shrink Volume. The selected volume will be queried for available shrink space.

4. After the volume is finished being queried, the volume statistics will be displayed as shown in Figure 7.1. In the Enter the Amount of Space to Shrink in MB field, type in the number of MB to shrink the volume or use the up and down arrows to adjust the shrink space.

5. Click Shrink to begin shrinking the volume.

6. When the shrinking process is completed, the new unallocated volume will need to be formatted. In the Disk Management console, right-click the unallocated volume and select New Simple Volume to initialize the New Simple Volume Wizard. Click Next in the New Simple Volume Wizard Welcome page.

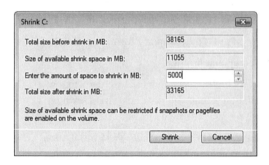

FIGURE 7.1
Shrinking a volume using Disk Management in Windows Vista.

7. Specify the volume size in MB or click Next to accept the default value.

8. Assign the drive letter to be used for this volume by selecting the Assign the Following Drive Letter button and then choosing a drive letter, such as S, in the drop-down selection option on the right. Click Next to continue.

9. On the Format Partition page, select Format This Volume with the Following Settings. Take the default settings for File System (NTFS), Allocation Unit Size, and Volume Name, and enable the Perform a Quick Format check box. Click Next to Continue and review the volume format settings.

10. Click Finish to complete the New Simple Volume Wizard. The New volume will now formatted and show up in the Disk Management console as New Volume (drive letter :), as shown in Figure 7.2.

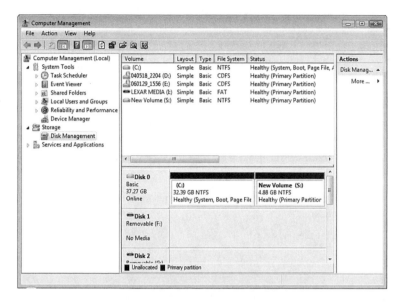

FIGURE 7.2
Viewing New Volumes using Disk Management in Windows Vista.

Turning on Basic BitLocker Drive Encryption

When the computer system meets the required software and hardware requirements, administrators can enable BitLocker Drive Encryption protection on a system with a TPM. After Windows BitLocker Drive Encryption in enabled and the volume is encrypted, users log on to the computer normally.

Administrators can turn on BitLocker Drive Encryption by performing the following steps:

1. Click Start, Control Panel, Security, and then click BitLocker Drive Encryption.

2. If the User Account Control message appears, verify that the proposed action is what you requested, and then click Continue.

3. On the BitLocker Drive Encryption page, click Turn On BitLocker to start the BitLocker Drive Encryption Wizard. Click Next on the Welcome page to continue.

Note

If the system's TPM is not initialized, the Initialize TPM Security Hardware wizard will display. Follow the directions to initialize the TPM and the restart the computer.

4. On the Save the Recovery Password page, the BitLocker Drive Encryption Wizard provides options for printing, displaying, or saving the 48-digit recovery password. The options are

■ Save the password on a USB drive.

■ Save the password in a folder on a network drive or another location.

■ Print the password.

Caution

Be sure to store the recovery password in a secure location. The recovery password will be required if the encrypted drive must be moved to another computer or if changes are made to the system startup information. The recovery password is also needed to unlock secured data when a volume enabled with BitLocker Drive Encryption enters a locked state. The recover password is unique to a specific BitLocker Drive Encryption session and cannot be used to recover data from any other session than the one with which it was created. For maximum security, store recovery passwords in a location away from the computer.

5. Click Print the Password to print the password. Store the printed password in a secure location.

6. Click Save the Password. In the Save BitLocker Drive Encryption Password As dialog box, type a filename for the password. Click Save to save the file. The default location for the saved password file is the user profile's Documents directory.

7. Click Next to display the Save the Recovery Key on a USB Device page. To save the recovery password to a USB memory device, insert the device and then select the device from the displayed list. Click Save Key.

8. Click Next to display the Save the Recovery Key to a Folder page. To save the recovery passwords to a network drive folder or a network

share, click Save and then use the Browse Folder options to locate and select the folder to save the recovery key.

9. Click Next. If the computer is TPM enabled, the Create a PIN for Added Security page will be displayed. If a PIN is desired for added security during system start, enter and confirm a PIN, and then click Set Pin. Make sure to remember the PIN; it will be required to start the computer. Click Next.

10. The Create a Startup Key for Added Security page will be displayed. Here, administrators have the option of creating a startup key. When using a startup key, administrators have a few options to think about:

   ■ On TPM-enabled computers, the startup key is optional. If a startup key is required for the computer to boot, insert the USB memory device and then select the device from the displayed list. Click Save Key.

   ■ On computers without TPM, a startup key is required. Insert the USB memory device and then select the device from the displayed list. Click Save Key.

   After a decision has been made, click Next.

Note

Remember, a startup key is different from a recovery key. A startup key is required for users who start the computer. A recovery key is needed only when BitLocker Drive Encryption enters recovery mode.

---

11. On the Encrypt the Selected Disk Volume page, click Encrypt to encrypt the selected volume. Confirm that the Run BitLocker System Check option is checked, and then click Continue. Confirm that you want to restart the computer by clicking Restart Now. The computer restarts and BitLocker verifies whether the computer is BitLocker Drive Encryption compatible and ready for encryption. If it is not, you will see an error message alerting you to the problem.

12. If the system is ready for encryption, the Encryption in Progress status bar is displayed. To monitor the status of the disk volume encryption, drag the mouse cursor over the BitLocker Drive Encryption icon in the toolbar at the bottom of the screen. Encrypting the volume typically takes between one and two minutes per gigabyte to complete.

When the encryption process is finished, the operating system volume will be encrypted and a recovery password unique to this volume will have been created. The next time a user logs on, the user will see no change. If a startup key or PIN were created, the PIN or startup key will be needed to start the computer. If the TPM changes or cannot be accessed, if there are changes to key system files, or if someone tried to start the computer from a disk to circumvent the operating system, the computer will switch to recovery mode until the recovery password is supplied.

Turning on BitLocker Drive Encryption on a System Without TPM

BitLocker Drive Encryption can also be enabled on systems without a compatible TPM. Instead of a TPM, a startup key is used for authentication. The startup key is located on a USB flash drive that is inserted into the computer before the computer is turned on. The computer must have a BIOS that will read USB flash drives at startup during the preoperating system environment. If administrators are uncertain whether the computer has compatible system BIOS, they can check by using the Hardware Test at the end of the BitLocker Wizard.

Before getting started, be sure to be logged on as an administrator and have a USB drive for storing the recovery password and startup key.

Tip

For maximum security, use two USB memory devices to store the startup key and the recovery password. Use one drive for the startup key and one drive for the recovery password. With the startup key and recovery password stored on two separate devices in two different locations, it will be harder for someone to compromise the BitLocker Drive Encryption security.

To use BitLocker Drive Encryption without a TPM, the computer's Group Policy settings must be modified so that BitLocker Drive Encryption without a TPM can be enabled.

> **Note**
>
> Group Policy (GP) is a powerful tool that allows administrators to control all aspects of BitLocker Drive Encryption. Using Group Policy, administrators can enable, disable, or make optional authentication scenarios and recovery mechanisms. Some of the settings that administrators can configure are
>
> - Set Group Policy to enable backup of BitLocker and TPM recovery information to Active Directory.
> - Configure UI policies to do the following:
>   - Establish which security scenarios are enabled, disabled, or optional and which recovery mechanisms are enabled, disabled, or optional.
>   - Modify default settings as required. By default, all settings are optional except for the recovery password, which is mandatory.
>   - Set up encryption and validation policies such as the disk volume's encryption method.
>
> For more details on configuring Group Policy, see Chapter 22, "Understanding Group Policy Basics to Manage Windows Vista Systems" and Chapter 23, "Expanding on the Use of Group Policies to Better Manage Windows Vista Systems," later in this book.

To turn on BitLocker Drive Encryption on a computer without a compatible TPM, administrators can perform the following steps:

1. Click Start, type **gpedit.msc** into the Start Search box, and then press Enter. If the User Account Control dialog box appears, verify that the proposed action is what you requested, and then click Continue.

2. In the Group Policy Object Editor console tree, click Local Computer Policy, click Computer Configuration, Administrative Templates, Windows Components, and then double-click BitLocker Drive Encryption.

3. Double-click the setting Control Panel Setup: Enable Advanced Startup Options. The Control Panel Setup: Enable Advanced Startup Options dialog box appears.

4. Select the Enabled option, select the Allow BitLocker Without a Compatible TPM check box, as shown in Figure 7.3, and then click OK. The policy setting has been changed to use a startup key instead of a TPM.

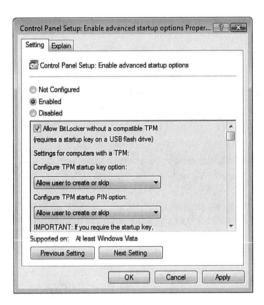

FIGURE 7.3
Enabling BitLocker Drive Encryption on a system without a TPM.

5. Click the red X in the upper-right corner to close the Group Policy Object Editor.

6. To apply the Group Policy immediately, click Start, type **gpupdate.exe /force** into the Start Search box, and then press Enter.

7. Click Start, Control Panel, Security, and then click BitLocker Drive Encryption. If the User Account Control message appears, confirm that the action is what you requested, and then click Continue.

8. On the BitLocker Drive Encryption page, click Turn On BitLocker. This will appear only under the operating system volume.

9. On the Set BitLocker Startup Preferences page, select the Require Startup USB Key at every startup option. This is the only option available for non-TPM configurations and requires the startup key to be inserted each time before the computer is started.

10. Insert your USB flash drive in the computer, if it is not already there.

11. Choose the location of your USB flash drive on the Save Your Startup Key page, and then click Save.

12. On the Save the Recovery Password page, you will see the following options:

- Save the Password on a USB Drive.

- Save the Password in a Folder.

- Print the Password.

13. Print or save the password using one of the following instruction sets:

- Click Print the Password to print the password. Store the printed password in a secure location.

- Click Save the Password to save the password. In the Save BitLocker Drive Encryption Password As dialog box, type a filename and set a location for the password. Click Save to save the file.

- Click Save the Password on a USB Drive to display the Save the Recovery Key on a USB Device page. To save the recovery password to a USB memory device, insert the device and then select the device from the displayed list. Click Save Key.

- Click Next to display the Save the Recovery Key to a Folder page. To save the recovery passwords to a network drive folder or a network share, click Save, and then use the Browse Folder options to locate and select the folder to save the recovery key.

   When you're finished saving the recovery password, click Next.

14. On the Encrypt the Selected Disk Volume page, click Encrypt to encrypt the selected volume. Confirm that the Run BitLocker System Check option is checked, and then click Continue. Confirm that you want to restart the computer by clicking Restart Now. The computer restarts and BitLocker verifies whether the computer is BitLocker-compatible and ready for encryption. If it is not, you will see an error message alerting you to the problem.

15. If the system is ready for encryption, the Encryption in Progress status bar is displayed. To monitor the status of the disk volume encryption, drag the mouse cursor over the BitLocker Drive Encryption icon in the System Tray. Encrypting the volume typically takes between one and two minutes per gigabyte to complete.

When the encryption process is finished, the operating system volume will be encrypted and a recovery password unique to this volume will have been created. The next time the system is started, the USB flash drive must be plugged into a USB port on the computer. If it is not, the data on the encrypted volume will not be accessible. For enhanced security, store the startup key away from the computer.

Note

If the USB flash drive containing your startup key is not available, users or administrators will need to use recovery mode and supply the recovery password to access the data.

Recovering Data Using BitLocker Drive Encryption

After BitLocker Drive Encryption has been enabled and an error condition occurs, administrators will need to perform the process for recovering system data after BitLocker has entered recovery mode. BitLocker locks the computer when a disk encryption key is not available. Recovery mode entry can be caused by any of the following issues:

- TPM errors.
- The TPM is accidentally turned off and the computer is turned off.
- The TPM is unintentionally cleared and the computer is turned off.
- Boot file modification.

When a computer is locked, the startup process is interrupted very early, before the operating system starts. Administrators are required to use the recovery password from a USB flash drive or use the function keys to enter the recovery password. At this point, because the computer is locked, a standard keyboard cannot be used to enter numerical keystrokes. In this case, the function keys are used for numerical input, where F1 through F9 represent the digits 1 through 9, and F10 represents 0.

Administrators should test their ability to recover volumes encrypted with BitLocker Drive Encryption. Heed the motto of the Boy Scouts: Be Prepared! To practice recovering volumes, administrators should perform the following steps in a test environment before the need arises in a production environment.

To test data recovery on system using TPM, administrators can perform the following steps:

1. Click Start, type **tpm.msc** into the Start Search box, and then press Enter. If the User Account Control dialog box appears, verify that the proposed action is what you requested, and then click Continue. The TPM Management console is displayed.

2. Under Actions, click Turn TPM Off. If required, provide the TPM password.

3. When the process is complete, the status panel in the TPM Management on Local Computer task panel will display the following message: `Your TPM is off and ownership of the TPM has been taken.`

4. Close the TPM console and all other open windows.

5. Safely remove the USB memory device that contains the recovery password that is plugged into the system using the Safely Remove Hardware icon in the notification area.

6. Click the Start button, and then click the Shutdown button to power off your computer.

Because the startup configuration has changed since encrypting the volume, the system will prompt for and require the recovery password when started.

Administrators can now use the following steps to recover access to data using BitLocker Drive Encryption:

1. Turn on your computer. Because the computer is in BitLocker Drive Encryption recovery mode, the computers start the BitLocker Drive Encryption Recovery console when powered on.

2. When prompted, insert the USB memory device that contains the startup or recovery key:

   - If you have the USB flash drive with the recovery password, insert it, and then press Esc. The computer will restart automatically without needing to manually enter the recovery password.

   - If you do not have the USB flash drive with the recovery password, press Enter. A prompt for the recovery password will display. If recovery password is known, type the recovery password and then press Enter. If the recovery password is not known, press Enter twice and turn off your computer.

Tip

If the recovery password is saved in a file in a folder away from the locked computer, or on removable media, use another computer to open the file that contains the password. First, find the Password ID on the recovery console display on the locked computer, and record this number. Next, locate the file containing the recovery key by using the Password ID as the filename on the remote folder or removable media. Last, open the filename that contains the Password ID and locate the recovery password in the file.

Turning Off BitLocker Drive Encryption

Administrators may have a need to turn off BitLocker Drive Encryption and decrypt the volume. The procedure for turning off BitLocker Drive Encryption is the same for all BitLocker Drive Encryption configurations on TPM-equipped computers and computers without a compatible TPM. When turning off BitLocker, administrators can choose to either disable BitLocker temporarily or to decrypt the drive. Temporarily disabling BitLocker allows TPM changes and operating system upgrades and takes only seconds to do. Decrypting the drive will make the volume readable and all the generated startup and recovery keys are discarded. Decrypting the volume will take a considerably longer amount of time, depending on the size of the volume. After a volume is decrypted, administrators must generate new keys by going through the encryption process again.

Administrators can turn off BitLocker Drive Encryption by performing the following steps:

1. Click Start, Control Panel, Security, and then click BitLocker Drive Encryption.

2. From the BitLocker Drive Encryption page, find the volume on which BitLocker Drive Encryption will be turned off. Click Turn Off BitLocker Drive Encryption.

3. In the What Level of Decryption Do You Want dialog box, click either Disable BitLocker Drive Encryption or Decrypt the Volume.

By completing this procedure, administrators have either disabled BitLocker or decrypted the operating system volume.

Reporting BitLocker Drive Encryption Problems

Microsoft spends much time and effort to make their products the very best in their field. Although development teams and quality assurance have performance rigorous lab, alpha, and beta testing to ensure the product performs as intended, problems and issues will exist that Microsoft did not encounter once the product is released to production. There will be many different test and production environments that introduce and discover new unknown bugs or "features" in BitLocker Drive Encryption. Because BitLocker Drive Encryption is a new feature of Windows Vista, Microsoft is interested in hearing feedback regarding user experiences and what issues and problems are encountered by their customers so that they can take a proactive approach to solving the issues and enhancing the current and future versions of BitLocker Drive Encryption security.

> **Note**
>
> To provide feedback on user experiences with BitLocker, problems encoun-
> tered, and the usefulness of the BitLocker Drive Encryption, contact the
> BitLocker Drive Encryption team by sending email to bdeinfo@microsoft.com.

BitLocker Drive Encryption Assistance and Resources

Without a doubt, Microsoft.com is packed with a wealth of information regarding the security features of Windows Vista. Administrators can access worldwide information in the Vista community made up of mailing lists, site forums, newsfeeds, and blogs that contain and express a tremendous amount of experience and expertise on Microsoft Vista. Some of the information is written by the people at Microsoft who worked on portions of Microsoft Vista.

Microsoft Vista Product Home Page

The best place to start for Microsoft Vista related content, information, tools, and updates is the Microsoft Vista Product home page at www.microsoft. com/windows/products/windowsvista/default.mspx. Here administrators can find links to everything and anything related to Windows Vista. Links to product information on Windows Vista and previous versions of the Windows operating system, help and how-to information, as well as Windows Vista downloads can be found here. There are also Quick Links to additional resources such as the download center, Help and Support, Microsoft Update and links to popular downloaded software such as Windows Defender and Internet Explorer.

Windows Vista TechCenter

The Windows Vista TechCenter can be found on the web at http://technet. microsoft.com/en-us/windowsvista/default.aspx. This page is the central area for all IT professionals and is an excellent technical clearing house of resources and information related to Windows Vista. Information on this site is broken into three categories:

- **Top Areas of Interest**—This section contains hot topics of interest in regard to Windows Vista.

- **Featured Resources**—This section contains documents relevant to Windows Vista.

- **Start Here**—This sections contains first-look content for evaluating, planning, and deploying Windows Vista.

BitLocker Drive Encryption Main Web Page

The BitLocker Drive Encryption main web page can be found on the Web at http://technet.microsoft.com/en-us/windowsvista/aa905065.aspx. This page is the central area for BitLocker Drive Encryption information. It contains the following primary areas of content:

- An Introduction to BitLocker Drive Encryption—This section contains links to introductory content on BitLocker Drive Encryption.

- Technical Information—This section contains technical review information for IT professionals.

- Setup, Deployment, and Frequently Asked Questions (FAQ)—This section contains setup and deployment-related content. It also contains a link to BitLocker Drive Encryption FAQ.

Windows Vista Security TechNet Forum

The Windows Vista Security TechNet Forum found on the Web at http://forums.microsoft.com/technet/ShowForum.aspx?ForumID=718&SiteID =17 is a good website for discovering the latest threads on Windows Vista security. IT professionals worldwide post questions and solutions here for troubleshooting difficult problems and issues. Use the provided search utility to locate BitLocker Drive Encryption specific threads and posts.

Summary

BitLocker Drive Encryption is a new hardware-enhanced feature in the
Microsoft Windows Vista operating system that provides offline data protection for computers in case they are stolen or lost. Available in only the
Enterprise and Ultimate versions of Windows Vista and in Windows Server
2008, BitLocker provides an extra layer of protection for the operating
system and data stores on the operating system drive volume. BitLocker
makes sure that data is protected against offline attacks made by disabling
and/or circumventing the operating system or by physically removing the
drive from the system to attack the data separately. Large or small enterprises
will benefit from using BitLocker Drive Encryption on any computer or
mobile PC that stores sensitive information. BitLocker Drive Encryption is
useful not only to meet legal requirements but also offers cost savings when
administrators need to take systems out of production service. It also saves
additional training costs by offering a transparent, secure solution for
encrypting computer drives without requiring additional end user training.

PART III

Windows Vista Mobility

IN THIS PART

CHAPTER 8

Configuring and Using Offline Files

Understanding Offline Files and Folders

First available in Windows 2000 as Offline Folders, Offline Files in Windows Vista facilitates users storing networks files on their computers when they are not connected to the network or when there is a network outage. When properly configured, Offline Files automatically use offline copies of files whenever the network files are unavailable. Even though the network files are not available, users can continue work uninterrupted until the network connection is restored. As soon as the network connection is reestablished, Windows Vista will automatically sync the local computer files with those in the network folder.

Changes are applied depending on how they were made. Depending on the time and date stamp of the version saved, users can run into version control issues. If many users make changes to a specific offline file, they must use set processes for how to deal with multiple versions. In some instances, users will save their version over the existing offline file. In other instances, users may keep the existing version or keep both copies of the offline file on the network. If a user deletes an offline file, the file will also be deleted on the network. The file will not be deleted if the version on the network has a more recent time and date stamp. In this scenario, the network file will not be deleted, but the version on the computer will be deleted. If users modify an offline file that others have deleted from the network, the users can either save the file to the network folder or delete the file from their computer.

To enhance the offline files experience, Windows Vista has improved the operation, usability, and reliability of offline files. In Windows Vista, Microsoft also improved the way offline files are used. Enhancing the performance of offline files, Windows Vista employs a new feature called Delta Sync for change-only synchronization and unavailable file and folder ghosting. Delta Sync, change-only synchronization, provides for faster synchronization by synchronizing only the blocks of data that have changed. In the previous version of Windows, Windows XP, the entire contents of the modified files were read from the computer and written to the server during synchronization. In contrast, Windows Vista reads and writes only the data blocks that have changed.

Unavailable file and folder ghosting in Windows Vista compensates for folders that have partial contents. Creating ghosted entries of missing files and folders helps preserve the online context for users that are not connected to the network. In this situation, users see ghost images of online files in addition to normal entries for offline items.

Administrators and users can control when offline files are synchronized. Synchronization can be automatically initiated when the user logs on and off or when the computer enters standby and hibernation modes. Synchronization settings can be set via Group Policy and user-configured settings.

Synchronization can also be performed manually via the Sync Center. The Sync Center is a new addition to Windows Vista that facilitates easy file synchronization. Sync Center is the tool for viewing the status of all sync activity, performing manual synchronizations, stopping an in-progress sync, modifying sync settings, or receiving a conflict notification when syncing. The Sync Center can be accessed by following these steps:

1. Click Start, Control Panel.

2. On the Control Panel home page, click the Network and Internet category link.

3. On the Network and Internet page, click Sync Center.

Configuring Files or Folders for Offline Availability

Network folders can be shared and made available for offline access by users. By default, all subfolders and files within a shared folder are also available offline. Individual files and folders can also be designated for offline access.

Administrators can configure offline files using the Computer Management console or Windows Explorer. The Computer Management console is typically the best tool for the job because it allows administrators to manage offline folders on any networked computer. Configuring offline files on Windows Vista systems requires that the user be a member of the Administrators. To configure offline files on Microsoft Windows 2000, Windows Server 2003, or Windows Server 2008, the user must be a member of the Administrators or Server Operators group.

Configuring file and folders for offline access is a three-step process:

1. Share the folders.

2. Configure Files and Folders for offline availability.

3. Specify offline file or folder for use.

Sharing Folders

Administrators must first share the folders containing the files and folders wanted for offline use. Using Computer Management, administrators can make a folder available for use by performing the following steps:

1. Click Start and highlight Computer.

2. Right-click Computer and click Manage. If prompted, confirm the action by selecting Continue. This will display the Computer Management console.

3. Right-click Computer Management in the console tree and then select Connect to Another Computer. Choose the computer to work with using the Select Computer dialog box. The default option is the Another Computer option. Administrators can use the Browse button to search for a computer if they don't know the name, or they can type the fully qualified domain name (FQDN) of the computer to work with, such as flyingv.airjimi.com, where flyingv is the computer name and airjimi.com is the domain name.

4. Expand System Tools, expand Shared Folders, and then select Shares. The current shares on the system are displayed in the details pane as shown in Figure 8.1.

5. Right-click Shares and then select New Share. This will start the Create a Shared Folder Wizard. The wizard is used to share folders and files. Click Next on the Welcome page to continue.

FIGURE 8.1
Viewing and creating Folder Shares in the Computer Management console in Windows Vista.

6. In the Folder Path field, type the path to the folder to share, such as **C:\Zip**. If the path is unknown, use the Browse button to find the folder to share. A new folder can also be created here and then shared if needed. Click Next to continue to the Name, Description, and Settings page.

7. Type a unique name for the share in the Share Name field. The name can be up to 80 characters in length and can contain spaces. To support legacy systems no longer supported by Microsoft (such as Windows 98, Windows ME, and Windows NT systems), use a unique name with 12 characters or less.

8. Type a description of the share's contents into the Description field. The more detailed the description is, the easier it is for users to recognize the folder contents.

9. To change Offline Settings such as performance optimization or to disable offline availability, click Change. If default settings are fine, click Next to continue to the Shared Folder Permissions page.

10. The Shared Folder Permissions page contains the following options:

   ■ **All Users Have Read-Only Access**—This is the default option and allows users permission to read data and view files but does not allow users to modify, create, or delete files or folders.

   ■ **Administrators Have Full Access; Other Users Have Read-Only Access**—This level of access gives administrators full access to the share and limits other users to read-only access. Administrators can create, modify, and delete file and folders. Other users can only view files and read data.

   ■ **Administrators Have Full Access; Other Users Have No Access**—This level provides only administrators full access to the share.

   ■ **Customize Permissions**—This level enables administrators to configure access for specific users and groups. Select the Custom button to set specific access rights for users.

11. When permissions setup is complete, click Next and then click Finish to share the folder. Click Finish a second time to complete the process.

Configuring Folders for Offline Availability

After the folders and files have been shared for use, administrators can make the folder available for offline use. Using the Computer Management console, administrators can make a shared folder available for offline use by performing the following steps:

1. Right-click Computer Management in the console tree and then select Connect to Another Computer. Choose the computer to work with using the Select Computer dialog box.

2. Expand System Tools, expand Shared Folders, and then select Shares.

3. Currently shared folders are shown in the details pane of the Computer Management console. Double-click the folder to be configured for offline use.

4. Click the Offline Settings on the General tab.

5. In the Offline Settings dialog box, select one of the following options, as shown in Figure 8.2:

   ■ **Only The Files and Programs That Users Specify Will Be Available Offline**—This setting lets users manually choose which files are available offline. This is the default option.

This option is the best option to use when multiple users will specify files in the same folder for offline use.

- **All Files and Programs That Users Open from the Share Will Be Automatically Available Offline**—This setting is best used for folders that contain programs and user data. Opened Files and programs are downloaded automatically and made available for use. This option also has an addition option for improving performance. Select the Optimized for Performance check box to enable caching of programs. The caching enables programs to be cached and run locally, improving application performance.

- **Files or Programs from the Share Will Not Be Available Offline**—This setting is used when files or programs are not meant to be available offline.

6. Click OK and then click OK again to finish configuring offline files.

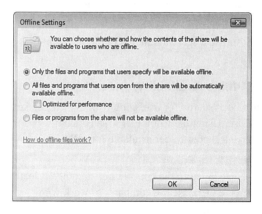

FIGURE 8.2
Configuring folders for offline availability in Windows Vista.

Specifying Offline Files and Folders for Use

After administrators have created the shares and configured settings for offline files, they can specify the file and folders to use offline. Users can then access the share as a network resource or connect to it by mapping a drive letter on the computer. When this is done, users can use the mapped drive as if it were a local drive. Drive mapping also adds additional benefits, such as making the network folder available to programs that don't use the Windows common dialog boxes and making the network drive available in the Computer folder alongside the local computer drives.

To map a drive, administrators can use the following steps:

1. Click Start and then Computer. Click the Map Network Drive button on the right side of the toolbar. This will display the Map Network Drive dialog box, as shown in Figure 8.3.

FIGURE 8.3
Mapping a share to a network drive in Windows Vista.

2. In the Drive field, select a free drive letter and then click the Browse button located to the right of the Folder field. In the Browse for Folder dialog box, expand the network folder field and select the workgroup or domain name to work with.

3. When the selected computer is expanded, a list of folders will be displayed. Select the shared folder to work with and then click OK.

4. Select the Reconnect at Logon option to enable Windows Vista to automatically reconnect to the shared folder at the start of each computer session.

5. To log on as a different user with appropriate access permissions, click Connect Using a Different User Name. Enter the proper username and password of the account to use for accessing the folder. Administrators will use this feature when they have logged on to the computer with limited account access and also maintain an administrative account for network management.

6. Click Finish.

Tip

If the network drive is not wanted later on, it can be easily removed. Click Start and then click Computer. Right-click the network drive icon located in the Network Location section and select Disconnect.

---

7. Click Start and then Computer to open the Computer console.

8. Create the offline file cache. Administrators have two options for creating the offline file cache:

   ■ **Copy the Entire Contents of a Shared Folder**—To copy the contents of a shared folder to a user's computer and make it available for offline use, locate the shared folder in the Network Location, right-click the share location, and then select Always Available Offline (see Figure 8.4).

   ■ **Copy Only a Selected Folder**—To copy a specific folder or file to a user's computer and make it available offline, use the Computer console to find the folder or file, right-click the folder or file, and then select Always Available Offline.

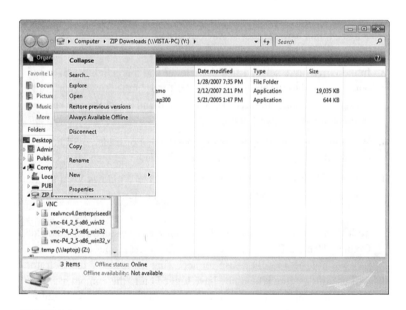

FIGURE 8.4
Viewing the Always Available Offline option in the right-click menu.

Allocating folders or files for offline use creates a local cached copy of the folder and file contents on the user's computer. It will also create a sync relationship between the sharing computer and the local computer. It can also extend an existing sync relationship to incorporate additional shared folder and files.

Working with Offline Files and Folders

Typically, working offline occurs whenever the computer is not connected to the local area network. When working offline, users can work with files as if they are connected to the network. Offline file permissions are the same as when using the files online; if a file has read-only access when connected to the network, the user will have read-only access when using the file in offline mode. A red X displayed on the notification area of the toolbar or over the Network Drives indicates to users that they are working in offline mode.

User can specify whether they want to work offline. To work in offline mode and work with files on the local computer instead of network shared files, use the following steps:

1. In Windows Explorer, open the network folder that contains the offline files to work with.

2. On the toolbar, click Work Offline. This will enable the user to work with the files as if in offline mode.

3. When working online is desired, click Work Online on the toolbar. This will sync any file changes that occurred when working offline.

Administering Offline File and Folder Synchronization

Sync is short for synchronization. In Windows, *sync* is the process of keeping two or more versions of the same file stored in different locations matched with each other. If users add, change, or delete a file in one location, Windows can add, change, or delete the same file in the other locations that they choose to sync with, whenever they choose to sync. Synchronization is an invaluable tool for users in enterprises and corporations.

The Sync Center, shown in Figure 8.5, in Windows Vista simplifies the management of cached offline files and folders. Sync Center displays the synchronization relationship between the locally cached files and folders on the local computer and the shared files and folders on the network. The Sync Center is a convenient central location in Windows Vista from which users can manage data synchronization between PCs, between PCs and servers, and between PCs and devices. Management of data between computers, devices, and locations has exploded in the past few years and will continue to do so as newer devices for storing data are developed. Previously, there was no easy way to manage all the individual sync relationships. Now, Sync Center provides a central tool for starting manual syncs, stopping in-progress syncs, viewing the status of all current sync activities, and receiving notification of any sync conflicts.

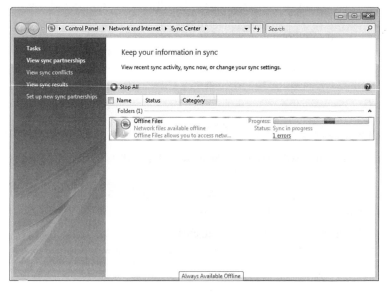

FIGURE 8.5
Using Sync Center to view synchronization.

Viewing Synchronization Partnerships

As outlined earlier in the chapter, the Sync Center can be accessed by following these steps:

1. Click Start, Control Panel.

2. On the Control Panel home page, click the Network and Internet category link.

3. On the Network and Internet page, click Sync Center.

4. In Sync Center, any existing sync partnerships are displayed according to name, category, progress, error count, and conflict.

In Sync Center, administrators and users can view existing sync partnerships, view sync conflicts, view sync results and errors, and create new sync partnerships.

Enabling Manual Synchronization

Offline file synchronization can be performed manually as well as automatically. Manual synchronization is performed using one of two ways and allows users to select which files are synchronized. Users may want to sync only certain files and folders because of time constraints, such as when they are leaving the office on short notice or will need only certain files available offline.

The first method is to synchronize all offline files and folders. In this method, all offline files and folders can be synced within Sync Center by clicking the Sync All option.

The second way to manually sync files is to synchronize a specific network share. In this method, a specific network share can be synced within Sync Center by selecting the sync partnership to work with and then clicking the Sync option.

Enabling Automatic Synchronization

Some times users can't be "bothered" with doing syncs manually. They want them to automatically happen; they don't care how and when as long as it happens. Generally, because Group Policy settings control how offline file syncing works, when a user reconnects to the local area network after being disconnected from the network or manually selecting to work offline, offline files are automatically synced. Automatic synchronization can be configured to sync when one of the following occurs:

- When a user logs on
- When the computer is idle
- When the user locks or unlocks Windows
- At a scheduled time

Using these time events, administrators can configure synching so that it occurs automatically without requiring a user intervention or interaction.

Syncing happens behind the scenes so that the most recent offline files and folders are available to the user.

Scheduling an Offline Synchronization

Administrators manage and create scheduled synchronizations using the Sync Center. To configure schedule synchronization from within Sync Center, use the following steps:

1. Click the partnership to work with and then click Schedule.

2. If a scheduled sync has already been completed, administrators can do one of the following:

   - **Create a New Schedule**—Click Create a New Sync Schedule and then perform steps 3–6.

   - **View or Edit an Existing Schedule**—Click View or Edit an Existing Sync Schedule and then click the schedule to modify. Click Next and then perform steps 3–6.

   - **Delete an Existing Schedule**—Click Delete an Existing Schedule, click the schedule to delete, and then click Delete. Click OK to finish and then skip the remaining steps 3–6.

3. Select configuration options and clear any unwanted options. When satisfied with the selected options, click Next and then click At a Scheduled Time. As shown in Figure 8.6, the At and Start On options are configured so that any scheduled synchronization will start on time. Use the time and date options provided to schedule syncing on a different time and date schedule. Use the right- and left-arrow keys for navigating the fields. Use the up and down arrows to change the field values.

4. The Repeat Every option is used for setting a recurring sync interval schedule. The default sync schedule is every day, and the time interval can be set in minutes, hours, days, weeks, or months. Click Next to continue when selections are completed.

Tip

Unlike Windows XP, Windows Vista syncs only folder or file changes, so users may want to synchronize more frequently. To keep important files up-to-date, users may want to sync every two to three hours.

FIGURE 8.6
Scheduling offline file syncing in Sync Center.

5. Enter a name for the sync schedule. Be sure to use a detailed name that describes the sync so that the sync schedule is easily distinguished from any other sync schedules.

6. When you've finished entering the scheduled sync name, click Save Schedule to save the scheduled sync.

Using Events or Actions to Synchronize Offline Files and Folders

Administrators can manage and create scheduled synchronizations using the Sync Center. They may also want to perform syncs of files and folders based on an event or an action, such as logging on to the computer or when locking the computer. To configure syncs based on actions or events from within Sync Center, use the following steps:

1. Click the partnership to work with and then click Schedule.

2. If a scheduled sync has already been completed, administrators can do one of the following:

   ■ **Create a New Schedule**—Click Create a New Sync Schedule and then perform steps 3–6.

- **View or Edit an Existing Schedule**—Click View or Edit an Existing Sync Schedule and then click the schedule to modify. Click Next and then perform steps 3–6.

- **Delete an Existing Schedule**—Click Delete an Existing Sync Schedule, click the schedule to delete, and then click Delete. Click OK to finish and then skip the remaining steps 3–6.

3. Select configuration options, clearing any unwanted options. When satisfied with the selected options, click Next and then click an event or action. Use the check boxes to specify the actions or events.

4. As shown in Figure 8.7, administrators can select which event or action to use by selecting or deselecting the appropriate check box. The selected options will be used to automatically start synchronization. Click Next when you've finished selecting configuration options.

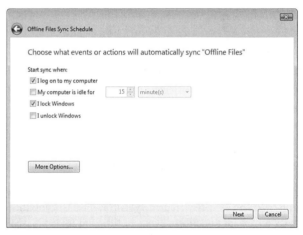

FIGURE 8.7
Offline file syncing using events or actions in Sync Center.

5. Enter a name for the sync schedule. Be sure to use a detailed name that describes the sync so that the sync schedule is easily distinguished from any other scheduled sync.

6. When you've finished entering the scheduled sync name, click Save Schedule to save the scheduled sync.

Viewing Synchronization Results

After syncs have been configured and performed using scheduled syncs or syncs based on events of actions, administrators will want to view the synchronization results. The sync results provide information regarding synchronization success, failures, conflicts, errors, and warnings. Additional info is also available, such as sync start and stop times and completion data. The synchronization warnings and errors are useful when troubleshooting sync configuration issues. To view the synchronization results, use the following steps:

1. Click Start, Control Panel, Network and Internet.

2. On the Network and Internet page, click Sync Center.

3. In Sync Center, click View Sync Results.

Resolving Synchronization Conflicts and Errors

Synchronization errors or conflicts can occur if a user modifies a file offline and that file that is updated by an online user. A sync conflict occurs because Sync Center is unable to reconcile differences between a file stored by the offline user and a version of the same file stored by the online user. Therefore, the synchronization is not completed. Typically, this occurs when a file has changed in both locations since its last sync, making it difficult to determine which changes to save. Sync Center displays this as a conflict and requests the user to determine which version should be kept as the master copy. When the user selects which copy to use, the conflict is resolved.

A sync error is a problem that prevents the sync from being completed as scheduled. For example, a network share is unavailable or a mobile device is not powered on. Sync errors are not caused by problems that occur because of the existence of two versions of a file. Sync errors are caused by problems with the folder, the computer, or the device that files are being synced with.

If a sync conflict exists, the Sync Center icon, located in the notification area of the taskbar, will change from a solid green circle with two white arrows to a solid green circle with two white arrows and a yellow caution sign and black exclamation mark. Highlighting the icon will display a summary of existing conflicts. To see a more detailed summary of sync conflicts and take steps to resolve the conflicts, users can right-click the icon and select View Conflicts to open Sync Center and view conflicts, or use the following steps:

1. To Open Sync Center, click Start, Control Panel, Network and Internet, Sync Center.

2. In the left pane, click View Sync Conflicts. Any conflicts will be displayed in the right pane with details such as name, date modified, and partnership details.

3. Click a conflict to resolve and the Resolve Conflict dialog box will be displayed.

4. The Resolve Conflict dialog box provides two options for resolving sync conflicts:

   ■ **Click the Version to Keep**—This option allows the user to choose to keep the computer version or the network version. To keep the local computer version and overwrite the network version, click the version listed as On This Computer. To keep the network version and overwrite the local computer version, click on the version listed as the network share version.

   ■ **Click Keep Both Versions**—This option allows the user to keep both versions by writing the local computer version to the share network location with a new name. Typically, Sync Center renames one version of the file and saves copies of both files in both locations using a suffix for version control and easy identification. If you're unsure about which version is the best one to keep, this option is great; it allows saving both versions, which can be reviewed later for merging or discarding of data.

Caution

Although the Keep Both Versions option keeps the entire information safe, offline and online files will not be in sync and users will end up with two different versions of the file in both locations. To avoid having too many versions floating around various locations, create a company policy that defines a standard for handling sync conflicts, such as by overwriting the older version of a file as determined by the modified date information.

Disabling Offline Files and Folders Availability

Administrators may want to disable offline files and folders altogether. As administrators, they have the ability to specify which files are or are not available for offline use. For example, administrators may want to prevent access to sensitive corporate files, such as accounting and human resources files, or financial data, such as company stocks and bonds, or merger and acquisition paperwork. Administrators can use the Computer Management console or Group Policy to restrict file access.

Administrators can make a shared folder unavailable in Computer Management using the following steps:

1. Open the Computer Management console by clicking Start. Right-click Computer and select Manage. If prompted, click Continue to display the Computer Management console.

2. In the console tree, right-click Computer Management and then select Connect to Another Computer. In the Select Computer dialog box, type in another computer to connect to or use the Browse button to select the computer to work with.

3. In the console tree, expand System Tools and then expand Shared Folders. Select Shares to display the current shared folders in the details pane.

4. Double-click the share to configure for offline use. Click the Offline Settings button on the General tab to open the Offline Settings dialog box.

5. In the Offline Settings dialog box, select the Files or Programs from the Share Will Not Be Available Offline option and then click OK to Finish.

Controlling Offline Files and Folders via Group Policy

Group Policy is used to centrally manage a large number of features and component behaviors. In Windows Vista, Microsoft has expanded the number of group policies available from 1,700 policies in previous versions of Windows to more than 2,400 group policies. The additional numbers provide administrators with enhanced control and management over functions and features available to users.

Primarily, administrators will want to configure Offline File policies that affect file and folder access, caching, encryption, and synchronization. These polices are found under Computer Configuration\Administrative Templates\Network\Offline Files and User Configuration\ Administrative Templates\Network\Offline Files, shown in Figure 8.8.

FIGURE 8.8
Viewing Offline File policies via Local Computer Policy in Windows Vista.

> **Tip**
>
> As a reminder, offline file policies are set at both the user and the computer levels. The policies are identical at both levels and can be easily mixed up. When working with identical policies, remember that user policies are over-ruled by computer policies. In addition, keep in mind that the policies can be applied at different times.

Configuring Policies for Offline Files and Folders

Using Group Policy, Administrators can control offline file configuration. Administrators can control and specify which files and folders are available for offline use, prohibit users from configuring offline file options on their own, or delete a user's local copy of offline files when the user logs on to the system. To configure offline files, administrators can use the following steps:

1. Access Group Policy for the OU, domain, site, or system to work with. The majority of offline file configurations are available in the computer or user policies by using the Offline Files node. Administrators can

access the policies by expanding `Computer Configuration\ Administrative Templates\Network\Offline Files` and `User Configuration\Administrative Templates\Network\Offline Files`.

2. To manage the availability of offline files, double-click the Allow or Disallow Use of the Offline Files Feature within `Computer Configuration\Administrative Templates\Network\Offline Files`. On the Setting tab, select Enabled or Disabled and click OK. When this option is enabled, users can select specific files or folders to make available offline. To prevent users from selecting files, disable this feature and administratively assign the appropriate offline files.

3. To prohibit users from setting offline file options, double-click the Prohibit Use of Offline Files Folder. On the Setting tab, select Enabled to prevent users from configuring offline file options.

4. To delete local copies of users' offline files at logoff, double-click the At Logoff, Delete Local Copy Of User's Offline Files. On the Setting tab, select Enabled to delete the locally cached offline files when the user logs off the computer. To delete only the temporary offline files, select the check box for enabling that feature.

Caution

Use caution when enabling the Delete Local Copy of User's Offline Files. When this feature is enabled, offline files are not synchronized before they are deleted. Any changes to local files since the last synchronization will be lost.

Preventing Users from Making Files Available Offline

Administrators may want to prevent users from being able to make files available offline and instead dictate specific offline resources. In doing so, administrators are able to effectively manage network resources and administratively control offline resources. Using policies, administrators can prevent users from making files available and instead assign specific offline resources. To do so, use the following steps:

1. Access Group Policy for the system to work with and then access the Offline Files node by expanding `Computer Configuration\ Administrative Templates\Network\Offline Files`.

2. Double-click Remove 'Make Available Offline' to prevent users from making files available offline. On the Setting tab, select Enabled. After it is enabled, this policy ensures users cannot designate files to be saved on their computer for offline use.

3. Double-click Administratively Assigned Offline Files to assign items that are automatically available offline. On the Setting tab, select Enabled. Click Show to display the Show Contents dialog box and then click Add to display the Add Item dialog box. Enter a descriptive name for the item to be added and then enter the value of the item to be added in the form of a UNC path, such as \\airjimi\music.

Enabling and Disabling Availability of Specific Files

Administrators may want to make some files automatically available while making other files not available for offline use. Using policies, administrators can make specific files automatically available offline and prevent others from being use offline by performing the following steps:

1. Access Group Policy for the system to work with and then access the Offline Files node by expanding Computer Configuration\ Administrative Templates\Network\Offline Files.

2. Double-click Administratively Assigned Offline Files to assign items that are automatically available offline. On the Setting tab, select Enabled. Click Show to display the Show Contents dialog box and then click Add to display the Add Item dialog box. Enter a descriptive name for the item to be added and then enter the value of the item to be added in the form of a UNC path, such as \\airjimi\music, as shown in Figure 8.9.

FIGURE 8.9
Administratively assigning offline file policies in Windows Vista.

3. Double-click Prohibit 'Make Available Offline' For These Files and Folders to specify resources that users should not be able to make available offline. On the Setting tab, select Enabled. Click Show to display the Show Contents dialog box and then click Add to display the Add Item dialog box. Enter a descriptive name for the item to be added and then enter the value of the item to be added in the form of a UNC path, such as `\\airjimi\music`.

4. Click OK three times to close out all dialog boxes and complete the policy changes.

Configuring Offline File Synchronization Policies

Offline file sync is controlled using the Sync Center. Sync Center is accessed by clicking Start, All Programs, Accessories, Sync Center. Administrators, however, can set specific sync techniques and timings by using policies. Syncing can be either fully synchronized (files are checked to complete and the most current version) or quickly synchronized (files are checked to be complete but not checked for being current version). Syncing can be triggered by events such as logoff, logon, hibernate, or standby. Although the Sync Center controls the behavior when one of the actions occurs, administrators can override the Sync Center actions using Group Policy.

Most often users will want to synchronize files when they log on so that they have the most current copies of the files. Even though this process may make the logon process longer, it ensures that the user have the latest data available. Laptop users may require a different syncing policy. Because laptop users are mobile and on the go, they may want to synchronize files on logoff so that they have the most current files available to them while traveling between home and office or between the office and client sites.

Administrator can configure offline file sync policies using the following steps:

1. Access Group Policy for the system to work with and then access the Offline Files node by expanding `Computer Configuration\Administrative Templates\Network\Offline Files`.

2. Three policies are available for controlling synchronization: Synchronize Offline Files Before Suspend, Synchronize All Offline Files When Logging On, and Synchronize All Offline Files Before Logging Off.

3. Double-click the policy for the sync technique to use on the computer. On the Setting tab, select Enabled. When selecting the Synchronize All Offline Files Before Suspend, make sure to select either Full or Quick for the synchronization type.

4. Click OK to complete the configuration.

Configuring Offline File Cache Policies

As part of their management duties, administrators must manage and control offline file caches as part of system and network maintenance. By configuring offline file cache policies, administrators can limit the maximum cache size when using offline files, encrypt the offline cache for security, or control which types of offline files are not cached. Administrators can configure offline file cache policies by performing the following steps:

1. Access Group Policy for the system to work with, and then access the Offline Files node by expanding `Computer Configuration\ Administrative Templates\Network\Offline Files`.

2. Double-click the Default Cache Size policy to set the maximum cache size. On the Setting tab, select Enabled. Then use the Default Cache Size Properties dialog box to set the default cache size. The value entered is the percentage of disk used times 10,000. To set a value of 20 percent, enter a value of 2000 into the Default Cache Size field.

3. Double-click the Encrypt the Offline Files Cache policy to encrypt the offline file cache. On the Setting tab, select Enabled. After this setting is enabled, any existing files and any new files in the cache will be encrypted, allowing the users to see their own files but preventing others from doing so. This option encrypts files in the local cache and does not affect the associated copy on the network.

4. Double-click the Files Not Cached policy to specify files to be excluded from the offline file cache. On the Setting tab, select Enabled. In the Extensions field, enter a list of extensions to be excluded. Each extension must follow an exact format: each extension must be preceded by an asterisk and a period such as `*.jpg`, `*.mp3`, or `*.wma`. To save storage space, administrators may want to exclude temporary files such `*.ndx`, `*.lnk`, and `*.tmp` files.

> **Tip**
>
> The Files Not Cached policy is a great way for administrators to enhance local system and network performance. By excluding certain files from being cached, administrators will improve logon times for the user, save on network storage space, and effectively manage network traffic performance, which can be affected by unnecessary file synchronizations.

Summary

First available in Windows 2000 as Offline Folders, Offline Files in Windows Vista facilitates users' storing of networks files on their computers when they are not connected to the network or when there is a network outage. When properly configured, Offline Files automatically uses offline files whenever the network files are unavailable. Even though the network files are not available, users can continue work uninterrupted until the network connection is restored. As soon as the network connection is reestablished, Windows Vista will automatically sync the computer files with those in the network folder.

A new synchronization algorithm called Delta Sync in Windows Vista syncs offline files and folders much faster, saving users extra time and improving file transfer speeds. Delta Sync transfers only the modified blocks of a file rather than the whole file when syncing file changes to the server. In addition, Delta Sync is more efficient at determining which files or directories need to be synchronized.

A godsend to mobile users and office users alike, with Offline Files in Windows Vista, taking remote folders offline is faster than ever, with smooth transitions between offline and online states. This feature is a boon for mobile workers who need data from office computers and servers while traveling and also for workers in remote offices with restricted bandwidth connections.

CHAPTER 9

Configuring Mobile Functionality in Windows Vista

Introduction to Mobile Computing

Industry studies have shown that mobile computers are the fastest growing computer category. Many consumer and business users are replacing their desktop computers with equally powerful mobile ones. In some vertical markets, palmtops or touch-screen PCs are even replacing laptops. Some power workers even avoid PCs altogether and work strictly from their cell phones.

Often, mobile computers are employed in a variety of situations. A single mobile PC will switch between various "nonwired" configurations—on battery power, with no network, or with a wireless connection—and "wired" configurations—plugged into a wall socket and physical network or in a docking station.

The new and improved mobility features in Windows Vista help users manage constant configuration changes, simplifying switching between network connections and workplaces. The mobility features also provide enhanced security, improved alternative input technologies such as ink and speech recognition, and facilitate easier synchronization with Pocket PC palmtops, Windows Mobile Smartphones, or Ultra Mobile computers. Using the all-new Sync Center, users can keep address lists, email, and appointments all in sync.

Microsoft defines the following categories of mobile computers running Windows:

- **Ultra-Mobile computers**—The smallest Tablet PCs and mobile computers capable of running Windows XP SP2 Tablet Edition and later, typically weighing one to three pounds and configured with a five- to eight-inch display.

- **Ultraportable computers**—The next smallest PC favoring small size, light weight, and battery life over processing power and screen size. This system is capable of running Windows XP SP2 Tablet PC Edition and later, typically weighs 2 to 5 pounds, and is configured with a 10- to 12-inch display.

- **Thin and light computers**—These computers favor battery life, screen size, and processing power over small size and light weight. This system is capable of running either Windows XP SP 2 Tablet PC Edition or Professional Edition and later, typically weighs 4 to 7 pounds, and is configured with a 14- to 15-inch display.

- **Transportable computers**—These computers favor processing power and graphics over small size, light weight, and long battery life. This system is capable of running Windows XP SP2 Media Center Edition and later, typically weighs 7 to 12 pounds, and is configured with a 14- to 17-inch display.

These mobile computer definitions do not include Smartphones or Pocket PCs, which use Windows CE and the Windows Mobile Platform.

A new Mobility Center makes Windows Vista easier to use on battery-powered, wireless-enabled, portable computers. Combined with the capability to protect data with BitLocker Drive Encryption, the Mobility Center and other features may prompt companies to move their mobile computers to Vista more rapidly than their desktops.

Using Windows Mobility Center

Available in the Home Basic, Home Premium, Business, Enterprise, and Ultimate editions of Windows Vista, Windows Mobility Center is a single location where administrators can adjust mobile PC settings. Mobility Center is especially useful when settings need to be quickly adjusted so the mobile PC can be used in different places, such as traveling from the office to home, work to school, or when going from home to the airport. For example, users can adjust the speaker volume of their mobile PC, check the status of their wireless network connection or battery, and adjust the display brightness—all from one location.

Windows Mobility Center, shown in Figure 9.1, consists of several of the most commonly used mobile PC settings. The Windows Mobility Center is available on all computers but is intended primarily for laptops. To access the Windows Mobility Center, click Start, All Programs, Accessories, Windows Mobility Center.

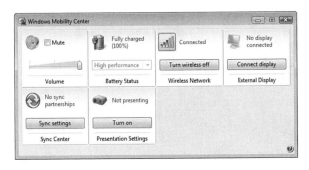

FIGURE 9.1
Using Windows Mobility Center to control mobility features in Windows Vista.

Depending on the system, the Windows Mobility Center window has some, but perhaps not all, of the following tiles:

- **Battery Status**—View how much charge remains on your battery or select a power plan from the list. Double-click the Battery icon to adjust power settings.

- **Brightness**—Move the slider to temporarily adjust the brightness of your display. To adjust the display brightness settings for your power plan, click the icon on the tile to open Power Options in Control Panel. Double-click the Display icon to adjust display settings.

- **External Display**—Connect an additional monitor to the mobile PC or customize the display settings. Double-click the Display icon to adjust display settings.

- **Presentation Settings**—Adjust computer settings, such as the speaker volume and the desktop background image, when giving a presentation. Double-click the Projector icon to adjust presentation settings.

Note

Presentation Settings, shown in Figure 9.2, are a boon for PowerPoint presenters. New configuration settings provide an easy way to prevent an embarrassing background from displaying, system notifications from popping up on screen, or having the screensaver start during the presentation. Presentation mode also kicks in when a network projector is connected or when an external monitor is connected. (A New Display Detected dialog box appears with an option to turn on Presentation mode.)

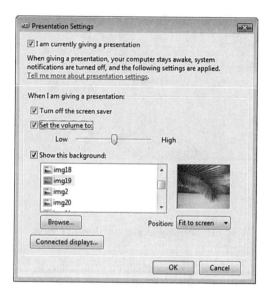

FIGURE 9.2
Using Presentation Settings in Windows Mobility Center to control system behavior during business meetings, lectures, or other presentations.

- **Screen Rotation**—Change the orientation, portrait or landscape, of the Tablet PC screen. Double-click the Primary Landscape icon to adjust display orientation settings.

- **Sync Center**—View the status of in-progress file syncs, start a new sync or set up a sync partnership, and adjust your settings in Sync Center. Double-click the Sync icon to adjust sync settings.

- **Volume**—Move the slider to adjust the speaker volume of the mobile PC or select the Mute check box. Double-click the Speaker icon to adjust volume settings.

- **Wireless Network**—View the status of the wireless network connection or turn the wireless adapter on or off. Double-click the Wireless icon to adjust wireless network connection settings.

Tip

Each of the features in the Windows Mobility Center can be accessed entirely from the keyboard. Press Alt + the letter of the feature to highlight the icon, and then press Enter to initiate the associated Control Panel applet. For example, press Alt +W to highlight the Wireless icon and then press Enter to load the Wireless Control Panel applet.

Using Power Management Settings

The Power Options program manages the power consumption of your computer. Of course, this is a big deal when the computer is a notebook or laptop. However, the power management features can also be used on desktop systems to help save electricity and the environment. Administrators will see different power options depending on the PC's system features. In Windows Vista, Microsoft has adopted a new name for managing system power settings. No longer does Microsoft called the settings Power Scheme; system power settings are now called Power Plans. A power plan manages how the computer goes to sleep, how bright the display is, the processor speed, and other energy and performance settings. A laptop can have multiple power plans defined but only one plan can be active at any time. In addition to power plans, most laptops have predefined settings for when the power button is pressed, when the laptop lid is closed, or when the Sleep button is pressed. Using the systemwide power plan options, administrators can customize the behavior of the power and sleep buttons or other power-related options. In some instances, users may want to reduce overall system performance and increase battery life, allowing the system to run on battery power for longer periods of time. In other situations, average battery life and performance or low battery life and maximum system performance may be preferred.

Using Power Plans

On laptop and Tablet PCs, a Power icon is displayed in the notification area of the taskbar. At a glance, users can determine the battery state and the power plan in use by hovering the mouse pointer over the icon. By right-clicking the icon, as shown in Figure 9.3, users can access the Power Options utility and the Windows Mobility Center.

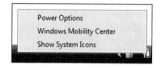

FIGURE 9.3

Right-clicking the Power icon to access the Power Options Utility and the Windows Mobility Center.

The default power plans are configured to meet most people's computing needs, but users can easily create a custom plan by using one of the default plans as a starting point. The three default plans shipped in Windows Vista are Balanced, Power Saver, and High Performance, described next:

- **Balanced**—This is the default power plan and offers full performance when more resources are used and saves power during low periods of inactivity. This plan is good for typical computer users who use Microsoft Office applications with low to moderate graphics intensity.

- **Power Saver**—This plan saves power by slowing down the processor and reducing system performance. This plan can help mobile PC users get the most from a single battery charge and is good for users of non-graphics-intensive applications such as Microsoft Word or Microsoft Outlook.

- **High Performance**—This plan maximizes system performance and responsiveness. Mobile PC users may notice that their battery doesn't last as long when using this plan because this plan makes sure that enough power is available for graphics-intensive applications or games. This plan is also good for arithmetic-intensive applications such as Microsoft Excel.

Power plans options are categorized into two areas: basic and advanced. Basic power settings control when a system turns off its display and when it turns it back on. For the Balanced and Power Saver plans, Windows Vista turns the display off after 20 minutes of inactivity. In the High Performance plan, the displays turns off after 20 minutes of inactivity but does not put the system in sleep mode automatically. Advanced power settings determine exactly when and where system components are shut down and also the performance configuration of the components. Following are some of the advanced power settings that can be configured:

- Password on Wakeup
- Hard Disk
- Wireless Adapter Settings
- Sleep
- Power Buttons and Lid

- PCI Express
- Processor Power Management
- Search and Indexing
- Display
- Multimedia Settings

Administrators have a lot of options here that can be set to manage and control system power usage. It is all these individual settings that really make the difference between power plans. When customizing or configuring power plans, administrators should remember to allow components to turn off after specific periods of inactivity. Also, configure power plans that suit a certain way a system is used at a particular time. Because administrators can configure multiple plans, each plan can be tailored for different situations, such as office versus home use or office versus business meeting presentations. The key is a configuration that optimizes laptop functionality for the particular use at hand.

Configuring Power Plans

Computers can have multiple power plans, but only one power plan can be in effect at any given time. Administrators can select, modify, or optimize power plans using the following steps:

1. Click Start and then click Control Panel.

2. In Control Panel, click the System and Maintenance category heading link and then click Power Options.

3. Select a plan to use on the Power Options screen. If the system is a laptop, Plans Shown on the Battery Meter is displayed. If the system is a desktop, Preferred Plans is displayed, as shown in Figure 9.4.

4. Select the plan to work with and then click Change Plan Settings to display the Edit Plan Settings page.

5. Use the Turn Off the Display option to configure when the display turns off. Choose the Never option to disable the display turn off feature.

6. Use the Put the Computer to Sleep option to configure when the computer goes into sleep mode. Choose the Never option to disable this feature.

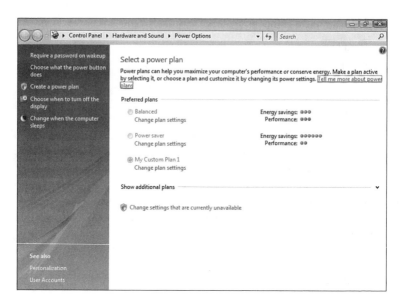

FIGURE 9.4
Selecting power plans and power options in Windows Vista.

7. To configure advanced options, click Change Advanced Power Settings. Modify the settings displayed in the Power Options dialog box and then click OK when finished.

8. Click Save Changes to save any changes that were made.

Creating Custom Power Plans

Administrators can also create custom power plans in Windows Vista to accommodate special needs that users may have when working on their systems. To create a custom plan, administrators can use following steps:

1. Click Start and then click Control Panel.

2. In Control Panel, click the System and Maintenance category heading link and then click Power Options.

3. In the left pane, click Create a Power Plan. If prompted, confirm the action to continue and display the Create a Power Plan page.

4. Select one of the default plans closest to the type of plan being created to use as a building block/template.

5. In the Plan Name field, type a descriptive name for the plan and then click Next to display the Edit Plan Settings page.

6. Use the Turn Off the Display option to configure when the display turns off. Choose the Never option to disable the display turn off feature.

7. Use the Put the Computer to Sleep options to configure when the computer goes into sleep mode. Choose the Never option to disable this feature.

8. Click Create to create the plan. The power plan page is updated with the newly created power plan (now the default selected plan) and replaces the plan that was selected as a template. The replaced plan will now be located underneath Additional Plans. Click the Expand button to display the additional plans.

9. On the newly created plan, click Change Plan Settings to display the Edit Plan Settings page. Click Change Advanced Power Settings and then configure the advanced power options as needed. Click OK and then Save Changes to save any changes made.

Configuring Power Plans Through the Command Line

Administrators can also configure power plans via the command line in Windows Vista. Microsoft includes the Power Configuration utility (Powercfg.exe). With this utility, administrators can configure a variety of power options:

```
powercfg [-a ] [-l ] [-q ] [-x ] [-changename ]
[-duplicatescheme ] [-d ] [-deletesetting ] [-setactive ]
[-getactivescheme ] [-setacvalueindex ] [-setdcvalueindex ]
[-h ] [-a ] [-devicequery ] [-deviceenablewake ]
[-devicedisablewake ] [-import ] [-export ] [-lastwake ] [-?]
[-aliases ] [-setsecuritydescriptor ] [-getsecuritydescriptor ]
```

The option details can be viewed by typing **powercfg /?** at the command prompt. The parameters that administrators will use most frequently are

- **a**—Lists all available sleep states.

- **d**—Deletes the power scheme with the specified Globally Unique Identifier (GUID).

- **h**—Turns the hibernate feature on or off.

- **l**—Lists all power schemes in the current user's environment.
- **q [GUID]**—Lists the contents of the power plan specified by the GUID.
- **s [GUID]**—Makes the power plan specified by the GUID the active power plan.

For example, typing **powercfg -l** at the command prompt displays the following information:

```
C:\Users\Vista>powercfg -l

Existing Power Schemes (* Active)
-----------------------------------
Power Scheme GUID: 381b4222-f694-41f0-9685-ff5bb260df2e
➥(Balanced)
Power Scheme GUID: 633f6e02-9d98-4499-b4a0-cb88738478c9
➥(My Custom Plan 1) *
Power Scheme GUID: 8c5e7fda-e8bf-4a96-9a85-a6e23a8c635c
➥(High performance)
Power Scheme GUID: a1841308-3541-4fab-bc81-f71556f20b4a
➥(Power saver)
```

The active plan is marked with an asterisk. From this information, administrators can determine that the system has four defined power plans and that the active power plan is the My Custom Plan 1.

Understanding Alarms and Alarm Actions

Alarms determine whether a laptop or tablet system sounds an alarm when a battery reaches a certain power level. In Windows Vista, administrators can configure two levels of alarms for laptops. The first level is the Low Battery Alarm and the second level is the Critical Battery Alarm. The Low Battery Alarm warns the user when the battery power is almost gone. Typically, the low battery state is reached when 10% of the full battery charge is remaining. The Critical Battery Alarm warns the user when the battery level is about to fail. The critical power state is reached when 3% or less of the full battery charge is remaining.

An alarm action is an event that can be set that tells Windows Vista what action to do or what program to run when an alarm level is encountered. Administrators may want to run certain programs or scripts upon receiving an alarm notification.

Configuring Low Battery Alarms

Administrators can configure the computer to take specific actions when a low battery state is reached. For example, instead of a text display and audible notification, the system may be configured to put the system into sleep mode when entering low battery power. To configure low battery notifications, administrators should perform the following steps:

1. Open the Microsoft Management console and then using the Add/Remove Snap-In option in the File Menu, add the Group Policy Object Editor under the Available Snap-Ins.

2. Open the Group Policy object to work with and then expand the Computer Configuration node to `Computer Configuration\Administrative Templates\System\Power Management\Notification Settings`, as shown in Figure 9.5.

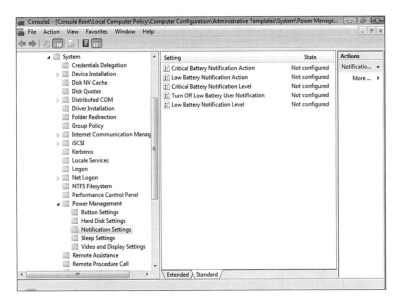

FIGURE 9.5
Configuring low and critical battery alarms and notifications in Windows Vista.

3. Set the low battery notification by double-clicking the Low Battery Notification Action option. Select Enabled and then select the appropriate action, such as sleep mode, to use via the Low Battery Notification Action list. Click OK.

4. Specify when the alarm is triggered by double-clicking the Low Battery Notification Level. Select Enabled and then select the appropriate alarm level via the Low Battery Notification Level Combination box. The alarm level is specified by the percentage of battery capacity remaining that triggers the low battery notification action.

5. To turn off the default user notification when the computer battery runs low, double-click the Turn Off Low Battery Notification, select Enable, and then click OK.

Configuring Critical Battery Alarms

Administrators can configure the computer to take specific actions when a critical battery state is reached. For example, instead of a text display and audible notification, the system may be configured to put the system into hibernation or shut-down mode when entering critical battery power. To configure critical battery notifications, administrators should perform the following steps:

1. Open the Microsoft Management console and then using the Add/Remove Snap-In option in the File Menu, add the Group Policy Object Editor under the Available Snap-Ins.

2. Open the Group Policy object to work with and then expand the Computer Configuration node to `Computer Configuration\ Administrative Templates\System\Power Management\ Notification Settings`, as shown in Figure 9.5.

3. Set the critical battery notification action by double-clicking the Critical Battery Notification Action option. Select Enabled and then select the appropriate action, such as hibernate or shutdown, to use via the Critical Battery Notification Action list. Click OK.

4. Specify when the alarm is triggered by double-clicking the Critical Battery Notification Level. Select Enabled and then select the appropriate alarm level via the Critical Battery Notification Level Combination box. The alarm level is specified by the percentage of battery capacity remaining that triggers the low battery notification action.

5. To turn off the default user notification when the computer battery reaches critical low levels, double-click the Turn Off Critical Battery Notification, select Enable, and then click OK.

Understanding Windows HotStart

A new feature in Windows Vista, Windows HotStart enables a user to click a button and immediately start a program regardless of whether the mobile PC is on, sleeping, in hibernation, or off. Within a few seconds of clicking a HotStart button, users can start a media program, such as Windows Media Player, to play a CD or watch a DVD that's been recorded, or browse and play audio and video files from the hard disk. At any point, the user can exit or pause the media program and return to the desktop without having to restart the mobile PC.

Although HotStart is ideal for playing media that's been recorded or stored on the hard disk, administrators can also configure the button to start other programs, such as a computer game program or third-party web browsers. HotStart works on mobile computers as well as on desktop computers. Similarly, manufacturers can take advantage of Windows HotStart to add consumer-friendly application-access buttons through chassis front panels or infrared (IR) remote controls to their system designs.

Administrators can configure Windows HotStart by completing the following steps:

1. Verify that the Advanced Configuration and Power Interface (ACPI) has enumerated all the application-launch buttons and stored the contents in the Registry correctly.

2. Set individual Registry keys or use Group Policy to configure the Windows HotStart button agent and application launch.

3. Verify that the Windows HotStart button agent is receiving the application-launch button-press event.

Verifying ACPI Has Enumerated HotStart Buttons Correctly

Administrators can verify that ACPI has enumerated the HotStart buttons correctly by checking the following:

1. Checking that the following registry entries exist on the system:

```
HKLM\SYSTEM\CurrentControlSet\Enum\ACPI\PNP0C32\<ButtonID>
HKLM\SYSTEM\CurrentControlSet\Enum\ACPI\PNP0C32
➥\<ButtonID>\Control
HKLM\SYSTEM\CurrentControlSet\Enum\ACPI\PNP0C32
➥\<ButtonID>\Device Parameters
HKLM\SYSTEM\CurrentControlSet\Enum\ACPI\PNP0C32
➥\<ButtonID>\LogConf
HKLM\SYSTEM\CurrentControlSet\Enum\ACPI\PNP0C32
➥\<ButtonID>\Properties
```

2. Checking that the UserHIDBlock value is set properly:

```
HKEY_LOCAL_MACHINE\SYSTEM\CurrentControlSet\Enum\ACPI\
➡PNP0C32\<ButtonID>\Device Parameters
```

```
Name: UserHIDBlock
Type: REG_BINARY
Data: <UsageID>
```

The UserHIDBlock value could be something like the following:

```
ButtonID: 1
UsageID: 04
```

Configuring the Windows HotStart Button Agent and Application Launch

Windows Vista provides a user-mode button agent that subscribes to application-launch notifications from the Windows kernel power manager and launches the application that is associated with a specific button usage ID in the Windows Registry. This behavior is implemented as a task named HotStart that is launched by Windows Task Manager when the user logs on.

The HotStart task can be viewed and configured in the Scheduled Tasks viewer management console in the Performance and Maintenance Control Panel application.

Administrators and manufacturers can configure the application that is associated with a specific UsageID by using the following Registry key:

```
HKLM\System\CurrentControlSet\Control\MobilePC\
➡HotStartButtons\<UsageID>
```

where *<UsageID>* corresponds to the value that is specified in the system's ACPI namespace. The GHID method returns this value for each application-launch button instance. This Registry key is not present in the Registry by default and must be added by the manufacturer when the system is configured to support direct application launch.

As described in the Microsoft whitepaper, "Direct Application Launch from System Startup on Windows Vista," the usage ID is encoded in Little Endian order. The proper *<UsageID>* key should be created in Little Endian byte order, with leading zeros truncated. For example, if UserHIDBlock of button 2 is '21 01 00 00', the key name in Little Endian would be '00000121' before truncation and '121' after truncation. If UserHIDBlock of button 0 is '04', the name in Little Endian would be '04' before truncation and '4' after truncation.

> **Note**
>
> Depending on which computing system is used, programmers have to consider the byte order in which multibyte numbers are stored, particularly when writing those numbers to a file. The two orders are called Little Endian and Big Endian. *Little Endian* means that the low-order byte of the number is stored in memory at the lowest address, and the high-order byte at the highest address. (The little end comes first.) Intel processors, found in PCs, use Little Endian byte order. *Big Endian* means that the high-order byte of the number is stored in memory at the lowest address, and the low-order byte at the highest address. (The big end comes first.) Motorola processors, found in Macs, use Big Endian byte order. For more detailed information on Endian orders, check out www.cs.umass.edu/~verts/cs32/endian.html and read Dr. William T. Verts, "An Essay on Endian Order."

Administrators must be sure to pay close attention to the syntax as they create a HotStart button agent application. To create the target application path, administrators must create a string value named `ApplicationPath` under the appropriate `<UsageID>` key. The value for this key must contain the full path to the application to be launched, enclosed in quotation marks. Additional command-line switches should be delimited by whitespace after the application-launch path. The maximum length of `ApplicationPath` string is 260 characters, which includes all executable launch paths and parameters.

For example, to launch `foobar.exe` with `/bar` and `/xyz` as parameters, specify the following:

```
"C:\Windows\System32\foobar.exe " /bar /xyz
```

Remember, Windows Vista does not populate the application-launch button by default, so Windows Vista makes no associations between usage ID values and target applications. Administrators can choose any value for usage ID and map it to any target application.

Verifying That the Windows HotStart Button Agent Receives the Button-Press Event

To verify that the Windows HotStart button agent is properly receiving the button-press event from the kernel power manager, administrators need to check the HotStart Timestamp value after pressing the button. To do so,

administrators should verify the Timestamp value stored under the
LastTimeStamp value at:

```
HKLM\Software\Microsoft\Windows\CurrentVersion\HotStart
```

The timestamp should match the time value at which the HotStart button was
pressed. If so, the HotStart button agent is working properly. If the value is
not recorded or does not match, administrators should revalidate that the
setup is properly configured and then rerun the testing procedures.

Configuring Networking

Many laptops require more than one network configuration for use at home
and at the office or when traveling. At the office, the system may use a
Dynamic Host Configuration Protocol (DHCP) assigned Internet Protocol (IP)
address and network settings set by the DHCP server. While at the home the
system may use a static IP address for access to a broadband network, print
server, and network communication. When a system is configured with DHCP
for its primary network settings, administrators can also set alternate network
configuration settings to use when a DHCP server is not available, such as
when the user is traveling or is on a home network. The alternate network
configurations can be assigned automatically, or they can be configured by a
user. Systems may also need to be configured for use in business settings
where a network projector may be required for business presentations.

Using Dynamic IP Addresses

DHCP addressing gives administrators centralized control of IP address
assignment and TCP/IP settings for the network. Using a DHCP server, available dynamic IP addresses are assigned to any of the properly configured
network interface cards (NICs) that supply the required TCP/IP network
settings, such as IP addresses, default gateways, primary and secondary DNS
servers, primary and secondary WINS servers, and more. When computers
use dynamic addressing, they are assigned a lease on a specific IP address.
The lease is good for a specific time period and must be renewed periodically. When the lease needs to be renewed, the computer contacts the DHCP
server that provided the lease. If the server is available, the lease is renewed
and a new lease period is granted. Administrators can also renew leases
manually as necessary on individual computers or by using the DHCP
server itself.

Administrators can configure a system for DHCP by performing the following steps.

1. Click Start and then click Control Panel.

2. In Control Panel, click View Network Status and Tasks located under the Network and Internet heading.

3. In the left pane of the Network and Sharing Center, click Manage Network Connections. This will display the Network Connections page, displaying a list of all network connections configured for use on the computer. Right-click the connection to configure and select Properties.

4. Select Internet Protocol Version 4 (TCP/IPv4) and then click Properties to display the Internet Protocol Version 4 (TCP/IPv4) dialog box. This can also be accomplished by double-clicking Internet Protocol Version 4 (TCP/IPv4).

5. From the General tab, verify that Obtain an IP Address Automatically and Obtain DNS Server Address Automatically options are selected. If alternate DNS server addresses are required, select the Use the Following DNS Server Addresses option and type in the IP address information for the Preferred and Alternate DNS servers.

6. Click OK when finished.

Using Static IP Addresses

When administrators configure static IP addresses, they need to provide the IP address, subnet mask, and default gateway in order for the computer to communicate properly across the network. These settings give the computer an identifier on the local network and allow it to interact with other computers. IP addressing schemes vary according to how the network is configured yet typically are assigned based on a particular network segment.

IPv6 and IPv4 addresses are designed differently. IPv6 addresses use the first 64 bits of the address to represent the network ID and the remaining 64 bits to represent the network interface. IPv4 addresses use a variable number of the first bits to represent the network ID and the remaining bits to represent the host ID. On networks connected indirectly to the Internet, IPv4 addresses may be assigned 192.168.10.10 with a subnet mask of 255.255.255.0. In this case the first three bits represent the network ID and the available range of IP addresses is between 192.168.10.1 and 192.168.10.254. The network broadcast address is 192.168.10.255.

Table 9.1 shows the four ranges reserved for private networks. All other IPv4 addresses are considered public IP addresses and must be purchased or leased from ISPs.

Table 9.1   **Private IPv4 Network Addressing**

Private Network ID	Subnet Mask	IP Address Range	Class Description
10.0.0.0	255.0.0.0	10.0.0.0 – 10.255.255.255	Single class A
172.16.0.0	255.240.0.0	172.16.0.0 – 172.31.255.255	16 contiguous class Bs
192.168.0.0	255.255.0.0.	192.168.0.0 – 192.168.255.255	256 contiguous class Cs
169.254.0.0	255.255.0.0	169.254.0.0 – 169.254.255.255	256 contiguous class Cs

Administrators can configure IPv4 or IPv6 addresses for a particular network connection using the following steps:

1. Click Start and then click Network. In the Network Explorer page, click the Network and Sharing Center link on the toolbar. Next, click Manage Network Connections in the left side.

2. Right-click the connection to work with and then select Properties. If prompted, confirm the action in question to continue.

3. Click Properties in the Local Area Connection Status dialog box. This displays the Local Area Connection Properties dialog box.

4. Select the IPv4 or IPv6 address scheme to work with by double-clicking IPv4 or IPv6.

5. If IPv4 was selected, complete the following items:

   ■ Click Use the Following IP Address. Enter the IPv4 IP address in the IPv4 address field.

   ■ Press Tab and then enter in the subnet mask for the network. Press Tab again and enter the default gateway setting. Use the address of the network default router as the default gateway entry. If necessary, configure Windows Internet Name Service (WINS) settings for WINS resolution.

6. If IPv6 was selected, complete the following items:

  ■ Click Use the Following IP Address. Enter the IPv6 IP address in the IPv6 address field.

  ■ Press Tab and then enter in the subnet prefix length for the network. Press Tab again and enter the default gateway setting. Use the address of the network default router as the default gateway entry.

7. Type an entry for the Preferred and Alternate DNS server fields. DNS is necessary for domain name resolution.

8. Click OK twice and then click Close to complete the steps.

Configuring Wireless Networking

Wireless networking makes it easy for users to take their laptops with them to business meetings, remote offices, or other office locations. Using a wireless network adapter and a wireless access point or wireless gateway, users can easily connect to the corporate network. Wireless adapters include devices such as wireless PCI cards for desktops, PC cards for notebooks, and USB devices that can be used on desktops, laptops, and notebooks. Each of these devices uses a built-in antenna to communicate with the wireless access point. The wireless access point itself is connected to the company's physical network. It may contain a switch and network router.

The primary types of network wireless adapters are PC cards for notebooks and PCI cards for desktops. Both types of adapters are easily configured and highly reliable. When using a USB wireless adapter, keep in mind that there are USB 1.0 and USB 2.0 versions of adapters, each with different speed performance. USB is the original design specification and USB 2.0 is the newest and fastest specification. For proper operation, connection speeds, and optimal performance, match port types to the appropriate USB specification.

Administrators may need to configure wireless security settings as well. Wireless Equivalency Protection (WEP), the most basic security setting, requires a network encryption pass phrase or network key to obtain network access. WiFi Protected Access (WPA) and WiFi Protected Access Version 2 (WPA2) provide a higher level of security because they are able to rotate the encryption keys and dynamic creation over time, providing added security.

Working with Wireless Networks

After the wireless adapter and wireless access point are installed, a connection can be made over the wireless network. Wireless network connections are similar to wired network connections and provide network access to corporate resources such as domains, servers, and peripherals such as printers and scanners. Computers that connect to both wired and wireless connections will show two active connections in the Network and Sharing Center. As shown in Figure 9.6, wireless connections provide additional network information, such as the Wireless Network Connection name, signal strength, and an option for disconnecting from the wireless network.

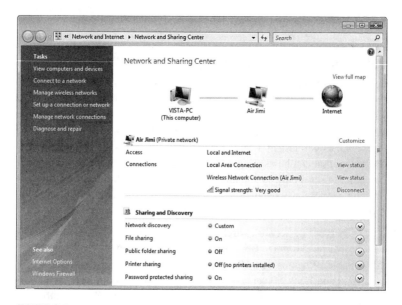

FIGURE 9.6
Viewing wireless settings in Network and Sharing Center.

Click View Status to check the status of the wireless connection and to monitor the connection status for connection speed and signal strength.

Connecting to Wireless Networks

Computers with a wireless network adapter should be able to connect to any wireless networks that are broadcast within their antenna's range limit. Windows Vista allows administrators to configure any network setting required, such as encryption settings, authentication, or other communication settings.

If a computer hasn't accessed a wireless network previously, administrators can create a connection by using the following steps:

1. Click Start, Network. Then click Network and Sharing Center on the toolbar.

2. In Network and Sharing Center, click Set Up a Connection or Network to display the Set Up a Connection or Network Wizard. Select Manually Connect to a Wireless Network and then click Next.

3. Enter the wireless network information in each of the provided fields for Network Name (SSID), Security Type, Encryption Type (automatically selected), and Security Key/Pass Phrase. If desired, select the Connect Even if the Network Is Not Broadcasting check box; the Start This Connection Automatically check box is selected by default.

4. If using security types such as WEP or WPA/WPA2, entering a Security Key/Pass Phrase is required.

5. Click Next to add and then connect to the wireless connection.

Managing Wireless Networks

Administrators can manage wireless network connections using the Manage Wireless Networks link on the left pane of Network and Sharing Center. To do so, complete the following steps:

1. Click Start, Network. Then click Network and Sharing Center on the toolbar.

2. In Network and Sharing Center, click Manage Wireless Networks to display the Manage Wireless Networks page, as shown in Figure 9.7.

3. Select the wireless connection to work with and modify settings as necessary.

Manage Wireless Networks displays the wireless connection in order of connection priority. The wireless connection at the top of the list is the first connection that will be accessed. If it is not available, Windows Vista will try the next connection in the list until a connection is successful or until a failure occurs if no wireless networks are available. To change the order preference, select a wireless connection and then click the Move Up or Move Down button on the toolbar. As needed, add new wireless connections using the Add button on the toolbar. Defunct wireless connections can be removed from the list by selecting the broken wireless connection and clicking Remove to delete the entry.

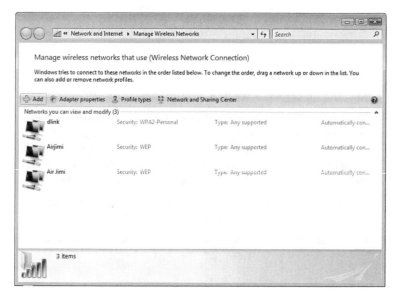

FIGURE 9.7
Viewing wireless connections using Manage Wireless Networks in Windows Vista.

Configuring VPN Connections

VPN connections are used to connect over a dial-up or broadband connection using secure communication protocols and channels. To connect, administrators must know the connection information such as IP address or fully qualified domain name (FQDN) of the remote access server. Administrators can create a VPN connection using the following steps:

1. Click Start and then Connect To.

2. Click Set Up a Connection or Network to display the Set Up a Connection or Network Wizard.

3. Scroll down the list and select Connect to a Workplace and then click Next.

4. Select Use My Internet Connection (VPN) on the Connect to a Workplace page, and enter the Internet address or FQDN of the

computer to connect to. Typically, this will look something like 192.168.10.100 or VPN.AIRJIMI.COM and will be the name of the corporate network.

5. Type a name for the connection in the Destination Name field. If the connection requires a smart card or if other users will be allowed to use this connection, select the check box for the Use a Smart Card or Allow Other People to Use This Connection options.

6. Click Next and enter the usernames and password for the connection. It is not recommended that the check box for Remember This Password is selected. Selecting this check box allows anyone with access to the computer to use the connections. This is a poor security practice and should be avoided.

7. If needed, specify the domain name in the Domain (optional) field and then click Connect. If the connection fails, click Set Up the Connection Anyway so the information will be saved and the connection can be tried later.

Configuring Network Projectors

Advances in computer technology have provided conference rooms and meeting centers with network-enabled projectors that can be used during business meetings. A network projector is traditional video projector connected to a PC either using a standard cabled network or a wireless network. When users want to send a presentation to the projector, Windows Vista streams the output over the network rather than over fixed video cabling. To use a networked projector, a laptop is connected to the Local Area Network (LAN) and then the projector is accessed over the network using the Connect to a Network Projector Wizard. The wizard automatically searches for, locates, and connects to a networked projector. The projector's IP address and subnet mask must be configured to allow it to operate on the LAN.

Administrators can configure and connect to networked projectors using the following steps:

1. Click the Start button, All Programs, Accessories and then select Connect to a Network Projector.

2. If prompted by the Windows Firewall, allow permission to connect to a Network Projector by clicking Yes.

3. Specify how to connect to the projector. The choices are Search for a Projector and Enter the Projector Address.

4. When searching for a projector, the wizard will produce a list of available projectors. Select the desired projector, input the password (if necessary), and click Connect.

5. When the address of the network projector is known, click Enter the Projector Address. On the Enter the Network Address of a Projector page, input the address for the projector, such as http://airjimi.intranet.local/projectors/conroom1-proj1. Input the projector password and click Connect.

6. After a projector connection is established, click Finish to exit the wizard and use the network-enabled projector.

Note

But how does this work? Network Presentation uses the same technology as the Remote Desktop Connection to communicate with the projector. It streams video output from the PC over the network to the projector using the Remote Desktop Protocol (RDP). A big advantage to using RDP is added security. The encryption techniques enforced by RDP that secure sensitive data from network sniffers and potential hackers also apply to Network Presentation. In addition, if the presentation is delivered over a wireless networking solution, underlying network security, such as Wireless Protected Access (WPA), is used to encapsulate the network traffic and force endpoint authentication. How cool is that!

Using Access and Connectivity Policies

Windows Vista provides many access and connectivity policies to control network connections, dial-up connections, and remote assistance connections. Using these policies, administrators can alter a system's connectivity to remote systems as well as the local network.

Setting Network Policies

Network Policies are designed to limit computer actions on the company network. Enforcing restrictions prevents users from using certain features within the corporate network, such as access to advanced TCP/IP settings. Network Policies are located under Computer Configuration\ Administrative Templates\Network\Network Connections and User

Configuration\ Administrative Templates\Network\Network Connections. By enabling these restrictions, administrators enforce security measures and protect the corporate network from potential security breaches.

To enable and disable the network policy restrictions, administrators can use the following steps:

1. Access Group Policy on the system to work with and then expand the Network node to display Configuration\Administrative Templates\Network\Network Connections.

2. To configure a policy, double-click the policy. Select Enabled or Disabled on the Setting tab and then click OK.

To enable and disable the user policy restrictions, administrators can use the following steps:

1. Access Group Policy on the system to work with and then expand the Network node to display User Configuration\ Administrative Templates\Network\Network Connections.

2. To configure a policy, double-click the policy. Select Enabled or Disabled on the Setting tab and then click OK.

Setting Remote Assistance Policies

Remote Assistance policies are used to permit or prevent the use of the remote assistance feature on computers. Typically, unsolicited remote assistance offers are rejected while requested offers are accepted. Item such as expiration time limits for remote assistance offers can be configured. Enhanced security options are available for users of Windows Vista and later releases of Windows operating systems.

Administrators can configure Remote Assistance policies using the following steps:

1. Access Group Policy on the system to work with and then expand the Network node to display Computer Configuration\Administrative Templates\System\Remote Assistance.

2. Double-click Solicited Remote Assistance. Select Enabled on the Setting tab to allow authorized users to respond to remote assistance invitations.

3. Specify the access level for remote assistance responders. The Permit Remote Control of This Computer section has two levels of access that can be configured:

   ■ **Allow Helpers to Remotely Control This Computer**—Permits viewing and controlling of remote computers.

   ■ **Allow Helpers to Only View This Computer**—Permits only viewing and no remote control of computers.

4. Set the Maximum Ticket Time (Value) and Maximum Ticket Time (Units) fields to set the maximum time limits for remote assistance invitations. By default, the time limit is set to one hour.

5. If needed, change the default method for sending email invitations. By default, the method for sending email invitations is set to Mailto. Click OK.

6. Double-click Offer Remote Assistance to open the Offer Remote Assistance properties dialog box. Select Disabled on the Setting tab to prevent unsolicited assistance offers. Click OK.

7. If strong security encryption is desired and restricting connections to only computers running Windows Vista or later releases is also desired, double-click the Allow Only Vista or Later Connections Group Policy setting and display the Allow Only Vista or Later Connections dialog box. Select Enable and then click OK.

Last, administrators can prevent remote control and remote assistance altogether. To do so, administrators can use the following steps:

1. Access Group Policy on the system to work with and then expand the Network node to display `Computer Configuration\Administrative Templates\System\Remote Assistance`.

2. Double-click Solicited Remote Assistance. Select Disabled on the Setting tab to disallow remote assistance.

3. Click the Next Setting button to open the Offer Remote Assistance Properties dialog box. Select Disabled and then click OK.

Summary

Mobile computers are the fastest growing computer category. Consumer and business users are replacing their desktop computers with equally powerful mobile ones. In some vertical markets, palmtops or touch-screen PCs are even replacing laptops.

Often, mobile computers are employed in a variety of situations. A single mobile PC will switch between various "non-wired" configurations—on battery power, with no network, or with a wireless connection—and "wired" configurations—plugged into a wall socket and physical network or in a docking station.

The new and improved mobility features in Windows Vista help users manage constant configuration changes and simplify switching between network connections and alternative workplaces. Windows Vista also sports improved power management, enhanced security, improved alternative input technologies, and facilitates easier synchronization using the Sync Center with Pocket PC palmtops, Windows Mobile Smartphones, or Ultra Mobile computers.

CHAPTER 10

Creating a Secured Mobile Communications Configuration

Introduction to Secured Mobile Computing

In recent years, mobile computers have become the fastest growing computer category. Consumer and business users are replacing their desktop computers with equally powerful mobile computers. In some vertical markets, palmtops or touch-screen PCs are even replacing laptops.

With an increasing number of mobile and at-home employees, it becomes more difficult to maintain network security and the confidentiality of corporate information. Windows Vista provides the latest wireless security protocols and improved layers of protection that safeguard the corporate network while providing secure remote access to documents and programs.

Users can connect remotely using a variety of connection methods, such as dial-up, broadband or over Virtual Private Network (VPN) connections. Dial-up allows user to connect to the corporate network using a modem and standard telephone line. Broadband allows users to connect mobile computers to the corporate network using a high-speed Digital Subscriber Line (DSL) or cable modems. VPNs use encryption to provide a connection over an existing connection such as dial-up, broadband, or LAN. Wireless connections are also being used to connect to corporate networks. Using a wireless adapter with an antenna enables the computer to connect to available wireless access points and corporate connectivity.

Understanding Mobile Computing and Remote Access

Dial-up, direct-dial, and broadband connections make it possible for remote users to access the corporate network and its resources from remote work locations. The underlying technologies for each method are different, but ultimately provide the user with a remote connection with the office network.

Understanding Direct Dial and Modem Pools

When using a direct-dial network connection, remote users utilize their computer's modem and a standard telephone line to connect to a modem pool on the office network. A Windows Server manages the modem pool and employs Routing and Remote Access Server to authenticate the user logon ID and allow the user to connect to the network. Once connected, the user accesses the network as if actually located in the office. With this connection method, analog modems are connected to telephone lines and connect users to the internal network at speeds up to 33 kilobits per second (Kbps). Digital modems use channels of a T1 line to connect users to the internal network at speeds up to 56Kbps. A typical configuration, shown in Figure 10.1, consists of 8 to 16 modems, each configured with its own line or channel. The modem pool has a main number that a user calls to connect to the first modem in the pool. If the first modem is busy, the user is rolled over to the next number, which is configured to the second modem in the pool. This pattern continues until a free modem is detected and the user is connected. This allows users to have a single number to dial for remote access.

Understanding Broadband Connections

Different from direct-dial connections, broadband connections are completed through Internet Service Provider (ISP) networks. The user's cable modem or DSL router connects to the ISP network, which traverses the public Internet, as shown in Figure 10.2. To establish a connection to the corporate network, users create a connection using a VPN to establish a "virtual tunnel" through the public Intent to the office network.

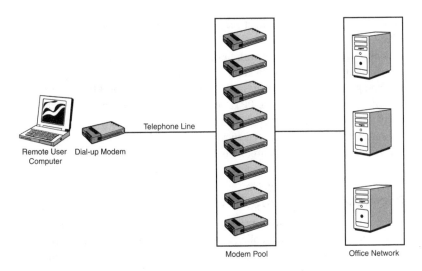

FIGURE 10.1
Accessing the corporate network using a modem pool.

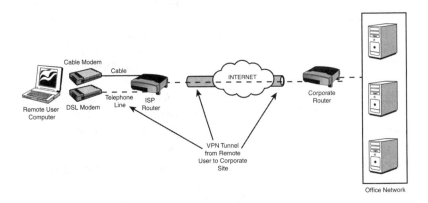

FIGURE 10.2
Accessing the corporate network using broadband and VPN technologies.

Understanding Virtual Private Networks

A VPN is a private network within the public Internet network or private local area network. When a user connects to the corporate network via VPN, the user experience is as if the user is directly connected to the corporate network and therefore has direct access to any available resources on the office network. The user is "virtually" in the office working because the user is connected to the office network through a virtual tunnel, and the routing of information over the public Internet is handled by the VPN technology. VPN technology typically uses Point to Point Tunneling Protocol (PPTP) or Layer 2 Tunneling Protocol (L2TP). PPTP and L2TP provide security from cyber attacks by offering encryption. L2TP, however, is more secure than PPTP because L2TP uses an advanced encryption technology, IP Security (IPSec). L2TP is more difficult to configure because it requires a certificate server to issue a certificate to each system that will access the network using L2TP.

Comprehending RADIUS Servers

Remote Authentication Dial-In User Service (RADIUS) (RFC 2865) is a widely deployed protocol enabling centralized authentication, authorization, and accounting for network access. Originally developed for dial-up remote access, RADIUS is now supported by VPN servers, DSL access, wireless access points, authenticating ethernet switches, and other network access types.

As shown in Figure 10.3, a RADIUS client (a dial-up server, VPN server, or wireless access point) sends user credentials and connection information in the form of a RADIUS message to a RADIUS server. The RADIUS server authenticates and authorizes the RADIUS client request and sends back a RADIUS message response. RADIUS clients also send RADIUS accounting messages to RADIUS servers. The RADIUS standards also support the use of RADIUS proxies—a computer that forwards RADIUS messages between RADIUS clients, RADIUS servers, and other RADIUS proxies. RADIUS messages are never sent between the access client and the access server.

RADIUS messages are sent as User Datagram Protocol (UDP) messages. Different ports are used to send authentication and accounting messages. Typically, UDP port 1812 is used for RADIUS authentication messages, and UDP port 1813 is used for RADIUS accounting messages. Some access servers might use UDP port 1645 for RADIUS authentication messages and UDP port 1646 for RADIUS accounting messages. Either way, only one RADIUS message is included in the UDP payload of a RADIUS packet.

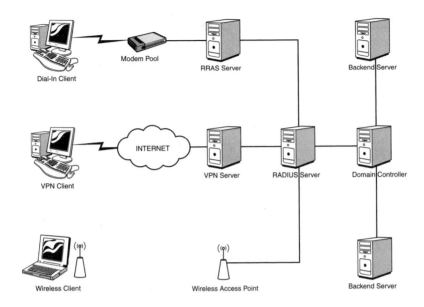

FIGURE 10.3
Accessing the corporate network using RADIUS server technology.

Configuring Remote Access Connections

Administrators can create dial-up and broadband connections for remote access. For additional security, administrators can configure the connection to use a VPN. Creating new connections is fairly easy using a wizard provided by Windows Vista. Accessing the wizard is easy via the Network and Sharing Center. Administrators can access the wizard by performing the following steps:

1. Click Start and then click Network.

2. In Network Explorer, click Network and Sharing Center in the toolbar.

3. In Network and Sharing Center, click Set Up a Connection or Network.

4. Select the appropriate option for a dial-up, broadband, or VPN connection and follow the prompts to complete the wizard.

Creating a Dial-Up to ISP Connection

In Windows Vista, administrators can a create dial-up connections to the workplace or an ISP. Similar processes are used to create each type of connection, and the settings are similar. However, there are differences between the two connections. A dial-up connection to the workplace uses the Client for Microsoft Networks and will not redial if the line connection is dropped. In contrast, a dial-up to an ISP does not use the Client for Microsoft Networks and will redial if the line connection is dropped. The Client for Microsoft Networks networking component allows Windows Vista to communicate with workgroups and domains. Most workplaces use a Windows domain or workgroup, and most ISPs do not; therefore, the component is configured for workplace connections and not for ISP connections.

Before setting up a dial-up connection, administrators should make sure that the computer is configured properly for phone and modem options. These settings are also known as the dialing rules and determine how phone lines are used and any special settings that may be needed, such as area code, carrier codes, the number needed to access an outside line (such as hotel or office), or dialing type such as dial or tone. The basic steps for creating a dial up connection are:

1. Set the Default Dialing Location.
2. Create, Modify, or Delete Additional Dialing Locations.
3. Create Dial-Up Connection.

> **Note**
>
> Administrators may notice that some of the settings for dialing rules and connections are created during the initial setup of the computer. Items like the country code and area code may not be properly configured to the specific user's location and may need to be changed to prevent long distance telephony charges.

Creating a Dial-Up Internet Connection

After you have configured the dialing locations and dialing rules, you can create a dial-up connection. To do so, follow these steps:

1. Click Start and then click Connect To.
2. In Connect to a Network, click Set Up a Connection or Network to start the Set Up a Connection or Network wizard.

3. Create a dial-up connection to an ISP by selecting Set Up a Dial-Up Connection and then click Next. Windows Vista will automatically search for a modem. If none is found, a dialog box will appear with an option to try again or set up a connection anyway. Select the Set Up a Connection Anyway option. This will save the configuration settings and allow them to be used later when a modem is present.

4. In the Dial-Up Phone Number text box, enter the phone number for the dial-up connection.

5. In the User Name text box, enter the username and then enter the password into the Password text box.

Caution

Using the Remember This Password and the Show Characters options is not recommended; it is a poor security practice because it allows anyone who uses the computer to view the password and to use this account and this dial-up connection.

---

6. In the Connection Name field, type a name for the connection. Typically, this is a descriptive name that prompts the user about where the connection is occurring; it should be 50 characters or fewer.

7. If other users of the computers should be able to use this connection, select the Allow Other People to Use This Connection check box.

Tip

If you want the connection to be available to all users of the computer, you can select Allow Other People to Use This Connection. This selection is preferred when using Group Policy to assign the connection and the user login information is not provided.

---

8. Click Create to create the dial-up connection. Then click Close to close the wizard.

Creating a Broadband to Internet or Dial-Up to Office Connection

Broadband connections are simpler to configure and use than dial-up connections. When using a broadband connection, dial-up rules and location settings are not needed. Redialing options, calling cards numbers, and dial-up access numbers are also not needed.

Typically, broadband providers provide users with a router or a modem to connect to the broadband service. The user then connects to the modem or router using a network interface card (NIC). The situation is typical of what is found in Local Area Network (LAN) environments, and in this configuration the user connects to the broadband connection and gains access to the Internet using the LAN.

Administrators may have the need to create specific broadband connections for their users. This is normally necessary when the ISP requires specific configuration settings such as secure authentication or when a specific username and password are required for access by the broadband provider.

You can create broadband connections to the Internet or a dial-up connection to the office using the following steps:

1. Click Start and then click Connect To.

2. In Connect to a Network, Click Set Up a Connection or Network to start up the Set Up a Connection or Network Wizard.

3. Choose one of the following options and then click Next:

   - Connect to a Workplace to connect via dial-up to the office.

   - Connect to the Internet to create a broadband connection to the Internet.

4. There may already be a configured connection. If so, you can either reconfigure this connection or create a new connection. Typically, you'll create a new connection. Click Set Up a New Connection Anyway and then click No, Create a New Connection. Click Next to continue.

5. On the How Do You Want to Connect dialog box, select Dial-Up to create a dial-up connection to the office, or click Broadband (PPPOE) to create a broadband connection to the Internet.

6. To set up a dial-up connection, configure the following and then click Next:

   - Set the dial-up phone number in the telephone text box.

   - Type the name of the connection into the Destination Name field. Use a descriptive name such as Rockridge Office or Emeryville Office. Keep the name to 50 characters or fewer.

   - If a Smart Card is used for authentication, select the Use a Smart Card option.

- If other users of the computers should be able to use this connection, select the Allow Other People to Use This Connection check box.

> **Tip**
> If you want the connection to be available to all users of the computer, you can select Allow Other People to Use This Connection. This selection is preferred when using Group Policy to assign the connection and the user login information is not provided.

7. By default, a user is prompted when making a connection. If you do not want the user to be prompted for the user login information, you can enter the username and password in the appropriate fields. Using the Remember This Password and the Show Characters options is not recommended because it is a poor security practice; it allows anyone who uses the computer to view the password for the connection. By not selecting the Remember This Password option, the user will be prompted to enter the password. For a dial-up connection, the logon domain should be entered in the Domain text field and then Click Create to create the connection. Click Close.

8. For a broadband connection to the Internet, click Connect to create the broadband connection. Typically, the connection fails because the connection is being set up for an alternative location such as the user's home office, and these settings do not work through a corporate office network. In this situation, select Skip to bypass activating the connection and then click Set Up the Connection Anyway. Click Close to finish the setup.

Creating a VPN Connection

VPN connections are used to connect over a dial-up or broadband connection using secure communication protocols and channels. To connect, administrators must know the connection information, such as the IP address or fully qualified domain name (FQDN) of the remote access server. Administrators with the proper host information can create a VPN connection using the following steps:

1. Click Start and then Connect To.

2. Click Set Up a Connection or Network to display the Set Up a Connection or Network Wizard.

3. Scroll down the list and select Connect To a Workplace and then click Next.

4. Select Use My Internet Connection (VPN) on the Connect to a Workplace page, and enter the Internet Address or FQDN of the computer to connect to. Typically, this looks something like 192.168.10.100 or VPN.AIRJIMI.COM and is the name of the corporate network.

5. Type a name for the connection in the Destination Name field. If the connection requires a smart card or if other users will be allowed to use this connection, select the check box for the Use a Smart Card or Allow Other People to Use This Connection options.

6. Click Next and enter the usernames and password for the connection. It is not recommended that you select the check box for Remember This Password. Selecting this check box allows anyone with access to the computer to use the connections. This is a poor security practice and should be avoided.

7. If needed, specify the domain name in the Domain (optional) field and then click Connect. If the connection fails, click Set Up the Connection Anyway so the information will be saved and the connection can be tried later.

Configuring Connections Properties

After creating a dial-up, broadband, or VPN connection, administrators may need to configure additional settings. Users may have specific individual needs that administrators can address by setting automatic or manual connections. When in the office, mobile users may like automatic connections because most offices have high-speed Internet connections. When out of the office on slower connections such as dial-up, which may or may not be available, users may prefer to have manual connections. The good news is that administrators can configure pretty much whatever the user wants.

Configuring Automatic Connections

Administrators can configure Windows Vista to automatically start a dial-up, broadband, or VPN connection when a user uses a program which accesses the Internet such as Internet Explorer 7. Automatic connections depend on how Internet Explorer 7 is configured in the Internet Options. Administrators can choose from the following options when configuring connections:

- **Never Dial a Connection**—When this option is selected, users must establish connections manually.

- **Dial Whenever a Network Connection Is Not Present**—When this option is selected, the connection is automatically established whenever the LAN connection is not available.

- **Always Dial My Default Connection**—When this option is selected, the default connection is established even if other connections are already connected.

To configure automatic connections, you can perform the following steps:

1. Click Start and then click Control Panel. In Control Panel, click Network and Internet.

2. In Network and Internet, click Internet Options, and then click the Connections Tab in the Internet Properties dialog box to display the Connections tab, as shown in Figure 10.4.

3. Select Dial Whenever a Network Connection Is Not Present to initiate connections automatically if a LAN connection is not available. Select Always Dial My Default Connection to always attempt to initiate connections.

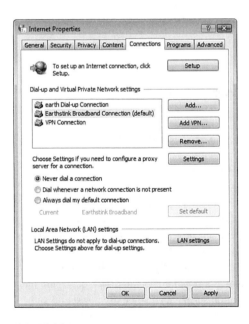

FIGURE 10.4
Configuring automatic or manual connections using the Connections tab.

4. The Dial-Up and Virtual Private Network Settings section shows the currently configured dial-up, broadband, and VPN connections.

5. Select the connection to use as the default connection and then click Set Default.

6. Click OK and then click OK again to complete the steps.

Configuring Manual Connections

Some users may always want to have control of establishing dial-up, broadband, or VPN connections. Administrators can configure the system so that the user must always manually initiate connections. Typically, this is not the case, but if users should request this setup, administrators can configure computers to connect manually by performing the following steps:

1. Click Start and then click Control Panel. In Control Panel, click Network and Internet.

2. In Network and Internet, click Internet Options and then click the Connections tab in the Internet Properties dialog box to display the Connections tab, as shown in Figure 10.4.

3. Select Never Dial a Connection.

4. Click OK to finish.

Configuring Proxy Settings for Mobile Connections

Internet proxy servers are deployed in most environments for security, performance, and usage tracking purposes. When an application makes a request to a resource on the Internet, the request is often routed through a proxy. The proxy server then makes the request on the computer's behalf and forwards the response back to the computer. This means that the application needs to know what proxy server to use when requesting a resource on the Internet. Users can either use an explicit proxy server name or take advantage of the automatic proxy detection capabilities. Similar to connections, proxy servers and their settings can be set automatically or manually. Automatic setup is easy because the computer attempts to detect and then configure the proxy server settings. A configuration script can also be used to set up and configure a proxy. Typically, configuration scripts are stored on the local computer or at an Internet address. Because the scripts can be preconfigured, they can save administrators a lot of time when configuring multiple users and proxy settings for each user. Proxy settings for VPN connections can also be scripted to include settings specific to the VPN connection.

Setting Up an Automatic Proxy Configuration

You can set up an automatic proxy configuration for a connection by completing the following steps:

1. Click Start and then click Control Panel. In Control Panel, click Network and Internet.

2. In Network and Internet, click Internet Options and then click the Connections tab in the Internet Properties dialog box to display the Connections tab, as shown in Figure 10.4.

3. In the Dial-Up and Virtual Private Network Settings section, select the connection to configure and then click Settings to display the Dial-Up Connection Settings dialog box.

4. Select Automatically Detect Settings in the Automatic Configuration section to attempt automatic detection of the proxy settings.

5. To use a configuration script, Select Use Automatic Configuration Script and then type the uniform resource locator (URL), such as proxy.airjimi.com/proxy.vbs, or the file path, such as C:\proxy.vbs, of the script. If desired, environment variables can be used for the file path, such as %userprofile%\proxy.vbs.

6. Clear the Use a Proxy Server for This Connection check box to ensure that the automatic settings are used.

7. Click OK and then click OK again to finish.

Configuring a Manual Proxy Setup

Administrators can also configure the proxy settings manually. You can manually set up a proxy configuration for a connection by completing the following steps:

1. Click Start and then click Control Panel. In Control Panel, click Network and Internet.

2. In Network and Internet, click Internet Options and then click the Connections tab in the Internet Properties dialog box to display the Connections tab.

3. In the Dial-Up and Virtual Private Network Settings section, select the connection to configure and then click Settings to display the Dial-Up Connection Settings dialog box.

4. Clear the Automatically Detect Settings and Use Automatic Configuration Script check boxes if they were selected in the Automatic Configuration section.

5. Select the Use a Proxy Server for This Connection check box to start the manual configuration. By default, the Bypass Proxy Server for Local Addresses option is not selected. Typically, a proxy is not used for server requests that reside on the same network segment. In this case, select Bypass Proxy Server for Local Addresses. If this option is not selected, users need additional permissions to access intranet servers through the proxy servers. Click Advanced to continue the manual configuration process and display the Proxy Settings dialog box as shown in Figure 10.5.

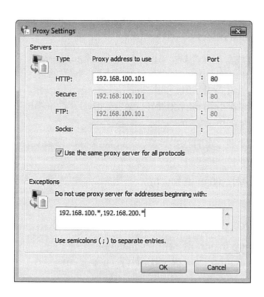

FIGURE 10.5
Manually configuring proxy server settings.

6. In the Servers section of the dialog box, administrators should enter the necessary information for the configuration of the proxy servers. In the Proxy to Use fields, type in the proxy address for the required proxies,

such as HTTP, Secure (Secure Sockets Layer (SSL)), FTP, or Socks. If multiple proxies are needed for a certain service, enter the IP addresses for each proxy in the order in which the web client should try to use them, separated by a semicolon. If a proxy is not required for a service, do not enter any server information in the related box.

7. In the Port field, set the port needed for the particular server. Although most proxies respond to requests on port 80, a unique port may be necessary. Typically, port 80 is used for HTTP, port 443 is used for Secure (SSL), port 21 is used for FTP, and port 1080 is used for Socks. In the Use the Same Proxy Server for All Protocols option, enable using the same IP addresses and ports for all proxy servers. If unique IP address and port settings are required for each proxy server, unselect the check box.

8. If the network has multiple segments or if specific servers should not use proxies, use the Exceptions list section to enter IP addresses or the IP address range. Again, separate each entry by a semicolon. If desired, a wildcard asterisk (*) can be used to specify an address range of 0 to 255, such as 10.10.10.*, 10.10.*.*, or 10.*.*.*.

9. Click OK three times to finish.

Configuring Connection Logon Information

Administrators can configure connection logon information for each connection that is created. You can set a username, password, and domain for each connection by completing the following steps:

1. Click Start and then click Control Panel. In Control Panel, click Network and Internet.

2. In Network and Internet, click Internet Options and then click the Connections tab in the Internet Properties dialog box to display the Connections tab.

3. In the Dial-Up and Virtual Private Network Settings section, select the connection to configure and then click Settings.

4. Type the username and password for the connection in the username and password text fields. If a domain is required, type the domain name into the domain text field.

5. Click OK and then click OK again to finish.

You can also configure options that determine whether users are prompted for a phone number or logon information. By default, the domain name is not passed with logon information. Because a user logon requires a logon domain, administrators should make sure that this information is passed with other login information. To do this, follow these steps:

1. Click Start and then click Control Panel. In Control Panel, click Network and Internet.

2. In Network and Internet, click Internet Options and then click the Connections tab in the Internet Properties dialog box to display the Connections tab.

3. In the Dial-Up and Virtual Private Network Settings section, select the connection to configure and then click Settings.

4. Click Properties in the Settings dialog box to display the Properties dialog box shown in Figure 10.6.

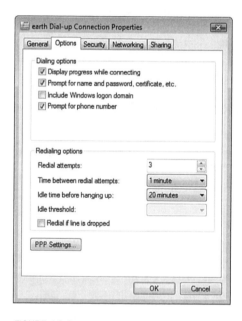

FIGURE 10.6
Configuring additional connection logon information.

5. Click the Options tab and then configure the following options as required:

- **Display Progress While Connecting**—Select this option to display status messages while making a connection.

- **Prompt for Name and Password, Certificate, Etc**—Select this option to ensure that users are prompted for logon information.

- **Prompt for Phone Number**—Select this option to prompt for a phone number when necessary.

- **Include Windows Logon Domain**—Select this option to ensure the Windows Logon Domain information is automatically included during the connection.

6. In the Redialing Options section, configure redialing options as needed:

- **Redial Attempts**—This option sets the number of times to redial a phone number automatically. Set the redial value to 0 to disable automatic redialing.

- **Time Between Redial Attempts**—This option sets the time to wait before making a redial attempt. Time values can be set in seconds (1, 3, 5, 10, and 30) or minutes (1, 2, 5, or 10).

- **Idle Time Before Hanging Up**—This option determines how long Windows Vista waits idle before severing the connection. Time values can be set in minutes (1, 5, 10, 20, 30), hours (1, 2, 4, 8, 24), or Never. The default value is 20 minutes.

- **Redial If Line Is Dropped**—This option specifies whether Windows Vista redials a connection if the line is dropped. For connections to the workplace, this option is cleared by default. Select this option to redial a dropped connection.

7. Click OK three times to finish.

Configuring Identity Validation

Mobile and network security can be compromised if the proper identity validation is not performed. When the integrity of a network is compromised, sensitive data can be stolen, deleted, or modified by hackers or other malicious bot type attacks. Remote user identities should be validated whenever possible. This is not the default configuration for most dial-up connections, and the user login information for connections should be validated. Administrators can use the following options to validate user logon information:

- **Allow Unsecured Password**—This option allows the user password to be sent over the connection in clear text.

- **Require Secured Password**—This option attempts to send logon information over a secure method of communication such as Challenge Handshake Authentication Protocol (CHAP) or MS CHAP 2, rather than over clear text.

- **Use Smart Card**—This option use a smart card to validate a user logon.

Dial-up or broadband connections can be configured using all these options. Secure connections such as VPNs can only be secured using secure techniques. When secure passwords are mandatory, administrators can automatically pass the username, password, and domain information included in the connection configuration. This is useful for remote users who connect to the network and are automatically required to authenticate to the domain. When using secure validation methods, administrators can require data encryption and force Windows Vista to disconnect if encryption cannot be used. Data encryption is automatically used for authentication with smart cards and secure passwords.

You can configure identity validation by completing the following steps:

1. Click Start and then click Control Panel. In Control Panel, click Network and Internet.

2. In Network and Internet, click Internet Options and then click the Connections tab in the Internet Properties dialog box to display the Connections tab.

3. In the Dial-Up and Virtual Private Network Settings section, select the connection to configure and then click Settings.

4. Click Properties in the Settings dialog box and then click the Security tab.

5. In the Security Options section, select Typical (Recommended Settings), or Advanced (Custom Settings). The Typical options are Allow Unsecured Passwords, Require Password, and Use Smart Card.

6. If secure passwords are required, configure automatic logon and require data encryption. These options are useful when logging on to a Windows domain. Be sure the domain supports the settings or user identities will not be authenticated and their connection will not be completed.

7. Data encryption should also be used with smart cards. Encryption protects the integrity of the remote computer and the authenticating computer. Selecting Require Data Encryption will force both computers to support a secure encrypted connection. If not, the connection will be dropped.

8. Click OK three times to finish.

Setting Up Networking Protocols and Components

As an administrator, you will encounter many different network environments. You will need to configure networking protocols to fit the type of connection needed by the enterprise company. Each connection type is associated with a connection protocol:

- **Dial–Up**—Uses the Point-to-Point Protocol (PPP) to establish connections to Windows servers over dial-up.

- **Dial-Up**—Uses Serial Line Internet Protocol (SLIP) to establish connections to UNIX servers over dial-up. Typically, additional third-party software is required to use SLIP.

- **Broadband**—Uses Point-to-Point Protocol over Ethernet (PPPOE) to establish connections over broadband connections.

- **VPN**—Uses the Automatic, Point-to-Point Tunneling Protocol (PPTP), or Layer 2 Tunneling Protocol (L2TP) to establish a virtual tunnel. Automatic will automatically detect the available protocol, PPTP or L2TP, and use that for a connection. PPTP is an extension of the PPP protocol. L2TP is an enhanced protocol that uses IPSec to enhance security.

When configuring mobile networking, you will be working with four network components in Windows Vista. By default, the four specific components are Transmission Control Protocol/Internet Protocol (TCP/IP), QoS Packet Scheduler, File and Print Sharing for Windows, and Client for

Microsoft Networks. The configuration of these components depends on the originally created connection. However, administrators can modify these components. Some networking components are considered advanced components and therefore are not installed by default. Advanced networking components, such as Internet Information Services (IIS), can be installed by through Windows Setup as described in the following steps:

1. Click Start and then click Control Panel. In Control Panel, click Network and Internet.

2. In Network and Internet, click Internet Options and then click the Connections tab in the Internet Properties dialog box to display the Connections tab.

3. In the Dial-Up and Virtual Private Network Settings section, select the connection to configure and then click Settings.

4. Click Properties in the Settings dialog box and then click the Networking tab.

5. On the Networking tab, you can configure the connection settings. In the This Connection Uses the Following Items section, you can configure the desired protocol and enable or disable networking components as desired. If additional networking components are required, you can install them by clicking the Install button and then selecting the component to use in the provided list.

6. Connections use DHCP by default for ease of use and configuration of network settings such as IP address, subnet address, default gateway, and DNS. To assign a static IP address or modify other default settings, select the TCP/IP protocol and then click Properties.

7. Click OK three times to complete the changes.

Using Windows Firewall with Network Connections

With any Internet connection such as dial-up, broadband, or VPN, administrators should always be concerned about security. The built-in Windows Firewall in Windows Vista will add additional security against attacks by unwanted intruders. The firewall restricts certain types of information and communications. By enforcing the proper restrictions, Windows Firewall allows administrators to reduce the attack surface of the computer and reduce security risks to the corporate networks when accessed by remote users.

Windows Firewall is enabled by default for all connections. It can be enabled or disabled per connection if desired by administrators. You can enable and disable Windows Firewall on a per-connection basis using the following steps:

1. Click the Start button, type Security Center into the Search box, and press Enter. In Windows Security Center, click Windows Firewall. Note the network location you are configuring and then click Change Settings.

2. In the Windows Firewall dialog box, make sure that firewall is set to On and then select the Advanced tab. If prompted, confirm the action by clicking Continue.

3. In the Network Connection Settings section, each of the configured network connections is listed. Clear the check box for a connection to disable Windows Firewall for that connection. Select the check box to enable Windows Firewall for a connection.

4. Click OK when finished enabling or disabling Windows Firewall connections.

Using Mobile Wireless Networking

To facilitate office productivity and office mobility, organizations are implementing wireless networking technologies. Wireless networks can be deployed in many configurations. Wireless standards are constantly evolving, with faster and more secure technologies being introduced. In basic terms, a wireless adapter with an antenna enables the computer to connect to available wireless access points, also known as wireless base stations or wireless gateways, and corporate connectivity.

Most wireless access points and wireless adapters are based on the Institute of Electrical and Electronics Engineers (IEEE) 802.11 specification and are Wi-Fi certified to demonstrate that they have passed certain performance tests and compatibility requirements. The 802.11 wireless standards are comparable to the IEEE 802.3 standard for ethernet for wired LANs. The IEEE 802.11 specifications address both the Physical (PHY) and Media Access Control (MAC) layers and are tailored to resolve compatibility issues between manufacturers of Wireless LAN equipment.

The 802.11 family currently includes multiple over-the-air modulation specifications that all use the same basic protocol. The most popular specifications are those defined by the 802.11b/g. These are amendments to the original standard in which security was originally purposefully weak because of multigovernmental export requirements. Security was later enhanced via the 802.11i amendment after governmental and legislative changes. 802.11n is a recently developed, multistreaming specification that is still under draft development, even though commercial products based on proprietary predraft versions of the standard are being sold. Although 802.11a was the first wireless networking standard, 802.11b was the first widely accepted wireless networking standard, followed by 802.11g, 802.11a, and 802.11n.

802.11b and 802.11g standards use the 2.4GHz band, which uses three non-overlapping channels. Because of this choice of frequency band, 802.11b and 802.11g equipment could occasionally suffer interference from microwave ovens, cordless telephones, Bluetooth devices, baby monitors, and other devices that operate in this spectrum. The 802.11a standard uses the 5GHz band, which is reasonably free from interference by comparison and offers 23 non-overlapping channels. 802.11a devices are never affected by products operating on the 2.4GHz band.

Tip

Before deploying wireless devices in the enterprise, be sure to take a close look at compatibility among devices. More and more wireless devices are being developed that may or may not be compatible with standard 802.11 devices and may operate on proprietary networking technologies that require specific wireless adapters and access points to achieve higher transmission rates. For more information on wireless devices, standards, and certifications, visit the Wi-Fi Alliance at www.wi-fi.org/.

Working with Security

Security on wired networks is pretty straightforward. Administrators mostly have to be concerned when the client is physically connected to the network via a network cable and associated switches. If rogue machines or unauthorized people connect to the network, it is fairly easy for administrators to detect and remove the intruder's computer from the network.

Wireless networks are a bit more complex because anyone within range of a wireless access point has access to the network. Hackers can intercept broadcast signals and also work their way into the network. For administrators, detecting and locating the suspected intruder is much more difficult because there is no physical cable to trace and disconnect. Additionally, if the intruder is connected to the wireless access point, the intruder is likely already inside of the network's firewall and the protection that it provides against attack. Administrators can provide protections against unauthorized access by configuring wireless devices to use wireless encryption.

The most basic encryption scheme is Wireless Equivalency Protection (WEP). WEP encrypts data with a 40-bit, 128-bit, or higher key encryption. Data is encrypted using a symmetric key derived from the WEP key or password before it is transmitted. Any computer that wants to read the data must be able to decrypt it using the key. Shared key encryption may be enough in wired access environment but in wireless environments this is not sufficient. Shared key encryption can be broken and because the shared key doesn't change over time automatically, intruders have continuous access to the corporate network.

Because WEP provides only basic security, it should be used in environments where no other alternatives are available. The situation where this occurs is limited and administrators should look to employ alternatives such as Wi-Fi Protected Access (WPA), which is based on the Draft 3 of the IEEE 802.11i standard, or Wi-Fi Protected Access Version 2 (WPA2). WPA was created by the Wi-Fi Alliance and is designed for use with an IEEE 802.1X authentication server that distributes different keys to each user. It can also be used in a less-secure preshared key (PSK) mode, where every user is given the same pass-phrase. WPA2 is based on the official 802.11i standard and is backward compatible with WPA.

WPA and WPA2 provide additional security by changing the way keys are derived and also by rotating keys. Changing key over time and changing the ways keys are derived so that no one single method is used ensures that the WPA and WPA2 security is much improved over WEP. Devices that are WPA and WPA2 compatible can be used in personal/Small Office Home Office (SOHO) or enterprise modes.

Enterprise mode provides authentication using 802.1x and Extensible Authentication Protocol (EAP). In this mode, devices have two sets of keys: session keys and group keys. Session keys are unique to each session between wireless clients and access points and create a virtual port between the two devices. On the other hand, group keys are shared among all clients connected to the same access point. Both types of keys are created dynamically and are rotated over time to preserve their integrity.

Personal mode provides authentication using a preshared key or password. In this mode, WPA uses a preshared key for encryption rather than a changing key. Administrators configure a group key (also known as master key) in the access point, and this key is then configured for all access devices. The master key is used to create a session-specific key. Key management occurs in the background so that the session key is changed regularly and the same session key is never used twice.

Administrators should keep the following in mind when working with WPA and WPA2:

- WPA and WPA2 have enterprise and personal modes of operation.

- WPA and WPA2 use 802.1x and EAP for authentication.

- WPA uses TKIP (Temporal Key Integrity Protocol) to provide strong data encryption.

- WPA2 uses Advanced Encryption Standard (AES), also known as Rijndael, for enhanced data encryption. This standard meets the Federal Information Processing Standard 140-2 requirement of many government agencies.

Note

The same encryption option must be used on all wireless devices on the network, such as access points, routers, network adapters, print servers, and the like. Be sure to pick the option that is supported by all the devices. If a handful of devices support only WEP and cannot be upgraded to support higher levels of security, consider removing or replacing those devices.

Configuring a Wireless Adapter

Wireless adapters are now included in the hardware of most laptops. For desktops and laptops that do not come equipped with wireless cards, PCI cards are available for desktops and PC cards are available for laptops. Manufacturers are also producing network adapters that can be connected to a desktop or a laptop via a USB cable. As with most USB devices, these adapters can come in either USB 1.0 or 2.0 specifications. USB 1.0 is the older, slower USB specification. USB 2.0 is the newer, faster USB specification. Wireless devices that are USB 2.0 compatible should be connected to USB 2.0 compatible ports for proper operation.

Windows Vista may not recognize many wireless USB devices, so when you install these devices be sure to have the installation disk handy. The best bet is to run the included installation CD prior to installing the USB wireless device.

After the installation is completed, the wireless device configuration can be completed. Typically, the installation wizard will provide guidance through this process. During the process, administrators will need to provide the name of the wireless network to connect to and the mode in which the device will run. The two modes the device can run in are

- **Ad Hoc**—Ad hoc mode allows the wireless device to be configured to communicate directly to computers with other wireless devices.

- **Infrastructure**—Infrastructure mode allows the wireless device to be configured for use on a wireless network. In this mode, the wireless device connects to an access point rather than directly to another computer.

After specifying the adapter's mode of operation, administrators may need to provide the security encryption key. If WEP is used, the key must be manually entered. If WPA or WPA2 is used, most likely a smart card or certificate will used to supply the encryption key.

Working with Wireless Connections and Networks

When the device is properly installed, users can establish a connection to any available wireless network. Similar to a wired NIC that displays a local area connection, wireless NICs display a connection as a public network, private network, or a domain network. Computers that have both a wired and wireless connection may have two active connections—one to the wired network and one to the wireless network.

The Network and Sharing Center, shown in Figure 10.7, provides information about the network and the connection. Here you can determine the names of the wireless network by looking at the parentheses in the Connector type field, the strength of the wireless connection (one bar is poor, five bars is excellent), and whether a connection is disconnected (red X in a link means disconnected).

If you click the View Status link, a status dialog box displays information about the status of the connection, such as IPv4 and IPv6 connectivity, media state, wireless network SSID, duration of the connection, speed of the connection, signal quality, and activity of the connection, as shown in Figure 10.8.

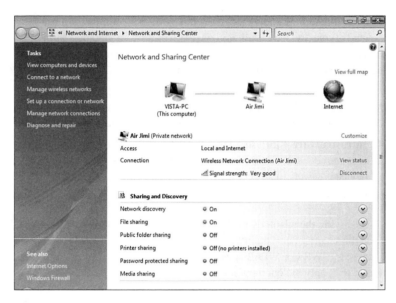

FIGURE 10.7
Viewing wireless connections and network information.

FIGURE 10.8
Viewing Wireless Network Connection Status.

Wireless connections have configurable properties. As with LAN connections, you can set the following properties for wireless connections:

- **Networking options for services, protocols, and clients**—In the wireless status page, click Properties and then click Uninstall or Install as appropriate for the desired configuration.

- **Configure network settings such as DHCP, static IP, dynamic IP addressing for TCP/IP versions v4 and v6**—In the wireless status page, click Properties and then double-click Internet Protocol Version 6 (TCP/IPv6) or Internet Protocol Version 4 (TCP/IPv4).

- **Disable or diagnose wireless connections**—In the Status dialog page, click Disable or Diagnose, as appropriate.

Connecting to Wireless Networks

Computers that have wireless adapters can establish connections with any wireless network that is broadcasting and is within range of the computer. In Windows Vista, administrators can configure any necessary settings that are required for authentication, encryption, and communication, as needed. If a new connection is required, administrators can use the following steps:

1. Click Start and then Network to display the Network Explorer page. In the Network Explorer page, click Network and Sharing Center in the toolbar.

2. Click Set Up a Connection or Network in Network and Sharing Center to start the setup wizard.

3. Select Manually Connect to a Wireless Network and then click Next.

4. Enter the appropriate network information for the wireless connection to be added. In the Network Name field, enter the network name. This is also known as the network SSID (Service Set Identifier).

5. Use the Security Type drop-down list to select the type of wireless security being used.

6. When WEP or WPA-Personal is selected, a security password or key must be entered in the Security Key/Passphrase field.

7. Click Next to connect to the wireless network.

In many cases, an existing wireless connection has already been created. Use the following steps to establish a connection to the existing connection:

1. Click Start and then Network to display the Network Explorer page. In the Network Explorer page, click Network and Sharing Center in the toolbar.

2. Click Connect to a Network in Network and Sharing Center.

3. Select the network to connect to. As the mouse moves over an entry, the network name, signal strength, and other wireless info will be displayed.

4. Click Connect to establish a connection to the wireless network. If desired, click Disconnect to drop the connection. Confirm the disconnection by clicking Disconnect again.

Managing Wireless Networks

Administrators can manage wireless connections using Manage Wireless Networks in Windows Vista. In Manage Wireless Networks, administrators can view, add, delete, or modify the wireless connections. You can access the tool by using the following steps:

1. Click Start and then Network to display the Network Explorer page. In the Network Explorer page, click Network and Sharing Center in the toolbar.

2. Click Manage Wireless Networks in Network and Sharing Center.

Manage Wireless Networks displays the wireless networks in the order in which the computer attempts to establish a connection to the available networks. The network listed at the top of the list is tried before any others in the list. If the first wireless network in the list fails to connect, the next wireless network is tried. This occurs until either a connection is established or all wireless networks have been polled and no connection has been established.

Administrators may want to change the preference order of a wireless network. This is done by clicking the appropriate network and then using the Move Up or Move Down buttons to set the wireless network in the appropriate connection order.

As needed wireless networks can be added or removed from the list. To add a wireless network, click Add. This creates a new wireless network and adds it to the list. Removing a network is accomplished by highlighting the appropriate network and then clicking Remove. This deletes and removes the wireless network from the wireless network list.

Summary

Mobile computers are the fastest growing computer category. Consumer and business users are replacing their desktop computers with equally powerful mobile ones. In some vertical markets, palmtops or touchscreen PCs are even replacing laptops.

Often, mobile computers are employed in a variety of different situations. A single mobile PC will switch between various nonwired configurations—on battery power, with no network, or with a wireless connection—and wired configurations—plugged into a wall socket and physical network or in a docking station.

With an increasing number of mobile and at-home employees, it becomes more difficult to maintain network security and the confidentiality of corporate information. Windows Vista provides the latest wireless security protocols and improved layers of protection that safeguard the corporate network while providing secure remote access to documents and programs.

PART IV

Backup and Recovery of Information

IN THIS PART

CHAPTER 11

Using Shadow Copy to Recover Lost or Damaged Files

What Is Shadow Copy?

Shadow Copy is a feature that was made available with Windows Server 2003. In a client/server environment, administrators were able to configure the Volume Shadow Copy Service to make copies of a shared folder at specified points in time, which were then stored on the server. Users were able to access these copies and restore the previous version of a document without administrator intervention. Windows Vista provides this functionality on the client computer, without the need of a domain environment, and it is enabled by default.

> **Note**
>
> Microsoft defines Shadow Copy as a read-only point-in-time replica of an original document. That concept is easy enough to understand; what should be clarified is that Shadow Copy is not another Undo command where you can roll back multiple edits made to a document in sequential fashion. It is a mechanism that allows you to go back in time to a previous version of a document that is known to be good when the snapshot was taken.

Benefits of Shadow Copy

In the past, one of the biggest concerns for users and IT groups was that data contained on a desktop or laptop was largely unprotected against loss of data. Although users could delete files and still recover them from the Recycle Bin, they had no protection against mistakes made in documents that were saved. Shadow Copy helps protect in these situations by allowing the user to open a previous copy of a file without having to get the IT group involved. This is a great boon to IT departments because users are able to "self-service" their restores.

It is important for administrators to be aware that the Shadow Copy functions of Vista do not have the same level of granularity as Windows Server 2003. In Windows Server 2003, you can modify the schedule of when Shadow Copies are made and configure the amount and location of the space that will hold the Shadow Copies. In Vista, you are limited to the default schedule and configuration.

How Does Shadow Copy Work?

Shadow Copy works in conjunction with another feature new in Vista, called System Restore. This feature will be discussed in more detail in its own chapter. The reason it is relevant here is that Shadow Copy is a part of the System Restore, which is enabled by default, and they both begin backing up their respective data (based on a schedule) soon after the operating system is installed.

The difference is that Shadow Copy targets documents and cannot create snapshots of system folders; this is the area that System Restore takes care of.

> **Note**
>
> Shadow Copy does not create a previous version of a file each time it changes. If a document has changed since the last restore point, this triggers a Previous Version save when the scheduled snapshot takes place.

What Can Shadow Copy Protect?

With Microsoft Vista, reliability of data protection has been enhanced at multiple levels. Shadow Copy focuses specifically on creating point-in-time copies of documents, directories, and volumes on the client computer. The concept is that multiple versions of files and directories are maintained so that a user can choose to read or restore the previous versions. This can be very helpful in situations where users are not in the habit of maintaining version control on their documents. Imagine that a user begins working on a PowerPoint document that the user has been developing all week. The user make a few changes and saves the file, only to discover that he or she managed to accidentally overwrite several existing slides. In a perfect world, the user would have been maintaining several local versions of the file to protect against exactly this situation, but in the real world, this rarely happens. In the case of Shadow Copy, the user could open a previous version of the PowerPoint presentation and copy it back into another location. Now the user would be able to open the secondary copy, cut the needed slides, and paste them back into the latest copy of the document.

Shadow Copy does not restore system files, which are the files used by Windows to run the operating system.

File-Level Protection

Shadow Copy can be used to revert to a previous version of a specific file or document. It can also be used to recover a document that was recently deleted; the only caveat is that you need to remember the directory where the document was stored before it was deleted. This is because Shadow Copy has to restore the entire directory, and then you can select the specific document you want to recover.

Directory-Level Protection

Shadow Copy can recover an entire directory, or it can be used to access a deleted document that was located in the directory. This is covered in the section, "Recovering Deleted Directories."

Volume-Level Protection

At the volume level, Shadow Copy begins to have more limited capabilities. At this level, you can restore an entire volume, replacing all files contained within the volume, but you cannot select a single directory or file.

Enabling Shadow Copy

One of the best things about Shadow Copy is that it doesn't require any administrator intervention to start. Shadow Copy is part of the System Restore feature that is activated by default when Vista is installed.

Soon after the operating system is installed, Shadow Copy makes copies of files that have changed since the last restore point created by System Restore. Restore points are created automatically as follows:

- Once every 24 hours unless the PC is turned off. In that case, the restore point is created when your PC is started.

- Before new software is installed. This includes new programs, device driver updates, and Windows Updates.

- Before a backup is made using Windows Backup.

- System Restore points can also be created manually; this is addressed in Chapter 14, "Microsoft Vista System Restore."

Enable Shadow Copy on an External Disk

If you have an external disk connected to your PC that you want to protect, it is as easy as checking a box. Remember that because Shadow Copy works in conjunction with System Restore, all you need to do is include the external disk in the System Restore set, as shown in these steps:

1. From the Control Panel, click System and Maintenance.

2. Click System.

3. In the left pane of the System window, click System Protection, as shown in Figure 11.1.

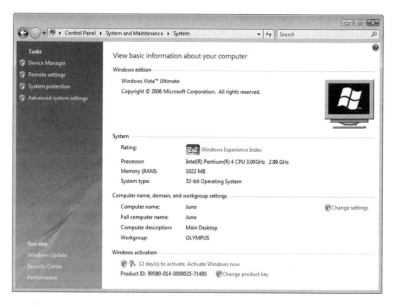

FIGURE 11.1
System window.

4. In the Automatic Restore Points list, select the drives you want to include in the System Restore, as shown in Figure 11.2.

5. Click OK to include the external drive in the System Restore.

FIGURE 11.2
Select drives to include in System Restore.

Configuring Shadow Copy

As previously discussed, Shadow Copy really doesn't require any intervention or configuration. The items that you need to taken into consideration are how much disk space you want to allocate on your local drive to store the Shadow Copies and how long you want to keep them around.

Allocating Disk Space for Shadow Copies

Although Shadow Copy is very efficient because it copies only files that have been changed since the last Restore Point was created, you want to be aware of the percentage of the volume it uses. By default, the system reserves 15% of *each volume* that has Previous Versions enabled. This means that if in addition to your PC hard drive, you use an external drive and have selected to enable System Restore on it, 15% of this drive is also be reserved for Shadow Copies.

Storing Copies on the Same Drive

One of the benefits of using Vista is having the capability to snapshot your files and directories onto your local PC. This eliminates the need for a domain environment to use the Shadow Copy feature. An additional consideration is that even if you do operate in a domain environment, you can save space on the shared drives by storing files locally. The downside to that is that if you lose your local drive, your back files are also lost.

Storing Copies on Separate Drives

If you are in a domain environment, you can use Windows 2003 Server to set up Volume Shadow Copy Services (VSS) and save the Previous Version to a shared drive on the server. The same self-service mechanism to access Previous Versions can be implemented, allowing the users to restore documents without administrator intervention.

Maintaining Enough Versions

For System Restore and Shadow Copy to work, you need at least 300 megabytes (MB) of free space on each hard disk that has System Protection turned on. As the amount of space fills up with restore points, System Restore deletes older restore points to make room for new ones. In addition, System Restore will not run on disks smaller than 1 gigabyte (GB). So the question really comes down to how much space you want to allocate for storing the Previous Versions.

Disk Cleanup

A good way to keep the number of files under control is to use Disk Cleanup. You can use this utility to reduce the number of unnecessary files on your hard disk, improving system performance. It removes temporary files, empties the Recycle Bin, and removes a variety of system files and other items that you no longer need. A nice feature is that it goes though a specified volume and then lets you pick and choose which files you want to delete.

To perform a disk cleanup, follow these steps:

1. From the Start menu, go to All Programs, Accessories, System Tools.

2. Click Disk Cleanup.

3. In the Disk Cleanup dialog box, select the disk you want to clean up, as shown in Figure 11.3.

FIGURE 11.3
Selecting drives to clean up.

4. In this window, you can view the files that are slated to be deleted, as shown in Figure 11.4. Determine whether they need to be deleted and click OK.

5. Click Delete Files to confirm that you want to delete the files.

FIGURE 11.4
Viewing files to be deleted.

> **Caution**
>
> If you happen to be one of the techies who likes (or needs) to have a PC
> that dual boots between XP and Vista, be aware that starting up in Windows
> XP will delete all your Shadow Copies, all your Restore Points, and all but
> the most recent of your Complete PC Backups. The workaround is to the
> turn off the hard drive that contains the multiple backup files before start-
> ing up in XP.

Recovering Items with Shadow Copy

Recovering items with Shadow Copy is very straightforward. The process is
wizard driven and very easy to follow. Steps for various scenarios are
outlined next.

When rolling back to a previous version, you will find three different options:

- **Open**—Use this option to open the document or directory and
  compare the content to determine whether it is the correct version.

- **Copy**—By copying the document or directory to another location, you
  can decide whether you want to restore all or just parts of the content.

- **Restore**—This option rolls back the file or directory to its previous
  version in full. Use this option only if you are completely sure you
  don't want any part of the current file. After you have restored using
  this option, there is no Undo.

Restoring Previous Versions of Files

This is the scenario where you have just saved changes to a document and
realize you really wanted to keep it as it was. To restore an older version of
the file, follow these steps:

1. Go to the directory where the file is located and right-click the file, as
   shown in Figure 11.5.

2. Click the Previous Versions tab.

3. Select which option you want to use to restore the file, as shown in
   Figure 11.6.

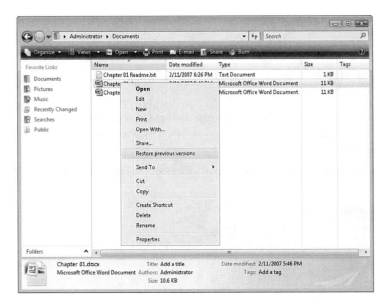

FIGURE 11.5
Right-clicking the file to restore a previous version.

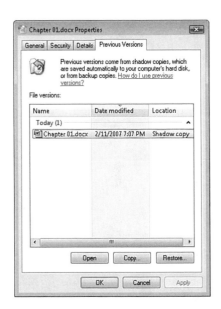

FIGURE 11.6
The Previous Versions tab.

Recovering Deleted Files

In this scenario, you just realized that you have (or someone else has) deleted an entire document! To restore the deleted file, follow these steps:

1. Go to the directory where the file was located and right-click within the Content pane of the window.

2. Select Properties, which pops up the dialog shown in Figure 11.7, and in the Documents Properties window, select the Previous Versions tab, as shown in Figure 11.8.

3. Select which option you want to use to restore the directory.

FIGURE 11.7
Documents Properties dialog.

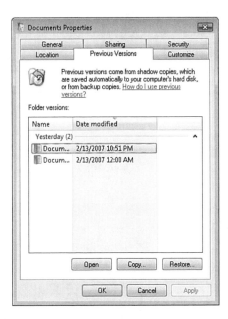

FIGURE 11.8
Previous Versions tab.

Recovering Deleted Directories

This is similar to the previous scenario where you find that an entire directory has been mistakenly deleted. To recover deleted directories, follow these
steps:

1. Go to the Volume or drive where the directory was located and right-
   click the drive within the Folders pane of the window, as shown in
   Figure 11.9.

2. Select the Open option, as shown in Figure 11.10.

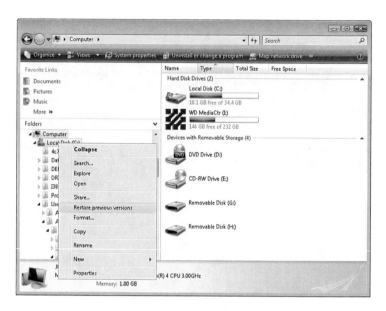

FIGURE 11.9
Right-clicking within the Folders pane.

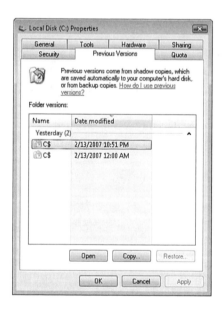

FIGURE 11.10
Selecting Open to bring up the list of directories.

3. Right-click the directory you want to restore and select Copy, as shown in Figure 11.11.

4. Copy the directory to the desired location.

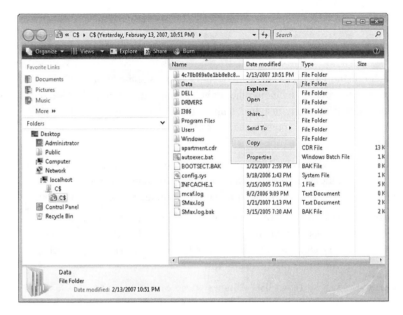

FIGURE 11.11
Selecting Copy to restore a directory.

Troubleshooting Shadow Copy

Occasionally you might run into situations where Shadow Copy is not running properly, or you may want to make changes to the default behaviors of Shadow Copy. Vista provides a utility called vssadmin.exe that allows a local administrator to query and modify Shadow Copy.

Vssadmin.exe offers several options:

- List Providers
- List Shadows
- List ShadowStorage
- List Volumes
- List Writers
- Resize ShadowStorage

Remember, to run `vssadmin.exe`, you must be running with elevated privileges. The easiest way to do this is to follow these steps:

1. Click Start.
2. Click All Programs.
3. Click Accessories.
4. Right-click Command Prompt and choose Run as Administrator.

The command `vssadmin list providers` outputs some basic information on the VSS provider, including the provider name and, more important, the version that is currently installed. This can be helpful when trying to determine why one system might be acting differently from the rest of your environment.

The command `vssadmin list shadows` displays the contents of the Shadow Copy sets on the local system. This includes information on the original volume, Shadow Copy volume, originating machine, and service machine.

`Vssadmin list shadowstorage` displays associate information for the volumes as well as showing the Maximum, Allocated, and Used Shadow Copy Storage space. This information can be helpful when trying to determine why a volume is unexpectedly full.

`Vssadmin list volumes` lists volumes where Shadow Copy is enabled. Although this information can be determined from the user interface, this command-line query can be useful when paired with a logon script to update client Shadow Copy information to a central location where administrators can audit this information to ensure that all Vista clients are properly protecting their local data.

`Vssadmin list writers` outputs information about the various Shadow Copy writers that are active on the system. Most important, it shows the current state of the writer as well as what the last error (if any) was.

`Vssadmin resize shadowstorage` allows a local administrator to alter the behavior of the Shadow Copy service. Various parameters can be altered, including the following:

- Location of the Shadow Copy
- Space allocated to store Shadow Copies

The syntax of this command is

```
Vssadmin resize shadowstorage /for=[drive letter]
➥/on=[location of shadowcopies] /maxsize=[size]
```

For example, if a system had multiple hard drives, you might run the following commands:

```
Vssadmin resize shadowstorage /for=c: /on=e: /maxsize=800MB
Vssadmin resize shadowstorage /for=d: /on=e: /maxsize=800MB
Vssadmin resize shadowstorage /for=e: /on=e: /maxsize=1TB
```

Acceptable suffixes for "MaxSize" include KB, MB, GB, TB, PB, and EB. For those not familiar with PB or EB, they refer to Petabyte and Exabyte, respectively. A Petabyte is 1024 Terabytes and an Exabyte is 1024 Petabytes. As you can see, Vista is looking pretty far forward in the areas of storage.

A clever administrator might wonder why, in the example, the Shadow Copies were all located on the E: drive. This is because a small amount of performance overhead goes along with maintaining multiple Shadow Copies. By placing them on another drive, the overall performance of the original disk is not compromised.

Summary

With Windows Vista, Microsoft has taken a great tool from the client/server environment, extended and improved its functionality, and made it available to the PC platform. When used in conjunction with the remaining backup and recovery tools (which are addressed in Chapters 12, 13, and 14), Shadow Copy can make the day to day recovery of data a minor task.

In closing, some of the best practices you should remember when working with Shadow Copies are

- **Don't use the Restore option as your first choice when recovering a document**—Open the document to compare the content or copy it to another location to avoid confusing the two sets of data.

- **Run the Disk Cleanup utility on a regular basis**—This helps keep the number of previous versions low and proactively save you disk space.

- **Remember to enable System Restore on any external disks you may have attached to your PC**—This enables Shadow Copy by default and ensures that all your files and directories are recoverable.

CHAPTER 12

Backing Up and Recovering Windows Vista Information

How Windows Vista Protects Your System

One of the biggest concerns that computer users face is the potential for the loss of data. Data can be lost through many ways, ranging from the accidental deletion to the corruption of files to a failure of the hard disk. Data loss isn't limited to unique files created by the users; you can be equally impacted by the loss of files that are needed by the operating system to keep the system running normally. Executables for the operating system, dynamic link libraries, hardware drivers, and application files are all critical parts of the computers that business users depend on every day. Keeping these files safe is a critical step in keeping users productive. Vista, like other versions of Windows, has provided many new mechanisms to maintain the integrity of data as well as to provide the capability to back up portions of the system so that they can be restored to a particular point in time. This is especially helpful to protect the system from changes that end up having a negative impact. Unstable updates, incorrect drivers, or even computer viruses can place a system into an unusual state. Vista provides ways for users to return the system to a "known good" state from before the change that caused the problems. This chapter explores and explains these options and gives both users and administrators suggestions about how to properly take advantage of Vista to protect the end-user workstations and help maintain their productivity.

Introducing Windows Vista Data-Protection Methods

Windows Vista does many things in the background to protect the data on the system. This is in addition to the user-configurable methods of data protection. Vista expands on the concept of Windows File Protection, which was available in Windows XP, with Windows Resource Protection. Vista has simplified the process of replacing detrimental drivers with the process of Driver Rollback and still gives users an environment where older data can be restored through Safe Mode. These background processes, when coupled with the user-configurable methods of data protection, work to make it even easier for users to recover data and restore the condition of their systems to keep them running properly.

Windows Resource Protection (WRP)

Vista introduces a new file-protection system called Windows Resource Protection (WRP). This is the next evolution of the Windows File Protection functions that were introduced in Windows 2000 and Windows XP. The purpose of WRP is to ensure that particular files and Registry key locations cannot be overwritten by an installer package. In this way, Vista is able to prevent another application from overwriting key bits of data that Vista needs in order to operate. This protects the user not only from malicious code but from poorly written applications as well.

More specifically, when an application attempts to issue an InstallFiles action, the installer will contact WRP to check whether a particular file or Registry key is protected. If it is, the file will be skipped and the installer will enter a warning in the application log. The remainder of the application installation will continue without generating any errors.

> **Note**
>
> It is very possible that the protected file will not be compatible with the application that is being installed. In this case, it is usually necessary to update the operating system. Applications that require updates to protected files are usually coordinated through Microsoft so that the protected file that needs to be updated can be fully evaluated by Microsoft before becoming available as an updated component. This helps to ensure the overall stability of the operating system.

One of the more interesting behaviors of WRP is that if an administrator were to delete a protected file from the operating system, it would reappear within a few seconds. This mechanism is meant to prevent well-meaning administrators from accidentally deleting a file that is needed by Vista to operate properly. If you browse to the \Windows\Winsxs\backup directory, you would find a list of nearly 2,000 files that are being protected by WRP.

Caution

WRP, although very helpful and well meaning, isn't magic. If an account with administrator-level access were to take ownership of a protected file, set the appropriate access control entry to prevent the system from writing to that location, and delete the file, the file won't be regenerated by the system. Although this isn't likely to be done by an administrator, it could potentially be done by a worm or virus.

Safe Mode

Not unlike previous versions of Windows, Vista has retained the concept of Safe Mode. Safe Mode is an option that is often used during troubleshooting and that allows a user to boot Vista so that only a very limited set of drivers and applications are loaded. More specifically, only the files and drivers necessary to run Windows itself are loaded. This allows the user the ability to uninstall new applications or drivers that may have been the cause of a failed load of Vista. When a system fails to boot normally into Vista, Safe Mode is usually the first thing that an administrator will try to boot into to determine the cause of the problem. To boot into Safe Mode, use the following steps:

1. Power on the computer.

2. Prior to the appearance of the Windows logo, press F8 on the keyboard.

3. When the Advanced Boot Options screen appears, use the arrow keys on the keyboard to select the Safe Mode you want to use and press Enter.

4. Log on to the system with an administrative-level account.

When booting into Safe Mode, you will have several options, including

- Safe Mode
- Safe Mode with Networking
- Safe Mode with Command Prompt

When troubleshooting a boot problem, Safe Mode with Networking can be very helpful because you are still able to access the Internet to download drivers or applications. If the network subsystem is suspected as the cause for the boot problems, trying both Safe Mode and Safe Mode with Networking may quickly narrow the list of suspects.

Safe Mode with Command Prompt can be useful when you already know which troubleshooting tools you plan to use to diagnose the system. For more information on troubleshooting Vista boot issues, see Chapter 17, "Troubleshooting Windows Vista."

Driver Rollback

One of the most common problems with computers is the replacement of an existing driver with one that ends up causing problems. In the past, you would have to uninstall the device, delete the drivers, reboot, let the system rediscover the device, and point the system to the previous version of the driver. This process is greatly simplified in Vista through the concept of Driver Rollback.

To roll back to a previous version of a driver, perform these steps:

1. Click Start.
2. Click All Programs.
3. Click Administrative Tools.

Note

If Administrative Tools isn't present in the Start menu, it can be enabled by clicking Customize in the Start menu properties.

---

4. Click Computer Management.
5. When prompted by User Account Control, click Continue.
6. Expand System Tools and click Device Manager, as shown in Figure 12.1.
7. Browse to the device for which you need to roll back the driver.
8. Right-click the device and choose Properties.
9. Click the Driver tab, as shown in Figure 12.2.
10. Click Roll Back Driver.

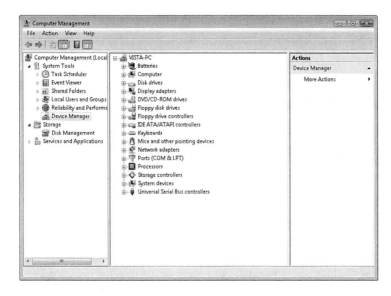

FIGURE 12.1
Viewing the Device Manager.

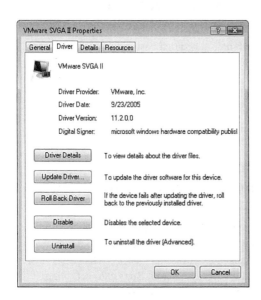

FIGURE 12.2
Viewing the Drivers tab.

11. When prompted for confirmation of the roll back action, click Yes.

12. Click Close when the process is completed. This may trigger a reboot depending on the driver that was replaced.

Automatic Backups

The most common method of protecting data on a workstation is the classic backup. A backup is a copy of important data that is placed in a physically separate location so that if the original data is lost through disk failure or accidental deletion, the copy of the data can be restored back to the original location. In the past, this type of backup was usually done only on file servers, and the data was usually copied to magnetic tape. Today the practice of workstation backup has become much more common. With the proliferation of DVD burners and external hard drives, it is almost a standard process for users to back up their important data on a regular basis. The classic problem with this type of backup is that users simply forget to do it. Vista has introduced tools to make it easy for users or administrators to set up backup jobs that will run on a regular schedule.

How to Set Up an Automatic Backup

One of the most useful abilities in the Vista backup function is the ability to automatically back up the system on a scheduled basis. Administrators can configure an automatic backup with the following steps:

1. Click Start.

2. Click All Programs.

3. Click Accessories.

4. Click System Tools.

5. Click Backup Status and Configuration (see Figure 12.3).

6. Click Setup Automatic File Backup. When prompted by User Account Control, click Continue.

7. If the backup will be placed on a local system device, click the option button for On a Hard Disk, CD, or DVD and use the drop-down menu to select the device. If the backup will go on a network location, click the option button for On a Network and click Browse to get to the location you want to use for the backup. Click Next.

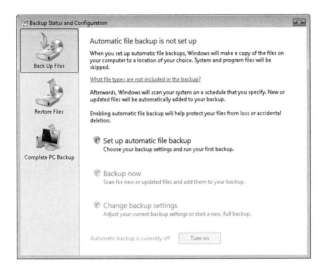

FIGURE 12.3
Backup Status and Configuration window.

8. Check the boxes next to all drives that you want to back up (see
   Figure 12.4). Click Next.

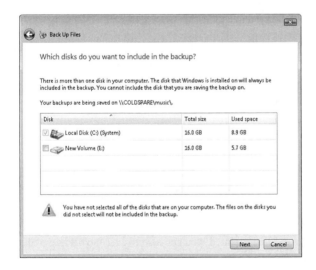

FIGURE 12.4
Selecting drives to back up.

9. Select the types of files you want to back up (see Figure 12.5). Click Next.

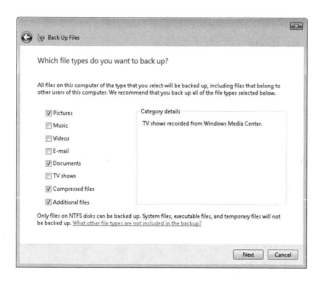

FIGURE 12.5
Selecting file types to back up.

10. Choose the schedule of when and how often the backup should occur.

11. Click Save Settings and Start Backup.

12. The Backup status is shown as well as an indication that Automatic Backup is currently enabled.

13. Close the Backup Status and Configuration page.

14. A balloon notification will inform you when the backup is completed.

If you check the destination location of the backup, you'll find a folder with the same name as the PC that was backed up. Inside this folder is a Backup Set folder named with the time at which the backup occurred. Inside this folder is a catalog of the backup as well as a compressed file that contains the files that were backed up.

If you are more command-line oriented, you can also trigger the backup with the following command:

```
C:\Windows\System32\wbadmin.exe start backup
➥ -backuptarget:[UNCPath] -include:[source]
```

For example:

```
C:\Windows\System32\wbadmin.exe start backup
➥ -backuptarget:\\fileserver\hddbackups\pc\ -include:c:
```

The advantage to triggering the backup in this manner is that you can place the command into a batch file and schedule the batch job to run on a recurring basis. Although at first glance this may seem to only mimic the functionality of the GUI, the advantage is that this method can be deployed in a remote fashion. The script can be scheduled on the workstation via logon script or Group Policy Object.

For example, a logon script called by a Group Policy could be as simple as

```
AT 23:00 /every:M,F "\\companyabc.com\workstation backup.bat"
```

In this example

AT calls the Task Scheduler 1.0 that is still available in Vista.

23:00 is the time value that simply means "11 p.m." Any 24-hour clock value is valid here.

/every tells the scheduler that the event will be recurring. Acceptable values here include days of the week such as M, T, W, TH, F, S, SU, or dates of the month such as 1, 15, 31.

The final value in the string is the command that is to be initiated on the schedule given. In this case we've chosen to run a batch file called Workstation Backup.bat that is located in the scripts directory of all domain controllers (thus the \\domain prefix). This command can call local or remote commands.

Updating an Existing Backup Job

In the course of managing a Vista workstation, it is very likely that the requirements for the scheduled backups will change. The Backup Status and Configuration Wizard allows for modifications to previously created jobs. To update a job, follow these steps:

1. Click Start.

2. Click All Programs.

3. Click Accessories.

4. Click System Tools.

5. Click Backup Status and Configuration (see Figure 12.6).

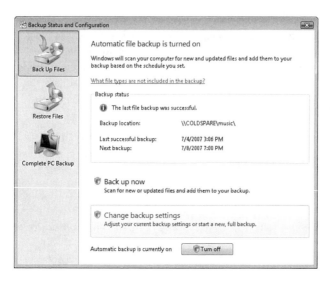

FIGURE 12.6
Backup Status and Configuration window.

6. Click Change Backup Settings. When prompted by User Account Control, click Continue.

7. If you need to change the destination location of the backup, do so now. Otherwise click Next.

8. Add or remove any new source locations that you want to include in the backup and click Next (see Figure 12.7).

9. Add or remove any new file types that you want to include in the backup and click Next (see Figure 12.8).

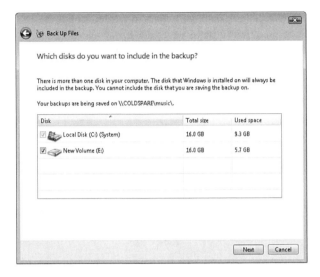

FIGURE 12.7
Selecting locations to include in the backup.

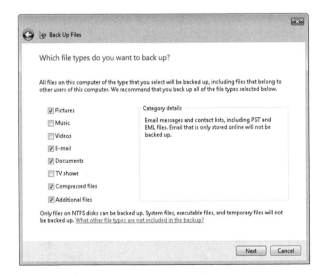

FIGURE 12.8
Selecting file types to include in the backup.

10. Modify the backup schedule (see Figure 12.9), if desired, and then click Save Settings and Exit. If items were added, consider checking the box to Create a New, Full Backup Now in Addition to Saving Settings.

The backup job is now modified.

FIGURE 12.9
Configuring the backup schedule.

Performing a Backup to Local PC

It is a fairly common practice to perform a local backup of files to protect against accidental deletion or modification. Although the Backup Status and Configuration Wizard is the newest and usually easiest way to create backups, it lacks the capability to back up files to the C: drive; thus it is a requirement to have a second location available to receive the backup. Although initially it might seem like an oversight to not be able to back up files to the local drive to protect against deletion or modification, the Shadow Copy functions already protect against this type of problem. For more information on Shadow Copy in Vista, see Chapter 11, "Using Shadow Copy to Recover Lost or Damaged Files."

Performing a Backup to External Drives or Removable Media

The most common scenario for backups for remote users will be a backup to either an external hard drive, usually connected via USB or FireWire, or to removable media such as a DVD-R. These backup targets are supported by the Backup Status and Configuration Wizard for both "one-time" and "recurring" backups. Administrators will quickly notice that neither tape devices nor USB flash drives are supported for backup targets in Vista.

To create a backup job that will utilize this type of media, perform the following steps:

1. Click Start.

2. Click All Programs.

3. Click Accessories.

4. Click System Tools.

5. Click Backup Status and Configuration.

6. Click Setup Automatic File Backup. When prompted by User Account Control, click Continue.

7. If the backup will be placed on a local system device, click the option button for On a Hard Disk, CD, or DVD, and use the drop-down menu to select the device. Click Next.

8. Check the boxes next to all drives that you want to back up. Click Next.

9. Select the types of files you want to back up. Click Next.

10. Choose the schedule of when and how often the backup should occur.

11. Click Save Settings and Start Backup.

12. The Backup status is shown as well as an indication that Automatic Backup is currently enabled.

13. Close the Backup Status and Configuration page.

14. A balloon notification will inform you when the backup is completed.

If the backup job is being stored on a DVD-R, the job may require more than one DVD-R disk to complete the backup job. If this is the case, when the first disk is filled, the backup wizard will prompt the user to insert another DVD-R disk to continue the backup.

Be sure that users place their backup device into a safe location when the backup has completed. Optimally, the backup device would be placed into a fireproof safe to protect the data against environmental dangers.

Performing a Backup to Network Location

For corporate-managed Vista workstations, it is probably most advantageous to perform backups to a network location. In this way, workstations can store their files on a file server which, in turn, can be backed up to tape for long-term storage. Then, workstations can still restore data even if that data is somewhat old. It is important to consider when and where backups will occur. Although a desktop can be easily backed up to a local file server, it might be a bad idea for a notebook to attempt to run a large backup when it is not in its local office. Because of bandwidth constraints, it is also a good idea to stagger workstation backups if possible. This is to say that administrators should aim to back up 20% of workstations each day of the week if weekly backups are what are called for. This will reduce the amount of bandwidth needed to support the backups.

To configure Vista to back up regularly to a network location, perform the following steps:

1. Click Start.

2. Click All Programs.

3. Click Accessories.

4. Click System Tools.

5. Click Backup Status and Configuration.

6. Click Setup Automatic File Backup. When prompted by User Account Control, click Continue.

7. Choose On a Network. Click Browse and navigate to the appropriate network location. Optionally, you can simply type in the UNC path. Click Next.

8. Check the boxes next to all drives that you want to back up. Click Next.

9. Select the types of files you want to back up. Click Next.

10. Choose the schedule of when and how often the backup should occur.

11. Click Save Settings and Start Backup.

12. The Backup status will be shown as well as an indication that Automatic Backup is currently enabled.

13. Close the Backup Status and Configuration page.

14. A balloon notification informs you when the backup is completed.

When preparing a network location to be the target of network backups, ensure that the appropriate NTFS rights are set and that the location is shared. Perform several test backups of various clients to get a feel for how large the backups are likely to be. This information will be critical in determining how much disk space to allocate for Vista workstation backups.

Backup Best Practices

When planning for and implementing backups for Vista workstations, many best practices exist that should be considered by administrators:

- Make sure the computer will be powered on during the scheduled backup.

  If client workstations are going to be backed up on a scheduled basis, the backup won't accomplish much if the system is offline when the backup job is scheduled to run. Consider either running backups during the lunch hour or train users to leave their computers on certain nights.

- Make sure that either the job fits onto a single DVD or that you are available to add DVDs.

  If a backup is going to be placed on a writable DVD, it is easiest if the backup will fit onto a single disk. If the backup is going to contain more information than will fit on a single DVD, be sure that the users are trained to replace the DVD with another to continue the backup job. If the backup will span multiple DVDs, it's helpful to have the user label them in case they need to perform a restore.

- If adding new drives or file types to a backup, kick off an immediate backup.

  If an administrator modifies a backup job to include additional source disks or new file types, it is helpful to initiate an immediate backup. The modification of an existing backup job includes the option to launch an immediate backup. Use this option whenever possible.

- Regularly test your ability to restore from a backup.

Note

As the old saying goes, backups are easy—it's restores that are the challenge. It is much less stressful to test the restore data when the data isn't critical. An emergency situation where data has been lost is the worst time to try to figure out how to restore a file or to discover that the backups haven't really been working. Administrators and remote users should get in the habit of regularly restoring data to ensure that their backup processes are working as intended. This will greatly reduce the chances of unwanted surprises.

- Revalidate systems when changes are made.

  One of the most classic problems with backups is when a significant change is made to a backup target and the process is not validated to ensure that it still works. Changes as simple as a service pack update, a hotfix, or a new application can result in the inability to restore information.

- Monitor the backed-up data.

  Many administrators take the backup process for granted and tend to not manage it actively. This can result in rampant consumption of disk space. Get in the habit of occasionally auditing the backup results and validate that systems being backed up are still in use. There is little benefit to backing up a system that isn't in use anymore.

- When possible, minimize the time it takes to perform a backup.

  The fastest way to back up a Vista system is to copy its data to another disk. This is significantly faster than a backup to tape, because the verification process doesn't take as long as the backup did. By keeping the backup times short, the users are less impacted by the backup, and it is much more likely to be completed before something happens to the computer. By spooling client backups to disk and later backing that disk up to tape, you can keep the backup windows small and can restore "current" data much more quickly. Backups to tape for longer-term archival can occur during the day because clients aren't affected by a backup of the "backup server."

How to Restore from a Backup

The real value in a backup of data is the capability to restore the data when it is needed. This may take the form of recovering a deleted file, or it could be an event as major as restoring the full contents of one computer onto another. As such, it is important to know how to restore data that was previously backed up. Windows Vista makes it easy to restore data that was backed up with its native Backup utility. To perform a restore, you will need several items:

- The object holding the backup data
- A computer running Vista
- Sufficient disk space to hold the restored data
- Permissions to read the backup (if placed on a network location)

To restore data with the Vista Backup and Restore tool, perform the following steps:

1. Attach to the backup file (that is, plug in the external drive or map to the network location).
2. Click Start.
3. Click All Programs.
4. Click Accessories.
5. Click System Tools.
6. Click Backup Status and Configuration.
7. In the left pane, click Restore Files.
8. Click Restore Files (see Figure 12.10).
9. Choose the type of backup to restore from and click Next (see Figure 12.11).
10. Use the Add Files and Add Folders buttons to select which items should be restored.
11. When the desired items have been added, click Next.

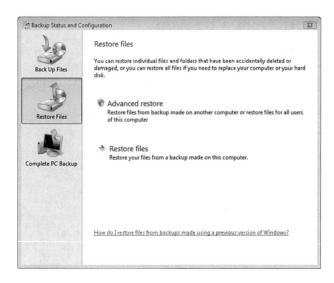

FIGURE 12.10
Restoring files.

FIGURE 12.11
Choosing a backup type.

12. When prompted, choose to either restore items to their original loca-
    tion or to an alternative location. Choose an alternative location when
    you do not want to lose the existing copy of the file. If you choose an
    alternative location, use Browse to navigate to the location where you
    want the restored file to go (see Figure 12.12). Click Start Restore.

13. When the files are successfully restored, click Finish.

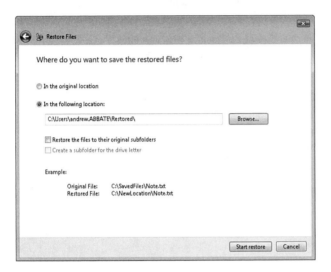

FIGURE 12.12
Choosing the restoring location.

The Advanced restore option can be chosen at step 9 with additional options.
You can choose to restore files from another computer's backup. This can be
helpful when extracting files for another user or for restoring files to a rebuilt
computer. To restore files in this manner, follow these steps:

1. Attach to the backup file (that is, plug in the external drive or map to
   the network location).

2. Click Start.

3. Click All Programs.

4. Click Accessories.

5. Click System Tools.

6. Right-click Backup Status and Configuration and choose Run as Administrator.

7. In the left pane, click Restore Files.

8. Click Advanced Restore.

9. Confirm the User Account Control prompt.

10. Click the option button to restore files from a backup made on a different computer. Click Next.

11. Browse to the location of the backup files and click Next.

12. Select the date to restore from and click Next (see Figure 12.13).

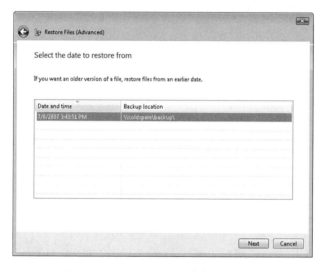

FIGURE 12.13
Choosing the date to restore from.

13. Use the Add buttons to select items to restore and click Next.

14. Choose a location for the file restore and click Start Restore.

15. When files have restored successfully, click Finish.

The capability to restore files from other computers can be very helpful when a user needs a file restored and needs assistance in doing so. A help desk employee could easily mount the user's backup file, restore the file needed, and email the file to the user.

Managing Backup Options via Group Policy

There may be situations in which an administrator doesn't want end users to be able to trigger or configure automatic backups on their Vista workstations. For example, computers that contain financial or human resources information may need to be handled differently in terms of local backups to ensure that information doesn't end up in uncontrolled locations. In these situations, it might be necessary to lock out some of the backup functions through Group Policy.

Vista provides many new Group Policy settings that can be accessed only from the Group Policy Management console (GPMC) on Vista or on Windows Server 2008. Running the GPMC on one of these systems exposes the new GPO settings. These settings include several that pertain to Vista backup.

To access these settings, an administrator will need to perform the following steps from a Vista or Windows Server 2008 system while logged in with a domain account that has sufficient rights to create or modify Group Policy Objects:

1. Click Start.
2. Click Run.

> **Note**
>
> If the Run option isn't in your Start menu, it can be added by customizing the Start menu. Alternately, pressing the Windows key and the R key at the same time will bring up the Run line.

3. Type **GPMC.MSC**.
4. Accept the User Account Control prompt.
5. Expand Forest and then Domain to reach the domain housing the Vista workstations that will be managed.
6. Click Group Policy Objects.
7. Right-click Group Policy Objects and choose New.
8. Enter a name for the new GPO and click OK.
9. Right-click the new GPO in the right pane and select Edit (see Figure 12.14).

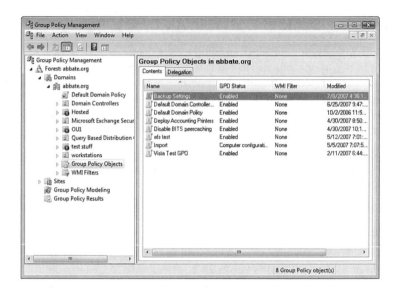

FIGURE 12.14
Editing the GPO.

10. In the GPO Editor, expand Computer Configuration.

11. Expand Administrative Templates.

12. Expand Windows Components.

13. Expand Backup.

14. Click Client.

15. Set client-based backup settings as desired (see Figure 12.15).

16. When finished, close the Group Policy Editor.

17. Link the GPO to the desired containers and close the GPMC.

By controlling backup settings through Group Policy, an administrator is able
to limit how a system can be backed up. For more information on managing
Vista workstations with Group Policy, refer to Chapters 22 and 23.

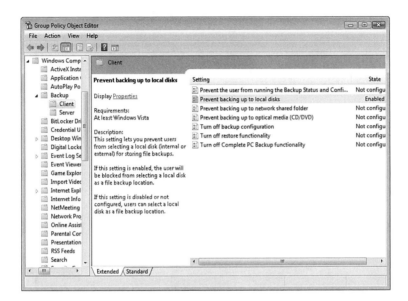

FIGURE 12.15
Seting the client-based backup settings.

Summary

As you've seen in this chapter, the protection of critical workstation files
continues to be a high priority for both users and administrators. Windows
Vista has continued the trend of Windows desktop products and has further
evolved the functions and utilities that serve to protect this critical data.
Administrators should take advantage of these functions whenever available
to reduce the chances of data loss for users. Vista has done a great job of
empowering end users to handle their own recovery of files, thus freeing up
administrators to do other tasks.

Clever administrators should take advantage of Group Policy Objects or
simple scripting to ensure that Windows Vista workstations are properly
protected against potential data loss. By following the best practices
presented in this chapter, administrators can all but eliminate the fear of data
loss among their end users.

CHAPTER 13

Using the Complete PC Backup Utility

What Is Complete PC Backup Utility?

The Complete PC Backup Utility is a new utility that ships with
Windows Vista Business, Ultimate, and Enterprise editions that
allows the user to initiate an image-level backup that contains all
information contained on the system disk. Unlike the backup and
restore functionality described in other chapters of this book, this
type of backup allows you to restore an entire system to a new
hard drive or even an entirely new computer. This style of backup
is meant to be used as a form of disaster recovery where a major
corruption or even a hardware failure could be recovered from.
Previously only available in server operating systems or from
third-party software providers, this functionality is now available
natively in Vista.

Recommended Uses for Complete
PC Backup

Although the concept of an image style "bare metal restore"
backup may be familiar to administrators who have used
Automated System Recovery (ASR), it is nonetheless a relatively
new concept for the desktop. As such, it is useful to talk about
situations where Complete PC Backup should be used.

Two of the largest challenges in supporting a computing environment are remote office users who do not have local IT support and
traveling users who are often out of the office for extended periods
of time. The biggest fear among these users is the possibility of a
total system failure. Traditionally, if their computers experience a

major failure, they are going to lose data and therefore productivity. Although some users are fairly good about backing up the data they work with, they invariably forget to back up some files, or they are unaware of important directories that need to be backed up. Complete PC Backup shines in this area because it's a foolproof backup in that it backs up all data on a system and can quickly and easily restore a system to a function state based on when it was last run.

There are two schools of thought on how best to use Complete PC Backup:

- Initiate a new Complete PC Backup when major changes are made to a system.

- Plan regularly scheduled occurrences of Complete PC Backup, such as every Friday afternoon.

The first school of thought works under the assumption that day-to-day files are being backed up with the normal backup functionality of Vista, such as the Volume Shadow Copy or the backup files functionality found in the Control Panel. If the user were to make a major change to the system, such as the installation of a new application or a new hardware device, the user would first initiate a Complete PC Backup so that if anything went wrong with the installation, the user would have a "known good" point in time to which to restore. To maximize the recoverability of this style of backup, it would be optimal to store the backup image on a device other than the local computer. This concept will be covered later in this chapter.

The second school of thought seeks to reduce the dependency on the user to remember to create a backup before major changes. This methodology also leverages existing file backup processes storing data in another location to ensure that if a user has to roll back several days, they won't lose any data. This situation could occur if a major system error occurred several days after a scheduled Complete PC backup. The primary advantage to this school of thought is that the dependency on the user's memory of running the utility is eliminated. As the saying goes, any method of protecting a system that is dependent on people following instructions is ultimately unreliable.

Configuring Complete PC Backup

To take advantage of the new Complete PC Backup functionality, it is necessary to perform a few tasks to be able to use the backup and restore features.

Create a System Image

The first step in leveraging Complete PC backup is to create a backup of the system you want to protect. This can be done with the following steps:

1. Click Start.

2. Click Control Panel

3. Under System and Maintenance, click Back Up Your Computer, as shown in Figure 13.1.

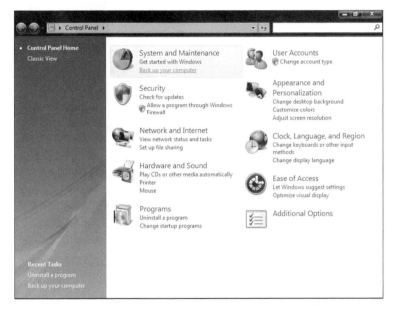

FIGURE 13.1
Choosing Back Up Your Computer.

4. Click Back Up Computer. User Account Control will ask you to confirm your action.

5. When Windows Complete PC Backup has finished looking for backup devices, select the location that will store the backup and click Next (see Figure 13.2). This must be a drive other than the system drive. It can be another partition on the system drive or it can be an external drive.

FIGURE 13.2
Choosing the location for your backup.

6. Choose which local disks should be backed up by placing a check in the box for the device. Click Next.

7. Confirm the settings and click Start Backup.

8. The backup will run through several stages:

   ■ Preparing to Create Backup

   ■ Backing Up Local Disk (C:)

   ■ Creating Shadow Copy on Backup Disk (F:)

   ■ Backup Completed Successfully

9. When the backup is completed, click Close.

Note

For comparison, a 72GB disk with 55GB of space filled took 45 minutes to run a Complete PC Backup to an external hard drive connected via USB 2.0.

Upon completion of the backup, the destination location will have a directory called WindowsImageBackup, and it will contain a subdirectory with the name of the host that was backed up. Below that will be the backup and catalog directories. The Backup directory contains the .vhd file that contains the actual image of the system. This directory can be seen in Figure 13.3.

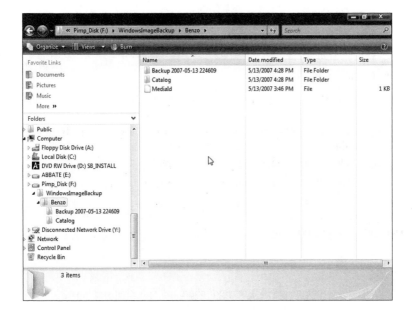

FIGURE 13.3
Location of the .vhd file.

> **Note**
>
> The backup image file is not compressed. You will need as much available space in the backup location as you have in use on the disks you plan to back up.

Using WBAdmin

In the previous section we saw how to use the User Interface to trigger a Complete PC Backup. In the case of wanting to schedule this event to occur regularly, it is simpler to perform the task from the command line. By using a command-line event, one can write a very simple batch file and place it into the task scheduler. In this way, the event can be scheduled to occur on a regular basis.

Vista provides a command-line interface into the Complete PC Backup process called wbadmin.exe. Wbadmin.exe provides several functions, including the following:

- Start Backup
- Stop Job
- Get Versions
- Get Items
- Get Status

The most common function will likely be wbadmin start backup. To run this, you will need to provide some parameters to tell the application what to back up and where to place the backup. For example:

```
WBADMIN START BACKUP -backuptarget:\\server1\backup -include:e:
```

In this example, we're creating a backup of the E: drive and placing the backup onto a network share.

Note

In order to run the backup to a network share, be sure that you have access to the network share. Also keep in mind that the backup may take longer to run depending on how fast the network connection is. For example, the 55GB of data that took 45 minutes to back up to a local USB 2.0 drive was equivalent to about 166Mb/sec, so running to a network location on 100Mb/sec ethernet would take longer. A 1Gb/sec network connection wouldn't run any slower than a local USB 2.0 backup.

By placing that command into a .bat file, you can schedule the .bat file to run regularly with the following steps:

1. Click Start.
2. Click All Programs.
3. Click Administrative Tools.
4. Click Task Scheduler. When prompted by User Access Control, click Continue.
5. In the right actions pane, click Create Task, as shown in Figure 13.4.

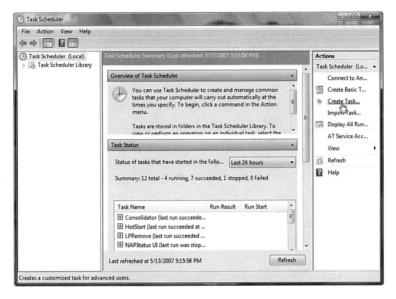

FIGURE 13.4
Creating a new task

6. Enter a name for the task.

7. Choose to run the task whether or not the user is logged in. Run the task with the highest privileges.

8. Enter a description for the task that explains what it's for, as shown in Figure 13.5.

9. From the Create Task window, click the Actions tab.

10. Click New.

11. Click Browse and browse to the location of the batch file, click Open, and then click OK.

12. Click the Triggers tab.

13. Click New.

14. Set the task to run weekly with a start time of noon and a recurrence on Fridays, as shown in Figure 13.6.

15. Click OK and you will be prompted for a password to go with the user account defined in the earlier step. Click OK.

16. Click OK again and the task will be scheduled.

FIGURE 13.5
Defining the task.

FIGURE 13.6
Configuring your schedule.

Restoring a System Image

As the saying goes, "Doing backups is easy; it's doing the restores that is a challenge."

Now that we know how to perform Complete PC Backups in Vista, it is helpful to know how to perform the restores. The first step in the restore process is making sure that a complete restore is actually the best plan of action. Unlike a file-level restore, a Complete PC Restore will completely overwrite the restored disks and return them to the state they were in when the backup was last performed. If the intent is just to restore files that were corrupted or deleted, there are better choices that will have less impact on the system. In the case of a failed hard drive or the total destruction of a computer, the Complete PC Restore is your best choice.

To trigger a system restore, perform the following steps:

1. Click Start.

2. Click Control Panel.

3. Under System and Maintenance, click Restore Computer, as shown in Figure 13.7.

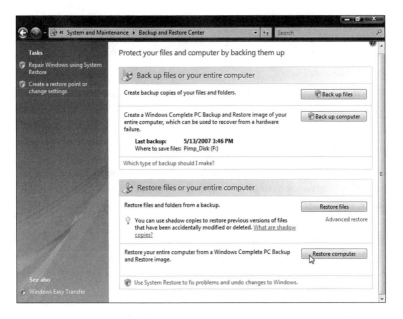

FIGURE 13.7
Triggering a computer restore.

4. A warning window will appear, asking if you are sure you want to restore your system. It will inform you that the process requires a reboot of the system after which you will need to access the System Recovery Options.

5. Reboot your system and press F8 prior to the start of Vista.

Enabling Logging of the Restore Process

In some situations administrators need to create a log file that tracks the restore process. This can be accomplished with the following steps:

1. Boot from the Vista DVD.

2. Go to Repair Computer, Command Prompt.

3. Go into Regedit.

4. Under HKEY_LOCAL_MACHINE\SOFTWARE\Microsoft\Windows NT\CurrentVersion\ create the key: Asr.

5. Under Asr create the key LogFileSetting.

6. Under LogFileSetting create the DWORD Value EnableLogging with the value 1.

7. Under LogFileSetting create the string LogPathName (string) with a value such as D:\Asr.log. You should specify a physical drive (for example, use the drive you are going to restore from).

8. Exit Regedit.

9. From the Repair menu, launch Complete PC Restore.

10. Perform the Complete PC Restore.

Using System Restore to Fix Problems

In the event that you suffer a complete hard drive failure or a catastrophic failure of the operating system, it will be necessary to restore the system from the latest Complete PC Backup. The surefire way to access the Startup Repair tools to access the CompletePC Restore is to follow these steps:

1. If applicable, attach the device that holds the Complete PC Restore files. (This is likely an external hard drive or a secondary local hard drive.)

2. Power on the computer.

3. Place the original Vista DVD into the DVD drive.

4. When prompted, choose to boot from CD/DVD.

5. When Windows has loaded its files, you will be prompted to select a language and keyboard input, as shown in Figure 13.8. Enter these and click Next.

FIGURE 13.8
Choosing the language and keyboard.

6. At the Install Windows screen, choose Repair your computer.

7. Vista will search for installed operating systems and allow you to choose which one you want to repair. Highlight the operating system you want to install and click Next.

Note

If you do not see any operating systems listed, it is likely that you need to install an additional driver in order to see your hard disks. This is especially common in systems that run RAID or SCSI drives for the operating system. You will need to provide the driver disk that was originally used when building the system. This is often referred to as the "F6" disk, because that's the key you had to press originally to specify an additional driver.

---

8. On the System Recovery Options screen, click Windows Complete PC Restore (see Figure 13.9).

9. Vista will scan for known backups and recommend the most recent image. If this is the image you want to restore, click Next, as shown in Figure 13.10.

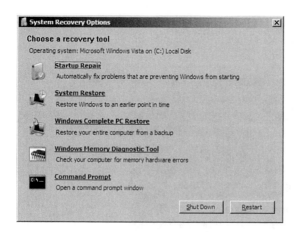

FIGURE 13.9
Choosing an OS to restore.

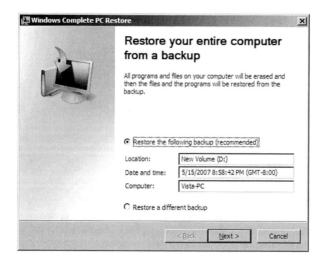

FIGURE 13.10
Selecting the image to restore.

10. Verify the information on the Windows Complete PC Restore screen and click Finish to initiate the restore.

11. You will receive one last warning to let you know that the restore will erase all data on the disks you chose to restore. If you are absolutely

certain that you aren't going to overwrite recoverable data, check the confirmation box and click OK (see Figure 13.11).

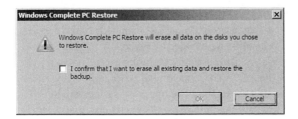

FIGURE 13.11
Confirming the restore.

12. At this point, the restore process initiates. Please be patient while the data is restored.

13. When the restore process is ended, the system will automatically reboot itself. The restore process is complete.

Complete PC Backup Requirements

Complete PC Backup and Restore is a useful tool to have access to. As such, administrators should plan out situations where this utility can do the most good and then ensure that users are properly equipped to take advantage of the process. There are several dependencies for Complete PC Backup that are detailed next.

Operating System Requirements

Unfortunately, not all versions of Vista offer the capability to perform a Complete PC Backup. The version that offer this functionality are

- Vista Business Edition
- Vista Ultimate Edition
- Vista Enterprise Edition

Although other versions of Vista are able to back up individual files and folders, only the preceding versions are able to take advantage of a full system image backup. If you have users who are likely to need the capability to restore a full system, strongly consider upgrading their version of Vista.

Hard Drive Backup

A Complete PC Backup to hard drive is likely to be the most common method of performing image backups in most companies. This would typically be a backup to either an external hard drive, a secondary hard drive inside the computer, or to a "recovery partition" on a single hard drive. Many prebuilt computers have been utilizing the idea of a recovery partition for many years. Although it is very convenient for restoring a system to a previous state, it has the disadvantage of not protecting the user from a physical hard drive failure, because the backup and live operating system would be on the same physical disk. A failure that ruined the OS would also ruin the backup.

As such, it is better protection to place the backup on a physically different device, such as a second hard drive. Many corporate desktops have multiple hard drives, and this would allow a backup to be placed on the secondary drive. This has several advantages in that it is a very fast connection to the computer and it is a physically different disk, so a disk failure of the system disk could be recovered from. Although handy for desktops, this is often not feasible for laptops.

In the case of computers with only a single internal hard drive, such as a laptop, the option of backing up to an external hard drive becomes very attractive. The external hard drive has the advantage of being not only physically separate from the system but it is portable as well. This means that the backup image can be stored in a physically secured location, such as in a fireproof safe. This would help to ensure that the data is available should the user need to perform a restore.

When considering external hard drives for backup/restore purposes, be sure that you get a large enough capacity to hold the entire system disk. Also try to use as fast a hard drive as possible. USB 2.0 is significantly faster than USB 1.1 and is widely available. If the system supports it, consider using eSATA, or *external serial ATA*, drives—they are even faster than USB 2.0 and are rapidly gaining in popularity.

Tape Device Backup

Interestingly enough, Vista provides no support for performing a Complete PC Backup to a traditional tape device. Microsoft explained that this is because of fundamental changes in the way it is now dealing with backup/restore. Users who want to reuse existing tape devices with their systems that have been upgraded to Vista will either have to switch to hard drive/DVD-based backups or else look to a third party for utilities.

DVD Backup

An alternative to backing up to hard disk is the option to back up the system to one or more DVDs. With the proliferation of DVD burners and the relatively low cost of DVD media, a backup to DVD is a viable option for users who do not need to run a backup too often. For users who are likely to run backups on a regular basis, DVD-RW is a better choice.

DVD has some advantages over hard drive backups in that the resulting backup takes up very little physical space (the size of a few DVDs instead of the size of a portable hard drive) and as such, the DVDs can be easily stored away in a safe location. DVD also has a stability advantage in that because it is a passive device, it can't crash. DVDs can handle the "rough handling" of users better than a portal hard drive can, so it may be a very good option for situations where a portable hard drive may be at risk.

Restoring to a New Hard Drive

In some situations, Complete PC Backup will be used to restore an existing image to an entirely new hard drive. This could be in a situation where a hard drive has failed, or it may be a situation where an administrator needs to "clone" an existing Vista computer for troubleshooting or some form of testing in a lab environment.

Generally speaking, Complete PC Restore works best when restoring to the same size hard drive that the image was made from. This is not a requirement, but it is certainly a simpler process. In the case of running a restore to a larger hard drive, additional steps will be needed.

Using DiskPart

One of the additional steps that may be needed when restoring to a different hard drive is the tool called DiskPart. To access DiskPart, follow these steps:

1. Power on the computer.
2. Place the original Vista DVD into the DVD drive.
3. When prompted, choose to boot from CD/DVD.
4. When Windows has loaded its files, you will be prompted to select a language and keyboard input. Enter these and click Next.
5. At the Install Windows screen, choose Repair Your Computer.

6. Vista will search for installed operating systems and allow you to choose which one you want to repair. Highlight the operating system you want to install and click Next.

7. On the System Recovery Options screen, click Command Prompt.

8. Type `x:\windows\system32\diskpart`.

DiskPart offers many options that can be used:

ACTIVE—Mark the selected basic partition as active.

ADD—Add a mirror to a simple volume.

ASSIGN—Assign a drive letter or mount point to the selected volume.

ATTRIBUTES—Manipulate volume attributes.

AUTOMOUNT—Enable and disable automatic mounting of basic volumes.

BREAK—Break a mirror set.

CLEAN—Clear the configuration information, or all information, off the disk.

CONVERT—Convert between different disk formats.

CREATE—Create a volume or partition.

DELETE—Delete an object.

DETAIL—Provide details about an object.

EXIT—Exit DiskPart.

EXTEND—Extend a volume.

FILESYSTEMS—Display current and supported file systems on the volume.

FORMAT—Format the volume or partition.

GPT—Assign attributes to the selected GPT partition.

HELP—Display a list of commands.

IMPORT—Import a disk group.

INACTIVE—Mark the selected basic partition as inactive.

LIST—Display a list of objects.

ONLINE—Online a disk that is currently marked as offline.

REM—Does nothing. This is used to comment scripts.

REMOVE—Remove a drive letter or mount point assignment.

REPAIR—Repair a RAID-5 volume with a failed member.

RESCAN—Rescan the computer looking for disks and volumes.

RETAIN—Place a retained partition under a simple volume.

SELECT—Shift the focus to an object.

> SETID—Change the partition type.
>
> SHRINK—Reduce the size of the selected volume.

In the case of a restore to a drive that is larger than the original, it is necessary to use DiskPart to convince Vista that it can properly restore. This is done in the following manner:

1. Get to DiskPart using the steps listed previously.

2. Type **List Disk**.

3. Based on the disk you want to recover, type **Select Disk=[*diskID*]**; for example, Select Disk=0.

4. Type **Create Partition Primary Size=[*size or original drive*]**; for example, Create partition Primary Size=40960.

5. Type **List Partition**.

6. Type **Select Partition=[*partitionID*]**; for example, Select Partition=0.

7. Type **Format fs=ntfs label="System Drive"**.

8. Type **Select Volume=1**.

9. Type **Assign Letter=C**.

10. Type **Exit** to exit DiskPart.

11. Type **Exit** to exit Command Prompt.

12. Run Complete PC Restore as per earlier instructions.

Summary

Microsoft has done the user community a great service in the introduction of the Complete PC Backup. No longer do users or administrators have to go through the hassle of building a workstation from the ground up just to access the backup/restore applications to restore the user's data to a system and make it usable again. The capability to quickly and easily perform a "bare metal restore" of workstations allows users to operate without the fear of a hardware failure or software corruption resulting in days of lost productivity.

As discussed in this chapter, administrators should strongly consider the needs of their users, weigh those needs against the availability of local IT support, and then pick a backup strategy that makes the most sense for that user community. Through something as simple as a scheduled task and an external hard drive, users are empowered to perform their own disaster recovery or even an upgrade to a larger hard drive without having to always involve the IT department.

Administrators should take advantage of the Complete PC Backup when performing testing or development work on Vista workstations. Rather than spending money on third-party imaging utilities, users can quickly and easily restore a system to a known state through the use of Complete PC Backup.

By taking advantage of Complete PC Backup as well as the Volume Shadow Copies functions of Vista, in conjunction with the capability to back up individual data drives, the days of lost user data may finally be at an end.

CHAPTER 14

Microsoft Vista System Restore

What Is System Restore?

In the imperfect world of computing, not all programs are created equal. Occasionally the installation of updates, hotfixes, hardware drivers, or third-party applications can have an adverse effect on a computer system, causing it to behave unpredictably.

In most cases, a simple uninstall of the recent modification is adequate to return the system to its formerly working order but, occasionally, more drastic measures are necessary.

Since the inception of Windows Me, Microsoft has included an application with its operating systems that allows users or administrators to easily return the system to a previous "known-good" configuration. Known as System Restore, this application enables users and administrators to remove or undo recent system changes without affecting personal files such as documents, photos, or stored email messages. Take a look at Figure 14.1 to see what the System Restore screen looks like.

What Is System Protection?

System Protection is the utility built in to the Vista operating system that creates restore points, allowing the user to use System Restore to roll back the operating system if needed. These restore points are saved on the workstation hard drive as insurance against future problems.

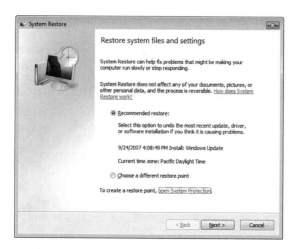

FIGURE 14.1
System Restore.

It is important to note that System Protection is not intended as a replacement for the regular use of a backup application to create and save copies of personal data. Because System Protection does not back up personal files in any way, System Restore cannot be used to recover lost or damaged personal files.

System Protection is enabled by default on all Windows Vista installations and it is highly recommended that the utility remain enabled for all drives (especially the system drive) on a workstation. Figure 14.2 shows the System Protection interface.

What Are Restore Points?

As previously noted, System Protection creates items called *restore points* that are basically copies of important system files. Using System Restore, these restore points can be used to return system files and settings to an earlier point in time if the need should arise because of the development of system problems.

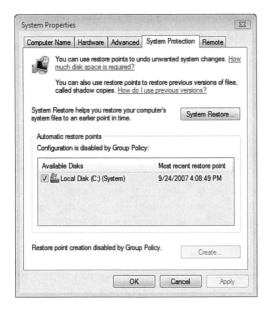

FIGURE 14.2
System Protection.

There are three basic types of restore points:

1. **System event restore points** are created just before significant events are implemented on a computer system. Examples of events that trigger the creation of a system event restore point include the following:

   - **Application Installations**—When an application is installed, a restore point is created that allows the user to roll the system state back to the time before the installation occurred. However, the application must use a current installer that is System Restore compliant for this feature to function reliably.

   - **AutoUpdate Installation of Critical Microsoft Windows Updates**—Prior to the application of AutoUpdate files provided by Microsoft, a restore point is created to allow the system to be rolled back to the point prior to the installation.

   - **Initiating a Restore Operation**—When a user restores the system state to a previous version, a new restore point is created before the event. This allows the user to return the system state to the point prior to the restoration, effectively allowing the user to undo the restore process.

- **Performing a Microsoft Backup Utility Recovery**—Before Microsoft Backup Utility performs a backup recovery, System Restore generates a restore point. If the user cancels the recovery, or if the recovery fails, a user can use this restore point to restore the system to the state it was in prior to the recovery attempt.

- **Unsigned driver installations**—The INF installer for Windows detects the installation of unsigned drivers and creates a restore point that users can use to restore the system to the state it was in prior to the installation of the driver.

2. Manual restore points are created by a user by using the System Protection feature of the operating system. By creating a manual restore point just prior to the implementation of a system change, a user can ensure that an up-to-the-minute restore point exists to fall back on if necessary.

3. Daily restore points are created automatically by the System Protection feature. By default, these restore points are created every 24 hours. Daily restore points are also created when the computer boots after being off for more than 24 hours. These restore points are created during periods of "idle" time, when no mouse, keyboard, or disk i/o activity is taking place. By keeping several revisions of the daily restore points, the System Restore feature allows a user to roll back the computer to one or more days in the past.

Each type of restore point serves a specific purpose, and each of them should be implemented to maximize the potential for recovery in the event of an operating system failure. Figure 14.3 shows the types of restore points.

Note

Restore points generated by different Windows operating systems are not created equal! Those created by Windows Vista are not recognized by previous versions of Windows. If you have a dual or multiboot system and start an earlier version of Windows (such as Windows XP), the earlier version deletes any restore points created by Windows Vista. When you start Vista again, those restore points are gone and cannot be recovered. However, the system resumes creating restore points automatically if System Restore has not been disabled.

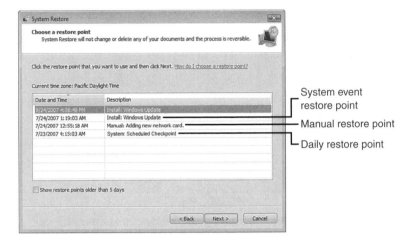

System event
restore point

Manual restore point

Daily restore point

FIGURE 14.3
Types of restore points.

Creating a Manual Restore Point

As previously noted, manual restore points are created by the user prior to implementing a system change. Creating a manual restore point is the safest way to ensure you have an up-to-the-minute restore point to fall back on in the event of a problem.

To create a manual restore point, perform the following steps:

1. Click the Start button and select All Programs.

2. Select Accessories, System Tools, System Restore. Alternatively, after clicking the Start button, type **System Restore** in the Start Search field and press the Enter key.

3. If prompted System Restore Has Been Turned Off. Do You Want to Turn on System Restore Now?, click Yes.

4. Locate the statement that says To Create a New Restore Point, Open System Protection; click the hyperlinked words that say Open System Protection.

5. Click the Create button.

6. Enter a description to help you identify the restore point (such as **Adding new video card driver**). The current date and time will be added automatically. When you are ready, click the Create button.

7. Click the OK button.

8. View the section that states Most Recent Restore Point to confirm that the process was successful. When ready, click the OK button.

9. Click Cancel to close the application.

Disk Space Requirements for System Restore

For System Restore to function on a particular disk, that disk must be at least 1 gigabyte (GB) in size and must have at least 300 megabytes (MB) of free space. System Restore reserves a certain amount of hard disk space (up to 15% of the space on the disk by default) to store restore points. Restore points are saved until this allocated space fills up. After the available allocated space has been filled, old restore points are deleted to make way for new ones.

What Is and Is Not Protected by System Restore?

System Restore is designed to affect files related specifically to the inner workings of the operating system. Specifically, the following types of files are protected:

- Windows system files
- Registry settings
- Profiles (local profiles only—roaming user profiles are not restored)
- Programs
- Executable files such as scripts and batch files

According to Microsoft, the following are not restored when using the System Restore feature:

- DRM settings.
- Passwords in the SAM hive.
- WPA settings (Windows authentication information is not restored).
- Specific directories/files listed in the Monitored File Extensions list in the System Restore section of the Platform SDK; for example, My Documents folder.
- Any file types not monitored by System Restore (for example, `.doc`, `.jpg`, `.txt`).

- Items listed in both Filesnottobackup and KeysnottoRestore (HKLM\System\CurrentControlset001\Control\Backuprestore\Filesnott obackup and Keysnottorestore) in the Registry.

- Contents of redirected folders.

- User-created data stored in the user profile.

Caution

Make special note of the last bullet point above. User-created data files are not recoverable utilizing System Restore, and conscientious users should employ regular and thorough backups to protect their personal data from loss. System Restore cannot be used to recover personal data files lost through accidental deletion, corruption, or system failure.

Note

System Restore cannot be utilized on disks formatted with the FAT32 or other FAT file system, because disks using any of the flavors of the FAT file system do not support the use of shadow copies. Shadow copy is the technology used to create and store the restore points. Only disks using the NTFS file system can be protected with System Restore.

Should You Use the FAT or NTFS File System?

A file system is the structure that computers use to organize data on a hard disk. Windows operating systems, including Vista, recognize three file system types: NTFS, FAT32, and the older (and rarely used) FAT, also known as FAT16.

Microsoft recommends the use of the NTFS file system for Microsoft Vista because it is truly a superior technology with several advantages over the earlier FAT32 file system, such as the following:

- Improved security that allows the restriction of specific files to approved users by implementing permissions and data encryption

- Improved support for larger disk drives

- The ability to recover from certain types of hard drive errors

Determining Whether a Disk Uses the NTFS File System

As previously mentioned, System Restore does not protect disks using the FAT file system. It can be used only for NTFS drives. To determine what file system each of your disks is using, you can perform the following steps:

1. Click the Start button, right-click Computer, and select Manage.

2. From the Computer Management screen, expand Storage and click Disk Management.

3. A list of the disks available on the system will be displayed. The properties of each disk are shown and, under the File System column, the type of file system used on each disk is displayed (see Figure 14.4).

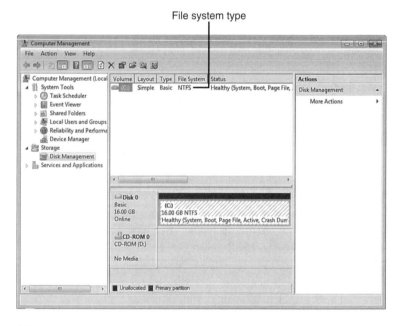

FIGURE 14.4
Determining file system type.

The NTFS file system is the preferred file system for use with Windows Vista, providing superior performance and security when compared to the older FAT and FAT32 file systems. If your Vista system is currently running on or contains FAT or FAT32 drives or partitions, they can be converted to NTFS by performing the following steps:

1. Close any open programs running on the partition or logical drive to be converted.

2. Click the Start button, click All Programs, Accessories, right-click Command Prompt, and then click Run as Administrator.

3. If you are prompted for an administrator password or confirmation, type the password or provide confirmation.

4. In the Command Prompt window, type **convert *drive_letter*:** **/fs:ntfs**, where `drive_letter` is the letter of the drive you want to convert, and then press Enter. For example, to convert the E: drive to NTFS, the following command would be used:

```
convert E: /fs:ntfs
```

5. Type the name of the volume you want to convert and then press Enter. To view the available volumes, click the Start button, and then click Computer. The volumes are listed under Hard Disk Drives.

If the disk or partition you are converting contains system files (as it would if you were converting your entire hard disk), you have to restart the computer upon completion for the new file system to be implemented. Also, users should be aware that the conversion process may fail on disks that are full (or almost full) of data. If the process does not complete successfully, the user can delete unnecessary files, relocate files to another location, or otherwise increase the available disk space.

Note

Although drives can be easily converted from FAT or FAT32 to NTFS, they cannot be converted back again. Returning a drive or partition from NTFS to a FAT file system requires a complete format of the disk, resulting in the loss of any data contained there.

Configuring System Restore and System Protection

System Restore is an extremely powerful tool, yet it is exceptionally easy to use. With very little effort, a workstation administrator can restore the system files to an earlier state, effectively "rolling back" the system to a time before certain changes were implemented that resulted in problems on the workstation.

This section focuses on the configuration of System Restore and System Protection.

Enabling and Disabling System Protection

As has been stated previously in this chapter, the installation of applications, updates, or drivers does not always end with the desired result. Having the ability to "undo" system changes is an extremely valuable asset, and users should have a very good reason before removing the System Restore tool from their system. If, after careful consideration, and despite repeated cautions, you desire to disable System Restore, it can be easily accomplished.

To Turn System Protection Off

To disable System Protection on one or more of your hard drives, perform the following procedure:

1. Click the Start button.

2. Select Control Panel.

3. Select System and Maintenance, then select System. Alternatively, if you are in the Classic View, double-click the System icon.

4. On the left pane, click System Protection. If you are prompted for an administrator password or confirmation, type the password or confirmation.

5. To turn off System Protection for a hard disk (or disk), clear the check box next to the disk in the Available Disks section (see Figure 14.5). Deselect all disks you want to disable protection for and then click OK.

Caution

If System Protection is turned off for a particular drive, all existing restore points on that drive are deleted and cannot be recovered. When System Protection is reenabled, new restore points can be created, but all old ones are gone.

Fortunately, System Protection is just as easy to enable as it is to disable.

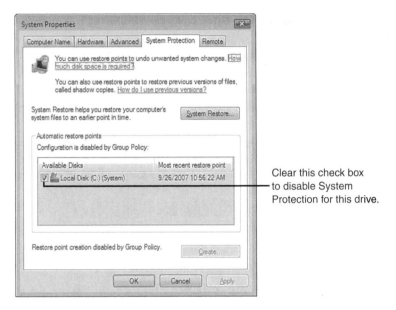

Clear this check box
to disable System
Protection for this drive.

FIGURE 14.5
Disabling System Protection.

To Turn System Protection On

To reenable System Protection on one or more of your hard drives, perform the following procedure:

1. Click the Start button.

2. Select Control Panel.

3. Select System and Maintenance, then select System. Alternatively, if you are in the Classic View, double-click the System icon.

4. On the left pane, click System Protection. If you are prompted for an administrator password or confirmation, type the password or confirmation.

5. To turn on System Protection for a hard disk (or disks), select the check box next to the disk in the Available Disks section. Select all disks you want to protect and then click OK.

Review and Configure the Disk Space Available to System Restore

As previously stated, by default System Restore reserves up to 15% of the space on a disk to store and maintain restore points. In previous versions of Windows (such as with Windows XP), this allocated disk space could easily be decreased using the settings configuration within the System Restore application.

With Windows Vista System Restore, this option no longer exists. If a user wants to change the disk space allocated for restore points, the user must use a command-line application called the Volume Shadow Copy Service Administrative Command-Line Tool.

To use this tool, log on to the workstation as a user with administrative privileges and perform the following steps:

1. Open a Command Prompt by clicking the Start button and, in the Start Search field, type **cmd** and press the Enter key.

2. From the command line, type **vssadmin /?**, and press Enter to see a list of supported commands.

Note

While the vssadmin /? command can be run by a nonadministrative user, the commands in the following sections require administrative access to run.

Determine the Disk Space Currently Used by System Restore

Users who are running low on disk space on a particular drive might want to know exactly how much space is being used by System Protection for the housing of restore points.

The vssadmin tool can be used to determine the maximum disk space System Restore is allowed to utilize, the amount of disk space currently allocated, and the amount of disk space currently used to house restore points. To generate this report, from the command line, type the following command:

```
vssadmin List ShadowStorage
```

The output of this command will list the following information for each volume currently protected:

- Used Shadow Copy Storage space
- Allocated Shadow Copy Storage space
- Maximum Shadow Copy Storage space

Modify the Disk Space Used by System Restore

The vssadmin tool can also be used to change the default behavior of the System Restore application, enforcing disk space utilization limits that the user mandates. To change the current settings, use the following command:

```
vssadmin Resize ShadowStorage /For=ForVolumeSpec
➥ /On=OnVolumeSpec /MaxSize=MaxSizeSpec
```

where

ForVolumeSpec is the drive that is being protected, OnVolumeSpec is the drive that will store the restore points, and MaxSizeSpec is the new maximum size System Restore can use for housing restore points.

The MaxSizeSpec must be at least 300 megabytes (MB) or greater. The following suffixes can be used (listed in increasing order of size):

B (bytes), KB (for kilobytes), MB (megabytes), and GB (gigabytes). Also available, but unlikely to be used in a workstation installation, are TB (terabyte), PB (petabyte), and EB (exabyte). K, M, G, T, P, and E are also acceptable suffixes.

Example:

To modify the settings for the C: drive, maintain the restore points on the C: drive (which is the default and recommended behavior), and set the available storage to a maximum of 1 gigabyte (GB), use the following command:

```
vssadmin Resize ShadowStorage /For=C: /On=C: /MaxSize=1GB
```

Caution

If a suffix is not applied to the MaxSizeSpec variable, the setting defaults to bytes. A user could easily intend to allocate 2GB, for example, and, by leaving off the suffix, restrict System Restore to a maximum of 2 bytes, rendering it virtually ineffective. Conversely, if MaxSizeSpec is not specified, the amount of disk space that System Restore can use is unlimited.

Decreasing the disk allocation for System Restore to a size smaller than currently used by restore points will result in the immediate deletion of the older copies until the size used is smaller than the size allowed. Users should be very cautious when modifying the behavior of the System Restore application.

Tip

After resizing the space available to System Restore with the `vssadmin Resize ShadowStorage` command, always perform a `vssadmin List ShadowStorage` command and view the results to ensure that the size configured is what was intended.

Enabling and Disabling System Restore via Group Policy

Administrators concerned with System Restore settings on workstations under their care can use Group Policy to enforce the enabling or disabling of System Restore. Additionally, administrators can enable or disable user access to the System Restore Configuration interface.

To do so, edit the policy that will be applied to the computers in question and navigate to Computer Configuration, Administrative Templates, System, System Restore.

There are two available configuration settings: Turn Off System Restore and Turn Off Configuration, each of which has three options—Not Configured, Enabled, or Disabled.

Selecting Not Configured for either setting results in that setting having no effect on the behavior of the workstations, allowing them to revert to their default local settings.

Without including the Not Configured option, these two settings can be configured in three combinations—each with a different result. To see the results of these combinations, see Figure 14.6.

Changes to these Group Policy settings take place at the time of the next workstation reboot.

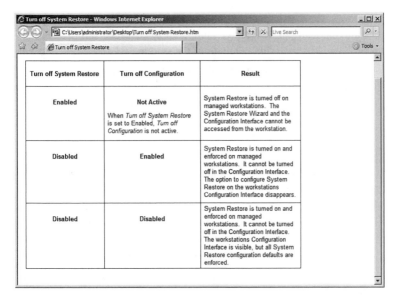

FIGURE 14.6
Group Policy settings and their results.

Using System Restore

Now that we have addressed the configuration of System Restore and System Protection, it is time to focus on the use of the applications.

When to Use System Restore

System Restore is a very powerful utility, sometimes more powerful than needed. By reverting the workstation to a previous state, it changes files and entries in the Registry and could potentially modify items that you would have preferred to leave alone.

Before performing a System Restore, some simple troubleshooting and problem resolution techniques should be tried. A few of the more common techniques are listed next:

- **Reboot the System**—It has been joked that computer help desks across the world could decrease their ticket entries and solve 99 percent of user reported problems by simply answering the phone and stating, "Shut up and reboot!" Although this is certainly stretching the truth, the reality is that a large number of system-related problems can be cleared up by a simple reboot of the system.

- **Reboot the System to the Last Known Good Configuration**—If you are unable to start your workstation in Normal mode, the machine can be rebooted and, by pressing the F8 key during the boot process, the user can select to boot to the Last Known Good Configuration. This option restores driver settings and Registry information that were implemented the last time the computer started successfully.

- **Uninstall**—If the problem you are experiencing manifested right after the installation of a new application, you can use the Uninstall or Change a Program feature in Windows Vista. To run this utility, click the Start button, select Control Panel, and double-click Programs and Features. From this utility, administrators can easily uninstall, change, or repair most of the nonoperating-system applications on the workstation.

  If the problem occurs right after the installation of a security update or hotfix, the Programs and Features page also has an option in the left pane to View Installed Updates. This option allows administrators to selectively uninstall Windows operating system and application updates.

  Additionally, if the problem is noticed after the installation or update of a device driver, an administrator can roll back the driver to a previous version. To do so, click the Start button, select Control Panel, and double-click Device Manager. Locate the device that you suspect is causing the problem, right-click it, and select Properties. Then, from the Driver tab, click Roll Back Driver.

After you have tried these (and other) troubleshooting techniques, if you are still experiencing difficulties, it may be time for you to perform a system restore.

Performing a System Restore

The System Restore tool can be extremely helpful in recovering from a system crash, especially if the crash is due to the recent addition of corrupt or damaged software. When you use System Restore to restore the computer to a previous state, programs and updates that were installed after the restore point are removed.

Because the System Restore tool creates a new restore point each time a significant change in the file or application structure occurs, there is a good possibility that a restore point was created immediately prior to the system change that is causing problems.

For the System Restore tool to be effective, it must be enabled and functioning properly—after a problem has been encountered, it is too late to enable System Restore and hope to do any good.

To implement a System Restore, perform the following steps:

1. Save and close any open files and close all applications. On completion of the restore process, System Restore restarts your computer.

2. Click the Start button, then type **System Restore** into the Start Search box and press Enter.

3. If you are prompted for an administrator password or confirmation, provide the information to continue.

4. From the Restore System Files and Settings screen, you are presented with two options: Recommended Restore or Choose a Different Restore Point, as shown in Figure 14.7. Select the appropriate choice and click Next. If you select Recommended Restore, skip to step 7; otherwise, continue to the next step.

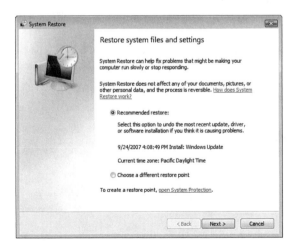

FIGURE 14.7
Running System Restore.

> **Tip**
>
> The goal is to roll back to the most recent restore point that will resolve the issues you are encountering. Selecting the Recommended Restore option will often meet this desired goal because System Restore automatically recommends the most recent restore point created before a significant change. Regardless of which option you select, however, if the problem is still occurring after the completion of the restore, the user can perform additional system restores, selecting older and older restore points with each step until the issue is resolved.

5. From the Choose a Restore Point screen, select the restore point you want to roll back to. If you want to see restore points that are older than five days, you must place a check mark in the box at the bottom of the screen.

6. After you have selected the restore point you want to roll back to, click Next to continue.

7. On the Confirm Your Restore Point screen, ensure all is correct and click Finish.

8. You will receive a notification stating, Once Started, System Restore May Not Be Interrupted and Cannot Be Undone Until After It Has Completed. Are You Sure You Want to Continue? Make sure you want to continue and click Yes.

9. After the System Restore has completed, the computer reboots. When prompted, log in to the system. You should see a message confirming the success of the System Restore process, similar to the one shown in Figure 14.8. Click Close to complete the process.

FIGURE 14.8
Successful system restore.

Undo a System Restore

After a system restore has completed, you should immediately determine whether the problem that was being addressed has been resolved. If the problem has not been resolved, you can run System Restore again and you will see a message similar to the one shown in Figure 14.9.

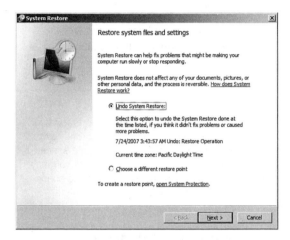

FIGURE 14.9
Undo a system restore.

You now have the option to Undo System Restore, which reverts you to the state you were in *prior* to performing the System Restore, or you can Choose a Different Restore Point. Select the desired option and click Next. Continue with the following remaining steps (if you selected Undo System Restore, start with step 3):

1. From the Choose a Restore Point screen, select the restore point you want to roll back to. If you want to see restore points that are older than five days, you must place a check mark in the box at the bottom of the screen.

2. After you have selected the restore point you want to roll back to, click Next to continue.

3. On the Confirm Your Restore Point screen, ensure all is correct and click Finish.

4. You will receive a notification stating, Once Started, System Restore May Not Be Interrupted and Cannot Be Undone Until After It Has Completed. Are You Sure You Want to Continue? Make sure you want to continue and click Yes.

5. After the System Restore has completed, the computer reboots. When prompted, log in to the system.

It may take several system restores before you find one that resolves the issues you are encountering. Carefully track which restore points you have tried.

> **Note**
>
> Each time you perform a new system restore, a new undo restore point is created. For systems without much disk space dedicated to restore points, it is possible for these repeated restore points to use all available space and cause the deletion of older (perhaps valid) restore points that you may need to resolve your problems. Whenever possible, ensure that the space allocated will allow the creation and storage of multiple restore points.

Using System Restore from Windows Safe Mode

On occasion, the operating system on a workstation can become so damaged that the machine cannot fully load the graphical user interface (GUI). Fortunately, Windows includes a diagnostic mode known as Safe Mode. Windows Safe Mode is a way of booting your workstation with the bare minimum of software that is required for the operating system to function. Loading only a limited set of files and drivers, Safe Mode even prevents the loading of programs designated as Startup Programs, which would normally load automatically as the operating system boots.

Although Safe Mode has reduced functionality when compared to the full-fledged version, the System Restore feature can still be used, enabling a user to recover from corruption that might otherwise prevent the operating system from functioning at all.

> **Note**
>
> When running System Restore from Safe Mode, a System Event Restore Point is not created, so you will be unable to undo the restore operation. However, you will be able run System Restore again and choose a different restore point if one exists.

To boot your Windows Vista workstation into Safe Mode, use the following procedure:

1. Remove all floppy disks, CDs, or DVDs from your computer, then restart the system. If you are unable to restart the system from within the operating system, power the workstation off, then back on.

2. If your computer only has one operating system installed (Windows Vista), press and hold the F8 key as the system boots. This key must be pressed before the Windows logo appears. If the logo has already appeared, you must shut down and reboot the workstation again.

3. If your computer contains more than one operating system, use the arrow keys to highlight Windows Vista, and then press the F8 key.

4. When the Advanced Boot Options screen appears, use the arrow keys to highlight the Safe Mode option, and then press Enter.

5. When prompted, log on to the workstation with an account that has administrative rights on the system.

You will know that you have successfully loaded your system in Safe Mode because the words Safe Mode will appear in all four corners of the screen. After you have logged in, you can run System Restore as detailed in the preceding section, "Performing a System Restore."

Using System Restore from Windows Safe Mode with Command Prompt

In the event that the system is so corrupt that the GUI cannot be displayed, there is still hope. Microsoft Windows also includes a recovery feature called Windows Safe Mode with Command Prompt. In this version of Safe Mode, the GUI is not loaded and the user is presented with a command line interface. To enter Safe Mode with Command Prompt, reboot the system as detailed in the previous section but, instead of selecting Safe Mode, select Safe Mode with Command Prompt.

After the command prompt has been presented, the user can attempt a system restore from there.

To do so, type **Rstrui.exe** and press Enter.

This starts the System Restore application. Use the same process that was detailed in the section titled "Performing a System Restore."

To exit Safe Mode with Command Prompt, press the Ctrl+Alt+Delete keys, and then click the arrow beside the shutdown options in the bottom-right corner. Select Restart to reboot the system.

Using System Restore from the Installation DVD

So, what can be done if the system won't even boot? There is one more method of implementing System Restore that may be used to roll back the system. By booting the workstation directly to the installation DVD, it is possible to select Repair Your Computer and, after clicking Next, to select System Restore from the System Recovery options. You should be presented with the same Choose a Restore Point screen that we have seen in previous sections.

Select the desired restore point and click Next. When prompted, select the drive that your operating system is installed on and click Finish. The System Restore process continues, rebooting your workstation upon completion.

Summary

With each updated version of its operating system, Microsoft has improved the tools and utilities to help prevent and recover from system problems. The Windows Vista System Restore tool is no exception. It is more powerful than its predecessors, easier to use, allows for a wider range of recovery options, and generates restore points based on a much more comprehensive list of system events.

Users should think long and hard before disabling or limiting this feature, especially if there are no overwhelming data storage needs that require such steps. Many people might never need to use this utility but any who do will be exceptionally happy to have it available.

PART V

Managing Vista

IN THIS PART

CHAPTER 15

Setting Up Users and Computers in Windows Vista

Types of User Accounts in Windows Vista

Whether you are a seasoned IT professional or consider yourself a beginner, one point of concern in the implementation and support of Windows Vista within a new environment is the choice between a workgroup and a domain. The answer to the question of which to choose is dependent purely on the environment that you are in. It is very common that most homes and small businesses will be set up in a workgroup configuration, whereas most mid- to large-sized organizations will take full advantage of a domain configuration when setting up their environment.

When faced with this choice, it is best to understand the differences between both modes of operation. Each mode presents contrasting features and capabilities (as well as limitations) and each serves a purpose. It is important to understand the distinction so that you can properly make a decision that factors in security features and convenience that is appropriate for your environment. As part of the decision-making process, things you need to take into consideration include the sharing of information, security, connectivity, the location of users and resources, as well as the general skill of your support staff.

After an appropriate decision has been made, the effects determine the level of effort necessary to administer your environment as well as the capacity to provide robust and reliable security for resources and services that may be provided within your organization.

Of the major differences between a workgroup and domain configuration in Windows Vista are the models that each configuration follows. As such, a workgroup follows the peer-to-peer model, whereas a domain configuration follows the client/server model.

By definition, a peer-to-peer communications model is one in which each participant has roughly the same capabilities and can initiate a communication session. In many instances, peer-to-peer communications are facilitated through granting each participant both server and client capabilities. This is a misnomer because peer-to-peer networking does not typically use the distinction of "clients" and "servers." Each is a disparate system that simultaneously provides both functions. Functionally speaking, this configuration is most desired when the environment contains very few participating nodes (10, but typically never more than 20), when supporting personnel do not have the skill to manage a domain, and when budget constraints do not allow for the purchase of server equipment.

In this configuration, resources and services such as file and print sharing will be located and secured at multiple systems within the environment. Node A may provide host Accounting files, Node B may host Engineering resources, and Node C may have a printer connected to it that your users may utilize. It is very important to note that in this scenario, every node that provides services is separately responsible for the security of those resources. If not for the sake of mass convolution of an environment, this reason alone makes a workgroup configuration not practical within environments hosting more than a handful of systems.

In contrast, a client/server communications model is one by which resources and services are located on dedicated systems, alleviating client nodes from the need to participate in this role. In some small, and most medium-to-large environments, this is the architecture model of choice. In a network that has been designed based on a client/server communications model, it is typical that most, if not all, resources will be hosted on high-end dedicated server systems. This model allows for simplicity in functionality, a means through which control and security are centralized, as well as greater ease of maintenance. Although this model provides the most convenient way to interconnect systems on a network, it does require your administrative staff to have the skill required to support it.

In network communications, the client/server communications model has become more or less the de facto standard for scalable networking of Windows systems. Because this convenient model has become one of the central ideas of network computing, many back-end systems and business applications in use today or being written target this model. Microsoft Windows Vista is no exception to this and was written to take full advantage of the client/server communications model when installed in an Active Directory domain.

Workgroups have several advantages, including the following:

- Useful in small environments (no more than 20 systems).
- Ease of use and setup.
- Purchase of server hardware is not required.
- Extensive skills are not required to administer and maintain.

Some of the disadvantages of a workgroup include the following:

- Lack of centralized security resulting in the requirement to set up and maintain users (synchronize passwords and the like) on every machine in the environment.
- Not practical in larger environments—The Workstation model does not scale well. If you're using more than a handful of nodes, administrative overhead for user maintenance becomes a nightmare.
- Additional time required to set up any new user in the environment.
- Resources can become unavailable if a peer reboots the system.
- When utilizing file-sharing services, you are limited to a maximum of 10 connections per node.

Some of the advantages of creating a domain include the following:

- Centralized management resulting in one location to set up and maintain user accounts and passwords that is available throughout the entire network.
- Less overhead maintenance required.
- Very scalable solution if your environment grows.

Some disadvantages of a domain include the following:

- Requires server hardware
- More complex to implement
- Requires more knowledgeable support staff

User Accounts in a Workgroup

As previously stated, workstations running Microsoft Windows Vista may be set up in a workgroup configuration or as members of a domain. When configured as a workgroup, the client is responsible for managing all user accounts that may be used. This is to say that each Vista workstation must contain the same set of local users with the same password on each system. This allows users to access resources on other systems through pass-through authentication. Alternatively, resources would have to be shared within the workgroup with no security set on the files or other resources.

User Accounts in a Domain

If the Vista workstations are participating in a domain, the user's accounts are located in the domain structure and not on the individual workstations. This is to say that all the workstations trust the domain for providing authentication. Because all the user objects and passwords are stored in a central location, there is no need to manually keep the passwords in sync across all potential resources.

Elevated Privileges

To protect Vista workstations from unauthorized changes, it is a best practice to always log in to the Vista system with a typical user account. In the past, administrators typically had local administrator rights on their workstations. The concern here was that if a malicious application were run by mistake, it would have full rights over the system and could accomplish whatever nefarious task it was written to do. In previous operating systems, it was more common for administrators to not have local administrator rights to a computer but to instead use the "runas" function when they needed to elevate their rights (as shown in Figure 15.1). The concept of "runas" is that the user can issue a different set of credentials to be used by a single executable. This would allow the executable to run as though the user were logged in with administrative rights. Vista has simplified this concept through the User Account Control (UAC). The UAC automatically prompts users if they need elevated rights to complete a task. Similarly, administrators will find that several tasks will tell them they lack the necessary rights even when they are logged in as a local administrator on a Vista workstation. In these situations, it is necessary to right-click the executable and choose Run as Administrator. Vista won't ask for additional credentials because this process is just an additional check to make sure the executable is being run intentionally. This functionality can greatly reduce the chances of malicious software getting installed on a Vista workstation.

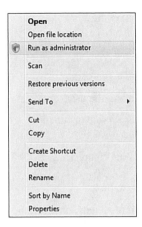

FIGURE 15.1
Using Run as Administrator.

Creating and Managing User Accounts

Whether managing Vista systems in workgroups or a domain, administrators will invariably have to deal with user account management. Commonly, administrators will have to provide for local logins for remote users, create local administrative accounts for help desk or desktop support, or even create local accounts to be used by management applications.

Creating and managing user accounts in Vista is very similar to how it was done in previous versions of Windows. Most administrators will find these tasks to be mostly "old hat," but with a few new twists, compliments of Vista's UAC functions.

Adding an Account

Adding a new account to a Vista workstation can be done several ways. Most administrators are probably familiar with using the Computer Management functions of Windows workstations to add a user through the graphical user interface (GUI). In Vista, this is performed with the following steps:

1. Click Start, All Programs, Administrative Tools, Computer Management.

2. When prompted by UAC, click Continue.

3. In the Computer Management console, expand System Tools and then Local Users and Groups.

4. Left-click Users. You will see the current Users on the Vista workstation.

5. Right-click Users and choose New User.

6. Enter a user name. This value will be the user's logon name.

7. Enter the user's full name. This is used for tracking the user.

8. Enter a description. This is especially useful for service or function accounts.

9. Type and confirm the user's password as shown in Figure 15.2.

10. When finished, click Create, Close.

If you don't require users to change their password immediately, uncheck the box next to User Must Change Password at Next Logon.

FIGURE 15.2
Creating a new user.

This method of creating a user through the GUI is the method that most administrators are familiar with. In some cases, it is more advantageous to create the user through a command-line interface. For example, an administrator might be deploying Vista workstations to a group of users in another location. Perhaps these users are managed by a remote help desk. This help desk needs to be able to work on the Vista workstations with local administrator rights, so the central administrator wants to place a help desk account on each Vista workstation and make it a local administrator. This could be accomplished with a script that is run at logon:

```
Net User [username] [password] /add
```

Then this account could be placed into the local administrators group with

```
Net Localgroup [groupname] [username] /add
```

This would ensure that the remote help desk had an account available with local administrator rights on each Vista workstation that they would manage.

A more likely scenario for this situation would be that the administrators would want to place an existing domain account into the local administrators group, rather than creating an additional account on each Vista workstation. In that scenario, the Localgroup command would instead be

```
Net Localgroup [groupname] [domain\username] /add
```

This places the existing domain account into the group specified in the command.

Changing/Editing an Account

In the course of maintaining accounts, it will be a somewhat common process to modify existing accounts. More often than not, the modification will be to reset passwords for users who have forgotten theirs or perhaps to reset the password of a common help desk account. This can be accomplished very easily through the computer management interface by following these steps:

1. Click Start, All Programs, Administrative Tools, Computer Management.

2. When prompted by UAC, click Continue.

3. In the Computer Management console, expand System Tools and then Local Users and Groups.

4. Left-click Users. You will see the current Users on the Vista workstation.

5. Right-click the user object and choose Set Password.

6. When prompted, accept the warning about the implications of setting the password in this manner by clicking Proceed.

7. Enter and confirm the new password and click OK.

8. If the password meets the requirements of the password policy, it will be successfully changed. Click OK to complete the process.

Other items that can be modified on a user object through the same interface are the following:

- Full name
- Description
- User must change password at next logon
- User cannot change password
- Password never expires
- Account is disabled
- Account is locked out
- Group memberships
- User profile path
- User logon script
- Home folder path

Security Groups

When managing users and computers in a corporate network, administrators will quickly find that as the environment grows, it becomes more and more difficult to manage users and computers as individual entities. Having to update multiple resource locations each time a new user is added to the environment becomes nearly impossible to manage in a consistent manner. In these situations, the use of groups can greatly simplify the administration of a network.

The concept of a security group is a relatively simple one. It is simply a new object that is able to represent multiple objects. For example, you could have a security group called Accounting that contains multiple user objects as its members. Now instead of granting access to a file share, for example, by adding users to it, you can simply add the group to it and delegate the permissions that way. Now when you add a new user to the existing group, the user automatically receives access to everything that the group is able to access.

To create a security group on a Vista workstation, perform these steps:

1. Click Start, All Programs, Administrative Tools, Computer Management.
2. When prompted by UAC, click Continue.

3. In the Computer Management console, expand System Tools and then Local Users and Groups.

4. Left-click Groups. You will see the current Security Groups on the Vista workstation, as shown in Figure 15.3.

FIGURE 15.3
Viewing existing groups.

5. Right-click Groups and choose New Group.

6. Enter a Name and Description for the group. Use a descriptive name for the group so that its purpose will be immediately evident. For example, the group could be called Accounting_Read_Only. In the description, it is helpful to list when and why the group was created and who created it.

7. Click Add to add members to the group.

8. Type the name of the object you want to add to the group and click Check Names. Vista workstations located in an Active Directory Domain will be able to add both local and domain users to their groups.

9. When all necessary users have been added, click OK.

10. Click Create to finish the creation of the group. If this is the last group you want to create, click Close.

Best Practices for Using a Shared Computer

There are many things that must be taken into account when sharing a Vista workstation between multiple users. Although this is a great way to get more done with fewer resources, it is very important to configure Vista to ensure that one user can't negatively impact other users of the same system.

In most situations where multiple people share the same system, there is often a pool of common shared systems. Situations such as a manufacturing floor or a nurse's station in a hospital are common examples. In these situations, it is useful to put systems into place that make it easy and safe for people to share the same pool of systems.

Initially the biggest challenge is maintaining a consistent view for users and ensuring that their resources are available no matter at which Vista workstation they sit down. If this type of functionality is required, administrators will want to configure the Vista workstations to participate in a domain. This will allow you to configure the Vista workstations so that they store the user's work on a network share rather than on the local system. This means that no matter where the user logs in, the user's work will be available. This is most commonly performed through folder redirection.

Similarly, it would be prudent to configure what's known as a *roaming profile* for the user. This is to say that the appearance of the user's desktop, shortcuts, and the like appear on any system the user logs in to. This gives users a consistent work experience and ensures that their applications and shortcuts are available to them.

Another key consideration is protecting local files from other users if the files are going to be stored locally on the Vista workstation. This is done through the use of NTFS permissions on the files and folders that need to be controlled.

Given that the NTFS permissions are based on the logon of the user, it is important to protect the user's credentials. As such, administrators will want to ensure that they've established a company password policy and to enforce those password policies.

Configuring Roaming Profiles in Vista

Roaming profiles are profiles that follow a user from workstation to workstation. Profiles include the following:

- **Windows Explorer**—All user-definable settings for Windows Explorer.

- **Documents**—User-stored documents.

- **Pictures**—User-stored picture items.

- **Favorites**—Shortcuts to favorite locations on the Internet.

- **Mapped network drive**—Any user-created mapped network drives.

- **Network Places**—Links to other computers on the network.

- **Desktop contents**—Items stored on the desktop and shortcuts.

- **Screen colors and fonts**—All user-definable computer screen colors and display text settings.

- **Application data and registry hive**—Application data and user-defined configuration settings.

- **Printer settings**—Network printer connections.

- **Control Panel**—All user-defined settings made in Control Panel.

- **Accessories**—All user-specific program settings affecting the user's Windows environment, including Calculator, Clock, Notepad, and Paint.

To enable a roaming profile for a user, perform the following steps:

1. From a domain attached system with Active Directory Users and Computer installed, click Start, Run, and type `dsa.msc`.

2. From within the Active Directory Users and Computers console, browse to the user for whom you want to enable a roaming profile.

3. Right-click the user and choose Properties.

4. Click the Profile tab.

5. Enter a UNC path under Profile Path to a shared location where the user has read/write access.

6. Click OK and close the console.

7. Have the user log off and back on to a workstation. The profile on the workstation the user logs on to will be copied to the User Profile path and used on all future logins.

Redirecting Folders

To ensure that users can access their documents from any workstation, it is recommended that administrators configure Redirected Folders for those users. The most commonly redirected folder is Documents. This is most commonly accomplished through Group Policy. To redirect Documents on a domain-joined workstation, perform these steps:

1. Click Start, Run, and type **gpmc.msc**. Click OK.

Note

If the Group Policy Management console isn't already installed, it can be downloaded from Microsoft at www.microsoft.com/downloads/details. aspx?FamilyID=0A6D4C24-8CBD-4B35-9272-DD3CBFC81887&displaylang=en.

This version works for Windows Server 2003 or Windows XP. Vista and Windows Server 2008 come with the GPMC preinstalled.

If Run isn't available in the user interface, Start Search works also.

---

2. When prompted by UAC, click Continue.

3. In the Group Policy Management console, expand the Forest object.

4. Below the Forest object, expand the Domains object.

5. Expand the domain for which you plan to alter the password policy.

6. Below the domain, right-click Group Policy Objects and choose New.

7. Enter a name for the GPO and click OK.

8. Right-click the new GPO and choose Edit.

9. In the Group Policy Editor console, expand User Configuration, Windows Settings, and then Folder Redirection. Entries for the folders that can be redirected will be displayed in the right pane.

10. To redirect any of these folders, right-click the folder name, click Properties, and then select one of the following options from the Setting drop-down box:

   - **Basic**—Redirect everyone's folder to the same location. All folders affected by this Group Policy object will be stored on the same network share.

■ **Advanced**—Specify locations for various user groups. Folders are redirected to different network shares based on security group membership. This option allows the administrator to populate locations for various security groups.

If you're using the Advanced setting, when adding groups and paths, you are asked to enter a Target Folder Location for each security group as shown in Figure 15.4. In the Target Folder Location drop-down box, you should select Create a Folder for Each User Under the Root Path. In the Root Path text box, type the name of the shared network folder to use, or click Browse to locate it.

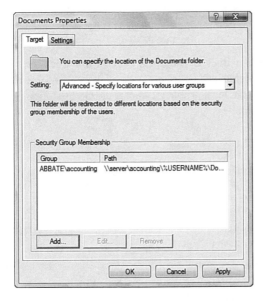

FIGURE 15.4
Redirection options.

9. In the folders Properties dialog box, select the Settings tab, configure the options you want to use, and then click Finish to complete the Folder Redirection. The available options for settings are the following:

■ **Grant the User Exclusive Rights to Documents**—If selected, this sets the NTFS security descriptor for the %username%

folder to Full Control for the user and local system only; this means that administrators and other users do not have access rights to the folder. This option is enabled by default.

- **Move the Contents of Documents to the New Location**— Moves any document the user has in the local Documents folder to the server share. This option is enabled by default.

- **Also Apply Redirection Policy to Windows 2000, Windows 2000 Server, Windows XP, and Windows Server 2003 Operating Systems**—This option is not enabled by default.

- **Leave the Folder in the New Location When Policy Is Removed**—Specifies that files remain in the new location when the Group Policy object no longer applies. This option is enabled by default.

- **Redirect the Folder Back to the Local User Profile Location When Policy Is Removed**—If enabled, specifies that the folder be copied back to the local profile location if the Group Policy object no longer applies.

Note

It is unnecessary to pre-create the directory defined by username. Folder Redirection will handle setting the appropriate ACLs on the folder. If you choose to pre-create folders for each user, be sure to set the permissions correctly.

Using NTFS Permissions

Way back in July of 1993, Microsoft released Windows NT. With the release of Windows NT came the introduction of the NTFS file system. NTFS was a big step for Windows because it allowed access permissions to be set at the file and folder level. Previously, Windows could control access only at Shares. The concept of NTFS permissions still exists in Vista. NTFS permissions are helpful in situations where you want to control access to specific files or entire folders. This is applicable to both local and network access. Take for example a Vista workstation that will sit on a manufacturing floor. The system needs to be available to all employees but it is important that users can't read or modify each other's files. This is a perfect task for NTFS permissions. By creating folders for each user and setting NTFS permissions, it is possible to grant the users access to their own folders and at the same time, protect those folders from other users.

An important consideration with NTFS permissions is the concept of *inheritance*. Inheritance is the behavior in which subfolders will mimic the settings of the folder above it. For example, if an administrator creates a folder called Documents and sets NTFS permission to give the Administrator account Full Control over the folder, any subfolder created below Documents will automatically grant Administrator the same Full Control over the folder. In some situations, it is useful to block this inheritance to prevent changes at a higher level from overwriting settings at a lower level. To determine whether a folder has inheritance set, perform the following steps:

1. Open Explorer and browse to the folder that you want to check for inheritance.

2. Right-click the folder and click Properties.

3. Click the Security tab.

4. In the bottom half of the Security view, click Advanced.

5. Near the bottom of the windows should be an entry Include Inheritable Permissions from This Object's Parent. If this box is checked, the folder has inheritance enabled.

To alter the inheritance settings:

1. Click Edit.

2. Check or uncheck, as needed, the box next to Include Inheritable Permissions from This Object's Parent, as shown in Figure 15.5.

As mentioned, NTFS permissions are used to control access rights of various users to various file and folder objects. The basic permissions that can be granted include

- Full Control
- Modify
- Read and Execute
- List Folder Contents
- Read
- Write

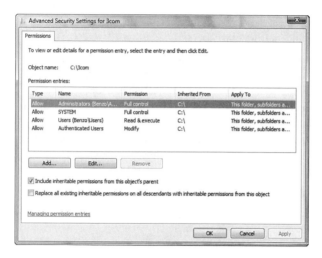

FIGURE 15.5
Checking for inheritance.

Each of these entries can be set to Allow or Deny to either grant or take away capabilities. NTFS permissions follow the concept of *least permissions*. Therefore, a deny always takes precedence over an allow. For example, if a user named TPope was a member of two groups, Accounting and HR, and a folder had security set with

```
HR - Full Control - Allow
Accounting - Read - Deny
```

TPope would be unable to read files in the folder because the deny would take precedent over the allow.

To set basic NTFS permissions on a file or folder, perform these steps:

1. Open Windows Explorer.

2. Browse to the file or folder where you want to set the NTFS permissions.

3. Right-click the file or folder.

4. Click Properties.

5. Click the Security tab, as shown in Figure 15.6.

6. Click Edit to alter the permissions.

7. Click Remove to remove an existing user or group object from the permissions.

8. Click Add to add a new user or group object to the permissions.

9. If adding, type the name of the user or group you want to add and click Check Names; then click OK.

10. Highlight the object you want to alter permissions for and use the check boxes to Allow or Deny the various permissions.

11. When done, click OK twice.

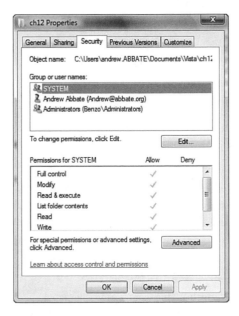

FIGURE 15.6
Viewing NTFS Permissions.

Password Policies

In most situations where Vista computers are being deployed, users will be required to maintain passwords. Passwords are critical in any system where any level of security is required. Passwords are a critical part of authentication that allows a system to determine that a user is who the user claims to be. This authentication is then utilized to access control to grant a user access to resources. As such, it is important to establish password policies to ensure that the identity of users is protected.

Implementation of password policies will vary depending on whether Vista systems are deployed in a Workgroup or Domain model. As mentioned earlier in this chapter, workgroups suffer from a lack of centralized management, so password policies must be configured on a per-workstation basis. Usually this can be done at the time of creation of the system. Environments where workstations are created from a common image should set the local password policy on the initial image to ensure that all "cloned" Vista workstations have the appropriate password policies in place.

To set a password policy on an existing Vista workstation in a workgroup, follow these steps:

1. Click Start, All Programs, Administrative Tools, Local Security Policy.

2. When prompted by UAC, click Continue.

3. In the Local Security Policy MMC, expand Account Policies.

4. Under Account Policies, highlight Password Policy.

5. In the right pane are six values that can be configured:

   - **Enforce Password History**—This value, set in number of passwords, is used to prevent users from recycling recent passwords.

   - **Maximum Password Age**—This value, set in days, is used to expire a current password.

   - **Minimum Password Age**—This value, set in days, is used to prevent users from quickly cycling passwords past the enforced password history value to return to the original password.

   - **Minimum Password Length**—This value, set in characters, determines the minimum number of characters that must be used to generate an acceptable password.

   - **Password Must Meet Complexity Requirements**—This value, set to Enabled or Disabled, determines whether a user's password must meet complexity requirements.

     If this policy is enabled, passwords must meet the following minimum requirements:

     - Not contain the user's account name or parts of the user's full name that exceed two consecutive characters

     - Be at least six characters in length

- Contain characters from three of the following four categories:
    - English uppercase characters (A through Z)
    - English lowercase characters (a through z)
    - Base 10 digits (0 through 9)
    - Nonalphabetic characters (for example, !, $, #, %)

    Complexity requirements are enforced when passwords are changed or created.

- **Store Passwords Using Reversible Encryption**—This value, set to Enabled or Disabled, determines whether a user's password can be stored using reversible encryption. Although some applications may require this for single sign-on, it is considered somewhat insecure because it greatly increases the chances for a user's password to be determined.

6. Configure the six values to match the company's security policy, as shown in Figure 15.7, and close the MMC.

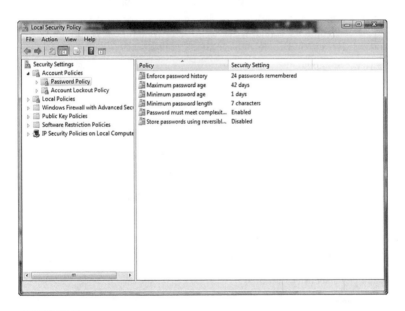

FIGURE 15.7
Local password policy.

Setting password policies in a domain model is handled in a different manner. As mentioned previously, one of the advantages to the domain model is that Vista workstations can be managed in a centralized manner. In an Active Directory domain, password policies are set at the domain level through the use of Group Policy. Important to note is that in Active Directories that are based on Windows 2003 or earlier, password policies can be set only at the domain level. This is to say that all computers in the domain get the same password policy. Windows Server 2008 introduces the capability to set different password policies at the Organizational Unit level.

To configure the password policy in a domain, complete the following steps:

1. Click Start, Run, and type `gpmc.msc`. Click OK.

Note

If you are using a Windows 2003 domain controller, and the Group Policy Management console isn't already installed, it can be downloaded from Microsoft at www.microsoft.com/downloads/details. aspx?FamilyID=0A6D4C24-8CBD-4B35-9272-DD3CBFC81887& displaylang=en.

This version works for Windows Server 2003 or Windows XP. Vista and Windows Server 2008 come with the GPMC preinstalled.

The view from gpmc.msc in Windows 2003 varies slightly from Figure 15.8.

---

2. When prompted by UAC, click Continue.
3. In the Group Policy Management console, expand the Forest object.
4. Below the Forest object, expand the Domains object.
5. Expand the domain for which you plan to alter the password policy.
6. Below the domain, expand the Group Policy Objects.
7. Right-click the Default Domain Policy and choose Edit.
8. In the Group Policy Object Editor, Expand Computer Configuration.
9. Expand Windows Settings, as shown in Figure 15.8.
10. Expand Security Settings.
11. Expand Account Policies.
12. Expand Password Policies.

13. In the right pane are six values that can be configured:

- **Enforce password history**—This value, set in number of passwords, is used to prevent users from recycling recent passwords.

- **Maximum password age**—This value, set in days, is used to expire a current password.

- **Minimum password age**—This value, set in days, is used to prevent users from quickly cycling passwords past the enforced password history value to return to the original password.

- **Minimum password length**—This value, set in characters, determines the minimum number of characters that must be used to generate an acceptable password.

- **Password must meet complexity requirements**—This value, set to Enabled or Disabled, determines whether a user's password must meet complexity requirements.

  If this policy is enabled, passwords must meet the following minimum requirements:

  - Not contain the user's account name or parts of the user's full name that exceed two consecutive characters

  - Be at least six characters in length

  - Contain characters from three of the following four categories:

    - English uppercase characters (A through Z)
    - English lowercase characters (a through z)
    - Base 10 digits (0 through 9)
    - Nonalphabetic characters (for example, !, $, #, %)

  Complexity requirements are enforced when passwords are changed or created.

- **Store passwords using reversible encryption**—This value, set to enabled or disabled, determines whether a user's password can be stored using reversible encryption. Although some applications may require this for single sign-on, it is considered somewhat insecure because it greatly increases the chances for a user's password to be determined.

14. Configure the six values to match the company's security policy and close the Group Policy Object Editor.

15. Close the Group Policy Management console.

To view the existing domain-level password policy, follow steps 1–6. Then left-click the Default Domain Policy object. In the right pane, click the Settings tab and then click the link for Show All.

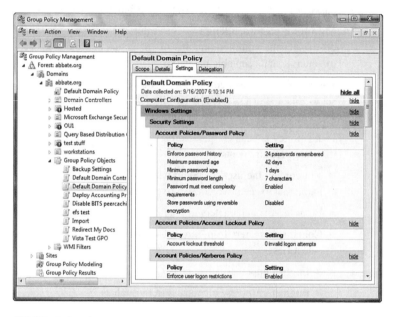

FIGURE 15.8
Viewing the domain password policy.

Summary

As we've seen in this chapter, Vista has continued to evolve the process of user and computer management. Common functions such as those in the Computer Management console have carried forward, as has the concept of "runas." Vista has improved on some of those features through User Account Control and has made it easier than ever to protect systems from themselves by not requiring users to have local administrative rights for commonly performed tasks.

NTFS permissions are still available to help protect data from unauthorized use and continue to be a key factor in simplifying the sharing of systems between multiple users. Through roaming profiles and redirection of common folders, Vista makes it easier than ever to take advantage of a small pool of workstations to service a larger number of users.

By utilizing these features, administrators can continue to provide improved usability to their users in both workgroup and domain models.

CHAPTER 16

Establishing Printer Management in Windows Vista

Introduction to Vista Print Management

Print Management is a new snap-in to Windows Vista, included by default. Print Management provides real-time details about the status of printers and print servers on your network. Administrators can leverage Print Management to automatically install printer connections to groups of client computers. Print Management can help administrators find printers that have error conditions through the use of filters or can even send email notifications or run scripts when a printer or print server needs attention. On printers that provide a web page, Print Management can access additional data, such as toner and paper levels, which can be managed remotely.

This chapter will focus on the use of the Print Management MMC snap-in. Although this MMC snap-in also allows administrators to manage any printer on Windows 20003 R2, this chapter will limit its scope to Windows Vista and how this tool can simplify and automate printer administration. This chapter covers the following topics:

- How to access the Print Management MMC and a basic overview on the tool
- The creation and use of custom filters
- Monitoring and email notifications
- Publishing printers to AD

- How to deploy printers to users via GPO
- Scripting and automation of tasks
- Frequently asked questions and troubleshooting

The Print Management MMC is geared toward individuals who manage printers and print servers throughout an organization. Following is a quick overview on each of the topics, geared toward making the task of locating information easier:

- **How to access the tool, and a basic overview on the tool**—We provide instruction on how to access the tool and how to use the tool.

- **Filters, and how to create custom filters**—What filters are, the benefits of filters, and how to create and use them.

- **Monitoring, and email notifications**—How to use Print Management to monitor printers and print servers and how to create and use email notifications.

- **Scripting, and automating tasks**—How to automate specific tasks using scripts.

- **Publishing printers to AD, and how to deploy printers to users via GPO**—How to publish printers to AD and deploy printers via GPO using the Print Management MMC.

- **FAQs/Troubleshooting**—When using Print Management, a number of frequently asked questions occur; this section addresses the most frequently asked questions and basic troubleshooting.

How to Access the Tool, and a Basic Overview on the Tool

Print Management should not be confused with the Printers interface that is located in the Control Panel. Print Management in Windows Vista is accessed through the Microsoft Management console, also referred to as the MMC. Although many admins will be familiar with the MMC available in earlier versions of Windows, the Vista MMC will seem a little different. What makes Vista's MMC feel different is the fact that the Action pane is enabled by default (see Figure 16.1). The functionality of MMC 3.0 remains the same; however, Print Management is included in Windows Vista, whereas it didn't exist in earlier versions of Windows. In this section, we will review how to access the Print Management MMC and its features.

To access Print Management within the MMC, complete these steps:

1. Click the Start menu, Run (or press the Windows key and the R key).

2. Type **MMC** into the Run dialog box and click OK.

3. When prompted by the User Account Control, click OK.

4. In the MMC window, click File, Add/Remove Snap-in.

5. Locate Print Management and click Add between the two panes.

6. Click Browse to locate the servers you want to manage, or click Add the Local Server to manage the system you are logged in to.

Note

If a message appears that states that network discovery and file sharing are turned off, click that statement and choose to enable those functions.

---

7. Click Finish.

8. Click OK.

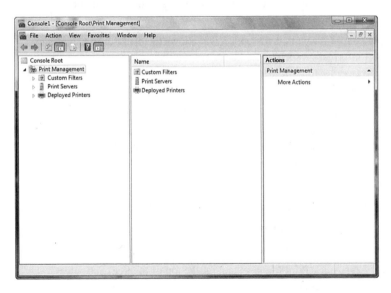

FIGURE 16.1
The Print Management MMC.

Using the Print Manager

In the left pane of the MMC, Print Management is present. Right-clicking this item will present you with the two most commonly accessed functions of the Print Management MMC:

- Add/Remove Servers
- Migrate Printers

Add/Remove Servers is used to add additional print servers that are to be managed by this console or to remove print servers that will no longer be managed.

Migrate Printers is the option used to import or export printer-specific information between various print managers.

There are two ways to add or remove servers in Print Management. The first method is to right-click Print Management (at the top of the tree) and select Add/Remove Servers.

The second method is to navigate to Print Servers, right-click Print Servers, and select Add/Remove Servers. Then specify the server to be managed. If there are no network-based servers to be managed, the Add the Local Server option is available.

Export/Import Printers is the option that allows the operator to export and import information specific to the printer (for example, queues, drivers, port, and processors) to a file with a `.printerExport` extension. The process is very straightforward with fewer than five wizard prompts to answer.

To begin Exporting or Importing printers, perform the following steps:

1. Click Start, Run; type `MMC` and press Enter. If Run is not available from the Start menu, it can be accessed by pressing the Windows key and the R key at the same time.

2. Confirm the User Account Control warning.

3. Click File, and then click Add/Remove Snap-in.

4. Select Print Management and click Add.

5. Add the server to be managed, click Finish, and then click OK.

6. Right-click Print Management (at the top of the tree) and select Migrate Printers.

   A new window appears, called Printer Migration, prompting you with two options: Export Printer Queues and Printer Drivers to a File or Import Printer Queues and Printer Drivers from a File. In this example, we are exporting. Select Export Printer Queues and Printer Drivers to a File and click Next (see Figure 16.2).

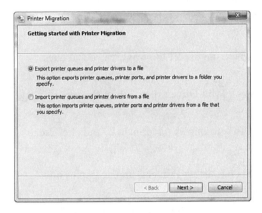

FIGURE 16.2
Printer Migration.

7. Select the server that the printer and information will be exported from and click Next.

8. Confirm the Print Queue(s), Print Driver(s), and Print Processor(s), and click Next.

9. Browse to the location where the file will be exported to and click Next.

   The process executes and a window confirming the export appears with a button to open the Event View for more detail.

10. Click Finish when you're ready to end the process.

To import the printers from an exported list, perform the following steps:

1. Click Start, Run; type **MMC**, and then press Enter.

2. When the User Account Control warning appears, click Accept.

3. Click File, Add/Remove Snap-in.

4. Select Print Management and click Add.

5. Add the server to be managed and click Finish. Then click OK.

6. Right-click Print Management (at the top of the tree) and select Migrate Printers.

A new window will appear, called Printer Migration, prompting you with two options: Export Printer Queues and Printer Drivers to a File or Import Printer Queues and Printer Drivers from a File.

7. Select Import Printer Queues and Printer Drivers from a File and click Next.

8. Browse to the location where the export file was created and click Next.

9. Confirm the Print Queue(s), Print Driver(s), and Print Processor(s), and click Next.

10. Choose which Print Server is to import the printer(s), and click Next.

11. Confirm the Import Options:

      ■ **Import Mode**—Keep Existing Printers; Import Copies or Overwrite Existing Printers.

      ■ **List in the Directory**—List Printers That Were Previously Listed, List all Printers, or Don't List Any Printers

      ■ Also confirm whether to Convert LPR Ports to Standard Port Monitors by clicking the check box, and then click Next.

    Settings will be imported and administrators will be offered the option to review the event log for any problems that may have occurred during the import.

12. Click Finish to complete the import.

More Functions of Print Management

Beyond just importing and exporting printers, there are additional functions of the Print Management MMC that administrators will find very helpful. If you double-click Print Management to expand its functional tree, you will find three main functions:

■ **Custom Filters**—Custom Filters provides "at a glance" monitoring, email notification, and scripting action to automatically mitigate issues (see Figure 16.3). By default, there are four custom filters: All Printers, All Drivers, Printers Not Ready, and Printers with Jobs. These default filters cannot be removed or modified; however, additional filters can be added.

■ **Print Servers**—This function allows the print administrator to manage all the print servers in the organization from one location. Provided is the capability to manage drivers, forms, ports, and printers and perform additional tasks, such as Add Additional Printers, Manage Print Server Properties, Import a Migrated Printer, and Set Notifications.

- **Deployed Printers**—Shows all the printers being deployed by the Group Policy Object (GPO).

Some of the less-used options with Print Management include the following:

- **Extended view**—Available on certain views (such as Print Servers, Print Server, Printers), this function shows more detailed information— in this example, all the jobs currently queued to the printer.

- **Export List**—This function will export the content of the right pane to a TXT or CSV file. It can be accessed by right-clicking a function listed in the left pane and selecting Export List.

- **Taskpad view**—When you're looking at GPO objects with gpedit.msc, a description of the GPO is listed to the left of the listed GPO objects in the same pane (using the extended view). With the ability to create, modify, and delete custom Taskpad views, you can provide the same text to detail printers or link commonly used tools, such as Shell Commands, Menu Commands, or Navigation. The Taskpad can be applied at any level.

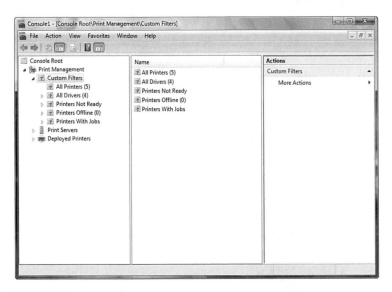

FIGURE 16.3
Custom Filters.

Creating a Taskpad View

To create a custom Taskpad, select the function Taskpad should be added to. In this example, we will be applying a Taskpad shell command to a print server. The print server in this example has been known for a failing print spooler after processing a number of large jobs. Although you can create an automated task to resolve this issue, this example will instead utilize a Taskpad.

1. Click Start, then Run, type **MMC**, and then press Enter. If Run is not available from the Start menu, it can be accessed by pressing the Windows key and the R key at the same time.

2. Confirm the User Account Control warning.

3. Click File, Add/Remove Snap-in.

4. Select Print Management and click Add.

5. Add the server to be managed and click Finish. Then click OK.

6. Expand Print Servers.

7. Expand the target server (for example, CorpHQ-Print-01).

8. Right-click the Printers icon and select New Taskpad View.

9. When the wizard launches, click Next.

10. Choose the default options for style and click Next.

11. On the Taskpad Reuse screen, choose Selected tree item, and click Next.

12. Name the Taskpad view and enter a brief description. Then click Next.

13. Notice that a check box is checked for Add New Tasks to This Taskpad After the Wizard Closes. Click Finish.

14. When the New Task Wizard launches, click Next.

15. The wizard presents three options:

    ▪ **Menu Command**—Similar to creating a shortcut on the desktop, this feature adds a shortcut to a function within the Print Management MMC.

    ▪ **Shell Command**—The capability to create a link to a script or web page that can be opened without having to navigate to the actual location.

    ▪ **Navigation**—The capability to navigate to a Favorite item.

16. Select Shell Command and click Next.

17. Populate all the necessary fields; for example, call a printer-related script and click Next.

18. Enter in a Task Name and Description. Then click Next.

19. Select an icon provided by MMC 3.0 or a custom-created icon, and then click Next.

20. Click Finish.

This will create an icon in the Print Servers view of the Print Management MMC, as shown in Figure 16.4. This type of Taskpad item is especially helpful for help desk employees that have common print tasks delegated to them. This allows administrators to provide employees with exactly the functions they need without granting them access to tools they shouldn't have.

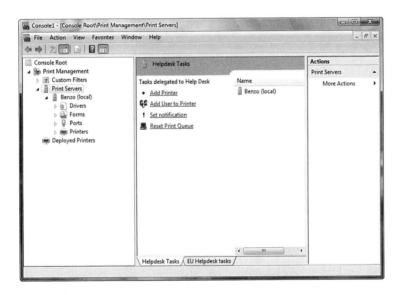

FIGURE 16.4
Taskpad view.

Adding Printers via Print Management
From inside the Print Management MMC, adding a local printer can be accomplished in two ways:

- Right-click the print server name and select Add Printer.

- Navigate to the print server, click Printers, then right-click and select Add Printer.

Adding a printer in either way launches the Network Printer Installation Wizard (see Figure 16.5). You will see four options for Installation Method:

- Search the Network for Printers

- Add a TCP/IP or Web Services Printer by IP Address or Hostname

- Add a New Printer Using an Existing Port

- Create a New Port and Add a New Printer

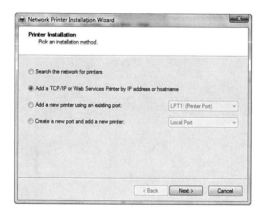

FIGURE 16.5
Options for installation.

In this example, we'll use Add a TCP/IP or Web Services Printer by IP Address or Hostname.

1. Select the option button and click Next.

2. Choose the type of device in the drop-down menu. Enter the printer name or IP address. If you enter Printer name, it needs to be resolvable via Domain Name Services (DNS). Optionally, alter the Port name. Click Next.

   The wizard will now contact the printer to detect the necessary configuration information.

3. Pick the appropriate driver for your printer and click Next.

4. Optionally, share the printer from the local system with the Share This Printer check box. Click Next.

5. Review the printer information and click Next.

6. When the wizard has completed, click Finish.

Filters, and How to Create Custom Filters

By using filters, you can quickly see issues at a glance. This comes in handy when managing a number of print servers and printers within an enterprise. One example is a state agency with more than 20 locations. Each location has multiple file servers, and each file server hosts 20 to 30 printers. By using this MMC, monitoring and performing printer administration suddenly isn't as overwhelming. As mentioned previously, by default there are four filters built in to the Print Management MMC to help you get started:

- **All Printers**—Shows all the active and installed printers on all the print servers managed

- **All Drivers**—All drivers in use by all print servers managed

- **Printers Not Ready**—All printers on all managed print servers that have a status of Not Ready

- **Printers with Jobs**—All printers on all managed print servers that have jobs

In this section, we'll focus on filters within the Print Management MMC.

Most administrators are probably familiar with filters. Filters allow you to identify conditions for which information is matched. In the Print Management MMC, administrators are limited to six selectable filter criteria fields, conditions, and values (see Figure 16.6). Within the criteria field are nine available filter options:

- Comments
- Driver Name
- Jobs in Queue
- Location
- Printer Name
- Is Shared
- Queue Status
- Server Name
- Share Name

Selectable conditions vary from field to field but contain some subset of the following:

- Is exactly
- Is not exactly
- Begins with
- Not begins with
- Ends with
- Not ends with

- Contains
- No contain
- Is less than
- Is less than or equal to
- Is greater than
- Is greater than or equal to

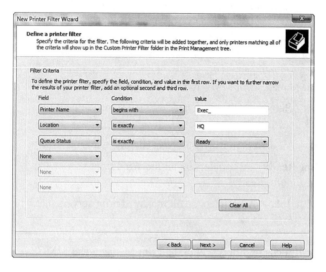

FIGURE 16.6
Options for filters.

These typical Boolean operators allow an administrator to create fairly powerful filters that greatly simplify common tasks. Take, for example, an administrator who is supporting an executive staff. The executives regularly send massive print jobs larger than 40MB to the printer and complain when print jobs do not print. An administrator could create a filter to deal with this issue in the following steps:

1. Click Start, Run; type **MMC**, and then press Enter. If Run is not available from the Start menu, it can be accessed by pressing the Windows key and the R key at the same time.

2. Confirm the User Account Control warning.

3. Click File, Add/Remove Snap-in.

4. Select Print Management and click Add.

5. Add the server to be managed and click Finish. Then click OK.

6. Expand Print Management.

7. Right-click the Custom Filters tree under Printer Management and choose Add New Printer Filter.

8. Name the filter and provide a description. Then click Next.

Note

Notice the check box for Display the Total Number of Printers Next to the Name of the Printer Filter. If this check box is enabled, the view will show the operator the total count of printers matching the filter in the left pane when the Custom Filters tree is expanded.

---

9. Select the criteria for the filter. For the preceding example, you would select the following:

   ■ Queue Status with a condition of Is Exactly and a value of Out of Memory

   ■ Jobs In Queue with a condition of Is Greater Than and a Value of 2

   ■ Location with a condition of Is Exactly and a value of Executive Office

   Select Next when you've completed your selections.

10. Optionally, choose an email notification or triggered script. Click Finish.

After completing this filter, administrators or help desk personnel will have the capability to actively monitor printers used by the executives for a specific reoccurring issue.

Monitoring, and Email Notifications

The previous section reviewed how to set up a custom filter for monitoring purposes. More specifically, it discussed how to monitor the printer status for the executive staff. As an administrator, you have enough to worry about.

Having to actively look at the status of a custom view wouldn't be very efficient! Microsoft has given administrators an easier way to deal with these
situations through the use of notifications based on filter criteria.

The Print Management MMC has the capability to send email through an
SMTP server. The email can include multiple email addresses separated by
semicolons, with a simple message. Typically, the message sent should be
descriptive enough to understand what the issue is at a glance. Building on
the previous example, we will modify the custom filter and configure an
email notification. To modify an existing filter to include a notification,
perform the following steps:

1. Click Start, then Run, type **MMC**, and then press Enter. If Run is not
   available from the Start menu, it can be accessed by pressing the
   Windows key and the R key at the same time.

2. Confirm the User Account Control warning.

3. Click File, Add/Remove Snap-in.

4. Select Print Management and click Add.

5. Add the server to be managed and click Finish. Then click OK.

6. Expand Print Management.

7. Expand Custom Filters.

8. Right-click the custom filter to be modified and choose Properties.

9. Click the Notifications tab.

10. Click the check box Send Email Notification.

11. Populate the Recipient Email Address(es). For this example, we'll send
    the email to ITSupport@companyabc.com.

12. In the Sender Email Address, populate a sender address.

13. Enter the SMTP server's address for your organization.

14. Insert the message that should be sent—for example, **Executive
    printer requires attention**.

15. Click Test to test the message.

16. Confirm message delivery and then click OK to save the modifications
    to the filter, as shown in Figure 16.7.

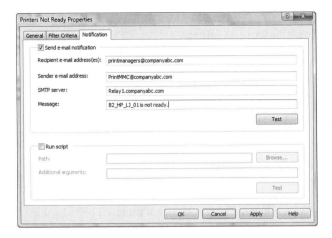

FIGURE 16.7
Configuring Notifications.

Scripting, and Automating Tasks

So far, this chapter has reviewed how to create a custom filter with specific criteria and then apply email notifications. In this next section, it will review how to go a step further by using scripts to automate the resolution of issues.

The Print Management MMC provides three layers of active management: Custom filters for at-a-glance reporting, email notifications for when the operator is away from the console, and scripts to automate the resolution of issues. In this section, we'll show how to add a script to a custom filter and provide some sample scripts to assist in the administration of printers.

Consider the previous example of executives submitting large print jobs that cause the printer not to print. You can automate the correction of this by adding a script to the custom filter that will simply delete all jobs over 40MB.

You can modify custom filters at any time by right-clicking the desired filter and selecting Properties. In Properties, select the Notification tab and check the Run Script check box.

The following is a sample script that can be applied to the custom filter example to delete all jobs over 40MB.

```
strComputer = "."
Set objWMIService = GetObject("winmgmts:" _
    & "{impersonationLevel=impersonate}!\\" & strComputer
➥& "\root\cimv2")
Set colPrintJobs =  objWMIService.ExecQuery _
    ("Select * from Win32_PrintJob Where Size > 41943040")
For Each objPrintJob in colPrintJobs
   objPrintJob.Delete_
Next
```

Although the focus of this book isn't on scripting, it's helpful for administrators to understand what kind of scripts can be applied. The preceding script deletes all print jobs over 40MB. Going back to our example, by using this script, when the printer's memory is maxed and print jobs can no longer be submitted, the executive staff will not have to wait for an administrator to clear the queue of nonimportant print jobs, because the script will do this automatically.

Another example of a handy script is one with the capability to transfer print jobs to another printer. Imagine the following: Traffic on a network printer HP01 hosted on FileServer1 has increased over the past three months. HP01 has been jamming because of worn rollers after printing 50 or so pages. By instituting this script on a custom filter, you can ensure that print jobs are redirected to network printer HP02 when specific conditions are met. This will enable an administrator to automatically maintain a high level of customer service without even being present and avoid situations in which the business is unable to print.

```
strComputer = "."
Set objWMIService = GetObject("winmgmts:" _
  & "{impersonationLevel=impersonate}!\\" & strComputer &
"\root\cimv2")
Set objPrinter = objWMIService.Get _
  ("Win32_Printer.DeviceID='<NETWORK PRINTER NAME>'")
objPrinter.PortName = "<IP OF ANOTHER NETWORK PRINTER>"
objPrinter.Put_
```

Publishing Printers to AD, and How to Deploy Printers to Users via Group Policy

A time-saving feature of the Print Management MMC is the capability to interface with Active Directory. Whether publishing the printer to the directory, deploying the printer to users, and/or deploying computers via GPO, managing printers has become an easier task, especially in enterprise environments.

Using the Print Management MMC, you are able to publish printers to the directory and deploy printers to users and/or machines following these steps:

1. Click Start, then Run, type **MMC**, and then press Enter. If Run is not available from the Start menu, it can be accessed by pressing the Windows key and the R key at the same time.

2. Confirm the User Account Control warning.

3. Click File, Add/Remove Snap-in.

4. Select Print Management and click Add.

5. Add the server to be managed and click Finish. Then click OK.

6. Browse to the desired printer (expanding the necessary Print Servers and Printers).

7. Right-click the printer to be modified.

    The right-click menu provides a number of options; listed next are the more advanced items:

    - **List in Directory**—Publish or remove from directory.

    - **Deploy with Group Policy**—Opens the Deploy with Group Policy window.

    - **Set Printing Defaults**—Modify Printer settings (Paper/Output, Document Options, Effects, Finish, Color, and so on).

    - **Manage Sharing**—Shortcut to the Sharing tab on the printer's property window.

8. Click List in Directory to publish the printer to Active Directory.

9. Right-click the printer and choose Deploy with Group Policy.

10. Click Browse to locate the GPO that will be used.

11. Check the necessary deployment option:

    - User specific

    - Computer specific

12. Click Add after all the information is correct. Then click OK to complete the process.

> **Note**
>
> Additional GPOs can be assigned to this printer by repeating the preceding steps.
>
> By clicking Deployed Printers, you will be able to see at a glance all the printers deployed by GPO.

FAQs/Troubleshooting

Administrators can find answers to the most commonly asked questions in the text that follows:

Q: Who can use Print Management?

A: Users without Administrative rights will not be able to perform any administrative functions; they will be granted View Only rights. Otherwise, administrative rights are required to perform all functions of the Print Management.

Q: How do I view my printer's web management interface within Print Management?

A: By enabling the Extended view, the web interface will be viewable.

Q: How do I suppress warning messages when viewing printer web interfaces within Print Management?

A: By adding the printer's web interface into Internet Explorer's trusted sites, the messages can be suppressed.

Q: Can printers be deployed to pre-Vista operating systems?

A: Yes, by using `PushPrinterConnections.exe` combined with a login script (user deployment) and/or computer start-up scripts (machine deployment).

Troubleshooting

Administrators can find basic troubleshooting steps next:

Q: I've deployed printers using Group Policy; however, users and machines are not receiving the policy.

A: Ensure that the GPO modified is applied to the specific OU and that the permissions are correct.

Q: Within the Print Management, I cannot connect to any servers.

A: Check your firewall settings and ensure that File and Print Sharing is allowed.

Q: I am unable to retrieve printer status on any of the printers hosted by one of my servers.

A: Check the Print Spooler service on the server in question.

Summary

Print Management is a tool that enables printer administrators to perform the task with ease. Administering print servers and printers becomes a bit easier by having a central location for monitoring, updating, and configuring. Administrators will also be able to take advantage of the additional functions within Print Management to automate tasks, such as deploying printers to a group of users and/or computers or automatically applying scripts to mitigate a reoccurring issue. Above all the benefits just listed, the most important benefit of Print Management is the savings in time this tool will bring to administering and troubleshooting errors.

CHAPTER 17

Troubleshooting Windows Vista

Supporting Windows Vista

As with previous versions of Windows, administrators need to troubleshoot, diagnose, and resolve software and hardware issues on computers running Windows Vista. Regardless of the location of the computers, administrators need to support computers and fix problems related to startup and shutdown, programs, disk drives, memory, network, security and even Windows Vista itself.

Administrators have to resolve common problems. For example, following are some of the more common problems computer users are facing:

- **Excessive hard drive activity**—This issue could be related to insufficient memory or to default tasks created by Vista, such as hard drive indexing.

- **Long system startup times**—This issue could be related to insufficient memory, insufficient hard drive space, or possibly because of attached external devices

- **Too many security messages**—This issue is a result of "not enough" security in previous versions of Windows. Microsoft has increased security notifications to inform users of potential security violations. This can be disabled but that is not recommended.

- **Connection issues with networked Windows XP computers**—This issue could be encountered when running third-party security programs. Updating these programs may solve the problem.

- **The Aero interface isn't working**—This issue could be related to the computer not meeting minimum system requirements for Vista for memory or video adapter, or because of incompatible third-party software.

Sometimes the problem is not really an issue but a matter of relearning new features and behaviors within Windows Vista. There are countless small changes in Windows Vista require relearning. The basic concepts presented in previous versions of Windows remain, but administrators and users alike should expect to spend time learning to do some essential small tasks all over again.

> **Note**
>
> The good thing about Windows Vista? Administrators should encounter no differences in working with hardware, installing devices, or troubleshooting issues on computers running different versions of Windows Vista. The steps followed for working with, installing, and troubleshooting computer problems are the same for all editions of Windows Vista.

Understanding System Information

Before resolving a computer problem, administrators typically like to discover as much information as possible about the computer they are about to work with: what type of hardware is installed, software installed, attached peripherals, and any other information administrators feel is valuable in resolving the system problem.

Windows Vista includes a variety of tools for looking at system information. Administrators can use the Computer Management console, the System console, or the System Information tool to gather different system information both basic and advanced. These tools are used to manage computers, diagnose problems, and troubleshoot support issues remotely and while administrators are at sitting at the physical computer.

Computer Management Console

The Computer Management console is a Microsoft Management console that provides services, system, and storage management tools and information. Administrators can use the Computer Management console to provide system administration on both local and remote systems. If the Administrative tools have previously been added to the Start menu computer, administrators can access the Computer Management console by clicking Start, Administrative Tools, Computer Management. Administrators can also start the Computer Management console by using the following steps:

1. Click Start and then click Control Panel.

2. In Control Panel, click the System and Maintenance category heading.

3. Click Administrative Tools and then double-click Computer Management. If prompted, confirm the action to continue.

The multipane console, shown in Figure 17.1, looks similar to other Windows programs such as Windows Explorer. A console tree is displayed in the left pane for easy navigation of the tools. The Actions pane is located on the far right and is similar to the shortcut menu displayed when right-clicking an item. The Actions pane can be toggled on and off by clicking the Show/Hide Actions Pane button on the console toolbar.

The tools are separated into three tool categories:

- **System Tools**—Contains tools for gathering system information and systems management. The tools include the following:

  - **Task Scheduler**—View and manage scheduled system tasks such as disk cleanup or disk defragmentation.

  - **Event Viewer**—View and manage the event logs on the selected computer.

  - **Shared Folders**—View and manage file shares on a computer.

  - **Local Users and Groups**—Manage local users and groups on the selected computer.

  - **Reliability and Performance**—View and examine how running programs affect the computer's performance using both real-time information and by collecting log data for analysis over time.

  - **Device Manager**—View and manage devices and device drivers installed on the selected computer.

- **Storage**—Contains tools for disk drive management. The tools include the following:

  - **Disk Management**—View and manage hard disks, disk partitions, and volume set on the selected computer.

- **Services and Applications**—Contains tools for monitoring services and applications. The tools include the following:

- **Services**—View and manage system services running on the selected computer.

- **WMI Control**—View and manage WMI settings on a remote or local computer.

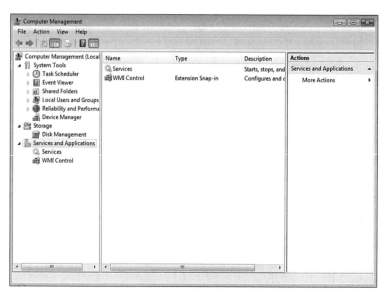

FIGURE 17.1
Using the Computer Management console to manage local and remote computers.

Administrators can use the Computer Management console to manage local or remote computers using the following steps:

1. Right-click the Computer Management node in the console tree and select Connect to Another Computer to open the Select Computer dialog box.

2. Choose another computer by entering the fully qualified domain name (FQDN), such as racerx.airjimi.com, where racerx is the computer name and airjimi.com is the domain name. Alternatively, use the Browse button to search for the computer to work with.

Basic System Information

Administrators can use the System console to view and manage basic system settings. Administrators can access the System console using the following steps:

1. Click Start and then click Control Panel.

2. In Control Panel, click the System and Maintenance category heading.

3. Click System.

Like other Windows applications and tools, the System console is divided into four panes of information. The four distinct areas provide links for accessing system information and completing common system tasks (see Figure 17.2).

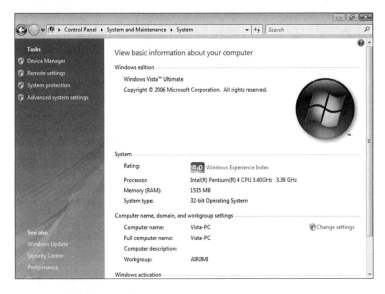

FIGURE 17.2
Using the System console to manage system properties.

The four areas are as follows:

- **Windows Edition**—Displays the operating system edition and version.

- **System area**—Displays system information related to the processor, memory, system type (32 bit or 64 bit), and the Windows Experience Index rating.

- **Computer Name, Domain, and Workgroup Settings**—Lists the computer name, full computer name, computer description, and domain information. To modify the settings, click the Change Settings option to display the System Properties dialog box.

- **Windows Activation**—Displays the status of the Windows Vista operating system and product key. If Windows Vista isn't activated, administrators can click the activation link to initiate the activation process and then follow the prompts. Click the Change Product Key link to change the product key.

The left pane provides easy access to the primary support tools, such as Device Manager, Remote Settings, System Protection, and Advanced System Settings.

The Windows Experience Index is one of the main indicators of a computer performance under Windows Vista. The rating is important in determining which Windows Vista operating system the computer will support. To rate a computer for performance, click Windows Experience under System and then click Update My Score on the Performance Information and Tools Page to start the performance testing process. After a computer is rated, administrators can click the Check Your Computer's Windows Experience Index Base Score link under System to access the Performance Rating and Tools console.

The Performance Rating and Tools console displays the system's overall rating and lists the installed hardware. The hardware information is displayed and categorized by each component: processor, memory, primary hard disk, graphics, and gaming graphics. Windows Vista uses the index rating to determine which features can be configured for use. If a system has a low rating, certain features, such as the Aero interface, will be turned off to improve performance. If the index rating changes over time, disabled features can be reenabled for use.

Performance issues can also be reviewed by using the Problem Reports and Solutions link in the left pane of the Performance Information and Tools page. To see possible solutions to a problem, select the check box for an issue and then click Check for Solutions. After a problem has been resolved, click Clear Solution and Problem History from within Problem Reports and Solutions, and then click Clear All.

Advanced System Info

Administrators can look at exhaustive system information using two similarly named tools, Systeminfo and System Information. Systeminfo is an EXE command-line tool that provides information in basic DOS-like text format. It displays information regarding the system Windows version, BIOS, memory, network configuration, and other system information. Administrators can run the utility by opening a Command Prompt window, typing **Systeminfo** and pressing Enter. This will display information such as that shown in Figure 17.3.

FIGURE 17.3
Using the command-line utility Systeminfo to view system settings.

Using the command-line switch, /Fo, along with a CSV or Table parameter, administrators can output the information to a file so that it can be used with other applications. For example, to output information to a file named User1pc.csv, administrators would enter the following command:

```
Systeminfo /fo csv > user1pc.csv.
```

Another handy switch, /S, allows administrators to get information about another computer on the network.

> **Tip**
>
> The Systeminfo command-line utility has a variety of switches enabling administrators to perform special functions. Type **Systeminfo /?** at a command prompt to display information regarding the following switch options:
>
> ```
> SYSTEMINFO [/S system [/U username [/P [password]]]]
> ➥[/FO format] [/NH]
> ```

Using Vista Troubleshooting and Diagnostics Tools

Many—if not most—administrators have spent a significant amount of time troubleshooting configuration errors in previous versions of Windows, such as Windows XP. In doing so, administrators have come to appreciate more commonly known tools and utilities, such as the System Configuration Utility and Disc Cleaner, or lesser-known troubleshooting utilities such as File Verification.

To help administrators, Windows Vista includes a variety of troubleshooting tools, which include the following:

- **Backup (SDCLT.exe)**—This utility runs the Backup Status and Configuration, which administrators use to back up and recover the Windows Vista system.

- **Built-in Diagnostics**—This tool scans the system, examining hardware and software configurations for problems, and is useful for troubleshooting performance-related issues.

- **Disc Cleanup**—This utility examines the disk drives for unnecessary files.

- **Disk Defragmenter**—This utility examines the disk drives for file fragmentation and is used to defragment the disk drives.

- **DirectX Diagnostics Tool (DXDIAG.exe)**—This tool is used for troubleshooting problems with DirectX.

- **File Signature Verification tool**—This tool checks files to see whether they are digitally signed. Critical files that are not digitally signed are displayed in a list of results.

- **System Configuration Utility (`MSConfig.exe`)**—This utility enables management of system configuration information. Administrators can manage and configure normal, selective, or diagnostic startup types.

- **System Restore (`RSTRUI.exe`)**—This utility is used to create system restore points and to roll the system back to a specific restore point.

Understanding System Configuration

Administrators have come to appreciate the System Configuration utility, also known as `MSConfig.exe`. Although familiar with the System Configuration tool in Windows XP, administrators will like the new and improved version of the System Configuration utility found in Windows Vista. The new System Configuration utility provides a simpler, more organized user interface than its predecessor. The utility also contains a Tools tab for accessing and running Windows Vista's advanced diagnostic utilities.

Just like in Windows XP, administrators can launch Windows Vista's System Configuration utility by pressing the Windows button +R to access the Run dialog box, typing `msconfig.exe` into the Open box, and then clicking OK. In Windows Vista, administrators can take advantage of the Start menu's Instant Search feature by pressing the Windows button and beginning to type the word `System`. As `sys` is typed, System Configuration will appear at the top of the results pane and administrators can immediately press Enter to start System Configuration. When prompted with the UAC dialog box, confirm the action to continue launching the System Configuration utility.

Tip

Although administrators can easily access the Run dialog box by pressing the Windows button +R, the Run command no longer appears on Windows Vista's Start menu by default. The command was removed to make room for other Start menu items. If desired, administrators can add it back to the Start menu using the following steps:

1. Right-click the Start button and select the Properties menu option.

2. When the Taskbar and Start Menu Properties dialog box appears, make sure that the Start Menu tab is selected. Click the Customize button adjacent to the Start Menu option.

3. Scroll down the list and select the Run Command check box and then click OK.

After System Configuration launches, as shown in Figure 17.4, administrators will see many differences when compared to the version in Windows XP, which is shown in Figure 17.5. A few of the differences are

- The word Utility has been removed from the name of the tool.
- The SYSTEM.INI and WIN.INI tabs have been removed.
- The BOOT.INI tab has been renamed to Boot.
- A new tab named Tools has been added.

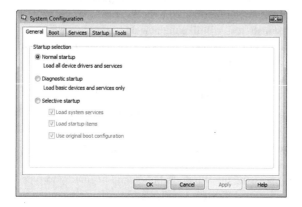

FIGURE 17.4
Viewing the System Configuration tool in Windows Vista.

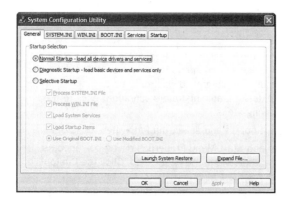

FIGURE 17.5
Viewing the System Configuration tool in Windows XP.

The General tab in System Configuration contains the same three startup options as the Windows XP version. The default configuration is the Normal Startup, which loads all the normal device drivers and services. The Diagnostic Startup option loads only the basic services and drivers. The Selective Startup provides you with the option to selectively load system services and startup programs. (The Use Original Boot Configuration check box stays selected unless you change the default setting on the Boot tab.)

The Boot tab in System Configuration contains boot configuration options that allow administrators to manipulate and manage the startup of Windows Vista. One big configuration options improvement over the Windows XP version is that the options and check box settings now use friendly names rather than using the cryptic syntax-based names used in the Windows XP Boot.ini file. In the lower-right of the dialog box, administrators can see a new check box titled Make All Boot Settings Permanent. When this check box is selected, System Configuration will not keep track of any configuration changes. Administrators must manually undo any changes made and will not be able to undo any changes by selecting Normal Startup on the General tab. Clicking the Advanced Options button brings up the Boot Advanced Options dialog box, which also uses friendly names and all the same settings. The major difference in the Advanced Options is that Windows Vista now has an option to choose and configure the USB port as part of the debugging options.

On the Services tab, administrators can see a list of all the services started when the computer boots. The current status of the application—Running or Stopped—is also displayed. Administrators can enable or disable individual services at boot for troubleshooting of services that might be contributing to system startup problems. One nice feature is that System Configuration also now keeps track of the date on which you disabled a particular service.

The Startup tab displays a list of all the applications that run when Windows Vista starts up. It lists applications that run when the computer boots, along with the name of their publisher, the path to the executable file, and the location of the Registry key or shortcut that causes the application to run. The Startup tab contains two new features—a Manufacturer heading and a Date Disabled heading. The Manufacturing heading helps administrators identify an application, whereas the Date Disabled heading helps administrators track the date on which you disabled a startup application. To troubleshoot startup issues, administrators can clear the check box for a startup item to disable it on the next system boot. If administrators have chosen Selective startup on the General tab, they must either choose Normal startup on the General tab or select the startup item's check box to start it again at boot.

The Tools tab is a new addition to the System Configuration and is a handy place for administrators to find an arsenal of diagnostic and troubleshooting tools. The list of tools is comprehensive and includes detailed descriptions for tools and also the exact syntax of the command-line executable. To use a tool, highlight the tool to use and click Launch.

For detailed information on troubleshooting startup issues, refer to the section "Understanding and Troubleshooting Vista System Startup" later in this chapter.

Using Disk Cleanup

The Disk Cleanup utility checks disk drives for unnecessary files and removes files that are not needed. Administrators can work with Disk Cleanup using the following steps:

1. Click Start, Programs or All Programs, Accessories, System Tools. Disk Cleaner can also be run from the command line using CLEANMGR.exe.

2. Administrators can choose to clean all files on the computers or to clean only the current user's files. Cleaning all files on the computer requires administrator privileges.

3. If multiple drives are present in the computer, the Drive Selection dialog box displays so that the appropriate drive can be selected for cleanup. Select the proper drive to clean using the drop-down list and click OK.

4. Disk Cleanup searches the selected drive for temporary files, files no longer needed, and files that can be compressed to maximize disk storage space. Larger drives will take longer times to search for appropriate files.

5. After the search process is complete, Disk Cleanup provides a report of the files that have been found and how much disk space will be gained by deleting the files. The report may contain the following file categories:

   - **Downloaded Program Files**—Programs downloaded by the browser, such as ActiveX controls, that can be deleted.

   - **Microsoft Office Temporary Files**—Temporary files and logs used by Microsoft Office that can be deleted.

   - **Offline Files**—Local copies of network files designated for offline use and stored to enable offline access. These files can be deleted.

- **Temporary Offline Files**—Temporary data and work files for recently accessed network files. These files can be deleted.

- **Recycle Bin**—Files that have been deleted from the computer but have not yet been purged. These files can be deleted. Emptying the Recycle Bin permanently removes these files.

- **Temporary Internet Files**—Web pages stored to support browser caching of web pages. These files can be deleted.

6. Select the appropriate check boxes in the Files to Delete list for the files to delete and click OK. If prompted to confirm the action, click Yes.

Using File Signature Verification

Critical system files in Windows Vista are digitally signed. Digital signatures provide administrators two important functions:

- Proof of file authenticity

- Easier tracking of file changes that may cause system issues

When troubleshooting suspicious computer behavior, administrators should check to see if critical files have been changed in any way and if the system file changes are the source of the computer problems. The File Signature Verification utility is a great method for administrators to check the status of file integrity.

Administrators can start the File Signature Verification utility, SIGVERIF.EXE, using the following steps:

1. Click Start, type **sigverif** in the Search box, and press Enter. Click Start to initiate the File Signature Verification utility with default configuration. The default configuration displays a list of files that are not digitally signed and writes the results to a file stored in c:\Users\ Public\DocumentsSIGVERIF.TXT.

2. The list of files shown in the File Signature Verification utility report do not have digital signatures and may have been changed or replaced by malicious applications such as viruses or spyware. Administrators should review error reports and event logs to see if these files show up on the error reports.

3. Administrators should also check the results that are stored in
SIGVERIF.TXT file. File are listed by status—signed, unsigned, and not
scanned—and any files that have been altered will be marked as
changed.

After reviewing the results, administrators may be able to determine the exact
cause of the computer problems and pinpoint the issue to specific files that
have been altered by malicious means.

Understanding and Troubleshooting Vista System Startup

When troubleshooting system startup issues, the System Configuration tool is
a good tool to use. System Configuration is an integrated tool for managing
system configuration information. Using the System Configuration tool,
administrators can manage system startup options, startup applications, and
startup services.

The System Configuration tool can be used to select one of three startup
modes for Windows Vista: Normal Startup, Diagnostic Startup, or Selective
Startup. The default configuration is Normal Startup, which loads all the
normal device drivers and enabled services for the operating system. The
Diagnostic Startup option loads only the basic services and drivers. After the
system is started in Diagnostic Startup mode, administrators can modify
system settings to resolve configuration issues. The Selective Startup
provides you with the option to selectively load system services and startup
programs and pinpoint problem areas in the configuration.

To change the startup mode, administrators can complete the following steps:

1. Click Start, type **msconfig** in the Search box, and then press Enter.
This launches the System Configuration tool.

2. Select either Diagnostic Startup or Selective Startup on the General
tab. If Selective Startup is chosen, administrators can modify different
options and can select from the following items:

   - **Load System Services**—Instructs the system to load Windows
   services on startup. Use the settings on the Services tab to
   specify which services are started.

   - **Load Startup Items**—Instructs the system to run applications
   designated as startup items. Administrators can enable and
   disable startup applications using options on the Startup tab.

- **Use Original Boot Configuration**—Instructs the system to process the original boot configuration instead of the modified boot settings created in System Configuration. Administrators can also change boot settings and additional boot flags on the Boot tab to control system startup. If any changes are made on the Boot tab, the Selective Startup option is automatically selected on the General tab.

3. When you're finished making changes, click OK and then reboot the system. If the system encounters startup problems, restart the system in Safe Mode and then make setting changes to correct. Safe Mode automatically appears as an option on the screen if the system fails to boot properly.

Configuring Boot Options

Unlike previous versions of Windows, Windows Vista no longer uses the Boot.ini or other boot files in a standard configuration. Windows Vista uses the Windows Boot Manager and a boot application to start up Windows Vista. When troubleshooting system issues, administrators can use the Boot tab, shown in Figure 17.6, to control the boot partition, boot startup method, and other boot options used by the operating system.

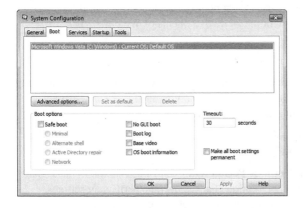

FIGURE 17.6
Using the System Configuration's Boot tab to modify boot options and control system startup.

Administrators can select the following options when working with operating system options:

- **Set as Default**—Sets the current boot partition as the default partition. The default partition is selected if the Timeout Value expires before another option is chosen.

- **Delete**—Deletes the selected operating system.

- **Timeout**—Sets the default amount of time the system waits before booting with the default partition.

- **Advanced Options**—Allows configuration of boot options for processors, memory, PCI locking, HAL detection, and kernel process debugging.

- **Safe Boot**—Starts the system in Safe Mode with options for Minimal (networking disabled with only critical services running), Alternate Shell (networking and GUI are disabled with only critical services running), Active Directory Repair (graphical user interface in safe mode running critical system services and Active Directory), or Network (graphical user interface in Safe Mode running only critical system services. Networking is enabled.) boots. This mode is useful for resolving configuration issues.

- **No GUI Boot**—Boots to Windows prompt and does not display the Windows splash screen when booting. This mode is useful for diagnosing problems with the GUI components of Windows Vista.

- **Boot Log**—Stores all information from the boot process in the file `%SystemRoot%Ntbtlog.txt`.

- **Base Video**—Forces the computer to use VGA (video adapter display) settings. This option is useful for resolving incorrect video display modes and monitor resolution issues.

- **OS Boot Information**—Starts the computer so that administrators can see detailed startup activities before the Windows GUI is loaded.

- **Make All Boot Settings Permanent**—Select this option to make standard or advanced boot option changes become permanent settings. Typically, troubleshooting and debugging options will not need to be made permanent, so be sure to deselect those options before setting this option and selecting OK.

If more than one operating system is present in the upper part of the dialog box, administrators will be able to select a different operating system to boot

Windows Vista with, and the Set as Default and Delete buttons will be active. If only one operating system is present, the Set as Default and Delete buttons will be grayed out and cannot be used.

After startup configuration changes are made, they are stored by the System Configuration utility and the system must be restarted for the changes to take effect. To roll back any changes made, select the Normal Startup option on the General tab and then click OK.

Configuring Startup Applications

Administrators will run into situations where startup applications are causing system problems. A simple way to determine which application is the problem is to disable the application from starting automatically and then reboot the system. If the problems cease, the offending program has been found and should be disabled permanently. If the problem still exists, repeat the process with other applications until the problem ceases. Administrators can disable programs using the following steps:

1. Click Start, type `msconfig` in the Search box, and then press Enter. This launches the System Configuration tool.

2. Click the Startup tab to display the list of programs currently loading at startup. Clear the check box next to the potential problem-causing application. This prevents the application from launching at the next system startup.

3. Click OK. The system may display a prompt to reboot the system. Confirm the reboot action to continue and make the modifications take effect at system restart. If not prompted, perform a manual reboot of the system.

4. Repeat this process as needed to pinpoint the offending program. If an application is not identified as the problem, look to other Windows components, services, and device drivers to locate the problem.

Configuring Startup Services

Similar to startup applications, system services can also cause system problems. To determine which service is the problem, temporarily disable the service from starting automatically at boot and then reboot the system. If the problems cease, the offending service has been found and should be disabled permanently. If the problem still exists, repeat the process with other services until the problem ceases. Administrators can temporarily disable services using the following steps:

1. Click Start, type `msconfig` in the Search box, and then press Enter. This launches the System Configuration tool.

2. Click the Services tab to display the list of services installed on the computer. The tab also includes information regarding the status of the service, running or stopped, and whether the service is critical to the operation of Windows Vista. Clear the check box next to the potential problem-causing service. This prevents the service from launching at the next system startup.

3. Click OK. The system may display a prompt to reboot the system. Confirm the reboot action to continue and make the modifications take effect at system restart. If not prompted, perform a manual reboot of the system.

4. Repeat this process as needed to pinpoint the offending service. If a service is not identified as the problem, look to other Windows components, startup applications, and device drivers to locate the problem

Understanding Remote Assistance

Remote Assistance is a collaborative Help tool that provides administrators with a method for viewing and controlling a user's desktop to assist in diagnosing and resolving computer problems. A feature of previous versions of Windows, such as Windows XP Windows Server 2003 and later versions, Remote Assistance in Windows Vista can be used to initiate and respond to Remote Assistance invitations from these operating systems. With Remote Assistance, a user initiates a remote invitation request. Similarly, administrators can initiate sessions and offer help to users. After a session is created, administrators can chat with the user, view their desktop screens, and, if permitted, control the computer. Invitations can be time limited from 8 hours to 30 days to allow administrators time to respond to the request for help. Be sure to set an appropriate time for system access that matches support service-level agreements.

Remote Assistance invitations can be created using email invitations or file invitations. Email invitations are sent as email messages to a specific email address. Administrators can configure a specific email address, such as RemoteHelp@mycompanyname.com, to allow users to send initiation requests to an easy-to-remote email address. The email address can also be a distribution list, which provides an easy way to send the request to multiple people or multiple addresses of the support team. The email message contains an attachment that is used to initiate the Remote Assistance session.

File invitations are saved as Microsoft Remote Control Incident Files (MsRcIncident) and are initiated by double-clicking the filename. File invitations are useful for web-based email where the attachment is made separately. File invitations may also be used in conjunction with a share network folder. For example, network administrators may automatically map a network drive, named HelpdeskAssistance or RemoteHelp, for users that is accessible by the support team. Users can then place their file invitations in this folder to request Remote Assistance.

For enhanced security in Windows Vista, Remote Assistance invitations must be created with a control password. This security control was not required in previous features of Windows. The control password provides an additional layer of security and ensures that users are authorized to provide remote assistance and that they know the control password. Administrators should create a corporate policy requiring the use of invitation passwords, regular intervals for changing passwords, and possible assigning per department within the company. Another security feature is that computers can be configured to grant different levels of access. System access can be unrestricted to allow remote access by any version of Remote Desktop (less secure) or restricted to only those computers running Remote Desktop with Network Level Authentication (more secure). By default, neither Remote Assistance nor Remote Desktop are enabled.

Configuring Remote Assistance

Remote Assistance must be enabled before Remote Assistance invitations can be used by administrators. To configure Remote Assistance, administrators should perform the following steps:

1. In Control Panel, click System and Maintenance, and then click System.

2. On the System page, click Remote Settings in the left pane to open the System Properties dialog box to the Remote tab, as shown in Figure 17.7. If prompted, confirm the action to continue.

3. Clear the Allow Remote Assistance Connections to This Computer check box to disable remote invitations to this computer. Click OK and then skip the remaining steps. Select the Allow Remote Assistance Connections to This Computer check box to enable remote invitations to this computer.

4. In the Remote Assistance section, click Advanced to display the Remote Assistance Settings dialog box.

FIGURE 17.7
Using the Remote tab options to configure remote computer access.

5. Clear the Allow This Computer to Be Controlled Remotely check box to disallow others from viewing and controlling the desktop. To provide viewing and desktop control, select the check box next to the Allow This Computer to Be Controlled Remotely setting.

6. In the Invitations section, configure the time allowance window for invitations to remain open. Administrators can configure a time value in minutes, hours, or days. The default maximum expiration limit is 6 hours and the maximum expiration time limit 30 days. To create invitations that can be used only by Windows Vista or later versions, select the check box next to the Create Invitations That Can Only Be Used from Computers Running Windows Vista or Later option.

7. Click OK twice to complete the configuration of Remote Assistance settings.

> **Note**
>
> Remote Assistance in Windows Vista in much improved over previous versions. It uses less bandwidth, it is faster, and it works effectively through Network Address Translation firewalls. Remote Assistance relies on the connection between the user's computers and the administrator's computer using the TCP communications protocol. It also requires communication over port 3389 to work properly. If administrators encounter difficult using Remote Assistance, they should check that port 3389 is not being blocked by software or hardware firewalls.

Using Remote Assistance Invitations

As discussed earlier, Remote Assistance invitations can be created by email or by file. Remote Assistance email invitations can be created using the following steps:

1. Click the Help and Support button on the Start menu toolbar and then click Windows Remote Assistance under Ask Someone. In the Remote Assistance Wizard, click Invite Someone You Trust to Help You, and then click Use Email to Send an Invitation.

2. Enter a secure password for connecting to the computer when asked. The secure password being created is good only for the Remote Assistance session and for the person being inviting to provide assistance.

3. Click Next to start the default mail program in Windows Vista and create a mail message with the Remote Assistance invitation. Enter the email address of the person to invite for assistance and click Send to deliver the mail message.

Remote Assistance file invitations can be created using the following steps:

1. Click the Help and Support button on the toolbar and then click Windows Remote Assistance under Ask Someone. In the Remote Assistance Wizard, click Invite Someone You Trust to Help You and then click Save This Invitation as a File.

2. Enter a path and filename in the field provided. For easy access by administrators, specify a designated network folder.

3. Enter a secure password for connecting to the computer when asked. The secure password being created is good only for the Remote Assistance session and for the person being inviting to provide assistance.

4. Click Finish to save the file invitation.

The default maximum expiration limit is six hours for Remote Assistance invitations, allowing administrators plenty of time to respond to the request. After the invitation is sent, the Windows Remote Assistance dialog box is displayed. The Remote Assistance dialog box provides the following options, which are useful for managing the assistance session:

- **Disconnect**—Disconnects and ends the help request.

- **Request Control**—Requests computer control or stops remote control of the computer.

- **Fit to Screen**—Resizes the remote user's display to fit the window.

- **Settings**—Allows configuration of the session settings, such as key controls, background displays settings, and bandwidth usage.

- **Chat**—Creates a chat window for sending messages between the current user and the remote assistance user.

- **Send File**—Transfers a file to the remote computer.

Offering and Answering Remote Assistance Invitations

Administrators can also offer assistance to users who they know are having computer problems. This allows the administrative staff to be proactive and offer assistance rather than wait for an invitation from a user. Use the following steps to offer assistance to a user:

1. Click the Help and Support button on the toolbar and then click Remote Assistance under Ask Someone. In the Remote Assistance Wizard, click Offer to Help Someone.

2. Enter the name or IP address of the computer to assist. Be sure that the computer you want to contact is enabled for Remote Assistance, or establishing a connection will not work.

3. Click Finish to establish a connection.

Administrators can also answer existing Remote Assistance invitations by double-clicking a file or email attachment. Administrators can answer invitations saved to a network location by using the following steps:

1. Click the Help and Support button on the toolbar and then click Remote Assistance under Ask Someone. In the Remote Assistance Wizard, click Offer to Help Someone.

2. Click Browse and use the Open dialog box to browse for an invitation. Select an invitation and click Open.

3. Provide the proper password when prompted to connect to the remote computer and click Finish. If the invitation time has not expired or the request for help has not been canceled, Remote Assistance will be allowed.

Detecting and Resolving Vista Errors

Managing computer systems and keeping them functioning properly can keep administrators very busy. Computers can have many components, services, and applications. Using the troubleshooting tools in this chapter is a big part of resolving common problems and resolving them. Unfortunately, not all problems can be automatically detected and resolved by the operating system itself. Administrators must still look at windows components, services, applications, and hardware devices, and determine which is causing the problem. Luckily, Windows Vista contains error logs for windows components, services, applications, and installed devices. These error logs are helpful for locating errors encountered by the operating system.

Using Event Logs for Error Tracking and Diagnostics

Windows Vista saves errors created by processes, applications, services, and hardware devices in log files. Windows Vista uses two types of log files, named Windows Logs and Applications and Services Logs. Windows Logs are used to record system events of applications, setup, security, forwarded events, and system components. Applications and Services Logs are used to log application and service-specific events.

Log file entries are recorded according to the warning level of the activity. The levels of event severity are classified by the following:

- **Information**—An informational event related to a successful system or application action.

- **Warning**—A warning of an event that may cause future system problems.

- **Error**—An error that indicates a problem such as the failure of a service to start properly.

- **Audit Success**—An event related to the successful completion of an action.

- **Audit Failure**—An event related to the failed completion of an action.

The summary and detailed event entries also contain the following information in addition to the date and time and severity level. The following information is also provided in the event entries:

- **Source**—The application, component, or service that logged the event.

- **Event ID**—A number that identifies the particular event type. The first line of the description usually contains the name of the event type.

- **Task Category**—The category of the event.

- **User**—The username of the user on whose behalf the event occurred. If a process or service caused the event, the username is identified as the process that triggered the event, such as System or Local Service or Network Service.

- **Computer**—The name of the computer on which the event occurred.

Viewing and Administering Event Logs

On computers that are configured to display the Administrative tools on the All Programs menu, administrators can access the event logs using the Event Viewer node within Computer Management (Start, All Programs, Administrative Tools, Computer Management). For systems not configured in this manner, type `Computer Management` in the Search box and press Enter. To access the event logs, perform the following steps:

1. Open Computer Management and expand the Event Viewer node.
2. Expand the Windows Logs node or the Applications and Services Logs or open both to view the logs.
3. Select the log to view.

Errors and warnings are the two primary types of events administrators will want to examine in detail. These types of events are indicative of future system failures and may contain helpful information regarding prevention of future system problems. When these types of errors occur, double-click to open the event and view detailed information about the event. Administrators can also use the provided link to learn more about the error or search the Microsoft Knowledge Base for the event ID or using part of the event description.

Resolving Startup and Shutdown Issues

Normally, administrators can shut down and restart Windows Vista by click-ing the Start button and then using the Options button to Shut Down or Restart a computer as necessary. Sometimes, computers seem to have a will of their own and refuse to respond as required. When this happens, adminis-trators need to take additional action to Shut Down or Restart the system. Before using last-ditch efforts such as pressing and holding in the computers power button or manually pulling the power cord out of the back of the system, administrators should try the following steps:

1. Press Ctrl+Alt+Del to display the Windows Screen. Click Start Task Manager to start the Task Manager application. If Ctrl+Alt+Del doesn't work, right-click the taskbar and select Task Manager.

2. On the Application tab, review the open applications listed for one app that is now responding. If the applications are all running normally, skip to step 4.

3. Select the application that is not responding and then click End Task. If the application fails to respond to the end task request, a dialog prompt appears that allows the administrator to end the application immedi-ately or to cancel the end task request. Click End Task Now.

4. At this point, try shutting down or restarting the computer by pressing Ctrl+Alt+Del and then using the Options button to gracefully shut down or restart a computer.

Understanding System Stop Errors

If a major system error occurs during the start, installation of programs, or while completing a system action, Windows Vista displays a system Stop Error across the monitor. When this occurs, administrators should record the information on the screen. This information can be helpful when attempting to fix the problem. The Stop error message contains useful information related to the Error Name (third line of the error message written in all CAPS), troubleshooting recommendations (following the Error name), Error Number (STOP, an error number, and parameters. That is, `STOP: 0x100000EA THREAD_STUCK_IN_DEVICE_DRIVER_M`).

After the error information has been gathered, try restarting the computer in Safe Mode. At the same time, administrators should look up the stop error on the Microsoft Knowledge Base and see if it is a known problem. If it is a common problem, there may be a set of instructions useful for resolving the issue.

Administrators should also check device drivers. A newly installed device driver may be causing the issue, and rolling back to a previous driver may solve the problem. Similar to troubleshooting device driver installations, administrators should also check recently installed applications and hardware. Make sure that new applications were installed completely and that hardware installations were properly performed and the correct device drivers were installed.

In addition, administrators should check system resources. Critically low amounts of random access memory (RAM) or hard disk space can cause system problems. Administrators can use tools such as Disk Cleanup to free disk space or Task Manager to close unnecessary programs.

Last, administrators should check all hardware components and BIOS versions. Check the BIOS settings, hard disk, memory, video cards, and other equipment for signs of incorrect configuration or installation, failure because of overheating, and general compatibility with Windows Vista.

> **Note**
>
> For detailed information about stop errors, check out http://aumha.org/ a/stop.htm. This website is a great resource for figuring out what generated the stop error in the first place!

Recovering from System Failures

Administrators are often faced with computers that will not start up properly and that display symptoms of system failure. Windows Vista needs specific files operating correctly for it to boot properly. If a file is missing or corrupted, the system may not start up properly or may undergo a complete system failure. Many times, systems problems are caused by improperly installed hardware, and the associated device drivers or the system configuration and system files or Registry have been improperly updated and are causing a system conflict. Sometimes the system hasn't really gone through a system failure but the user thinks it has because the user's data is suddenly incorrect or missing. Using tools such as System Protection, System Restore, and Previous Versions, administrators can avoid most system failures and problems. Additionally, the capability to resume semi-gracefully from a filed hibernation or sleep mode and reinstall system files without loss of user data are a big plus for administrators managing Windows Vista systems.

Understanding the Vista Previous Versions Feature

From Windows Server 2003, Vista inherits a nifty feature known as Previous Versions. Previous Versions are either backup copies—copies of files and folders that you back up by using the Back Up Files Wizard—or shadow copies—copies of files and folders that Windows automatically saves as part of a system restore point. Administrators can use previous versions of files to restore files that were accidentally modified or deleted or that were damaged. Depending on the type of file or folder, administrators can open, save to a different location, or restore a previous version.

Shadow copies can be copies of files on your computer or shared files on a computer on a network and are automatically saved as part of a restore point in System Properties. If System Protection is turned on, Windows automatically creates shadow copies of files that have been modified since the last restore point was made. Typically, restore points are made once a day. If the hard disk is partitioned or if more than one hard disk is on your computer, administrators will need to turn on System Protection on the additional partitions or hard disks.

> **Note**
>
> To save hard disk space, only one version of a file is saved as a shadow copy. For example, if users modify a file several times in one day, only the version that was current when the restore point was made is saved. System Restore points typically require at least 300MB of disk space for each saved checkpoint, up to a total of 10% of the total disk capacity. Because the amount of space allocated to System Restore is not configurable, System Restore frees up space as needed for user data and overwrites existing restore points if the disk runs out of space.

To use System Restore management on a computer, complete the following steps:

1. Click Start, Control Panel, and then select the System and Maintenance category link. Next, click System.

2. Click Change Settings under the Computer Name, Domain, and Workgroup Settings section of the System Console. Alternatively, administrators can select the Advanced System Settings in the left pane.

3. In the System Properties dialog box, select the System Protection tab.
Select the check box next to the volume to enable System Restore and
create automatic restore points. To manually create a restore point,
click Create and enter a name for the restore point.

4. To disable System Restore for a volume, clear the check box next to
the volume to work with. If prompted, click Yes to confirm disabling
System Restore. Be sure that this is what you want to do before
confirming the action. When System Restore is turned off, all associated restore points are removed and the action cannot be reversed.

5. Click OK when you're finished making changes.

Restoring a file or folder to a previous version is as simple using the following steps:

1. Right-click the file or folder to work with and then select Properties.

2. In the Properties dialog box, select the Previous Versions tab to display
previous versions of files or folders.

3. Select a file or folder version to work with and then choose the Open
button (to open a previous version), Copy button (create a copy of a
previous version), or Restore button (to revert a file or folder back to a
previous version).

If a previous version is not seen, check the following possibilities:

■ **System Restore may not have been enabled on the volume**—If
System Protection is not turned on, Windows can't create shadow
copies.

■ **The file might be an offline file**—Offline files are copies of files that
are stored on shared network folders. Shadow copies are not available
for offline files.

■ **The file might be a system file**—Shadow copies are unavailable for
Windows system files and folders, such as the system folder where
Windows is installed and files in the system folder, which is typically
C:\Windows.

■ **The file or folder has been deleted or renamed**—Use the System
Restore feature to restore the deleted or renamed folder or file.

Reinstalling System Files Using the Repair Option

As a last ditch effort to recover a system, administrators may need to reinstall Windows Vista using the repair option. The repair option tells Windows Vista to reinstall the base operating system over the existing installation. Using repair and install should not affect user settings, applications, or existing data. To prevent data loss, be sure to back up any existing data before using this option. To reinstall Windows Vista using the repair option, administrators can use the following steps:

1. Insert the Windows Vista installation disk into the appropriate drive and perform a manual reboot of the system from the CD/DVD.

2. When the Setup begins, do not select any repairs options. Press Enter to start the normal setup process. Press F8 to accept the license agreement, and Windows Vista then searches for existing operating system installations.

3. Press R to start the repair process and then proceed as if completing a fresh installation of Windows Vista. When finished, the system files are repaired and all user settings and data are available.

Recovering from a Failed Resume

When a Windows Vista system enters hibernation or sleep mode, a snapshot of the system state is created. In sleep mode, the snapshot is created and saved in memory and then read from memory when a user wakes the system. In hibernation mode, the snapshot is written to disk and is read from the disk when a user wakes the computer. In both situations, the Windows Resume Loader handles the operations. If there is a problem with system resume, Windows Resume Loader displays a warning message like the following:

```
Windows Resume Loader
The last attempt to restart the system from its
➥previous location failed.
Attempt to restart again?

Continue with system restart
Delete restoration data and proceed to system boot.

Enter=choose
```

At this point, administrators can choose to restart the system again by selecting Continue with System Restart and pressing Enter. Administrators can choose to delete resume data and boot the system by selecting Delete Restoration Data and Proceed to System Boot and pressing Enter. This option performs a full system restart and most likely resolves the problem but could cause data loss if the data was not saved prior to entering hibernation or sleep mode.

Recovering and Enabling System Startup

Administrators are often faced with computers that will not start up properly. Windows Vista needs specific files operating correctly for it to boot properly. If a file is missing or corrupted, the system may not start up properly. Many times, system startup problems are caused by improperly installed hardware, and the associated device drivers or the system configuration or Registry have been improperly updated and are causing a system conflict. Using the Startup Repair tool and Safe Mode, administrators are often able to recover computer systems suffering from startup problems.

Using the Startup Repair Tool

As administrators know from firsthand experience, startup problems are some of the most difficult to troubleshoot. In many instances, the best way to resolve the problem is to perform a fresh reinstallation of the operating system. Although effective for resolving startup issues, this problem-solving method is time consuming and can usually be avoided if administrators could simply find the errant file setting or corrupted file.

One of the new features in the Windows Vista operating system is a utility called the Startup Repair tool. The Startup Repair tool is designed to jump into action when an operating system startup problem is discovered. When a startup problem is detected, the Startup Repair tool launches an automated, diagnostics-based troubleshooter that requires minimal user intervention.

The Startup Repair tool can automatically repair problems such as missing/ corrupt/incompatible drivers, missing/corrupt system files, corrupt disk meta-data (master boot record, partition table, or boot sector), corrupt Registry settings, and missing or corrupt boot configuration settings.

The Windows Vista's Startup Repair tool automatically kicks in when it detects a startup failure. The Startup Repair tool takes control and analyzes startup log files for hints about what is causing the problem. The Startup Repair tool then launches a series of diagnostic tests to determine the exact cause of the startup failure. When the cause of the failure is found, the Startup Repair tool automatically attempts to fix the problem.

If the Startup Repair tool successfully repairs the problem, it reboots the system and notifies the user of the repairs. In the Windows Vista event log, a detailed report is filed that identifies the cause of the problem and also the solution. If the Startup Repair tool can identify the cause of the problem, but can't repair the problem, it provides access to a set of tools that administrators can use to manually troubleshoot the problem.

If the Startup Repair tool is unsuccessful in its attempt to identify or repair the problem, it will roll back the system to the last known good configuration and will add detailed information about the problem to the Windows Vista event log.

Using Safe Mode

In Safe Mode, Windows Vista loads the minimal amount of files, services, and drivers necessary. The drivers for monitor, mouse, keyboard, video, and storage are loaded, and the basic settings for monitors and video are set. Networking drivers and services are disabled unless Safe Mode with Networking is selected. This limited set of configuration setting helps administrators when they are troubleshooting issues.

Administrator can restart a computer in Safe Mode by performing the following steps:

1. Restart the computer exhibiting problems. Click Start and then click the Options button next to the Power and Lock buttons, selecting Restart.

2. During the system restart, press F8 to display the Advanced Options display. If the Recovery Console has been installed or multiple operating systems exist, the Windows Boot Manager screen will display and F8 can be pressed.

3. Select the Safe Mode to use and then press Enter. The primary options are as follows: Safe Mode (no networking), Safe Mode with Networking, Safe Mode with Command Prompt (no networking or driver started), Enable Boot Logging, Enable Low Resolution Video (maximum 640×480 display mode), Last Known Good Configuration, and Disable Driver Signature Enforcement.

4. A successful boot in Safe Mode eliminates basic settings and device drivers as potential issues. If a newly installed driver or hardware device is causing the problem, administrators can use Safe Mode to reverse the driver installation or remove the device.

5. If the system issues still persist, administrators may want to try using the System Restore while in Safe Mode to reverse recent system changes. If problems still exist, administrators can also try modifying system startup options using the System Configuration utility.

Summary

As with previous versions of Windows, administrators need to troubleshoot, diagnose, and resolve software and hardware issues on computers running Windows Vista. Regardless of the location of the computers, administrators need to support computers and fix problems related to startup and shutdown, programs, disk drives, memory, network, security, and even the Windows Vista operating system itself.

Administrators will have to resolve common problems such as long system startup times, too many security messages, connection issues with networked Windows XP computers, and problems with the Aero graphical interface. Sometimes the problem is not really an issue but a matter of relearning new features and behaviors within Windows Vista. There are countless small changes in Windows Vista that require relearning. The basic concepts presented in previous versions of Windows remain, but administrators and users alike should expect to spend time learning to do some essential small tasks all over again.

The good thing about Windows Vista is that administrators will encounter no differences in working with hardware, installing devices, or troubleshooting issues on computers running different versions of Windows Vista. The steps followed for working with, installing, and troubleshooting computer problems are the same for all editions of Windows Vista.

CHAPTER 18

Using Internet Explorer 7

Understanding the New Features of Internet Explorer

Internet Explorer version 7 in Windows Vista is a newly redesigned version of Microsoft's popular web browser. Browsing the Web is one of the top activities of PC users. Because the Web has become more complex and more mission critical, computer users are no longer satisfied with being able to navigate to one page at a time. In addition, users want easier ways to search for information from multiple places. The capability to easily search and consume multiple sources of information daily has become a necessity when looking for favorite news sites, performing research, shopping, and blogging or sending email.

The new, clean redesigned interface of Internet Explorer 7 makes everyday tasks easier, allowing consumer and business users and IT professionals to perform tasks more productively and efficiently. Computer users can use new features such as tabbed browsing, inline toolbar searching, new printing capabilities, and RSS feeds to enhance their web-browsing experience.

All these basic web-browsing features are available in Internet Explorer 7 for Windows XP, but Windows Vista adds a new level of security called Protected mode, not available in previous versions of Internet Explorer. Protected mode builds on the User Account Control (UAC) security built in to Windows Vista. The browser operates with reduced rights and permissions to protect against surreptitious program installations, program communications, or any hostile program that attempts to alter system settings or files. The new security features also defend against malware and protect users from fraudulent websites that phish for personal user data.

Internet Explorer 7 also contains an enhanced web development and manageability platform. Large and small enterprise environments will benefit from improved cascading style sheets, a new RSS web feed platform, and new full-featured tools for managing and deploying Internet Explorer 7.

User Experience

Microsoft listened to the user community in regard to enhancing the web-browsing experience. Competition in the web-browser arena has also prompted Microsoft to produce a new and improved version of Internet Explorer. In Internet Explorer 7, Microsoft created a cleaner, sleeker user interface and introduced a bunch of new features to improve usability and created a more user-friendly web surfing environment.

Improved Interface

The user interface of Internet Explorer 7 is significantly improved over previous versions of Internet Explorer. In web browsers, a *frame* is a word that refers to the way a browser's user interface is displayed. In Internet Explorer 6, the default frame included a menu at the top of the browser with a row of buttons for Back, Forward, Stop, Refresh, Home, Search, and other commonly performed tasks. Below the menu bar was the Address bar and any other additional information bars.

In Internet Explorer 7, the frame is reorganized to make the user interface simpler, sleeker, and uncluttered by unnecessary items. The web browser real estate is maximized to reveal as much as the screen as possible so that users can view more of their favorite websites.

Internet Explorer 7 reduces the toolbar "creep" where consecutive rows of buttons and tools can take up much needed screen real estate. By default, the menu is hidden in Internet Explorer 7. The redesigned toolbar contains commonly used functions consolidated into a compact Command bar located above the contents pane. As shown in Figure 18.1, the Back and Forward buttons have been redesigned to take up less space and have been moved next to the Address bar. Noticeably missing is the Windows flag icon, which has been removed to make room for the Instant Search box. On a clean install, Live Search (search.live.com) is the default search provider, yet the search tool can be configured to use other search providers, such as Google Search or Yahoo Search.

FIGURE 18.1
Viewing the Improved Internet Explorer 7 graphical user interface.

Tabbed Browsing, Quick Tabs, and Tab Groups

Unlike previous versions of Internet Explorer, Internet Explorer 7 now contains tabbed browsing. Tabbed browsing is the most-requested browser navigation feature among users seeking to manage multiple websites within one browsing window. To create or open tabs in Internet Explorer 7, click the empty tab on the toolbar or right-click any hyperlink on a web page and choose Open in a New Tab. Information in individual tabs can be refreshed by right-clicking a tab and selecting Refresh. All tabs can be refreshed at once by right-clicking a tab and selecting Refresh All.

The behavior of tabbed browsing can be customized using the Internet Options within Internet Explorer 7. Settings for enabling or disabling, handling pop-ups, and opening links can be modified and saved. To see the configurable settings, as shown in Figure 18.2, use the following steps:

1. In Internet Explorer 7, click Tools and then select Internet Options.

2. On the General tab, click the Settings button located in the Tabs section.

3. Select the configuration to change.

4. Click OK to save and exit.

FIGURE 18.2

Viewing the Tabbed Browsing configuration settings in Internet Explorer 7.

Quick Tabs are introduced in Internet Explorer 7 for management of multiple tabs. Quick Tabs allows viewing thumbnail images of all open tabs in one window. By clicking the Quick Tabs icon located to the right of the Favorites icon, all open tabs can be displayed. Within the Quick Tabs view, a tab can be opened by clicking anywhere on the tab, and the tab can be closed by clicking the X in the upper-right corner. One nice feature of Quick Tabs is the single display view, which will automatically scale to the number of open tabs by adjusting the size of the displayed tabs. Smaller-sized thumbnails are used if more than 20 tabs are open, thus allowing all the tabs to be viewed in one window.

Tabbed groups can also be used for managing multiple tabs. Tabbed groups allow organization of multiple tabs into the same category as a single Tab group saved as a Favorite. Tab groups can be created for items such as news, sports, finance, music, or entertainment. For example, Fender, Marshall, Gibson, and VOX can all be saved as a music Tab group in Favorites. When the folder is clicked, the Tab group expands to display the sites organized in the music Tabbed group. An unlimited amount of sites or tabs can be saved in a Tab group, and an unlimited amount of Tab groups can be created within Favorites.

Advanced Printing

Internet Explorer 7 includes enhanced functionality that makes printing web pages easier. The advanced printing feature will cut down on paper waste created by printing multiple copies to get information that may be cut off on left and right margins.

Internet Explorer 7 automatically shrinks web pages just enough to ensure that the entire page is printed properly. This also means that third-party programs will not be needed for cut-and-paste operations just for proper printing and editing web information. The enhanced printing capability allows adjusting of the web page margins, changes to the page layout, modifying of headers and footers, and modification of the print space.

Instant Search

Internet Explorer 7 provides different ways to search for information on the Web without actually going to a website. By entering the search terms in the Instant Search box, in the top-right corner of the browser, and then clicking the Search button, Internet Explorer 7 facilitates quicker and easier web searching directly from the browser frame using a favorite search provider. Additional search providers can be added to Internet Explorer 7. Administrators can use the following steps to add an additional search provider:

1. Click the Instant Search drop-down menu arrow located next to the Instant Search box.

2. Click Find More Providers.

3. On the Windows Search Guide web page, select a search provider. The web page includes many broad and vertical search providers, such as Google, AOL, eBay, and Expedia.

4. To make this the default search provider, click the Make This My Default Search Provider option box. If not, click Add Provider in the Add Search Provider dialog box, shown in Figure 18.3, to continue and add this search provider to the Instant Search.

FIGURE 18.3
Adding a Search Provider in Internet Explorer 7.

RSS Feeds

Internet Explorer 7 provides new integrated support for Really Simple Syndication (RSS). Internet Explorer 7 users can find, subscribe to, and read RSS feeds directly in Internet Explorer 7. Web publishers create RSS feeds using links, summaries, and headlines. Using a RSS reader, users can subscribe to many feeds and read new feeds all in one place, eliminating the need to constantly visit news sites and web logs.

Previous versions of Internet Explorer displayed RSS feeds in XML format, which requires advanced technical knowledge and expertise, eliminating all but the technically savvy user. Using Internet Explorer 7, the RSS feed is read directly into the browser, allowing the user to scan headlines for articles of interest. The Feed button on the Command bar in Internet Explorer 7 changes from the default gray color to bright orange when the presence of a web feed is detected on a web page. As shown in Figure 18.4, by clicking a feed, indicated by a little RSS icon dot on web pages, users can subscribe to a feed. This is similar to adding a website Favorite. Some web pages will contain a link with a label XML or RSS. The feed is displayed by clicking the link or the Feed button; the browser then applies a style sheet to the page and the feed is displayed in the contents pane.

Tip

Users can update feeds on demand by bypassing the scheduled updates. To perform on-demand feed updates, point to the feed item in the Favorites Center and then click the blue Refresh This Feed icon to the right. Right-click any feed item or folder, and then select Refresh All to initiate an immediate update of all subscribed feeds.

FIGURE 18.4
Subscribing to a RSS feed in Internet Explorer 7.

Dynamic Security Protection

Internet Explorer 7 is the most secure browser ever developed by Microsoft. Internet Explorer 7 provides protection against malicious core and software, worms, viruses, spyware, and adware. It also protects personal user data by protecting users from phishing attacks, preventing websites from stealing user information or divulging personal data unintentionally. When combined with other security features in Windows Vista such as Windows Firewall or Window Defender, Internet Explorer 7 provides users with the highest level of security protection.

Malware Protection

Malicious software, also known as malware, is software code or software programs designed to damage, slow down, or disrupt a user's system. The proliferation of malware is increasing and security issues related to malware are on the rise. The new version of Internet Explorer has been enhanced, reducing the potential for a browser or system to be compromised by computer hackers. The browser's architecture has been fortified at the core to defend against exploitation and improve the way the browser handles information. Internet Explorer 7 also includes several technical features, such as URL Handling Protections, Active X Opt In, Cross-Domain Scripting, Protected Mode, and Fix My Settings, which are designed to defend against hackers' attempts to gain access to users' personal data.

URL Handling Protection prevents malformed URLs containing extra code or malformed characters from creating a buffer overflow and executing malicious code of the hacker's choice. Microsoft has rewritten the browser code, defining a single function for processing URL data. This rewritten code reduces the potential attack surface of Internet Explorer 7. The reduced attack surface ensures higher security and reliability.

Active X Opt In is a new security mechanism for the ActiveX platform. In Internet Explorer 7, Active X Opt In deactivates classes of controls not enabled by the user. This further reduces the attack area of the browser and mitigates unwanted misuse of the preinstalled controls. When a potentially hazardous preinstalled control is activated for the first time, the user is provided a notification in the Information Bar. Using the Information Bar, users can allow or deny the control from being used when visiting websites. If unwanted attacks are made, Active X Opt In automatically kicks in, preventing unwanted access and providing the user with the control to permit or deny the action.

Cross-Domain Scripting is an attack where a script from one Internet domain manipulates data from another domain. This new feature prevent hackers from obtaining information fraudulently by pretending to be a legitimate site but really being a malicious site with the intention of stealing personal user account information. Internet Explorer 7 prevents this behavior by appending the domain name where the original script lives and limits the script's ability to only interact with windows and content from the same domain. This barrier helps ensure that user information stays where the user intends it to stay when entered on a web page.

Internet Explorer Protected mode, available only in Windows Vista, provides a new level of security and data protection for computer users. Protected mode defends against elevation of privilege attacks and provides a robust Internet browsing experience while preventing hackers from taking control of the browser and executing code through the use of administrator rights and permissions. See the section "Understanding Internet Explorer 7 Protected Mode" in this chapter for more information regarding Protected mode.

Protecting Personal Data

The risk of exposing personal and/or company data is a serious issue in corporate America. As web developers and website operators create content-rich websites and use new technologies, the risk of unknowingly transmitting sensitive data continues to grow. Users are having more and more trouble seeing differences between bogus and fraudulent sites versus a valid website. Malicious website operators abuse search listing services to attract unsuspecting web surfers to knockoff websites designed to imitate the appearance and function of well-known and trusted businesses.

Unlike previous versions of Internet Explorer, Internet Explorer 7 provides a number of improvements and solutions to better protect against malicious website operators and help prevent users from becoming victims of phishing attempts. Items such as the Security status bar helps users quickly differentiate authentic websites from suspicious or malicious ones. Some of the additional improvements involve SSL certificates, a new Phishing Filter, Parental controls, and more.

Internet Explorer 7 gives more emphasis on the security and trust levels associated with websites. Unlike previous versions of Internet Explorer, where the gold padlock was located in the lower-right corner of the browser window, Internet Explorer 7 uses the Security Status Bar to display the gold padlock on a yellow background directly in users' sight. By clicking the padlock, users can read information about the security certificate. If the website is deemed suspicious or irregularities are found in the certificate information, the padlock appears on a red background in the Security Status Bar. Certificates that are trusted are clearly displayed with the certificate owner's name on a green background to indicate the site is trusted, and it is okay to provide personal or confidential data.

Using an online update, the new Phishing Filter in Internet Explorer 7 consolidates the latest industry information about fraudulent websites and shares it with Internet Explorer 7 customers to proactively warn and help protect them. The Phishing Filter combines client-side scans for suspicious website characteristics with an online service that user subscribe to. The Phishing Filter protects web surfers by comparing visited websites against a stored list of legitimate websites and performs an additional check of the website against an online service provided by Microsoft. The Phishing Filter also heuristically analyzes websites as users visit the sites, checking for characteristics frequently found on phishing websites. If Internet Explorer 7 suspects a suspicious website, the Security Status Bar alerts users with a yellow shield and exclamation mark. Administrators or users can enable or disable the Phishing Filter at any time by clicking Tools and using the options on the Phishing Filter menu to perform a manual check against Microsoft's servers, to report suspicious websites, or to turn off automatic checking. To disable the Phishing Filter entirely, open the Internet Options dialog box, click the Advanced tab, and then in the Settings box scroll down to the Security section. Next, find the Phishing Filter settings and select Disable Phishing Filter. Click OK to finish disabling the Phishing Filter.

Hackers are constantly looking for new ways to fool Internet users into thinking the information displayed in the browser is from a known and trusted site. As a result, these website names look very similar to known and trusted websites, fooling users into submitting info to the website. Common methods include hiding the proper URL information and domain name information for users. To combat this, Internet Explorer 7 now displays an address bar in all browser windows. Internet Explorer 7 also delivers support for International Domain Names (IDN). This protects against domain names using international characters that look similar to characters in the English language.

Most browsers have options for deleting browser history information and cleaning the Internet cache, temporary files, and completed form history. Typically, this involves independent functions within the browser to accomplish protection of passwords and privacy information. Internet Explorer 7 uses a method called Delete Browsing History, which instantly erases personal information and provides enhanced data privacy on computer systems. Users can use one click within Internet Explorer 7 to easily clean up and erase personal data.

One of the newest features with Internet Explorer 7 is the new Parental Controls. Internet Explorer 7 now has a network layer service that filters objectionable content not appropriate for young Internet users while allowing a specific set of allowable websites. The Parental Controls service provides a single interface for managing settings. The controls can be set to block file downloads to prevent malware form being downloaded accidentally. The objectionable content is blocked from being downloaded unless an administrative password is supplied. When blocking inappropriate content, Internet Explorer 7 displays a message in the Information page that requests parental permission to approve the download.

Improved Platform and Manageability

Unlike previous versions of Internet Explorer, which frustrated developers in areas such as web application and development support, Internet Explorer 7 has a reengineered architecture that addresses application compatibility and supports a rich end-user experience. Internet Explorer 7 is more standards compliant than Internet Explorer 6 and makes it easier for developers to create and develop new web applications. In addition, administrators can manage Internet Explorer 7 centrally via Group Policy. The release of Internet Explorer Administration Kit 7 enables even more configuration and deployment options.

Cascading Style Sheets (CSS) support had also been improved in Internet Explorer 7. The improvements eliminated problems found in previous versions of Internet Explorer and provided CSS 2.1 support. These fixes resolve previous issues with fixed positioning, HTML 4.01 improvements, and the capability to hover on all elements and other issues that arise when creating content rich, interactive websites.

Portable Network Graphics (PNG) image file format support has also been improved by adding support for alpha channel transparent PNGs. A PNG file supports transparence through a measurement called the alpha channel. The alpha channel provides web designers with another tool with which to create dazzling special effects.

RSS feed support has also been improved in Internet Explorer 7. The RSS platform has been enhanced to accommodate an expected increase in the use of RSS feeds through Internet Explorer 7. Microsoft has improved the Common Feed list, which is responsible for storage of subscribed sites, and the Command Data Store, which is responsible for delivering of subscribed information such as calendar info, pictures, podcasts, and other subscription information.

Platform administration has also been improved. Administrators have better browser manageability in Internet Explorer 7 by using Group Policy to gain centralized control over Internet Explorer 7 settings. Group Policy allows administrators to manage old and new features, such as browser add-ons and other features to keep browsers compliant with enterprise standards.

Reviewing System Requirements for Internet Explorer 7

In Windows Vista, Internet Explorer 7 is included as a feature within Windows Vista and is configured as the default web browser. Any machine with the recommended amount of memory for Windows will meet the memory requirements for Internet Explorer 7.

Minimum System Requirements

Internet Explorer 7 will run on Windows XP Service Pack 2 (SP2), Windows XP Professional x64 Edition, and Windows Server 2003 Service Pack 1 (SP1). Memory requirements listed next are for Internet Explorer itself. Below are the minimum requirements your computer needs to run Internet Explorer 7. Some components may require additional system resources not outlined here. The Internet Explorer 7 requirements are the following:

- Computer with a 233MHz processor or higher (Pentium processor recommended)

- Windows XP Service Pack 2 (SP2), Windows XP Professional x64 Edition, Windows Server 2003 Service Pack 1 (SP1)
- CD-ROM drive (if installation is done from a CD-ROM)
- Super VGA (800×600) or higher-resolution monitor with 256 colors
- Microsoft Mouse, Microsoft IntelliMouse, or compatible pointing device
- Modem or Internet connection

Memory for Internet Explorer 7:

- **Windows XP Service Pack 2 (SP2)**—64MB
- **Windows XP Professional x64 Edition**—128MB
- **Windows Server 2003 Service Pack 1 (SP1)**—64MB
- **Windows Server 2003 Service Pack 1 ia64**—128MB

Recommended System Requirements

Internet Explorer 7 in Windows Vista will run using the minimum require-ments. For the best web browsing experience, it is recommended to not have a system that only meets the minimal settings for memory, graphics card and graphics card memory, and processor speed. To get the optimal web browsing experience, use a system that meets the recommended system requirements for Windows Vista using the Aero interface. The recommended requirements for the Windows Vista Aero interface are as follows:

- 1-gigahertz (GHz) 32-bit (x86) processor or 1GHz 64-bit (x64) processor
- 1GB of system memory
- Windows Aero-capable graphics card
- 128MB of graphics memory that supports Direct X 9 or later
- 40GB hard disk with 15GB of free hard disk space (temporary file storage during the installation or upgrade)
- Internal or external DVD drive
- Internet access capability
- Audio output capability

> **Note**
>
> A Windows Aero-capable graphics card must meet specific hardware specifications. Be sure that the video card meets the following requirements:
>
> - Windows Display Driver Model (WDDM) driver support
> - DirectX 9-class graphics processor unit (GPU) that supports Pixel Shader 2.0 and 32 bits per pixel and also passes the Windows Aero acceptance test in the Windows Driver Kit

Administering Internet Explorer 7 Internet Options and Security

The feature-rich Internet Explorer 7 in Windows Vista includes a variety of old and new tools for administrators to configure, administer, and customize browser settings. Administrators can configure file cache settings, security zones, privacy and security settings, default programs, and many other advanced options that control browser features. Administrators can manage and administer Internet Explorer 7 for individual users using the Internet Properties dialog box, accessed via Control Panel, Network and Internet, Internet Options. Alternatively, administrators can use Group Policy to manage and configure settings for multiple users. Many policies can be implemented via Group Policy, making an administrator's job easier and at the same time enhancing the user's computing experience and improving security. See Chapters 22 and 23 on Group Policy later in the book for more information on working with Group Policy settings.

Configuring Default Programs

Administrators can configure default Internet programs in Internet Explorer 7 using the Programs tabs of the Internet Properties dialog box. Using this button, administrators can define programs for use through Windows, not just Internet Explorer 7. Administrators can manage and administer Internet Explorer 7 for individual users using the following steps:

1. Click Start and then select Control Panel.
2. Select Network and Internet and then select Internet Options.
3. On the Internet Options page, select the Programs tab.
4. In the Internet Programs section, click the Set Programs button to define programs to be used for Internet services.

5. On the Default Programs page, click the Set Your Default Programs link to display the Set Default Programs page as shown in Figure 18.5.

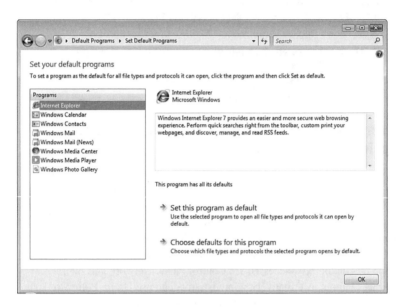

FIGURE 18.5
Configuring Default Programs in Internet Explorer 7.

6. Select any program in the Programs list and see information displayed about that program on the right side of the page. On this page, administrators can set a program for all file types and protocols that are available to the program.

7. To set file type associations for a program, administrators can click Choose Defaults for This Program, select which program to run for features specific to the program, and then click Save to save changes.

8. As we know, many times too much customization leads to odd program behavior, and troubleshooting can become hit or miss. Internet Explorer 7 helps reduce this headache by allowing administrators to clean the slate and return Internet Explorer 7 to its default setting. To do this, highlight the troublesome application and then click Set This Program as Default.

Managing Cookies and Temporary Internet Files

When users browse the Internet, many file types of temporary Internet files, such web pages and images, cookies, browser history, passwords, and form data are stored locally on the computer. Administrators can manage browser cookies and other type of temporary Internet files using the Internet Options dialog box. User who spend a large amount of time surfing and have disk size limitations may need their temporary files managed closely to prevent running out of disk space.

Administrators can clean out temporary files by using the following steps:

1. Click Start and then select Control Panel.

2. Select Network and Internet and then select Internet Options.

3. On the Internet Options page, select the General tab. In the Browsing History section, click the Delete Button.

4. In the Delete Browsing History dialog box, delete the individual types of temporary files by clicking the related button and then click Yes when asked to confirm the action.

5. To delete all browsing history temporary files, click the Delete All button. When prompted, select the option box to Delete Files and Settings Stored by Add-Ons. This will delete temporary files created by browser add-on applications. Click Yes to confirm this action.

Administrators will also want to restrict the amount of disk space available for storing temporary Internet files. This will prevent additional problems caused by running out of local disk space. Administrators can restrict the amount of available disk space by performing the following steps:

1. Click Start and then select Control Panel.

2. Select Network and Internet and then select Internet Options.

3. On the Internet Options page, select the General tab. In the Browsing History section, click the Settings button.

4. Using the Disk Space to Use combo box, specify the amount of disk space to use for temporary Internet files.

5. Temporary Internet files are stored in the `C:\users\%user%\appdata\local\microsoft\windows\temporary internet files`. Administrators can modify the folder location if needed by clicking the Move Folder button and then using the Browse for Folder dialog box to select a new folder location.

6. Click OK twice to finish and close the open dialog boxes.

> **Tip**
>
> When users request a web page, Internet Explorer checks first in the tempo-
> rary internet files to see whether a recent copy of the page, images on the
> page, and other related items already exist. In the "old days" of Internet
> access, dial-up access and small hard disks were the norm. To accommo-
> date the systems at the time, Microsoft allocated 10% of the hard drive for
> the Temporary Internet Files disk cache. In today's computing environment
> where 200GB hard drives and high-speed Internet access (DSL/Cable) are
> available in most areas, 10% is unreasonably low. To accommodate
> systems using DSL and Cable Internet access, use a cache setting of
> 20–75MB. If using dial-up access, use a setting of 100–200MB.

Securing Browsing and Internet 7 Lockdown

The foundation of security in Internet Explorer 7 is the use of Windows
permissions and rights to limit the freedom of add-ons and web pages. The
security fence surrounding Internet Explorer 7 is the new feature called
Protected mode. In addition, as with previous version of Internet Explorer,
Internet Explorer 7 uses security zones to save and apply group security
settings. The addition of an integrated Pop-Up Blocker and Add-On Manager
are other methods administrators can use to manage browser security.

Understanding Internet Explorer 7 Protected Mode

Available only to users running Internet Explorer 7 in Windows Vista,
Internet Explorer Protected mode provides new levels of security and data
protection for Windows users. Using a web browser exposes a computer to
many security risks. By mistyping a URL or unintentionally clicking a link in
an email, users can be redirected to a malicious website containing malicious
scripting or downloadable code that adversely affects the computer. Protected
mode, which runs in all Internet Explorer 7 security zones except the Trusted
Zone, is designed to defend against "elevation of privilege" attacks and takes
advantage of Windows Vista security enhancements such as User Account
Control. Protected mode severely limits the privileges available to programs.

In Protected mode, Internet Explorer 7 runs as a low-privilege process as
defined by the Mandatory Integrity Control (MIC) feature (for more information on MIC, check this link at http://blogs.technet.com/steriley/archive/
2006/07/21/442870.aspx. Because MIC limits the privileges of Internet
Explorer 7, Internet Explorer 7 is unable to modify system files and the
Registry, which requires a higher privilege. All communications occur via a
broker process that mediates between the Internet Explorer browser and the
operating system. The broker process is initiated only when the user clicks

the Internet Explorer menus and screens. The highly restrictive broker process prohibits workarounds from bypassing Protected mode. Any scripted actions or automatic processes will be prevented from downloading data or affecting the system. Whenever a user action requires a higher-level access level such as an ActiveX installation or saving a file, the broker process kicks in. Typically, this action is displayed to the user as the UAC dialog box asking for confirmation to continue.

Protected mode may prevent a website or program from working properly. If all attempts to work around the application or website compatibility fail, Protected mode can be disabled. Administrators can disable Protected mode using the following actions:

1. From within Internet Explorer 7, click Tools, and then click Internet Options.

2. Click the Security tab and clear the Enable Protected Mode check box.

3. Click OK to continue and save the changes. Windows will display a warning box as shown in Figure 18.6. Click OK to continue.

FIGURE 18.6
Warning displayed when disabling Protected mode in Internet Explorer 7.

When Protected mode is disabled, users will see a warning message in the Information Bar when visiting any web page. Users can reenable Protected mode by clicking the Information Bar and then clicking Open Security Settings. Select the Enable Protected Mode check box and then click OK. To make the changes take effect, Internet Explorer 7 must be closed and reopened.

Caution

Disabling Protected mode in Internet Explorer 7 is not recommended. If Protected mode must be disabled for any reason, it is recommended that Protected mode be reenabled immediately after the activity conflicting with it is completed. If a particular website is conflicting with Protected mode *and* it is known to be a safe site, administrators can add this site to the Trusted Zone, where Protected mode is not in effect. Again, use this option with caution; it does enable a wide range of potentially risky behaviors.

Understanding the Browser Information Bar

In Windows Vista, the browser Information Bar is used in place of pop-up warnings, dialog boxes, and confirmation prompts. The Information Bar is designed to help guide users through security enhancements for pop-up windows, add-ons, and Active X content. When the Information Bar is displayed, users can click or right-click on the bar to display a shortcut menu. The shortcut menu contains additional options that allow the user to enable or disable the related feature and also complete other related tasks.

Some of the common messages displayed in the Information Bar are as follows:

- Active X Control Blocked
- File Download Blocked
- Pop-Up Blocked
- Software Install Blocked
- Software Blocked

More information on specific browser Information Bar messages can be found at windowshelp.microsoft.com/Windows/en-US/Help/91b1038d-3f53-43a3-8bd8-9551e7c0b7c61033.mspx#EEF.

Using Add-On Manager

Internet Explorer 7 functionality can be enhanced and extended through the use of browser add-ons. Developer's add-ons can extend the capability of Internet Explorer 7 by adding toolbars, menus, explorer bars, and buttons. Programmer may also hook into core browser features and extend search capabilities, "automagically" filling in forms, or saving bookmarks. Usually, add-ons take the form of browser helper objects, browser extensions, Active X controls, toolbars, or Java applets.

Poorly written add-ons, however, may adversely affect the operation of Internet Explorer 7, resulting in random crashes, unnecessary pop-up windows, slow system performance, and unexpected glitches. Malicious add-ons may reveal personal data and information to an untrusted outsider.

In Windows Vista, administrators manage add-ons using the Manage Add-Ons dialog box. The Manage Add-Ons dialog box shows information about currently installed add-ons and allows disabling or enabling of add-ons through this interface. Administrators can open the Manage Add-Ons dialog box and control add-ons by using the following steps:

1. From within Internet Explorer 7, click Tools, and then click Internet Options.

2. Click the Programs tab.

3. In the Manage Add-Ons section, click the Manage Add-Ons button.

The Manage Add-Ons dialog box will be displayed as shown in Figure 18.7. In the dialog box, administrators can view and manage installed add-ons using the following options:

- **Enable Add-Ons**—To enable an add-on that has been disabled, select the add-on and then click Enable. If the feature is not available, indicated by a dimmed-out button, the Do Not Allow User to Enable or Disable Add-Ons option might be enabled within Group Policy. This setting in Group Policy is located in User Configuration\ Administrative Templates\Windows Components\Internet Explorer.

- **Disable Add-Ons**—To disable an add-on, select the add-on and then click Disable.

- **Delete an Active X Control**—To delete an Active X control, select the Active X control and then click Delete. This option is not available for Active X controls installed by Windows Vista or a Windows program such as Microsoft Office or Windows Live toolbar. To remove these programs, use the Uninstall feature in Control Panel.

Configuring Pop-Up Blocker

Because many pop-ups are unwanted ads, Windows Vista includes the Pop-Up blocker within Internet Explorer 7. A default setting, pop-up blocking is enabled to block most types of automatic pop-ups and operates in the Internet, Trusted Sites, and Restricted Sites security zones. It does not suppress pop-ups in the Local Intranet Zone. The browser Information Bar displays a message whenever a pop-up is blocked. Users can then click the browser Information Bar to display the pop-up or configure additional settings to allow pop-ups from the site automatically.

FIGURE 18.7

Viewing, enabling, and disabling browser add-ons using the Manage Add-Ons dialog box in Internet Explorer 7.

Administrators can configure pop-up blocking by performing the following steps:

1. From within Internet Explorer 7, click Tools, and then click Internet Options.

2. Click the Privacy tab.

3. To disable Pop-Up Blocker, deselect the Turn On Pop-Up Blocker check box and then click OK. Ignore the remaining steps.

4. To enable Pop-Up Blocker, click the Settings button in the Pop-Up Blocker section. The Pop-Up Blocker settings dialog box shown in Figure 18.8 will displayed.

5. To allow a site's pop-ups to be displayed, type the website address, such as www.airjimi.com, into the Address of Website to Allow field and then click Add. The site is now allowed to use pop-ups regardless of the settings in Internet Explorer 7.

6. To stop displaying a message in the browser Information Bar when pop-ups are blocked, deselect the Show Information Bar When a Pop-Up Is Blocked check box.

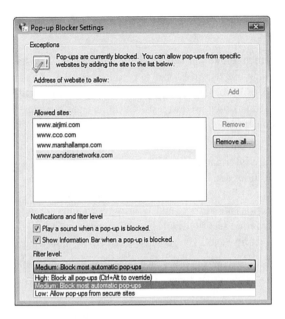

FIGURE 18.8
Using the Pop-Up Blocker Settings dialog box to configure that pop-ups are blocked in Internet Explorer 7.

7. Most pop-ups are blocked by default when Pop-Up Blocker is enabled. Administrators can also configure pop-up controls by selecting one of the following options in the Filter Level drop-down box:

- **High**—Pop-Up Blocker tries to suppress all new windows and may affect Active Content. If a link is clicked that would normally pop up a window and it is necessary to see the pop-up, press Ctrl+Alt while clicking the link to allow the pop-up.

- **Medium**—Pop-Up Blocker allows new windows resulting from clicked links but blocks most types of pop-ups used to display ads and other unwanted content. If a link is clicked that would normally pop up a window and it is necessary to see the pop-up, press Ctrl+Alt while clicking the link to allow the pop-up.

- **Low**—Standard HTTP connections will have their pop-ups blocked, preventing pop-ups used to display ads and other unwanted content. Pop-Up Blocker will allow pop-ups when accessing a secure HTTP (HTTPS) connection.

Understanding and Managing Security Zones in Internet Explorer 7

Internet Explorer 7 zones are an important part of security for Windows Vista computers. Administrators can use security zones to permit or restrict access to web content, file downloads, Java programs, applets, and Active X content and scripts. Security zones can also be used to restrict actions that users can perform when viewing web content.

Security zones control web content permissions for web servers depending on the server location and known information about the servers. Each zone is configured with a default security level ranging from low to high. High security means most actions are not allowed and security restrictions are tight. Low security means most actions are allowed and security restrictions are very loose. Administrators can override security levels by setting a new security level or creating a custom security level. The security zones are the following:

- **Internet Zone**—This zone controls users' access to web content on all sites not placed in any of the other zones. The default security level is Medium High.

- **Local Intranet Zone**—This zone controls users' access to web content on the local area network and includes local intranet sites, network paths, and sites that bypass any proxy servers. The default security level for the Local Intranet Zone is Medium Low.

- **Trusted Sites Zone**—This zone controls users' access to web content on sites that are explicitly trusted and are considered to be free of malicious content or data. The default security for the Trusted Zone is a custom version of Low. This setting allows downloading of unsigned Active X controls and configures the Java permissions to Medium-level security.

- **Restricted Sites Zone**—This zone controls users' access to web content on sites that potentially contain malicious content or data.

Administrators can manage and administer security zones for individual users using the Internet Properties dialog box, accessed via Control Panel, Network and Internet, Internet Options, and selecting the Security tab. Alternatively, administrators can use Group Policy to manage and configure settings for multiple users. Many policies can be implemented via Group Policy, making an administrator's job easier and at the same time enhancing the user's computing experience and improving security. See Chapters 22 and 23 on Group Policy later in the book for more information on working with Group Policy settings.

Configuring the Internet Zone

Administrators can configure the Internet Zone security using the following steps:

1. From within Internet Explorer 7, click Tools, and then click Internet Options.

2. Click the Security tab.

3. Select Internet from the zone list.

4. To restore the Internet Zone to its default level, click the Default Level button and then click OK. Skip the remaining steps.

5. To configure a custom level, click Custom Level. Use the Security Settings list to set a custom level of individual security options. Use the Reset Custom Settings drop-down box to reset the zone to a preset level. The preset levels for this zone are Medium, Medium High, and High.

6. Click OK when finished.

Configuring the Local Intranet Zone

Administrators can configure the Local Intranet Zone security using the following steps:

1. From within Internet Explorer 7, click Tools, and then click Internet Options.

2. Click the Security tab.

3. Select Local Intranet Zone from the zone list.

4. To restore the Local Intranet Zone to its default level, click the Default Level button and then click OK. Skip the remaining steps.

5. To configure a custom level, click Custom Level. Use the Security Settings list to set a custom level of individual security options. Use the Reset Custom Settings drop-down box to reset the zone to a preset level. The preset levels for this zone are Low, Medium, and Medium Low. Click OK to continue.

6. Next define which sites are included in the Local Intranet Zone by clicking the Sites button. This will display the Local Intranet dialog box.

7. By default, Internet Explorer 7 attempts to automatically detect the intranet network. If Internet Explorer 7 is unable to detect network settings, they might need to be manually configured. To do so, uncheck

the box for Automatically Detect Intranet Network and then include (select the option) or exclude (deselect the option) local intranet sites not listed in other zones, sites that bypass the proxy server, or network paths.

8. To configure specific additional sites or sites that require HTTPS secure verification, click Advanced. Add sites by entering the IP address or URL in the Add This Web Site to the Zone text field and clicking Add. Remove sites by selecting the site in the website list and clicking Remove. To require secure verification using HTTPs, select the Require Server Verification (HTTPS:) For All Sites in This Zone check box.

9. Click OK twice to close the Local Intranet dialog boxes.

Configuring the Trusted Sites Zone

Administrators can configure the Trusted Sites Zone security using the following steps:

1. From within Internet Explorer 7, click Tools, Internet Options. In the Internet Options dialog box, click the Security tab and then click Trusted Sites in the zone list. Set the security level as explained in the "Configuring the Internet Zone" section earlier in this chapter.

2. Next define which sites are included in the Trusted Sites Zone by clicking the Sites button. This will display the Trusted Sites dialog box.

3. In the Trusted Sites dialog box, add or remove trusted sites from this zone. Add trusted sites by entering the IP address or URL in the Add This Web Site to the Zone text field and clicking Add. Remove sites by selecting the site in the website list and clicking Remove. To require secure verification using HTTPS, select the Require Server Verification (HTTPS:) For All Sites in This Zone check box.

4. Click Close and then click OK to finish.

Configuring the Restricted Sites Zone

Administrators can configure the Restricted Sites Zone security using the following steps:

1. From within Internet Explorer 7, click Tools, Internet Options. In the Internet Options dialog box, click the Security tab and then click Restricted Sites in the zone list. Set the security level as explained in the "Configuring the Internet Zone" section earlier in this chapter.

2. Next define which sites are included in the Restricted Sites Zone by clicking the Sites button. This will display the Restricted Sites dialog box.

3. In the Restricted Sites dialog box, add or remove trusted sites from this zone. Add restricted sites by entering the IP address or URL in the Add This Web Site to the Zone text field and clicking Add. Remove sites by selecting the site in the website list and clicking Remove.

4. Click Close and then click OK to finish.

Exploring the Internet Explorer Administration Kit

For years, enterprises have been using the Internet Explorer Administration Kit (IEAK) to control and customize their installations of Internet Explorer. Similarly, Internet Service Providers (ISPs) also use this tool to provide customized versions of Internet Explorer that are branded with the ISO logos, naming, and hyperlinks unique to the ISP. Available in several languages, such as Chinese, Japanese, and Hebrew, for worldwide use, IEAK is useful where customizing the Internet Explorer 7 interface and modifying browser settings is desired. IEAK provides administrators with options designed to save time and money in deploying and managing enterprise web solutions.

IEAK 7 allows enterprise administrators to

- Establish version control across the organization.

- Centrally distribute and manage browser installations.

- Configure automatic connection profiles for users' machines.

- Customize Internet Explorer features such as communications settings, security, and other browser items.

New features are also included within the latest version of IEAK 7. Some of the new features in IEAK 7 are:

- Customization of features such as web feeds, multiple home pages, and antiphishing using the Internet Explorer 7 Customization Wizard or IEAK Profile Manager.

- Single package creation that can automatically install and configure Internet Explorer 7 or configure an existing installation of Internet Explorer 7.

- Improved Internet Explorer 7 Customization Wizard pages and text.

- Improved access to Auto-Complete and Feeds discovery settings using the Internet Explorer 7 Customization Wizard and the IEAK Profile Manager.

Internet Explorer Administration Kit 7 is a free program that is installed separately from Windows Vista. It is downloadable at http://technet. microsoft.com/en-us/ie/bb219543.aspx. Administrators must use IEAK 7 because it is the only version that works with Internet Explorer 7.

After IEAK 7 is downloaded and installed, administrators can begin using IEAK 7 by using the following steps:

1. Click Start, All Programs, and then click Microsoft IEAK 7.

2. Select one of the following options and then follow the wizard prompts to configure one of the options:

   - Click Internet Explorer Customization Wizard to start creating a custom package as shown in Figure 18.9.

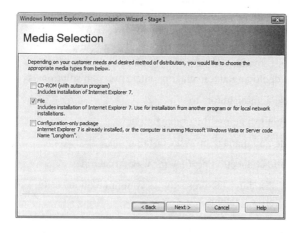

FIGURE 18.9
Choosing a media option within Windows IEAK 7.

Note

Administrators who like the command prompt or using scripting can also open the Internet Explorer 7 Customization Wizard from the command line by typing `ieak7wiz`.

- Click IEAK Profile Manager to edit existing settings.
- Click IEAK Help to access the IEAK 7 product documentation.

The wizard-driven interface of IEAK 7 simplifies the process of creating custom distribution packages of Internet Explorer 7. IEAK 7 also allows greater flexibility and greater control of the Internet Explorer features configuration with an organization. As shown in Figure 18.10, administrators can configure features such as the default home page, the default browser, Favorites, and Security Zones.

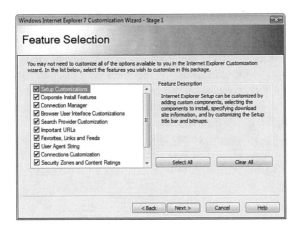

FIGURE 18.10
Customizing Internet Explorer options using Windows IEAK 7.

Tip

If possible, administrators should install IEAK on the same version of operating system as the destination computer or computers for which they are creating a package. Mixing and matching operating systems and packages may not produce desired results. Also, this version of the IEAK builds custom browser packages only for 32-bit or 64-bit versions of Windows. Administrators should use IEAK 5 when building a custom package for a 16-bit version of Windows or for a UNIX operating system.

Summary

Internet Explorer version 7 in Windows Vista is a newly redesigned version of Microsoft's popular web browser. Because the web has become more complex and more mission critical, computer users are no longer satisfied with being able to navigate to one page at a time. In addition, users want easier ways to search for information from multiple places. The capability to easily search and consume multiple sources of information daily has become a necessity when looking for favorite news sites, performing research, shopping, and blogging or sending email.

Enabling savvy Internet users to perform everyday tasks more productively and efficiently, Internet Explorer 7 is redesigned with new and enhanced capabilities. The new, clean interface of Internet Explorer 7 makes everyday tasks easier with new features such as tabbed browsing, inline toolbar searching, new printing capabilities, and RSS feeds. Internet Explorer 7 also adds a new level of security called Protected mode that builds on the User Account Control security built in to Windows Vista. The browser operates with reduced rights and permissions to protect against surreptitious program installations, program communications, or any hostile program that attempts to alter system settings or files. The new security features also defend against malware and protect users from fraudulent websites that phish for personal user data.

With all the new features and security enhancements, Internet Explorer 7 is the browser for users looking for an effective, efficient, and enhanced web browsing experience.

PART VI

Deploying Vista

IN THIS PART

CHAPTER 19

Creating Windows Vista Images

Image Creation Requirements and Preparation

The release of Windows Vista is complemented by an overhaul to Microsoft's imaging and image distribution technology for ease of deployment by customers. Imaging systems, maintaining those images, and establishing a solid distribution mechanism can yield prosperous results for IT administrators. Imaging systems and image distribution have several advantages. Developing an imaging process should be in place for any Enterprise environment. Small to medium businesses should also consider developing a process to create and distribute system templates, although the method of deployment can vary depending on the size of the install base and how frequently systems are replaced with new ones. Home users don't often image systems; however, with the increase in home networks serving more than one system, having a snapshot of systems can again be beneficial. Although most PC manufacturers include an image to restore the system to factory defaults, a customized image can include software, customized settings, and more—allowing systems to be restored or rebuilt much faster than a step-by-step installation.

In previous releases of Windows, organizations may have had multiple images to support different hardware platforms. Windows Imaging Format (WIM) is a new imaging technology designed specifically for Windows Vista. WIM makes it possible to deploy the same image file to multiple computers where those computers may run on different hardware and contain differing hardware components, require the operating system to run in a different language, require different Windows components, or updates. Managing a WIM image is easy since any of these components can be added or removed off-line—without booting into the image. WIM is a file-based imaging technology, unlike some competitive products that are sector-based, which can be much slower, require reformatting of the hard drive, can be larger in size, and not as easy to deploy.

Microsoft has combined all the necessary tools and information, available in one of these two "packages"; the Windows Automated Installation Kit (WAIK), which contains several tools for customizing and automating the installation of Windows Vista into an image file, and the Microsoft Solution Accelerator for Business Desktop Deployment 2007 (BDD), which installs the WAIK and adds several tools and guidance documents to provide reference to those responsible for deploying Windows Vista in an automated fashion, generally to hundreds or thousands of computers. The BDD is covered in Chapter 21, "Deploying Windows Vista in an Automated Fashion," of this book. Windows Deployment Services, which replaced Remote Installation Services (RIS) with the release of Windows Server 2003, is discussed in Chapter 21. Windows Deployment Services is available on the WAIK DVD. Other functionality of the WAIK is covered in the next section.

Developing, maintaining, and testing an imaging process addresses several important scenarios for organizations planning a migration to Windows Vista and maintaining consistency in deployment of workstations. For instance, having an imaging and deployment process is often a requirement of a company's business continuity and disaster recovery plans. Images and deployment software are frequently used in organizations to upgrade legacy Windows systems on a network and quickly roll out new customized systems when old or broken ones need replacing. Having a "clean" snapshot can also prove useful when systems have been infected with a virus or other malicious program and need to be restored.

Note

Today applications, operating systems, networks, hardware, and even malicious programs like spyware and adware are including "self-healing" mechanisms. Self-healing can be compared to restoring a system from an image or when Windows automatically checks and repairs a disk volume when errors are detected. These products or programs are configured to replace or fix vital components if specific errors or other erratic behavior is detected.

Malware authors incorporate self-healing mechanisms into their programs to evade detection by antivirus and anti-malware scanners such as Windows Defender and Microsoft Forefront. The malicious program senses it is being tampered with (removal) and either allows this, but hides the executable, or removes itself first and then restores a copy when it is able and safe to do so—sometimes undetected. In some cases, the malicious program will even report that it has been removed when in fact it hasn't.

Working with the Windows Automated Installation Kit (WAIK) and Windows Setup

The Windows Automated Installation Kit (WAIK), discussed in the next section, includes all the tools necessary to create and manage Windows Vista packages. The WAIK can be downloaded separately (1GB image for DVD) and is also included with the BDD typically used by small- to enterprise-size organizations and businesses.

The Windows Setup routine in Windows Vista has changed dramatically from previous releases to support Microsoft's new imaging and image deployment technologies, security enhancements, and flexibility for including items in addition to the operating system. Windows Setup uses a collection of configuration passes and an XML-based answer file to install Windows Vista.

The Windows Automated Installation Kit (WAIK)

The WAIK is a comprehensive set of tools designed for IT administrators, system developers, and original equipment manufacturers (OEM) to design and maintain a reliable, often automated, imaging process for upgrades and new system builds. The WAIK can be downloaded from the Microsoft website at www.microsoft.com/downloads/. The download is located in the Windows product family category; searching for "WAIK" displays the download page. The WAIK is downloaded in image file format (IMG) and is approximately 1GB in size. To install the WAIK, the downloaded IMG file must be extracted and burned to a DVD. Each program included with WAIK is discussed later in this chapter, with the exception of Windows Deployment Services, which is covered in Chapter 20, "Imaging Tools and Processes."

Programs included with the WAIK are the following:

- Windows Preinstallation Environment (PE) version 2.0
- Windows Deployment Services
- ImageX

- Windows System Image Manager (SIM)
- Package Manager

Tip

If your DVD burning software doesn't recognize IMG files when creating a DVD from an image file such as ISO or CIF, rename the file to have an ISO extension and try again. This trick usually works with most CD and DVD recording software. An update to support IMG files may also be available from the software manufacturer.

If you don't have a DVD burner or would like to save some time, simply mount the ISO file that would have been used to create the DVD. Mounting an ISO file reveals its contents and allows it to be used as if it were on a DVD.

Installing the WAIK is effortless. Simply insert the WAIK DVD and run the StartCD.exe program, choose Windows AIK Setup when the Welcome screen appears, and follow the onscreen instructions. There are no customizable options during setup other than the location where WAIK will be installed.

Supported operating systems are the following:

- Windows XP SP2 with KB926044
- Windows Server 2003 SP1 with KB926044
- Windows Server 2003 SP2
- Windows Vista

Several other items are available on the WAIK DVD as the Welcome screen in Figure 19.1 shows. Items included on the DVD are the Getting Started guide, WAIK Release Notes, Windows Deployment Services, .NET Framework 2.0, and MSXML 6.0.

Windows Setup

Windows Setup is exactly what the name implies—the setup routine for Windows Vista. However, Windows Setup includes several new enhancements and features to ensure stability, ease of deployment, and reduced administrative overhead, especially for creating and deploying images. Windows Setup is used to install a clean copy of Windows Vista or upgrade an existing system.

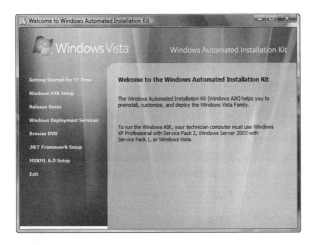

FIGURE 19.1
Welcome to the Windows Automated Installation Kit.

The Windows Setup routine now uses an image-based setup built on new technology that is contained in a single file (WIM), and that file can hold multiple copies of the Windows Vista operating system also supporting multiple platforms. So, a company with four different laptops and six different desktop models with a plan to deploy two different versions of Windows Vista can do so using a single image file. Image-based installations are faster, more reliable, and can be customized based on deployment requirements.

> **Note**
>
> During an installation of Windows Vista, files from the previous operating system are copied to the C:\Windows.old directory.

The Windows Setup Routine

The Windows Setup process runs through a variety of steps to install Windows Vista and can end the installation in one of two boot modes: Audit mode or Windows Welcome. Windows Welcome is the default for new Windows Vista installations and boots the system with the Welcome to Windows Vista screen displayed, allowing further customization of the operating system. Audit mode is used by corporations and original equipment manufacturers to customize the Windows Vista installation and can include additional device drivers, applications, and system settings. Audit mode also provides the capability to validate the installation.

Windows Setup is accomplished through different configuration passes that apply the settings contained in an answer file. When building an answer file in Windows System Image Manager (Windows SIM), the setting being applied must be assigned to the appropriate configuration pass. Thankfully, Windows SIM makes the supported configuration passes available only when configuring an item for the answer file. Understanding the different configuration passes is important when you're building and deploying image files.

Windows Setup configuration passes are as follows:

- **WindowsPE**—Applies basic Windows Setup options, configures hard disk drives, and can also include the Windows Vista product key.

- **OfflineServicing**—Installs Microsoft updates, patches, and hotfixes.

- **Specialize**—Used to configure specific system settings such as network configuration.

- **Generalize**—Removes system-specific information such as the Security ID (SID).

- **AuditSystem**—Available if the system is started in Audit mode. See the sysprep section for more information.

- **AuditUser**—Available if the system is started in Audit mode. See the sysprep section for more information.

- **OobeSystem**—Applies settings in the Oobe.xml file before Windows Welcome.

Caution

Typically an answer file is named unattend.xml; however, for the answer file to be applied during the Windows PE configuration pass, the answer file must be named autounattend.xml. This allows the Windows PE configuration pass to recognize the answer file and apply the settings. For example, Autounattend.xml should be used if the target hard drive will be formatted and partitioned, which is only possible during the Windows PE configuration pass before Windows Setup files are copied to the hard drive. Storing the Autounattend.xml file on a USB flash drive is the easiest way to include these settings.

Windows Setup works in conjunction with sysprep, an answer file (Unattend.xml), a Windows PE boot environment for image and DVD-based installations, and a content file named oobe.xml for customizing the "out-of-the-box" installation. The Windows Setup process is further outlined next.

1. Configuration options for Windows Setup are applied, such as the product key (either input manually or silently using Unattend.xml).

2. Windows PE applies settings from the answer file (Unattend.xml).

3. Hard disk drive is configured.

4. Windows image is copied to the disk.

5. Prepare system boot configuration.

6. OfflineServicing applies settings from the answer file (Unattend.xml).

7. Online configuration occurs.

8. The oobeSystem applies settings from the answer file (Unattend.xml).

9. Settings are applied from the oobe.xml file.

10. Windows starts and the Welcome screen is displayed.

Running Scripts in the Windows Setup Routine

Windows Setup can run custom scripts or other commands specified inside of the SetupComplete.cmd file, located in the %WINDIR%\Setup\Scripts\ directory. The SetupComplete.cmd file is launched after Windows has finished installing and before the user is presented with the logon prompt. Results from the SetupComplete.cmd file are logged to the Setupact.log file located in the same directory.

Windows Setup can also launch customized scripts or a command if an error is encountered that prevents installation from finishing. When this occurs, Windows Setup searches for the ErrorHandler.cmd file in the %WINDIR%\ Setup\Scripts\ directory and, if present, runs the file and then exits Windows Setup. The system may return to the previous operating system or Windows PE boot environment.

Running Windows Setup in Audit Mode

Audit mode is a network-enabled Windows Setup routine that disables the Welcome screen and allows further customization of image-based Windows Vista installations. Audit mode provides functionality for installing software, adding drivers, running scripts, and validating the Windows installation. An administrator can reduce the number of customized images needed by developing a baseline image or template and applying customized settings and delivering applications in Audit mode.

Note

The Welcome screen must be displayed by system manufacturers because the end user must accept the license agreement. Corporations and other organizations may bypass the Welcome screen.

Audit mode can be enabled in three different ways. For example, one way of enabling audit mode is to use the /audit switch with the sysprep command (for example, sysprep /audit). Audit mode can also be enabled by modifying the Microsoft, Windows, Deployment, Reseal to Audit mode setting in an answer file created with Windows System Image Manager (SIM). Lastly, audit mode can be invoked by pressing SHIFT+CTRL+F3 at the Windows Welcome screen. Windows System Image Manager and sysprep are covered in Chapter 20, "Imaging Tools and Processes."

Command-Line Options for Windows Setup

Windows Setup includes several command-line parameters for executing specific tasks and to support certain functionality during installation. The following lists define each command-line option available to Windows Setup.

Command-line options for Windows Setup:

- **/dudisable**—Disables dynamic updating of setup files.

- **/m:folder_name**—Specifies an alternative location for setup files. Network paths are not supported.

- **/noreboot**—Setup will bypass the first reboot, allowing time for further customization or configuration of the installation. This applies only to the first reboot.

- **/tempdrive:drive_letter**—Specifies an alternative local partition for Windows Setup to place temporary installation files.

- **/unattend:answer_file**—Enables Windows Setup to run in unattended mode and specifies the location of the answer file. Network paths are supported.

Command-line options for debugging:

- **/1394debug:channel baudrate:baudrate**—Activates kernel debugging over a FireWire connection. Valid baud rates are 19,200 (default), 57,600, and 115,200.

- **/debug:channel baudrate:baudrate**—Activates kernel debugging over a specific communications port (COM). The default COM part is 1. Valid baud rates are 19,200 (default), 57,600, and 115,200.

- **/usbdebug:hostname**—Enables debugging for a specific host on a USB port at the next system restart.

Windows Setup Log Files

Windows Setup creates several log files during installation. These log files contain invaluable data for troubleshooting issues and identifying the order in which tasks occur or occurred during the setup process. Before the Windows Setup routine configures the hard drive, log files are stored in the $windows.~bt directory, accessible by browsing to C:\$WINDOWS\. After Windows Setup has finished configuring the hard drive, log files can be found in various locations of the standard C:\Windows directory, unless Windows has been installed to a different location. Some of the more commonly referenced log files are outlined next, although others do exist.

Windows Setup logs:

- **$windows.~bt\sources\rollback**—Log files when a fatal error results in a rollback to the current operating system.

- **C:\Windows\memory.dmp**—Location of memory dump.

- **C:\Windows\system32\sysprep\panther**—Sysprep log files.

- **C:\Windows\Panther\setupact.log**—Actions taken by Windows Setup during installation.

- **C:\Windows\Panther\setuperr.log**—Setup errors encountered during installation.

- **C:\Windows\Panther\miglog.xml**—Information about the user directory structure.

- **C:\Windows\INF\setupapi*.log**—Information about Plug and Play devices.

- **C:\Windows\INF\setupapi.app.log**—Application installation details.

- **C:\Windows\Performance\Winsat\winsat.log**—Detailed testing results from the Windows Vista System Assessment tool.

Creating Windows Vista Images

Creating Windows Vista images is fairly easy given the similarity of the process with other imaging technologies. The basics to creating a Windows Vista image are installing and customizing Windows Vista, running sysprep, restarting the system to be imaged using Windows PE, and running ImageX to create the WIM file. The system being imaged is commonly referred to as the *Master Installation*. In addition, an answer file can be created with Windows SIM to further customize the installation, join an Active Directory domain, include update packages, and so on. Answer files are covered in the next section. Windows SIM is covered in the next chapter.

With the capability to support multiple hardware platforms and configurations with one image file, larger organizations will need to invest more resources in image development, customization, maintenance, and testing. Leveraging the benefits of using an answer file and the other tools available, the process is much less involved and more flexible than other imaging solutions and previous Windows deployment solutions released by Microsoft.

Creating an Answer File

Windows SIM is used to create and maintain answer files for WIM images. The new single answer file format based on XML (unattend.xml) replaces the previous set of files used for deploying previous versions of Microsoft Windows.

Using an answer file for an unattended installation of Windows Vista eases deployment by including custom settings specified by component in the answer file. Creating an answer file is the first item to address when customizing Windows Vista for imaging. The process to create an answer file using Windows SIM is outlined in the following steps. The Windows SIM program is discussed further in Chapter 21.

To create an answer file with Windows SIM, follow these steps:

1. Download and install the WAIK.
2. Copy the install.wim file from a Windows Vista Setup DVD to the computer.
3. Open Windows System Image Manager.
4. Click File and choose Select Windows Image from the list.
5. Navigate to the location of the install.wim file copied from the DVD.

> **Caution**
>
> To work with the `install.wim` image file, the file attribute of read-only must be removed, Windows SIM needs to run with Administrative credentials, and the account should have full access to the folder containing the file.

6. When the Select an Image dialog box appears, choose the correct version of Windows Vista and click OK.

7. Click OK to the Catalog Does Not Exist warning to have a catalog created.

8. Click File and choose New Answer File (see Figure 19.2).

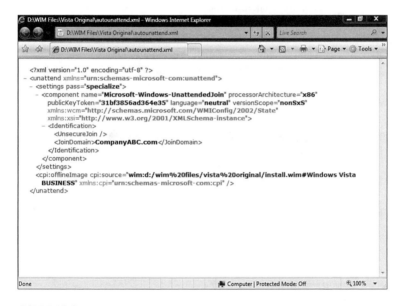

FIGURE 19.2
Answer File created with Windows SIM.

Configuring Windows Vista Components and Settings

Adding and configuring components for Windows Vista images is easily accomplished using Windows System Image Manager.

To configure Windows Vista components with Windows SIM, follow these steps:

1. Expand the Component list in the Windows Image pane of Windows SIM.

2. Select the component to add, right-click the component, and select the correct configuration pass (only valid ones are available).

3. The component is then added to the answer file.

4. After it is added, the value of the component can be modified in the Answer File pane.

For example, to have the computer join a domain, expand to Microsoft, Windows, UnattendedJoin, Identification, JoinDomain and specify the domain name (for example, CompanyABC.com). To specify the credentials for joining a domain, add and specify values for the Microsoft, Windows, UnattendedJoin, Identification, Credentials, Domain, Username, and Password component options. The settings for joining a domain are applied during the "specialize" configuration pass. Figure 19.3 shows an answer file with the necessary settings for joining the CompanyABC.com domain.

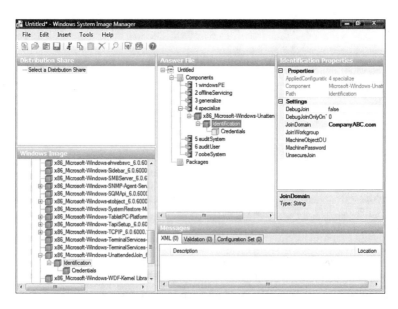

FIGURE 19.3
Adding Windows Vista components to an answer file.

> **Caution**
>
> Answer files can contain usernames and passwords. Because XML files by default are not encrypted, anyone could potentially gain access to this information. Access to this account information can pose a serious security risk. When adding passwords and accounts to answer file, be sure to hide this information using Tools, Hide Sensitive Data in Windows System Image Manager.

For a complete list of Windows Vista components, subcomponents, their options, values, and the configuration pass to apply, visit the Microsoft Windows Vista Deployment Center at TechNet (http://technet.microsoft.com/en-us/windowsvista/default.aspx/) and browse to the Unattended Windows Setup Reference section located under Windows Vista: Deployment, Windows Automated Installation Kit (Windows AIK).

Validating the Answer File

To avoid potential issues and reduce troubleshooting efforts, Microsoft considers it a best practice to validate the answer file after it has been created and customized. Validation of an answer file will reveal any missing or incorrect settings, allowing time to correct them. Steps to validate an answer file are outline next.

To validate an answer file with Windows SIM, follow these steps:

1. Click Tools, Validate Answer File in the Windows SIM program. Windows SIM compares the answer file and settings against the image file.

   - A No Warnings or Errors entry appears in the Messages pane if no errors are encountered.

   - Any discovered errors are also displayed in the Messages pane, as shown in Figure 19.4. Double-clicking an error takes you to the location of the incorrect setting.

2. When finished, click File, Save to save a copy of the answer file that has been created and validated. Save the file as `autounattend.xml` if the answer file contains items that will be configured during the Windows PE configuration pass, such as hard drive partitioning and formatting.

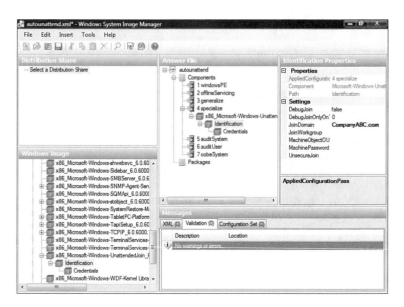

FIGURE 19.4
Validating an answer file.

Creating a Master Installation

Master Installation is the term used by Microsoft to define the reference or source computer that will be imaged and then distributed. The Master Installation can be created in only a few steps or can take some time, depending on what's being included in the image. For example, larger organizations may have a broader range of standardized settings and applications, whereas smaller companies most likely won't. Personnel responsible for developing and maintaining images should take detailed notes and keep relevant resources and materials organized. This will prove especially useful when validating and troubleshooting image deployments.

A separate system with the WAIK is typically used for the creation of answer files for the Master Installation, Windows PE CDs, and so on. Microsoft refers to this as the *Technicians Computer*. The hardware for the Technicians Computer and Master Installation should match, with the differences for target systems that will be imaged in a production environment (for example, drivers or updates) being delivered using the other tools discussed in the next chapter. To build a Master Installation, follow these steps:

1. Create an answer file and include any configuration and settings desired (`autounattend.xml`).

2. Store the answer file on a USB drive or other media.

3. Install Windows Vista using the Installation DVD and answer file.

4. Install additional software and make any other desired changes.

5. Prepare the computer using sysprep /generalize to remove unique settings.

6. Shut down the system.

Adding Hardware Drivers to the Master Installation

There are different ways to add hardware drivers to a Windows Vista installation, providing administrators with flexibility in developing an imaging process. Using the different tools provided for updating drivers allows Windows Vista to be delivered to different hardware platforms using a single image (WIM) file.

Drivers can be installed directly onto the Master Installation as they will be included in the image; however, it is recommended that driver updates be installed during the Windows Setup routine or offline. The difference is that Windows Setup will install the driver, whereas an imaged driver has already been installed and could possibly be overwritten. This also allows for easier maintenance when updating existing images.

Use the Package Manager program to update drivers on an offline Windows Image File (WIM). The Sysprep command can install drivers in Windows Setup Audit mode. For information on checking drivers into a distribution share, see the "Windows System Image Manager (SIM)" section in the next chapter. For more information on Sysprep and Package Manager, see the Chapter 20, "Imaging Tools and Processes" for further details and proper usage.

Adding Other Programs to the Master Installation

Some programs can be installed before the Master Installation is cut into an image file; however, sometimes this is not supported or recommended. For example, common agent software for centralized management applications should be imaged only if the unique identifiers of that agent are removed, such as a Globally Unique Identifier (GUID) used with Microsoft Systems Management Server (SMS).

Using ImageX, applications can be converted into a single WIM file and then applied to the Master Installation through a Distribution Share in the Windows System Image Manager program. These WIM files are called *Data Images*. See the "Imaging Tools" section in the next chapter for more information on Image X and Windows System Image Manager.

In some cases, applications must be applied after the target system is imaged and online. For example, if the application is in Microsoft Installer (MSI) format, OCSetup must be used with Package Manager. Service packs also fall into this category and must be installed online with the Windows Update Stand Alone (WUSA) installer or Microsoft Windows Software Update Services. For more information on OCSetup and Package Manager, see the "Imaging Tools" section of the next chapter.

Adding Microsoft Update Packages to the Master Installation

Use the Package Manager program to include Microsoft Updates such as security updates for known vulnerabilities, hotfixes, and Anti-Malware definition files, all of which are distributed in CAB format. For more information on Package Manager, see the "Imaging Tools" section in the next chapter. Online systems should use the Windows Update services from Microsoft or an internal Windows Update server.

Adding Service Packs to the Master Installation

As previously mentioned, service packs must be installed online using the Windows Update Stand Alone (WUSA) installer. At the time of writing, no service packs had been released for Windows Vista, although one is planned. Service packs can also be obtained directly from Microsoft or an internal update server; however, it is a best practice to first install the operating system and then any full Windows service packs. To include a service pack, follow these steps:

1. Explode the image onto a target system and log on.

2. Download the service pack.

3. Run the command `wsua C:\path_to_service_pack\sp1.msu /quiet` in an administrative command prompt window.

4. Include any additional items or configuration the image should contain.

5. Unmount and save (commit) the changes to the WIM file.

Validating the Master Installation and Customizations

Because the answer file contains almost everything needed for a Windows Image file to be applied and processed, validation is highly recommended. To validate an answer file, click Tools, Validate in Windows System Image Manager with the WIM file and Answer file both open. After it is validated, any discrepancies can then be corrected and if necessary, a new WIM file can be created from the Master Installation. Error messages created from validation link directly to the section of the answer file containing the setting. More detailed and visual verification can be performed manually after the image has been applied to a system.

Capturing an Image

Creating a WIM file from the Master Installation is accomplished in a few simple steps. Boot the system into the Windows Preinstallation environment, start the Master Installation, run ImageX, and copy the WIM file to a distribution location for deployment.

Follow these steps to create an image from the Master Installation:

1. Create a WIM image of Windows PE on removable media, such as a USB flash drive (remember to include all necessary tools, such as Image X). See the Windows Preinstallation Environment (PE) section of Chapter 20 for detailed instructions on creating Windows PE images.

2. Start the Master Installation computer in the Windows PE Environment. See Chapter 20 for detailed instructions on creating Windows PE images.

3. Run `ImageX.exe /capture` at the Windows PE command prompt, adding any additional command-line options as necessary. See the ImageX section of Chapter 20 for detailed instructions.

   Example: E:\WinPE\Tools\imagex.exe /capture c:\vistaimage_ABC.wim "Vista Business Edition for CompanyABC"

4. Copy the Windows Image File to the desired location.

The next two chapters of this book outline and describe each of the different tools and scenarios for deploying Windows Vista image files.

Updating and Maintaining Windows Vista Images

A critical part to any imaging process, especially for larger organizations, is to include a maintenance plan for keeping images up-to-date. Maintaining images to include new drivers, programs, security updates, and settings as they become necessary or available will be beneficial in the long run. Imaged systems, for example, wouldn't have to download as many security updates after Windows Vista is running, new corporate policy changes or systems settings can be included out-of-the-box, and new applications could replace outdated versions so a current system can be immediately delivered to the end user.

Over time, tools for imaging and deploying Windows, such as ImageX and Windows System Image Manager, will be updated and released by Microsoft. Administrators should take note to monitor the release of newer versions of these tools and test them against existing images and planned changes accordingly.

Using sysprep in Audit mode means that administrators have fewer images to maintain and keep updated. With sysprep's audit mode, a baseline or reference image is used for all systems, and driver updates are added as necessary. Upon deployment of the image, administrators can more accurately pinpoint issues with device drivers. For example, if all models of one desktop work with an updated video card driver, but all laptops are failing with an updated network card driver, administrators can quickly and accurately identify the problem and resolve it without affecting the reference image or systems that were upgraded successfully.

Updating and maintaining images normally includes adding new drivers or updates. This is accomplished using Package Manager, Windows System Image Manager, and an answer file. The tools to complete each of the tasks described next are discussed in Chapter 20. See each respective section for technical details.

Follow these steps to update a Windows Vista Image with a new package:

1. Create an answer file using Windows System Image Manager.

2. Mount an image using ImageX.

3. Add the packages(s) using Package Manager.

4. Commit (save) the changes and unmount the image using ImageX.

After updating images, system administrators will want to take advantage of the System Integrity Check and Repair program (`sfc.exe`) included with Windows Vista in the `C:\Windows\System32` folder. When validating an image, only the reference image needs to have system files validated in this manner. If any issues are encountered, they will be reported and should be researched prior to making changes to an image.

Caution

The sfc.exe program is normally executed with the /verifyonly option because Microsoft recommends against having sfc.exe automatically repair system files.

Note

The sfc.exe program can take a considerable amount of time to complete a scan.

The sfc.exe program has a few additional command-line options. For example, the /SCANNOW option can be used to verify and repair all system files, /SCANFILE=..\path_to_file\ can be used to scan and repair a single file, and /VERIFYFILE=..\path_to_file\ can be used to verify a single file. For more sfc.exe options, type **sfc.exe /?** at a command prompt. Figure 19.5 shows a completed sfc.exe scan using the /VERIFYONLY option.

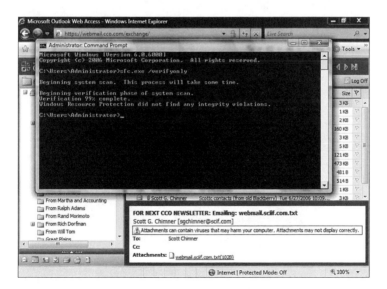

FIGURE 19.5
A completed SFC.exe scan executed with the /verifyonly option.

Alternatively, administrators can rely on other online tools, such as Microsoft's Windows Update Services to deploy Microsoft updates, Systems Management Server (SMS) to deploy software packages and updates, and Distribution Services to deploy the Windows Vista operating system. Distribution Services is covered in Chapter 21 of this book. Larger organizations are more likely to implement technologies such as these; however, Windows images should be updated offline as well to maintain a consistent standard and prepare for automated online systems possibly being unavailable.

Summary

Creating and maintaining Windows Vista images is a crucial part of a system maintenance and deployment strategy. When configured and tested properly, Windows Vista images can streamline the system deployment process by significantly reducing administrative overhead and deployment time. Maintaining Windows Vista images reduces the amount of images that need to be archived and completely rebuilt each time a new update or system change needs to be incorporated. This chapter focused on providing guidance for creating, testing, and maintaining images using the WAIK and building and using unattended answer files during the Windows setup routine.

CHAPTER 20

Imaging Tools and Processes

Imaging Tools

The release of Windows Vista and an improved imaging process is made possible by the simultaneous release of several new and updated tools. As mentioned in the previous chapter, there are a couple of ways to obtain all the imaging tools and information needed to create Windows Vista images. This primarily depends on the size of the target install base and existing deployment technologies at an organization. For example, an administrator with only 200 systems may want to distribute the image manually on DVD using bootable USB flash drives running Windows PE. For that deployment scenario, only the Windows Automated Installation Kit (WAIK) would be needed, whereas an organization with thousands of computers may choose to implement Microsoft Deployment Services first and would start with the customizable Business Desktop Deployment (BDD) package. Regardless, the right tools are available, flexible, and easy to interact with. Having a good understanding and hands-on experience with these imaging tools will make a migration to Windows Vista much easier to launch and maintain.

The WAIK and Windows Setup, covered in the previous chapter, work along with the subset of tools covered in this chapter to deliver Windows Vista installations that encompass virtually every possible combination of configuration and the vast array of different platforms and user requirements that exist today. The primary tools used for creating Windows Vista images are the Windows Preinstallation Environment (Windows PE), ImageX, Windows System Image Manager (Windows SIM), and Package Manager.

Although it's technically not a tool, the answer file is a required component that makes imaging systems possible. Answer files were covered in the previous chapter.

The Microsoft Solution Accelerator for Business Desktop Deployment 2007 (BDD), also updated with the release of Windows Vista, is an all-in-one imaging and deployment package with larger organizations in mind. The BDD includes the WAIK, several other tools, documentation, and technical guides for designing and executing an automated large-scale deployment of Windows Vista—successfully. The BDD is covered in Chapter 21, "Deploying Windows Vista in an Automated Fashion."

Caution

Even if you are logged on with an Administrative account, User Account Control is enforced, requiring imaging tools launched in a command prompt to be run with elevated privileges. Because most of these tools run in a command prompt, launch the command prompt using the Run as Administrator option by right-clicking the command prompt link in the Accessories menu under All Programs.

ImageX

ImageX is a tool that provides administrators with the capability to create, manage, and deploy Windows Image Files (WIM). ImageX also allows modification of files within an existing image without extracting or re-creating the entire image. This is accomplished through the use of the Windows Imaging File System Filter (WIMFS Filter).

Although possible, ImageX doesn't require reformatting of the target hard drive. This allows certain information to be retained during an upgrade. ImageX has multiple compression options and quick extraction during installation to help reduce overall image creation and deployment time. ImageX accomplishes this by combining multiple images for multiple platforms into a single WIM file.

ImageX is also used to create Data Images, which are smaller WIM files that don't contain the Windows operating system, but rather, files or applications for installation later. To include files or install applications to Windows Vista during the Windows Setup process, a Data Image must be used. The Data Image file (WIM) that contains the application, files, or the like can then be checked in through a Distribution Share in Windows System Image Manager (SIM). SIM is covered later in this chapter.

To create a Data Image, follow these steps:

1. Place the data, such as the copy of an application installation package from a CD into an accessible location (for example, `C:\temp\Office2007\`).

2. Launch a command prompt (with Administrator credentials) and change to the `C:\Program Files\Windows AIK\Tools\x86\`folder.

3. Run the following command to compress the files into a single WIM file:

   ```
   imagex /capture C:\temp\Office
   ➥C:\Temp\Office2007.wim "Office2007"
   ```

4. Everything in `C:\temp\Office2007` will be added to the `Office2007.wim` file.

5. Using Windows SIM, check the `Office2007.wim` file into a Distribution Share and add the WIM file to Windows System Image Manager for inclusion in the answer file.

6. Make sure that a copy of the WIM data image file (for example, `Office2007.wim`) is available in the location specified in the answer file so it is available during Windows Setup.

Caution

ImageX can apply only full versions of the Windows Vista operating system or an application—not upgrades.

Before using ImageX, a WIM must first be created using Windows SIM. The WIM file can then be captured with ImageX. More information on Windows SIM is available later in this chapter.

The `ImageX.exe` program is located in the `C:\Program Files\Windows AIK\Tools\x86\` folder after the WAIK has been installed. `ImageX.exe` is run from the command prompt and includes several options for working with WIM image files. The commonly used ImageX command-line options are listed next. For more options, advanced settings, and parameters, run `ImageX.exe /?`, or add a specific operation such as `ImageX.exe /Capture /?` at a command prompt. Most of these options must be executed in the Windows Preinstallation (PE) environment, covered later in this chapter.

Command-line options for `ImageX.exe`:

- **/capture**—Creates a new WIM file by capturing a volume image from a drive. Empty directories and extended attributes are not captured. Use /compress to switch to Maximum (longer capture and slightly longer extraction time) or None from the default setting of Fast.

- **/apply**—Applies an image to a drive. Run in Windows PE.

- **/append**—Combines a volume image and a WIM file into one file. Run in Windows PE.

- **/delete**—Removes a volume image from a WIM image file that contains multiple images. Run in Windows PE.

- **/dir**—Lists files and folders in a volume image. Useful to run before mounting an image.

- **/mountrw**—Mounts the contents of a WIM image file to a directory with read and write permissions. The contents can then be viewed in Windows Explorer and modified. Running /mount instead provides read-only access to the contents.

- **/unmount**—Dismounts a mounted image from the directory. Use the /commit option to save any changes.

- **/split**—Spans the image file across multiple disks.

Caution

When unmounting an image file, make sure the /commit option is also executed; otherwise, any changes will not be saved.

Tip

In addition to the /split option, you can also use the createspannedshares.cmd file in the C:\Program Files\Windows AIK\Samples\ directory to span an image into multiple files. For example, this can be useful when the WIM image file is larger than 4.7GB—the size of a single-layer DVD.

Configuring the Out-of-the-Box Experience Using Oobe.xml

Out-of-the-box experience is the meaning behind the acronym OOBE, used in the oobe.xml filename. The oobe.xml file is used by commercial computer manufacturers and corporations to add settings to the desktop, customize the Welcome Center, include support for multiple languages, and deliver the End-User License Agreement (EULA), if necessary. A lot of the options in the oobe.xml file are also available in the Unattend.xml file used by Windows Setup, covered later in this chapter.

The oobe.xml file is normally placed in the C:\Windows\system32\oobe\info directory. This is the first place Windows Setup checks for this file. If found, settings are applied. To use oobe.xml to specify a different language for installation, an oobe.xml file must be present in the C:\Windows\system32\oobe\info\default\default language\ folder or the appropriate country folder underneath.

> **Tip**
>
> The C:\Program Files\Windows AIK\Samples\OOBE directory contains an oobe.xml file example based on a fictional company (Fabrikam) to use as a template.

> **Tip**
>
> A list of ISO 639 language codes and ISO 3166 region codes can be obtained from the International Organization for Standardization (ISO) website at www.iso.org, the Unicode Consortium website at www.unicode.org, or the Internet Assigned Numbers Authority at www.iana.org.

Package Manager

Package Manager is a tool that adds, updates, or removes Microsoft Update packages such as hotfixes or security updates in Windows images (offline Windows Image file only). Package Manager is executed in a command prompt using the pkgmgr.exe file located in the C:\Program Files\Windows AIK\Tools\x86\Servicing\ directory. Package Manager adds or updates CAB files to Windows images only. Package Manager can use the Unattend.xml answer file for input and can enable or disable certain features of Windows Vista. When the Unattend.xml file is used, only settings in the offlineServicing section are recognized. Some sample uses and instructions for Package Manager are listed next.

Caution

The path Package Manager can use is limited to 126 characters in length, including the filenames and their locations inside the package, which can sometimes quickly reach 126 character limit. Microsoft strongly recommends using a folder in the root of the drive named using five or fewer characters. Microsoft also strongly recommends against placing the package directly at the root of the Windows installation partition.

To add a driver using Package Manager, follow these steps:

1. Create an answer file and add the Microsoft-Windows-PnpCustomizationsNonWinPE component with the path to the driver in the offlineServicing pass section.

2. Run Package Manager in a command prompt against the offline image:

```
Start /w pkgmgr /n:C:\Unattend.xml /o:
➥"C:\Images\;C:\Windows"
```

To enable or disable Windows features using Package Manager, follow these steps:

1. Create an answer file and add the entry for enabling or disabling a component. For example, adding <DisableAntiSpyware>false </DisableAntiSpyware> enables Windows Defender.

2. Use ImageX to mount the image.

3. Run Package Manager in a command prompt against the offline image, referencing the answer file:

```
Start /w pkgmgr /n:C:\Unattend.xml"
```

4. Unmount the image using ImageX with the /commit option to save changes.

Note

Windows service packs cannot be added using Package Manager because they can be installed only after Windows Vista is running on the system (online). Service packs can be delivered through the Windows Update Stand Alone (WUSA) installer. The basic command is given next and is also covered in the previous chapter.

For example: wsua C:\service_packs\sp1.msu /quiet

Pkgmgr.exe includes a few options for working with WIM image files. A handful of the commonly used options for pkgmgr.exe are listed next. For more options, advanced settings, and parameters, run pkgmgr.exe at a command prompt.

Command-line options for pkgmgr.exe include the following:

- **/m:Package Directory**—Location of the package. Multiple entries can be made separated by semicolons.

- **/ip:Package Name**—Installs a package or packages using the /p or /m parameters, respectively. When installing multiple packages, entries in the command line must be separated by a semicolon. Package names are case sensitive.

- **/up:Package Name**—Uninstalls packages. Multiple entries can be made separated by semicolons.

- **/iu:Windows feature**—Identifies the command-line name of the Windows feature to enable. Multiple entries can be made separated by semicolons.

- **/uu:Windows feature**—Identifies the command-line name of the Windows feature to disable. Multiple entries can be made separated by semicolons.

- **/n:Answer File**—Location of Unattend.xml.

- **/norestart**—Prevents Windows Setup from rebooting.

- **/quiet**—Runs the updated package in quiet mode.

Installing MSI Packages with OCSetup

OCSetup is a tool for installing Microsoft Installer (MSI) packages after Windows Vista is running on the system. OCSetup works with an answer file to install or remove MSI packages. The OCSetup.exe program could be scripted to run after Windows Vista is installed on the system, providing administrators with a means of installing MSI packages during an image process. The OCSetup program is run in this syntax: start w/ ocsetup MyProgram.msi /unattendfile:unattend.xml, with any additional options added as needed. The OCSetup.exe program is located in the C:\Windows\System32 folder and includes several options for use.

Command-line options for OCSetup include the following:

- **/unattendfile:filename**—Filename of the answer file to use (runs the installation in passive mode, showing a progress indicator (/passive) unless /quiet is used).

- ■ /**norestart**—Suppresses a system reboot.
- ■ /**quiet**—Hides progress indicator of MSI installation.
- ■ /**uninstall**—Uninstalls an MSI package.
- ■ /**x:<parameter>**—Configuration parameters to be used when installing a component.
- ■ /**passive**—Displays the progress indicator only.
- ■ /**log:file**—Specifies a location other than the default, for creating log files.
- ■ /**h, /?, or /help**—Displays helpful information about OCSetup.

Working with Sysprep

Sysprep, short for "system preparation," is a command-line tool used for preparing system images that will be used to deploy Windows Vista. The sysprep.exe file is located in the C:\Windows\system32\sysprep directory after Windows is installed on a system. Sysprep is generally used to remove data unique to systems for creating an image that will be deployed to multiple machines. This is often referred to as a baseline template or reference image. ImageX or a similar imaging tool is needed to capture the image. Sysprep is also used to boot to the Windows Welcome screen, boot into Audit mode for adding drivers and other items, and to reset product activation.

Note

Windows product activation can be reset only three times using sysprep. Run sysprep /generalize at a command prompt to reset the activation clock.

Because sysprep.exe is a command-line tool, several options are available for its use and are listed along with a description in the following list. If sysprep.exe is run without adding any additional commands, the Sysprep window appears, where actions for sysprep can be specified and executed (see Figures 20.1 and 20.2).

Command-line options for sysprep:

- ■ /**generalize**—Prepares the operating system for imaging. Unique system information is removed or reset. This includes the security identifier (SID) of the system, event logs, and system restore points. After the image is deployed, system activation will be reset and a new security identifier will be created.

- **/unattend:answerfile**—Specifies an answer file to use with sysprep.

- **/audit**—Runs the computer in Audit mode on the next reboot, which allows for the inclusion of additional drivers or applications and validation of the installation.

- **/oobe**—Displays the Welcome screen at logon.

- **/reboot**—Reboots the system after sysprep has completed.

- **/shutdown**—Shuts down the system after sysprep has completed.

- **/quiet**—Runs sysprep without any confirmation or dialog boxes.

- **/quit**—Closes sysprep after sysprep has completed.

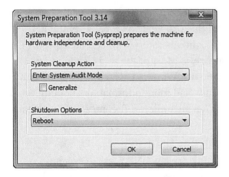

FIGURE 20.1
System Preparation Tool.

FIGURE 20.2
Sysprep is working.

> **Caution**
>
> If ImageX is used to create the image, the hard drive partitions (partition number, type, and active partition setting) must match on both the reference image and the destination computer. To clarify, if Windows was imaged from drive C:, the image must be extracted to drive C: on the destination computer.

> **Caution**
>
> Do not use any encryption on the reference image because any encrypted files and folders will be unreadable after sysprep runs.

Additional Command-Line Tools

ImageX, Sysprep, Package Manager, and several Windows PE command-line based tools were discussed throughout this chapter; however, several other command-line tools also exist to assist administrators with certain aspects of the imaging and image-distribution process. Most of the tools listed in the sections that follow are either included with Windows Vista or included with the WAIK. To obtain optional commands and more information about these tools, visit Microsoft TechNet at http://technet.microsoft.com/WindowsVista/.

Adding Drivers to Windows PE with `Drvload.exe`

Drvload is a program designed for adding drivers (INF files) to systems running in the Windows PE environment, whereas PEImg is used to add drivers to Windows PE images prior to boot (offline). To add a driver using `drvload.exe`, enter the following at a Windows PE command prompt:

```
drvload.exe path_to_inf_file
```

Extracting Cabinet (CAB) files with `Expand.exe`

The `Expand.exe` program is used for extracting the contents of compressed (CAB) Microsoft Updates for review, such as security patches and hotfixes. `Expand.exe` is located in the `C:\Windows\System32\` directory.

The following options are available when running `Expand.exe`:

- **expand.exe ("CAB file name", for example) `sample_file.cab`**— Extracts the specified CAB file. Can also be used with wildcards and the path to the file.

- **-d sample_file.cab**—Displays the files that will be extracted.

- **destination**—Specifies the location the files should be extracted to.

- **-r**—Renames the expanded files.

- **-f**—Expands only the specific file or files from the compressed CAB file. Can also be used with wildcards and the path to the file.

Installing Language Packs with Lpksetup.exe

Lpksetup.exe is used to install language packs. Lpksetup can be executed only on a system running Windows Vista (online). Lpksetup.exe is located in the C:\Windows\System 32 directory. In addition to running lpksetup.exe from a command line, double-clicking it presents a Window for installing or removing languages. Parameters that are used with Lpksetup.exe in a command-line are listed next.

The following options are available when running Lpksetup.exe:

- **/I language-REGION**—Installs the specified language using ISO 639 language codes and ISO 3166 region codes. Using an asterisk (*) in place of ISO codes will install all available languages.

- **/U language-REGION**—Uninstalls the specified language using ISO 639 language codes and ISO 3166 region codes.

- **/p path**—Path to language pack files.

- **/s**—Installs the language pack silently.

- **/f**—Forces the computer to restart after the language pack has been installed.

- **/r**—Prevents a system reboot from occurring after a language pack has been installed.

For example, to install the Armenian language silently and restart the system, the following syntax would be used:

```
lpksetup.exe /i arm-AM /s /f
```

Tip

A list of ISO 639 language codes and ISO 3166 region codes can be obtained from the International Organization for Standardization (ISO) website at www.iso.org, the Unicode Consortium website at www. unicode.org, or the Internet Assigned Numbers Authority at www.iana.org.

Modifying Windows PE Images with `PEImg.exe`

The `PEImg.exe` tool is used to modify an offline Windows PE image (`WinPE.wim`), for example, adding new drivers. With `PEImg.exe`, you can also optimize the image file size and add or remove packages from the WindowsPE image file. Running `PEImg.exe /?` at a command prompt displays the available options and samples for their use (also included in the following list). Any of the options can be used with the `/silent` option to suppress the progress indicators.

The following options are available when running `PEImg.exe`:

- **`/import=path_to_package` (CAB file or folder)**—Imports a package for Windows PE that will be available for installation later (use the /install=package option after import).

- **`/install=package_name`**—Installs the specified package by package name.

- **`/uninstall= package_name`**—Installs the specified package by package name.

- **`/list`**—Displays all packages in the current image and whether they are installed (denoted with a plus (+) sign; not installed is denoted with a minus (–) sign). To obtain the full name of the package, use the /verbose option.

- **`/inf=path_to_inf_file`**—Installs drivers (INF).

- **`/prep`**—Optimizes the Windows PE image file. This command cannot be reversed, and after execution, /install, /uninstall, /import, and /list will no longer function. This option requires the change to be confirmed through the presented dialog box. This command should be run last.

Configuring Power Settings with `Powercfg.exe`

`Powercfg.exe`, installed with Windows Vista in the `C:\Windows\System32` folder, is used to configure power settings such as hibernate and sleep options. `Powercfg.exe` has a large number of options that can be configured. A few examples are given next. Other options are available by running `Powercfg.exe /?` at a command prompt.

The following options are available when running `Powercfg.exe`:

- **`-list`**—Displays all currently available power schemes.

- **`-change` *setting value***—Used to change the configuration of a component such as a monitor or hard drive. The *value* is always entered in minutes. Available configuration options to use for the *setting* parameter are listed next.

- `-monitor-timeout-ac` (or) `-dc`
- `-disk-timeout-ac` (or) `-dc`
- `-standby-timeout-ac` (or) `-dc`
- `-hibernate-timeout-ac` (or) `-dc`

- **-lastwake**—Provides information regarding the last time the computer resumed operation from a sleep state and what event caused it.

- **-deviceenablewake**—Configures a device such as a mouse, keyboard, or network card so it is allowed to wake the computer from a sleep state.

Running Windows PowerShell in Windows PE Using `Winpeshl.ini`

`Winpeshl.ini` allows for the replacement of the standard command prompt with a shell, such as Windows PowerShell in the Windows PE environment. `Winpeshl.ini` isn't a tool, but rather a file that can be created in Notepad and placed in the System32 directory of the Windows PE image. When Windows PE starts, the shell is loaded instead of the standard command prompt. Create the file `winpeshl.ini` and include this section providing the path to the shell to be used. The sample file shown next launches Windows PowerShell 1.0. Command-line options for the shell executable are not supported.

```
[LaunchApp]
AppPath = C:\Windows\System32\powershell.exe
```

Controlling System Settings Using Wpeutil

Wpeutil is a tool used to call several useful administrative commands within a running Windows PE environment. A couple of examples for its use include enabling or disabling the firewall, restarting Windows PE, creating a swap file, initializing the network, or running scripts. Some of these options are listed next. Run `Wpeutil /?` at a Windows PE command prompt to obtain a complete list of options and proper usage. This tool is not available in a Windows Vista session.

The following options are available for use with `Wpeutil.exe`:

- **createpagefile**—Must be used with `/path=path_to_pagefile` or `/size=size_of_pagefile`.

- **enablefirewall or disablefirewall**—Enables and disables the Windows Firewall.

- **initializenetwork**—Assigns the computer a randomly generated name and activates networking components.

- **reboot or shutdown**—Restarts or shuts down WindowsPE.

Windows System Image Manager (SIM)

Windows System Image Manager (SIM) is included with the WAIK. SIM is the main console for managing and creating unattended answer files (unattend.xml). SIM allows creation and modification of answer files using the information contained in an existing image file (WIM) and a catalog file (CLG), which contains settings and packages. SIM also provides a means for validation of an answer file against an image, adding software, drivers, and more.

Using an answer file and Windows Package Manager, Windows SIM is able to update an offline image file with a new service pack, patch, or software package from Microsoft. Package Manager is used to create, install, and uninstall packages in CAB file format and was discussed earlier in this chapter. Unattended Answer Files are covered in detail in an upcoming section of this chapter.

To help ease deployment of images, Windows SIM also creates *configuration sets* from Distribution Shares. Distribution shares typically contain copies of drivers, software, and more. Windows SIM uses a Distribution Share to house packages that do not currently reside in an image file (WIM). A configuration set is simply a copy of all of the items called in the answer file that reside in a Distribution Share. This reduces the amount of time needed to deploy a Windows Vista image and any extras specified in the answer file. Configuration sets are especially useful for systems that can't access the Distribution Share.

The Windows System Image Manager (SIM) Interface

Navigating around and using Windows SIM is a fairly straightforward process. The interface is laid out in a manner that is easy to understand and work with. All pertinent options and functionality of SIM are laid out in one window, further divided into multiple panes for each area. The SIM interface is shown in Figure 20.3. The Distribution Share pane at the top left of Windows SIM is used to create, modify, and view Distribution Shares. Items listed in the Distribution Share section of Windows SIM can be added to an answer file by right-clicking the item and selecting Add to Answer File.

The Answer File pane located in the middle provides a space for creating, viewing, and modifying unattended answer files and the actions that will take place during each configuration pass in the installation process. The Windows Image pane displays the contents of the Windows Image file being used as the source for installation. Components and packages from the image can be added to the answer file from this area. The Properties pane shows information related to a selected package or other item. In the Properties pane, settings can be modified and Windows features can be included or removed. The Messages pane displays messages and errors related to the answer file (XML tab), issues encountered after an answer file has been tested (Validation tab), and the contents of a configuration set (Configuration Set tab).

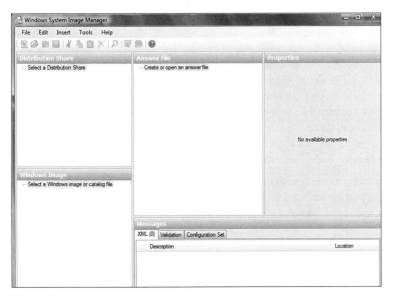

FIGURE 20.3
Windows System Image Manager (SIM) interface.

Distribution Shares and Configuration Sets

As mentioned earlier, SIM uses Distribution Shares to create a reference point in the unattended answer file for installing packages, Windows settings, and more. A Distribution Share could be a pre-existing location like a network share or local folder, or new ones can be created within the SIM program. When an item is added to an answer file from a Distribution Share, the answer file contains the path to the item added.

To create a Distribution Share, follow these steps:

1. In the Distribution Share pane of Windows System Image Manager, right-click Select a Distribution Share.

2. From here an existing share can be selected or one can be created.

Caution

If a preexisting location is referenced as a Distribution Share, it must contain at least one of the following folders: `..\$OEM$\`, `..\Out-of-Box Drivers\`, or `..\Packages\`. These folders allow Windows SIM to recognize the location as a Distribution Share for use with imaging. Any Distribution Share created within Windows SIM contains these folders by default.

The OEM folder and subfolders are retained from previous releases of Microsoft Windows. These folders are designed for configuration sets and are typically used by computer manufacturers to include applications, logos, and custom settings. The Out-of-the-Box Drivers folder exists to house additional drivers or updated drivers (INF files) to be called during Windows Setup. The Packages folder is a location for storing Microsoft Updates (CAB format), like Service Packs, hotfixes, and security updates.

A configuration set is a compiled collection of the items in a Distribution Share that are included in the answer file only. Configuration sets can vary in size and are very useful when network distribution isn't an option.

Caution

When using a preexisting location as a Distribution Share (for example, a UNC network share), the path to the share will automatically be added to the answer file when the item is added to a Distribution Share in Windows SIM. Ensure that the location will be available to the computer during the Windows Setup process.

Windows Preinstallation Environment (Windows PE)

Windows Preinstallation Environment (Windows PE) was designed to over-come the limitations of an MS-DOS–based boot disk and to streamline Windows Vista migrations through an imaging process. Windows PE contains all the necessary items to start a system and get it ready for a Windows Vista installation. Using bootable media such as a USB jump drive, DVD, CD, or even another hard drive, the system is started in the Windows PE environment (resident in memory only). Windows PE prepares a computer for Widows Vista installation, copies image files from a local or network share, and initializes Windows Setup.

Windows PE includes support for the NTFS file system, TCP/IP networking, 32- and 64-bit drivers, Windows Management Instrumentation (WMI), and the Windows Scripting Host (WSH). Windows PE can be launched from a CD, DVD, or USB device. Windows PE also includes support for Systems Management Server (SMS), Windows Deployment Services (Windows DS), and the Windows Recovery Environment. Using Windows PE with these technologies is covered in Chapter 21.

Windows PE is built on the Extensible Markup Language (XML) architecture and is backed by several command-line programs to create and manage Windows PE images. This includes partitioning the hard drive, setting the boot configuration, installing packages, and more.

The Windows PE Tools command prompt can be launched under the Start, All Programs, Microsoft Windows AIK, Windows PE Tools Command Prompt link (`C:\Program Files\Windows AIK\Tools\PETools\`) after the WAIK has been installed. All the command-line tools included with Windows PE are explained next, along with optional parameters.

Creating and Using Bootable Windows PE Media

The Windows PE environment can be stored on a bootable CD, DVD, or USB drive. Although Windows PE itself is relatively small, using a DVD, CD, or large jump drive provides enough space to accommodate additional software packages, drivers, and so on. To create a bootable Windows Media USB jump drive, follow these steps:

1. Launch the Windows PE Tools Command Prompt in Administrator mode: Start, All Programs, Microsoft Windows AIK, Windows PE Tools Command Prompt.

2. Run the `copype.cmd` file for the desired architecture (x86, ia64, or amd64) and provide a destination for `copype.cmd` to extract the Windows PE files for the selected system architecture.

```
Copype x86 d:\winpe_dump_x86\
```

> **Note**
>
> When specifying the destination folder, that or any higher-level folder cannot already exist; otherwise, the message Directory Already Exists is displayed and the files aren't copied. Instead, a directory path that doesn't exist must be provided.

3. Add applications or scripts that may be needed when working in the Windows PE environment, such as ImageX or Package Manager.

```
Copy "C:\Program Files\Windows AIK\Tools\x86\imagex.exe
➥" d:\winpe_dump_x86\winpex86_iso\
```

4. Using Notepad, create a list of files to exclude from being captured with ImageX, and save the file as `wimscript.ini`, and save it in the same location that `imagex.exe` was copied to in the previous step so it can be recognized by ImageX. Several sample exclusions are shown next in a sample list:

```
[ExclusionList]
Hiberfil.sys
Pagefile.sys
"System Volume Information"
RECYCLER
C:\WINDOWS\TEMP

[CompressionExclusionList]
*.zip
*.cab
```

5. This step must be performed on a Windows Vista system or Windows PE session. Format the USB flash drive using DiskPart. The device will need to be formatted with the FAT32 file system, use all available space, and the partition must be set as active. The disk number is needed to carry out this procedure. Run `diskpart`, `list volume` to obtain the disk number for the USB device. Steps to format the device

in DISKPART are outlined next. A successfully completed DiskPart routine is shown in Figure 20.4 and listed here:

A. `Select disk 1`

B. `clean`

C. `create partition primary size=976`

D. `active`

E. `format fs=fat32`

F. `assign`

G. `exit`

FIGURE 20.4
USB flash drive for Windows PE configured with DiskPart.

6. Copy or use a program such as xcopy to duplicate the contents of the folder created previously in step 3 (for example, `d:\winpe_dump_x86\winpex86_iso\`):

   A. `Xcopy d:\winpe_dump_x86\iso\*.* /s /e f:\`

7. The USB flash drive can now be used to start the computer in the Windows PE environment.

Note

Windows PE is assigned a drive letter of X:, which cannot be changed because it is connected with a virtual disk in memory created by Windows PE.

Windows PE Command-Line Tools

To accomplish specific tasks, Windows PE also includes several command-line tools designed to work in the Windows PE environment. BCDEdit, for example, manages the system boot configuration. Bootsect can create or repair a damaged master boot record (MBR), DiskPart is used to configure and manage hard disks and arrays, Oscdimage is used to make ISO files from Windows PE images, PEImage creates and modifies Windows PE images offline (a WIM image file), and WPEnit can be used to process an answer file in the Windows PE environment. Each of these tools, their purpose, and optional parameters are outlined next.

BCDEdit

BCDEdit.exe is a tool that manages boot configuration data and settings contained within stores for Windows Vista systems. Stores contain the information necessary to boot into Windows, for example, the correct drive or partition. Each store lists multiple objects and elements that can be modified using different commands. Information contained in these stores is similar to that of the boot.ini file used with previous versions of Windows. The BCDEdit.exe program includes several command-line options for working with stores and their objects. Following are the commands to create and work with stores and modify settings for the boot manager. For additional options, such as support for Emergency Management Services (EMS), run BCDEDit.exe /? at a command prompt to list the available options. BCDEdit.exe is located in the C:\Windows\System32\ folder.

The BCDEdit store options include the following:

- /**createstore**—Creates a new, empty, non-system store.
- /**export**—Exports the system store to a file.
- /**import**—Imports a backup of the system store generated with the /export option.
- /**store**—Specifies a store for use other than the system store (default).

BCDEdit store entry options include the following:

- /**copy**—Copies a specific boot entry in the system store.
- /**create**—Creates a new entry in the store.
- /**delete**—Removes elements from entries in the store.

BCDEdit boot manager options:

- ▣ /**bootsequence**—Displays the boot sequence once on reboot.

- ▣ /**default**—Entry the boot manager uses when a different option isn't selected by the user.

- ▣ /**displayorder**—Displays the boot sequence every time on system start.

- ▣ /**timeout**—Seconds the boot manager waits for a selection from the user.

Bootsect

Bootsect.exe is located in the C:\Program Files\Windows AIK\Tools\ PETools\x86\ directory and is used to load master boot record code for compatibility with either NTLDR for earlier versions of Windows or BOOTMGR for Windows Vista. Bootsect.exe can also be used to fix or restore the boot sector on a computer. Bootsect.exe has a few options for use, listed next:

- ▣ /**nt52**—Loads master boot code compatible with NTLDR for previous versions of Windows.

- ▣ /**nt60**—Loads master boot code compatible with BOOTMGR for Windows Vista.

- ▣ **SYS**—Specifies the system partition as the target.

- ▣ **ALL**—Specifies that all partitions should have the master boot code updated.

- ▣ **Drive Letter**—Specifies a drive as the target.

- ▣ /**force**—Forces the volume to be dismounted during the update.

DiskPart

DiskPart.exe is located in the C:\Windows\System32\ directory and has multiple options for working with disk volumes, partitions, RAID arrays, and more. Type **diskpart** at a command prompt and the DISKPART prompt appears, allowing you to enter commands.

DiskPart can automate a lot of tasks normally undertaken to prepare hard drives, volumes, and partitions for use. Commonly used options for DiskPart are listed next, along with a brief description. The select disk, partition, or volume should be used first to select the desired component, disk, partition, or volume. Microsoft refers to this as assigning *focus* to the component. For more options and their use, type **DiskPart /?** at a command prompt.

Common commands for DiskPart are the following:

- **select disk=**—Used with the disk number to select a disk.

- **select partition=**—Used with the partition number or drive letter to select a partition.

- **select volume=**—Used with the volume number or drive letter to select a volume.

- **active**—Marks the partition as active so it is recognized as a valid system partition.

- **assign**—Specifies a drive letter to use with a volume. This option cannot be used on system or boot volumes and those containing the Windows pagefile (pagefile.sys). Use the letter= option to specify the drive letter to be assigned. Use the mount= option to specify the path to the volume that will be mounted with the designated drive letter.

- **create partition primary**—Creates a primary partition on the disk. The assign command must be used when creating a primary partition. Use the size= option to designate the amount of space to use in megabytes (MB) for the primary partition. Use the offset= is option for disks that contain the master boot record (MBR) to specify the location (in bytes) for the extended partition to begin.

- **create partition extended**—Creates an extended partition to later be used as a logical drive. Use the size= option to designate the amount of space to use in megabytes for the extended partition. Use the offset= is option for disks that contain the master boot record (MBR) to specify the location (in bytes) for the extended partition to begin.

- **create partition logical size=**—Creates a logical drive in the extended partition. Use the size= option to specify the amount of space to use in megabytes for the logical drive.

- **create volume simple**—Used to create a simple volume. Can be used with the size= option to specify the size in megabytes for the volume and the disk= option to designate a dynamic disk to hold the volume.

- **delete partition**—Deletes partitions, with the exception of system or boot partitions or those that contain the Windows pagefile or memory dumps.

- **delete volume**—Deletes volumes with the exception of system or boot volume or those that contain the Windows pagefile or memory dumps.

- **detail disk**—Shows properties of selected disks and volumes.

- **detail partition**—Shows properties of the selected partition.

- **detail volume**—Shows the disks the current volume is configured on. Can be used with the recommended option to use the FS= option to format with a specific file system.

- **format**—Formats a volume or partition for use. Can be used with the FS= switch to specify the file system. Use the RECOMMENDED switch to format with the recommended settings and size. Label= can be used to specify the volume label. Using the QUICK switch performs a quick format; otherwise, a full format is invoked.

- **list disk**—Shows all disks, their size, free space, and type. Disks marked with an asterisk (*) signify the currently selected item. This command also displays the numbers corresponding to each disk, which can then be used with other commands.

- **list partition**—Shows the partitions of the current disk. This command also displays the numbers corresponding to each partition, which can then be used with other commands.

- **list volume**—Shows all volumes (basic and dynamic) for all disks. This command also displays the numbers corresponding to each volume, which can then be used with other commands.

Tip

DiskPart can also be used in conjunction with a script that can automate most or all of the preceding tasks. To invoke a script for use with DiskPart, run diskpart /s *example.txt*, where *example.txt* designates the name of the script to be executed.

Oscdimg

Oscdimg is a simple command-line tool with the sole purpose of creating an ISO file of a Windows PE build for use on a CD or DVD. For the ISO file to work and the disk to be bootable, the ISO file must be burned to a CD or DVD using burning software. `Oscdimg.exe` is located in the `C:\Program Files\Windows AIK\Tools\PETools` folder after the WAIK has been installed. Commonly used options for Oscdimg are outlined next. For more options and their use, type **oscdimg /?** at a command prompt.

Command-line options for Oscdimg include the following:

- **sourceroot**—This is a required setting that identifies the location of the source Windows PE files for the ISO image file.

- **-b*location***—Location of the boot sector file (ETFSboot.com). Do not separate the -b and *location* with spaces.

- **-d**—File names in lowercase will not be changed to uppercase.

- **-g**—Use Universal Coordinated Time (UCT).

- **-h**—Include all hidden directories and files.

- **-j1**—Generates DOS compatible 8.3 filenames for 64 character filenames.

- **-j2**—Does not create DOS compatible 8.3 filenames.

- **-l*labelname***—Assigns a volume label. Do not separate the -b and *labelname* with spaces.

- **image_file**—This is a required setting that identifies the location of the source Windows PE files for the ISO image file.

PEImg

PEImg is another command-line tool for Windows PE that is designed for modifying and creating Windows PE images offline. `Peimg.exe` is located in the `C:\Program Files\Windows AIK\Tools\PETools` folder after the WAIK has been installed. Commonly used options for PEImg are outlined next. For more options and their use, type **peimg /?** at a command prompt.

Command-line options for PEImg include the following:

- **%WINDIR% or /image=path to image file**—Location of the Windows directory for the base Windows PE image. ImageX must be used to mount an image to a local directory before this command can be executed.

- **/import=path to package**—Location of CAB files or directories containing packages for installation. Packages are installed using the /install option (see later in this list).

- ■ /**list**—Displays a list of imported packages.

- ■ /**install=package name**—Name of the package to be installed.

- ■ /**inf=path to inf file**—Location of drivers (inf files) to install.

- ■ /**quiet**—Hides the progress indicator.

Wpeinit

Wpeinit is command-line tool that processes the unattend.xml answer file, initiates Windows PE on each system boot, loads network settings, and installs plug-and-play devices. Wpeinit.exe is available at a Windows PE command prompt after a Windows PE image has been loaded. The only option available to Wpeinit is /unattend=*patch to unattend.xml answer file*. Wpeinit creates the wpeinit.log file in the C:\Windows\System32 directory for review.

Windows Recovery Environment (RE)

The Windows Recovery Environment (Windows RE) is an extension of Windows PE, previously discussed. Windows RE is designed for troubleshooting and in some cases automatically repairing failed Windows Vista installations. Windows RE can be launched manually (pressing F8 at system startup) or automatically when Windows has detected a problem with an installation or when a system fails to boot.

Windows RE can also recover a system from a pre-canned image file. Computer manufacturers commonly include this functionality on a specific hard drive partition or CD/DVD with new systems. Using the backup tool, end users and administrators can also create an image of the system. Alternatively, the image can be provided on a DVD, hard drive, partition, or network share.

When the Windows RE is invoked, several options become available to troubleshoot or rectify a problem. This includes the Startup Repair option, System Restores (uses restore points), Windows Backup Disaster Recovery (restore from an image), command prompt, and custom tools when applicable.

The Startup Repair option is typically invoked automatically when Windows detects a boot failure. Startup Repair automatically fixes most common problems with the following Windows Vista components; Registry, damaged system files, hard drives and partitions, file system, and drivers. More information on recovering from Windows Vista issues and backing up Windows Vista systems is available in Part V, "Managing Vista," of this book.

> **Tip**
>
> Several customizable sample scripts are included with the WAIK to support the Windows RE. These scripts can be found in the `C:\Program Files\ Windows AIK\Recovery` folder and includes `buildwinre.cmd` (creates a Windows RE image from a Windows PE image), `configdiskwinre.cmd` (configures the hard drive for Windows RE), `installwinre.cmd` (dumps a Windows RE image), `setautofailover.cmd` (sets automatic failover to Windows RE), and more.

Summary

Understanding and testing imaging tools is critical to successful creation and deployment of Windows Vista images. The tools provided for deploying Windows Vista provide administrators and IT personnel with the necessary components for supporting a complete image creation, deployment, and maintenance cycle. This chapter focused on providing guidance for using the wide array of imaging tools available, and it provided instructions for the use of Windows PE, Windows SIM, ImageX, and much more. Taking the time to learn how these tools work together is essential to creating reliable Windows Vista images.

CHAPTER 21

Deploying Windows Vista in an Automated Fashion

The Microsoft Business Desktop Deployment Kit (BDD) 2007

The Microsoft Business Desktop Deployment Kit (BDD) 2007 is an all in-one solution for deploying Windows Vista images. The BDD also integrates deployment of the Office 2007 suite into Windows Vista images as a core OS application because most companies have previous versions of Office running in their environments. The BDD also deploys other operating systems and includes Windows Deployment Services, which has taken the place of Remote Installation Services (RIS). Those familiar with Microsoft Management consoles (MMC) and Windows Systems Image Manager (Windows SIM) will be pleased to find that the Deployment Workbench—the primary component of the BDD— is very similar.

Microsoft has designed the Desktop Deployment Center at TechNet (www.microsoft.com/technet/desktopdeployment/ gettingstarted.mspx) around the Business Desktop Deployment (BDD) 2007 kit. Microsoft created both the TechNet Deployment Center and BDD 2007 to support businesses that need to migrate hundreds or thousands of systems to Windows Vista. Deployment of Windows Vista can be accomplished in different ways:

- Manually at the local system using Windows PE and a DVD

- In an automated fashion using Active Directory and PXE boot with a Windows Deployment Services boot image

- Using Systems Management Server (SMS) 2003 SP2+ and Microsoft Operations Manager (MOM) 2005

- Systems Center Configuration Manager 2007 (SCCM) and Systems Center Operations Manager 2007 (SCOM)

It is worth noting that Microsoft refers to these deployment scenarios as Lite-Touch Installations (LTI) and Zero-Touch Installations (ZTI), respectively, throughout the documentation written for BDD 2007 and the TechNet Deployment Center.

Note

Microsoft Systems Management Server (SMS) 2003 SP2+, System Center Configuration Manager 2007, Systems Center Operations Manager 2007, and Windows Server (2003 and 2008) are beyond the scope of this book. However, to illustrate certain mechanisms or processes, features included with those products may be covered. For more detailed information regarding any of these Microsoft Solutions, see the product's documentation.

Administrators can use the different components of the BDD 2007 to obtain an inventory of currently running hardware and software and test both for compatibility with Windows Vista before deployment. The BDD 2007 includes the necessary components for designing customized application packages, automating image and image deployment processes, cataloging drivers, deploying strong security out-of-the-box, migrating user settings and data, and validating deployments. In addition, the BDD also includes detailed technical documentation on setting up a lab environment for testing and troubleshooting.

For large scale deployments, the BDD is packed full of information, not only regarding the technologies and how to use them, but it also provides direction for anyone who is responsible for developing and supporting a migration to Windows Vista in an enterprise. From project managers to IT staff, the information for each person's role in the BDD is easy to follow and helps companies get a running start on their rollout of Windows Vista. Furthermore, developing and maintaining a sound imaging process reduces the total cost of ownership (TCO) an organization directly inherits when managing its system's life cycles and addressing upgrades to newer operating systems. To help companies get started with their Windows Vista deployments, Microsoft included the Plan, Build, and Deploy Guide, Feature Team guides specific to team roles, and job aids such as Microsoft Project templates and checklists.

After the BDD has been installed, all the documents, templates, scripts, MOM management packs, downloaded software, scripts, and samples can be found in the C:\Program Files\BDD 2007\ folder.

> **Note**
>
> BDD 2007 includes support for Microsoft Systems Management Server (SMS) 2003 SP2+ and its forthcoming replacement, System Center Configuration Manager 2007. BDD 2007 also supports Deployment Services on Windows Server 2003 and 2008. This allows organizations the flexibility of using existing architecture to deploy Windows Vista without having to also replace deployment and asset management software.

> **Note**
>
> BDD 2007 includes support for Microsoft Office 2007 by default, not Office 2003. Guidance around Office 2003 can be obtained from the Upgrading to Microsoft Office 2003 package available in the Office section of the Microsoft Download Center, www.microsoft.com/downloads (specifically, www.microsoft.com/downloads/details.aspx?FamilyID=d3c5977f-fb14-4cc4-b54e-321283e3c0f4&DisplayLang=en).

> **Tip**
>
> Large organizations that use Systems Management Server (SMS), Microsoft Operations Manager (MOM), or the newer System Center Configuration and/or Operations Manager along with the BDD, should take advantage of the BDD Management Packs to monitor the deployment of Windows Vista. More information on the BDD Management Pack can be found here: technet.microsoft.com/en-us/library/bb490132.aspx.

System Requirements for BDD 2007

The BDD 2007 kit can be installed on systems running Windows XP (Professional and Tablet PC only, SP2 recommended), Windows Vista (Business, Enterprise, and Ultimate only), or Windows Server 2003 (at least SP1 and with Active Directory if Windows Deployment Services and auto-mated deployment support is needed).

In addition, Microsoft Word (or .doc file reader) is needed to review the included documentation, Windows Script Host 5.6 is needed, and version 3.0

of the MMC is required to run the Deployment Workbench (3.0 is the default version of the MMC in Windows Vista and Windows Server 2003 R2). Last, the following tools should be downloaded and installed throughout the Components section of the Information Center in the Deployment Workbench after the BDD has been installed. Additional components can be downloaded and installed as necessary. Downloading and installing software in the Components section of the Information Center in the Deployment Workbench is covered in the next section.

- Windows Automated Installation Kit (Windows AIK), available in 32- and 64-bit versions
- Application Compatibility Toolkit (ACT)
- User State Migration tool, available in 32- and 64-bit versions
- MSXML version 6.0, available in 32- and 64-bit versions

Caution

During installation of the BDD 2007, the location of the Distribution Share software, operating systems, and so on are checked in to using the Deployment Workbench. The default location is X:\Distribution, where X represents the volume with the most available free space. Although this setting can be changed later, take into consideration that it can fill quite quickly given the amount and potential size of the items being checked in.

The Deployment Workbench

The Deployment Workbench, as mentioned previously, is the hub of the BDD 2007 that connects everything related to desktop deployment. The Desktop Workbench comprises four main areas: Information Center, Distribution Shares, Builds, and Deploy, as reflected in the task pane of the MMC shown in Figure 21.1.

The Deployment Workbench is the nucleus of the BDD. In the Deployment Workbench, administrators can find documented guidance and step-by-step instructions, project plan and other templates, a news feed from the Microsoft website, and a list of the relative software that can be downloaded and installed. The Deployment Workbench also provides a place to distribute the software necessary for supporting the deployed images, a collection of the system builds that have been created, and more.

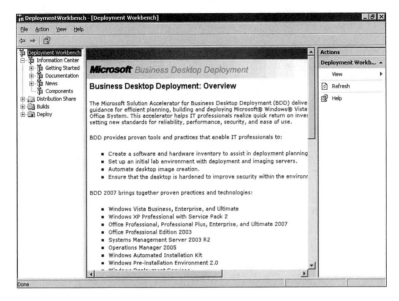

FIGURE 21.1
The Deployment Workbench.

Information Center

The Information Center of the Deployment Workbench houses the Getting Started page, links to documentation, a news feed regarding desktop deployment, and the Components section, which highlights the software that is required and others that are available to support a Windows imaging and deployment solution.

Documentation

The Documentation section of the Information Center contains a roadmap that links the major stages of desktop deployments and migrations to the appropriate documentation. The Documentation section, shown in Figure 21.2, helps Administrators visualize the process involved when deploying Windows Vista images with quick access to the right information and tools.

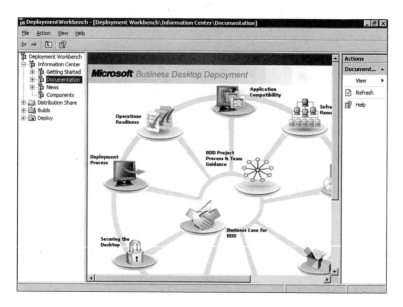

FIGURE 21.2
Documentation links in the Deployment Workbench.

News

The News section displays summaries and links to the most recent news and releases fed from Microsoft's website regarding desktop deployments. Administrators should glance at this page on occasion to review any new and/or pertinent information regarding desktop deployments.

Components

The Components section, as mentioned earlier, lists all the software needed to support imaging and deployment of Windows Vista. This is one of the first places to check after the BDD has been installed. The WAIK is one of the required components and should be downloaded first; it is approximately 1GB in size. After programs have been downloaded, they appear in the Downloaded list and are available for installation. The Unavailable for Download section displays items that are not available to the current installation of BDD, and the Installed section lists programs that are already installed.

To download and install a component, highlight the desired item, click the Download button, and wait for the program to be listed in the Downloaded section, as displayed in Figure 21.3. To install a component, highlight the desired item in the Downloaded section and click the Browse button to open the folder containing the executable needed for installation. After the program has been installed, it is detected by the BDD 2007, and the program is listed in the Installed field.

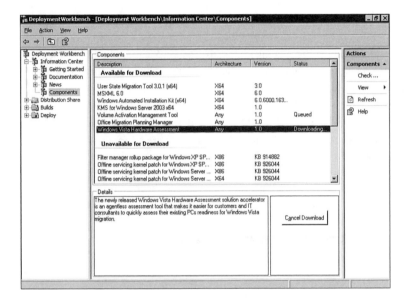

FIGURE 21.3
Downloading and installing components in the Deployment Workbench.

Working with Distribution Shares

Working with Distribution Shares in the Deployment Workbench application differs in several ways from the Distribution Share component in Windows System Image Manager, covered in Chapter 20, "Imaging Tools and Processes." Although both serve the same purpose, creating and configuring locations to house applications, drivers, and so on, the Deployment Workbench focuses on a more automated approach for larger installations and as such, includes additional support for SMS and Deployment Services for Windows Server.

Checking items into the Distribution Share is the first step to configuration. As mentioned earlier, the Distribution Share location is specified during the installation of BDD 2007. The items checked in are later used to create system builds. The Distribution Share can house these items:

- Operating systems and language packs
- Applications
- Security updates and other updates
- Drivers

To add any one of these items to the Distribution Share in the Deployment Workbench, right, simply expand the Distribution Share category in the task pane, right-click the category for the item you will add (for example, Applications) and select New. The wizard appears, walking you through the process, displaying the different options available for each category.

Windows Vista can be added to a Distribution Share by following the steps listed next. To demonstrate this process, the steps add a Windows image file to the Distribution Share. Alternatively, operating systems can also be added using the full set of operating system source files, such as from a DVD or a Deployment Services image, as shown in Figure 21.4.

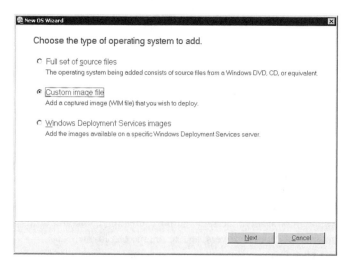

FIGURE 21.4

Adding Windows Vista using a WIM image file in the Distribution Share in the BDD 2007 Deployment Workbench.

> **Note**
>
> The Windows Deployment Services Images option shown in Figure 21.4 doesn't actually copy the files used for installation, but instead sets up a pointer to the Windows Deployment Services share. Windows Deployment Services is covered later in this chapter.

To add Windows Vista to a Distribution Share, follow these steps:

1. Launch the Deployment Workbench.

2. Expand the Distribution Share category, right-click Operating Systems, and select New.

3. Select Custom image file and click Next.

4. The Mandatory Components Missing warning might appear, indicating that components necessary to carry out the task are not installed. If this message appears, go to the Components section of the Deployment Workbench to download and/or install the missing items. If this warning does not appear, all necessary components are already installed.

5. Specify the location of the source Windows image file and click Next. (Files can also be moved to this location, instead of copied, by selecting the check box.)

6. Specify whether Windows Vista setup or sysprep files will be used.

7. Specify the name of the directory to be created (for example, ..\Vista64_Business).

8. The WIM image file will be copied to the Distribution Share (for example, D:\Distribution\Operating Systems\Vista64_ Business\install.wim).

9. After the file has been copied, it appears in the Operating Systems section of the Distribution Share. Right-clicking an operating system and selecting Properties displays the details of the WIM image file (for example, SMS 2003 compatibility, setup and sysprep file usage, image size, and so on).

> **Caution**
>
> When an operating system is removed from the Distribution Share in the Deployment Workbench, the files are also deleted from the system.

Applications, update packages, and drivers are added in the same manner. Simply right-click one of the options, select New, and follow the steps in the wizard. For more detailed information on checking items into the Distribution Share, see the Desktop Deployment product documentation or Desktop Deployment Center at Microsoft TechNet (www.microsoft.com/technet/desktopdeployment/gettingstarted.mspx).

Note

If Windows Deployment Services is already configured to distribute images, the BDD can check them in to the Distribution Share. The BDD doesn't copy any files but simply creates a pointer for the target system to obtain its image file from the Windows DS server, not BDD.

To accomplish this, copy the files `wdsclientapi.dll`, `wdscsl.dll`, and `wdsimage.dll` from the Windows Vista DVD's Sources folder to `C:\Program Files\BDD 2007\bin`. Next, check in an image and select Windows Deployment Services, associate a catalog file with its build, and follow the prompts.

Working with System Builds

Creating custom System Builds in the Deployment Workbench provides a way to compose various Windows Vista systems for different deployment scenarios. For example, organizations that will be deploying Windows Vista 64- and 32-bit editions would need two different builds created in the Deployment Workbench. The steps for creating a Build in the Deployment Workbench are outlined next:

1. Launch the Deployment Workbench.

2. Check in a Windows Image file (WIM) using the steps outlined in the previous section (required).

3. Expand the Distribution Share, right-click Builds, and select New.

4. Follow the prompts in the New Build Wizard, shown in Figure 21.5.

5. Provide a Build ID, Build Name, and Comments (all required).

   Note: The Build ID cannot be modified after the build has been created.

6. Select an Operating System Image (WIM) to use.

7. Enter a product key to use with the build or choose to provide one later.

8. Enter a Full Name, Organization, and Home Page (all required).

9. Enter an administrator password to use with the build or choose to provide one later.

10. Click the Create button and the build is created and listed in the Deployment Workbench.

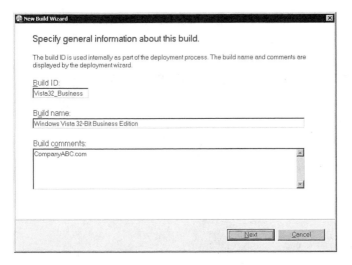

FIGURE 21.5
The New Build Wizard in the Deployment Workbench.

Right-clicking and selecting Properties on a build in the Deployment Workbench will display the <Build Name> Properties window, where settings such as the product key can be changed, the unattend.xml file (if used) can be edited, drivers can be assigned for installation, and the task sequence for the build can be defined.

The task sequence for a build breaks down the work into groups of tasks that the image installation must go through before a deployment is considered finished. The Task Sequence tab of a build's properties, shown in Figure 21.6, outlines the tasks that will be completed and allows administrators to change the order of tasks, add and remove individual or groups of tasks, and change options for existing groups and tasks. For example, applications can be added, automatic reboots configured, and so on.

To access the task sequence of a system build, follow these steps:

1. Check a Windows Image file (WIM) into the Distribution Share as outlined in the "Working with Distribution Shares" section of this chapter.

2. Create a custom build as outlined in the previous section, "Working with System Builds."

3. Right-click on the system build you created and select Properties.

4. Select the Task Sequence tab at the top.

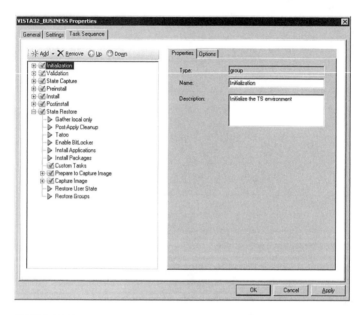

FIGURE 21.6
Task Sequence of a system build.

A couple other convenient features available with the Task Sequencer are the capability to filter tasks by the type of operating system and run WMI queries. Operating systems can be identified by configuring the condition (equals, doesn't equal, greater than, and so on) for Operating System Version by clicking Add in the Options tab. To add a WMI query, click Add in the Options tab of the Task Sequencer, select WMI query, and configure the options accordingly.

Working with Deployment Points and Databases

Deployment points in the Deployment Workbench define the location(s) where systems will retrieve the Windows Vista operating system, applications, drivers, update packages, and anything else checked into the Distribution Share(s) from during initial deployment. Distribution points are used in larger networks and when configured properly localize the traffic generated by installing these rather large items over the network.

The Deployment Workbench includes four different types of deployment points: Lab or Single-Server Deployment (Lab), Separate Deployment Share (Network), Removable Media, and SMS 2003 Operating System Deployment (OSD).

The Lab or Single-Server Deployment option configures a deployment point using the Distribution Share created on the local system. The Separate Deployment Share (Network) option allows for creation of Distribution Shares and points on remote computers. The Removable Media option creates a DVD ISO image for deployment. Last, the SMS 2003 OSD option will create a directory containing all the files needed to create an SMS 2003 compatible Operating System Deployment Program. Deploying Windows Vista using SMS 2003 is covered in the next section.

Caution

When deploying multiple platforms of Windows Vista (32 or 64 bit), a deployment point for each platform (x86 and x64) must always be created in the Deployment Workbench.

Creating Deployment Points

The following steps illustrate the procedures to create a deployment point using a single server (local Distribution Share):

1. Right-click the Deployment Points category in the Deployment Workbench and click New.

2. Select the appropriate deployment method (Lab or single-server deployment (Lab), and click Next.

3. Enter a name for the deployment point and click Next.

4. If users should be provided with a list of applications to install after deployment (default), leave the Allow Users to Select Additional Applications on Upgrade box checked; this is not applicable when creating a media deployment point. Click Next.

5. If an image of the computer should be created after deployment (default), leave the Ask if an Image Should Be Captured box checked and click Next.

6. If the user should assign a password to the local Administrator account, check the Ask the User to Set the Password option and click Next.

7. If the user should enter a product key, check the Ask User for a Product Key option and click Next.

8. For the Lab or Single-Server Deployment option, the server name displayed will be the local system (for example, DEPLOYMENTSRV1), the share name and path will reflect the Distribution folder created when BDD 2007 was installed. For example, the share name would be Distribution$ ($ hides the share from network browsing); the local path would be D:\Distribution and accessible on the network from \\DEPLOYSRVR1\Distribution$. Click Next.

9. On the Specify User Data Defaults page, select the appropriate option for retaining user state data (files, settings, and so on). User migration and upgrades to Windows Vista are covered later in this chapter.

    - Allow the user to configure user state options (default)— Prompts user for the location.

    - Automatically determine the location (based on available disk space).

    - Determine whether data and settings should be saved locally (default is yes) by checking or unchecking the Allow Data and Settings to Be Stored Locally When Possible check box.

    - Specify a location. Enter the appropriate data into the Location box or browse to a location (for example, \\FILESERVER1\ UserData$\).

    - Do not save data and settings. User data and settings will not be retained.

10. Click the Create button to create the Deployment point.

11. The deployment point is created and appears under the Deploy heading in the Deployment Points category.

Configuring Deployment Points

Deployment points, after they are created, can be further configured by right-clicking the deployment point and selecting Properties, as shown in Figure 21.7. On the General tab, the name of the deployment point, network path, local path, and supported platforms can all be set. The Rules tab of a deployment point's Properties window, displayed in Figure 21.7, displays the contents of the `CustomSettings.ini` file, which resides in the Control folder of the deployment point.

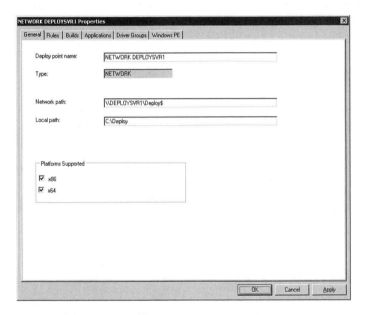

FIGURE 21.7
Deployment point Properties.

The Builds, Applications, and Driver Groups tabs appear after they have been configured in the Deployment Workbench, as shown in Figure 21.7. For example, creating a system build adds the Builds tab to the Deployment Point Properties window (not available for Lab/single-server deployment points). The tabs exist to provide a place to associate a particular build, application(s), or driver(s) with a deployment point. After these items are chosen and associated with the deployment point, they are copied to the deployment point.

The Windows PE tab provides a place to include similar items like drivers, fonts, and other customizations for use in the Windows PE environment. The Windows PE tab also provides for the selection of the type of image(s) that should be created.

Updating Deployment Points

Once a deployment point has been created, it must be updated to finalize its creation on the file system. When a deployment point is updated, it creates the folder structure and copies files, creates Windows PE images, and other items that have been marked for inclusion in the deployment point.

To update a deployment point, right-click the deployment point and click Update. As any files change or get added in the future to Distribution Shares that are connected to builds and further assigned to deployment points, right-click the deployment point and select Update (files only).

Deployment Methods and Requirements

Microsoft defines two deployment scenarios that administrators can use when rolling out Windows Vista: Lite Touch and Zero Touch. These terms are used throughout the Microsoft Deployment website and their documentation. A Lite Touch deployment means that the Administrator IT person could be installing Windows Vista using Windows PE, a Windows Deployment Services server, and the Windows Deployment Wizard. The term *Lite Touch* could also be spun to include local installations using Windows PE bootable media and a DVD; however, Microsoft's intention is to educate the IT world that a Lite-Touch deployment simply means that the process isn't entirely automated.

A Zero-Touch installation equates to a hands-off approach using Windows Deployment Services or SMS 2003. The Lite Touch and Zero Touch deployment methods are outlined in the next sections of this chapter by technology. Realistically, the larger the install base, the more preparation, testing, and the need to use automated tools and apply a Zero-Touch deployment become necessary.

Deploying Windows Vista with Windows Deployment Services (Windows DS) for Windows Server 2003 (SP1 or SP2)

Windows Deployment Services is included with the BDD 2007 software and runs on Windows servers to deploy Windows operating systems, including

Windows XP, Vista, and Windows Server 2008. Full coverage of Windows Deployment Services is outside the scope of this book; however, the basics that need to be understood for installing and using Windows Deployment Services on a Windows 2003 server are outlined next.

Caution

Windows Deployment Services is included with Windows Server 2003 SP2. Windows Server 2003 SP2 will automatically upgrade Remote Installation Services (RIS) when SP2 is installed. If RIS is not installed when SP2 is loaded, Windows Deployment Services must be added through the Add/Remove Windows Components option found in the Add/Remove Programs category.

The Windows DS server is responsible for starting the target computers from the Windows PE environment and installing the Windows Vista operating system from the Windows DS server. Target computers should not be managed by SMS. SMS-managed computers should use the SMS OSD package instead. This is discussed in an upcoming section of this chapter.

Installing Windows Deployment Services

Windows Deployment Services (shown in Figure 21.8) is included in Windows Server 2008, Windows Server 2003 SP2, and the WAIK. Windows Deployment Services has several requirements that must be met before its installation and use. These requirements are typical of any business environment that relies on Active Directory for directory services.

Requirements for installing Windows DS include the following:

- Windows DS cannot be run in a Workgroup; it must be a member of an Active Directory Domain or installed on a Domain Controller.

- An active DHCP scope and server (supports PXE boot used by target systems that will be upgraded to Windows Vista through Windows DS).

- An active DNS server.

- Windows Server 2003 SP1 with RIS installed or Windows Server 2003 SP2, with or without RIS.

To install Windows DS, follow these steps:

1. Download the WAIK or Windows Server 2003 SP2.

2. If installing Windows DS from the WAIK, use one of the following:

   ■ windows-deployment-services-update-x86.exe (32-bit Intel)

   ■ services-update-amd64.exe (64-bit AMD)

3. If installing Windows SP2:

   ■ If RIS is currently installed, Windows DS is automatically
     installed and current RIS settings are retained.

   ■ If RIS is not installed, use the Add/Remove Windows
     Components option in Add/Remove Programs to add Windows
     Deployment Services.

4. Restart the server.

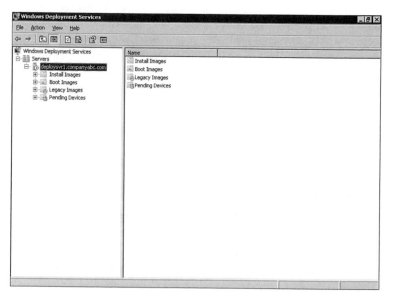

FIGURE 21.8
The Windows Deployment Services console running on a Windows 2003 R2 SP2
Server.

Preparing the Windows Deployment Services Server

Before Windows DS can be used to deploy Windows Vista, several preparation
tasks must be completed. This includes selecting the appropriate operation

mode, adding images to the server, and prestaging the target systems that will receive the install packages.

Windows DS can run in three operational modes: legacy, mixed, and native. For the purpose of using WIM image files and deploying Windows Vista, native mode should be used. Native mode provides no support for legacy RIS tasks. If necessary, mixed mode can be used if an environment is migrating from an older deployment process to the newer one. Legacy mode is essentially Remote Installation Services running under Windows DS and provides no support for WIM image files or Windows PE (which means no Vista deployment support). More information regarding the different modes of Windows DS can be found in the Windows Deployment Services Update Step-by-Step Guide and Windows DS help, both included with an installation of Windows DS.

WDSUTIL is a command-prompt utility for configuring components of Windows DS from the command line. For example, WDSUTIL can be used to add images using the /ADD option, auto-approve new computers using /APPROVE, and manage settings of Windows DS. For a list of all available commands and the correct syntax for use, type **WDSUTIL /AllHelp** at a command prompt.

Adding Windows Vista Images to Windows DS

Depending on the mode (native, mixed, or legacy) that Windows DS is running in, different types of images can be added for distribution. Windows Vista supports only Windows images (WIM); therefore, mixed or native mode must be used. To deploy Windows Vista using Windows DS, a boot image and install image must be checked in.

To check in a Boot Image, in the Windows Deployment Services console, right-click the Boot Images folder under the Windows DS server that will deploy the image and select Add Image. To check in an Install Image, simply repeat this process using the Install Images folder (and the right WIM file). Images can also be added using WDSUTIL /add-image /<../path to file> /imagetype:boot (or) install. After an image is checked-in, right-click the image and select Properties to display information about the image and change options.

> **Note**
>
> For Windows 2003 servers running Windows Deployment Services, the boot image file (boot.wim) that should be used for Windows Vista is located on the Windows Vista DVD in the D:\Sources\ folder. For servers running Windows 2008, the boot.wim file included with Windows 2008 should be used because it contains newer functionality.

Image Deployment Process

As discussed earlier, the use of BDD 2007 and Windows Deployment Services delivers a Lite-Touch installation. When deploying Windows Vista in the Lite-Touch scenario, the Windows Deployment Wizard is launched on the target computer when the target system is started one of two ways:

- Booting from the LiteTouchPE_x86.iso locally on a DVD

- Booting the computer with PXE enabled in the BIOS (required), which uses the LiteTouchPE_x86.wim file on the Deployment Services server

Both the LiteTouchPE_x86.iso and LiteTouchPE_x86.wim files can be found in the Boot folder underneath the Distribution Share.

> **Note**
>
> In order to have computers restart and locate the Windows DS server, PXE (Preboot Execution Environment) must be supported and enabled in the system BIOS. PXE allows a computer to restart and essentially broadcast its existence to a system, like Windows DS that is configured to provide a program that the computer will use to start, like Windows PE used for Windows Vista (LiteTouchPE_x86.wim). This is accomplished using Trivial File Transfer Protocol (TFTP), installed with Windows Deployment Services.

> **Tip**
>
> The Control folder in the Distribution Share of a system running BDD 2007 contains the CustomSettings.ini, Builds.xml, Deploy.xml, DriverGroups.xml, OperatingSystems.xml, and TS.xml files, which can be customized to automatically answer questions normally presented by the Deployment Wizard.

When the computer restarts, the Welcome to Windows Deployment Wizard appears and walks the user through the Windows Vista installation process. In most cases, administrators will want some or all of these questions to be answered for the user in an effort to avoid inaccurate input—for example, specifying the computer name or capturing an image. In some cases, this may be the opposite desire of an organization. Either way, Microsoft again shows that its solution is flexible enough to accommodate most scenarios. This can be accomplished through the use of an Unattend.xml file that is stored on the Windows Deployment Services server in the X:\Deploy\WDSClientUnattend folder.

Deployment Services for Windows Server 2008 (Beta)

Windows Server 2008 improves on the previous versions of Windows Deployment and Remote Installation Services. For example, Windows 2008 running under the Deployment Services and Transport roles, delivers the capability of multicasting to target computers for transmission of data and images. Windows 2008 also includes an upgraded Trivial File Transfer Protocol (TFTP) server, supports network boots for 64-bit computers, and detailed reporting to monitor deployment status. For more information on Windows DS for Windows 2008 Server, see the Windows 2008 Server documentation.

Caution

For Windows 2008 servers running Windows Deployment Services, the boot image file (boot.wim) that should be used is located on the Windows 2008 DVD in the D:\Sources\ folder. This file is required over the Windows Vista boot.wim file because it contains added functionality to support the new features of Windows DS on Windows 2008 servers.

Deploying Windows Vista with Microsoft Systems Management Server (SMS) 2003

Organizations that currently rely on Systems Management Server (SMS) 2003 to maintain their operating system and application deployment can also make use of the Business Desktop Deployment Kit and Windows Deployment Services functionality to roll out Windows Vista. The forthcoming release of SMS 2007 also supports this configuration, with some changes. SMS 2007 in this scenario is briefly discussed at the end of this section.

> **Caution**
>
> Deploying Windows Vista with BDD 2007 and SMS 2003 requires that SMS 2003 servers be at the SP2 level or later and that the SMS 2003 Operating System Deployment (OSD) Feature Pack Update is installed. The OSD feature pack includes support for Windows Vista, 64-bit hardware, modified Windows PE images, and the creation of Windows image files (WIM) using the OSD feature pack image capture utility. The OSD feature pack can be downloaded here: http://technet.microsoft.com/en-us/sms/bb676770.aspx.

Deploying Windows Vista using SMS 2003 involves a few steps. First, an OS deployment point must be created in the BDD, an Image Capture CD must be made, a reference image must be prepared and then captured with the SMS 2003 ODS Feature Pack's Image Capture Wizard, and a Windows PE boot image must be created.

Configuring the SMS 2003 OSD Deployment Point

To create a SMS 2003 deployment point, follow the steps outlined earlier in this chapter to create a new deployment point in the BDD, and select SMS 2003 OSD as shown in Figure 21.9. Follow the prompts to complete the process. When finished, a directory will be created containing all the necessary files for implementing an SMS 2003 deployment solution.

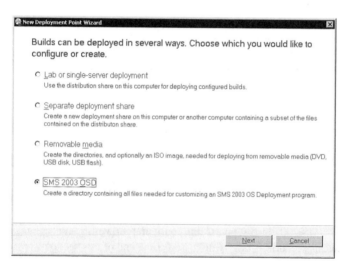

FIGURE 21.9

SMS 2003 OSD option in the New Deployment Point Wizard of BDD.

Preparing and Capturing a Windows Vista Image for Use with SMS 2003

To support deployment with SMS 2003, a Windows Vista image must be captured in a specific manner. In addition, a customized version of Windows PE for use with ODS and an Image Capture CD created by SMS are needed to capture the image. The following steps outline the processes necessary to prepare and capture a Windows Vista image for use with SMS 2003.

To customize Windows PE for use with the SMS 2003 OSD, follow these steps:

1. Add the operating system(s) to the BDD Deployment Workbench.

2. Make any necessary changes under the deployment point's Windows PE tab (for Windows Vista and SMS 2003, use the 2005 version).

3. Right-click the deployment point and select Update, and an ISO file will be created.

4. Create a CD with the bootable ISO image on it or place the Windows PE image on a Windows DS server.

Prepare a Windows Vista image for capture by following these steps:

1. Boot the reference computer using Windows PE media (DVD or a Windows DS image using a PXE boot).

2. When the Welcome to Windows Deployment Wizard starts on the reference computer, select Run the Deployment Wizard and click Next.

3. Enter the user credentials that have rights to the Distribution Share and click Next.

4. Enter a computer name and join the computer to a Workgroup. Click Next.

5. Select Do Not Restore User Data and Settings and click Next.

6. Select the appropriate version of Windows Vista to install and click Next.

7. Select No Product Key Is Needed and click Next.

8. Select a Locale and Keyboard layout and click Next.

9. Set the time zone and click Next.

10. Install any applications on the Select One or More Applications to Install page and click Next.

11. Enter the local Administrator password and click Next.

12. Select Prepare to Capture the Machine and click Next.

13. Select Do Not Enable BitLocker and click Next.

14. Click Begin and Windows Vista is installed.

Creating an Image Capture CD

The SMS 2003 Image Capture CD boots a computer into the Windows PE environment so an image of the hard drive can be captured and stored in a network location.

To create and use an Image Capture CD, follow these steps:

1. Open the SMS 2003 console.

2. Right-click Image Packages and select Create Operating System Image Capture CD under All Tasks.

3. Burn the ISO image to a CD.

4. Start the reference computer using the CD.

To capture a Windows Vista image, follow these steps:

1. After the computer starts, the SMS 2003 Image Capture Wizard appears. Click Next.

2. Enter a name for the WIM file.

3. Enter the path of the network server that will hold the image, enter a valid account name and password with rights to the share, and click Next.

4. Enter the local administrator's password and any sysprep parameters, and click Next.

5. The SMS 2003 Image Capture Wizard will run Sysprep and shut down the computer.

6. Start the computer using the Image Capture CD and an image is automatically captured.

Image Deployment Process

After an image has been captured and placed on the network, Windows Vista can be deployed to the systems. The procedures are identical to that of deploying Windows Vista using Windows DS alone. The difference lies in the Windows PE boot image and Windows Vista install image being used.

The repackaging of these components delivers support for SMS features such as reporting and SMS agent compatibility.

Start the computer (in PXE boot mode) and it contacts the Windows Deployment Services server to complete the installation. If the system cannot contact a Windows DS server, or the organization doesn't use one, the computer can be started locally using a Windows PE boot CD or other media created in the preceding steps.

System Center Configuration Manager 2007 (Beta)

Windows Vista image deployment to new or existing computers with or without being managed by System Center Configuration Manager is supported. Window Vista installations are very efficient, using a single image for all hardware that is further customized through sequential tasks and a driver catalog. The BDD 2007 program currently includes this functionality. System Center Configuration Manager 2007 includes a new account, the Capture Operating System Image Account to use for capturing images, a process discussed earlier in this section with SMS 2003. For more information on System Center Configuration Manager 2007, visit the System Center Configuration Manager 2007 website at http://technet.microsoft.com/en-us/configmgr/default.aspx.

Migrating Systems to Windows Vista

The BDD 2007 kit includes support for migrating user data, settings, and applications to Windows Vista. The same infrastructures are supported for Lite Touch and Zero Touch installations; however, some new tools and processes are introduced to support upgrades to Windows Vista versus a clean installation and minimize the impact to the end user, in turn reducing administrative overhead.

Larger organizations will no doubt have a tougher task of creating a migration strategy, and in some cases an accompanying rollback plan, to Windows Vista than smaller companies will. Nonetheless, Microsoft took both scenarios into account and with some well-orchestrated planning, testing, documentation, and support, a Windows Vista migration should be fairly smooth for any size installation. Part I, "Windows Vista Health Check," of this book covers the system requirements and considerations to note when upgrading a computer to Windows Vista.

To break a migration to Windows Vista into a simple process, administrators start by assessing the hardware using the Windows Vista Hardware

Assessment tool and address any incompatibility issues. Next, administrators assess applications that are to be retained or installed and address any incompatibility issues using the Application Compatibility toolkit. Last, an imaging process needs to be developed and deployed that incorporates the findings of these tools and the necessary configuration to migrate existing data, settings, and applications for end users.

Assessing Windows Vista Readiness with the Windows Vista Hardware Assessment Tool

The Windows Vista Hardware Assessment Tool is designed for organizations that migrate from Windows XP to Windows Vista; it is not designed for home use. The Windows Vista Hardware Assessment tool is an agentless scanner that uses Windows Management Instrumentation (WMI) to create a comprehensive inventory of systems on a network. This inventory highlights systems that are incapable of running Windows Vista and/or Office 2007. The report also includes guidance from Microsoft on where to resolve any identified issues. Any hardware incompatibility issues can also be cross-referenced using the Microsoft Windows Vista Hardware Compatibility List, located at http://winqual.microsoft.com/hcl/.

> **Note**
>
> The Windows Vista Hardware Assessment tool can only inventory and report on a maximum of 25,000 systems. All data is encrypted during transit between the inventoried systems and the system running the assessment tool.

> **Caution**
>
> The Vista Hardware Assessment tool can be installed only on a computer running Windows XP SP2, Windows Vista (Business, Ultimate, or Enterprise), and Windows 2003 Server R2. 64-bit versions are not supported.

The Windows Vista Hardware Assessment Tool categorizes its results into systems that are ready for Windows Vista and systems that require hardware upgrades first (except CPU). The computers that are capable of running Windows Vista are further defined by their capability of running Windows

Aero. The reporting function of the Windows Vista Hardware Assessment tool generates a summary for management (Word) and a detailed report for the IT staff (Excel).

The Windows Vista Hardware Assessment tool, shown in Figure 21.10, can find systems using Active Directory, computers in workgroups (nonroutable broadcast, repeat on each subnet), and other domains. The Windows Vista Hardware Assessment tool can also import an inventory of systems to target.

> **Caution**
>
> The Windows Vista Hardware Assessment tool requires Microsoft Word and Microsoft Excel 2007. The Vista Hardware Assessment tool also requires a database and offers to download and install SQL 2005 Express.

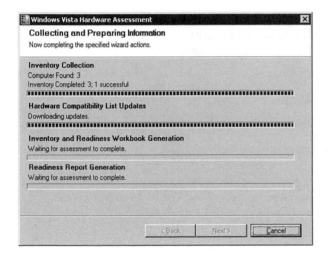

FIGURE 21.10
The Windows Vista Hardware Assessment tool.

Working with the Application Compatibility Toolkit 5.0

The Application Compatibility Toolkit (ACT) is discussed in detail in Chapter 6, "Using User Account Control to Establish System Security," because that is one primary focus of the ACT—compatibility with Windows Vista's new User Account Control security feature.

The ACT, like the Windows Vista Hardware Assessment tool, can be deployed to systems on a network to collect and analyze data derived from application compatibility checks to recommend solutions for incompatibility issues discovered with Windows Vista and currently installed applications. The ACT 5 Deployment Guide, available on the Microsoft download site, contains a wealth of detailed information specific to deploying DCPs on a network.

ACT 5.0 requirements include the following:

- **Operating System**—Windows Vista, Windows XP SP2, Windows 2003 Server SP1, or Windows 2000 SP4

- **Database**—SQL Server 2005, SQL Server 2005 Express, or SQL Server 2000

- **Recommended Hardware**—2.8Ghz processor with 2GB of RAM

- **Microsoft.NET Framework 1.1** (Windows Vista)

- **Microsoft.NET Framework 2.050727** (Windows XP SP2, Windows Server 2003 SP1, Windows 2000 SP4)

To obtain a comprehensive report of any application compatibility issues that may arise from a migration to Windows Vista, administrators deploy executable Data Collection Packages (DCPs) to computers using the Application Compatibility Manager (ACM) central console. The DCP sends the results of its findings to a log file in a shared location during the evaluator checks pass. The ACT Log Processing service formats the log files and uploads them to a SQL database. The ACM provides the results and potential resolutions to the administrator for analysis. The DCP can perform the following compatibility checks on a target computer:

- **Internet Explorer Compatibility Evaluator**—Checks for any issues with websites or web applications.

- **User Account Control Compatibility**—Checks application compatibility when running without elevated privileges.

- **Update Compatibility**—Reports on the Automatic Update status.

- **Windows Vista Compatibility**—Checks for other application compatibility issues running under Windows Vista.

Caution

The Data Collection Package's evaluators will not run on a 64-bit platform.

Migrating User Accounts with the User State Migration Tool 3.0

The User State Migration tool (USMT) was designed to automatically transfer accounts, data, applications, settings, and more, and then reload them onto a computer after Windows Vista has been installed. The USMT is designed for automated deployments of Windows Vista, whereas the File Settings and Transfer Wizard program is designed for home use. Both tools contain similar technologies; however, only USMT is appropriate for nonhome use. USMT uses two primary programs to complete its job: the ScanState program, which gathers information, and LoadState, which restores the items when Windows Vista is installed. ScanState and LoadState both use XML files (`config.xml`, `miguser.xml`, `migapp.xml`, and `migsys.xml`) to record and reference the items collected. LoadState and ScanState and the XML files can be found in the `C:\Program Files\ USMT301\` folder after USMT has been installed.

Before migrating user data, settings, and the like, careful planning should take place. Planning for a migration to Windows Vista should include discussions around what should be migrated, where those items should be stored, and how to resolve any potential issues.

Note

USMT 3.0 no longer requires a separate scan for all accounts on the target computer (domain and workgroup). All accounts and settings can now be captured during a single scan. For detailed information on accomplishing this, see the "Migrate Data on Computers with Multiple Users" section in the USMT product documentation.

Assessing a System and Collecting Items Using ScanState

ScanState is the executable program that works with several XML files (outlined next) to collect specific items for transfer by LoadState after a migration to Windows Vista has been performed. ScanState is a command-line program that can be run using a script or deployed using management software, such as SMS 2003. ScanState uses the following XML files and syntax to perform a scan. For more information on ScanState, sample XML files, and proper usage, see the USMT help documentation or Microsoft TechNet center.

Sample ScanState syntax is as follows:

```
scanstate /targetxp /c /i:migapp.xml /i:miguser.xml
➥ \\FILESVR1\USMT\store /encrypt /key:091199 /progress:prog.log
➥/l:scanlog.log
```

The preceding ScanState example logs errors, optimizes the scan by specifying that the target computer is running Windows XP (/targetxp), collects application settings, collects user files and folders, and uploads and encrypts them using Secure Hash Algorithm (SHA-1) in a share labeled store on a file server. The preceding syntax also displays a progress indicator and logs the results to a file.

XML files used by ScanState:

- **MigSys.xml**—Specifies operating system and browser settings to migrate from a Windows XP system.

- **MigApp.xml**—Specifies application settings to migrate.

- **MigUser.xml**—Specifies folders, files, and settings that should be migrated for end users.

- **Config.xml**—Created using scanstate/genconfig. Specifies which items should be skipped during the migration by setting the migrate = "no" option.

- **Custom.xml**—Can be used to define specific items to migrate, not included with other XML files.

Caution

Use the /c option with ScanState and LoadState; otherwise, the export or import will fail when it encounters errors. The /c option allows ScanState and LoadState to log the errors and continue running.

Note

Any files or folders that are collected from a drive (for example, separate local partition) and are placed on a new system where that same drive will not exist, and will be placed in the same location on the C: drive (system drive).

> **Caution**
>
> USMT will not migrate installed applications by design, only application settings. For the application settings to be properly restored, the same version (not newer) of the application must exist on the new computer before LoadState imports the settings.

Items That Can Be Migrated with the User State Migration Tool 3.0

USMT supports migrating of user folders, such as Documents, the Start menu, and Favorites. USMT migrates operating system components, depending on the source computer's operating system. This can include items such as accessibility options, wallpaper, fonts, screensavers, and folder options, among other things. USMT also supports migration of file types to maintain any present application specific file types or file type associations outside the Windows defaults. USMT can also migrate access control lists (ACLs), although this has specific requirements to work successfully. For a complete list of items that can be migrated along with a list of applications and versions that support migration of settings, see the Getting Started with USMT 3.0 section of Microsoft TechNet.

Items That Won't Be Migrated with the User State Migration Tool 3.0

Although USMT supports migrating of many items, some items cannot be migrated. For example, although application settings can be migrated, this is restricted to a compatibility list and as mentioned earlier; the applications themselves will not be migrated. Some of the items that won't be migrated using USMT include mapped network drives, locally installed printers, DLLs, permissions on shared folders, taskbar settings from Windows XP, and more. For a complete list of items that won't be migrated, see the Getting Started with USMT 3.0 section of Microsoft TechNet.

Restoring Collected Items Using LoadState

LoadState is the executable program that works with the same XML files (see previous section) that were used to collect items with the ScanState scan. In fact, LoadState should include all files used by ScanState when restoring items on the new system. LoadState is a command-line program that should be run after Windows Vista has been installed. For more information on ScanState, sample XML files, and proper usage, see the USMT help documentation or Microsoft TechNet center.

Sample LoadState syntax is as follows:

```
LoadState /c /i:migapp.xml /i:miguser.xml
 \\FILESVR1\USMT\store /decrypt /key:091199 /progress:prog.log
➥/l:scanlog.log
```

The preceding LoadState example logs errors, restores application settings, restores user files and folders, and decrypts and downloads them from a share labeled store on a file server. The preceding syntax also displays a progress indicator and logs the results to a file.

Caution

Use the /c option with ScanState and LoadState; otherwise, the export or import will fail when it encounters errors. The /c option allows ScanState and LoadState to log the errors and continue running.

Caution

After LoadState has finished importing settings, files, folders, and other items, the system should either be restarted or run through the logoff routine.

Working with the Volume Activation Management Tool

Using the Volume Activation Management tool, Windows Vista makes use of product keys, which reduces the risk of piracy, increases system security, and eases license-management for administrators. These new product keys are encrypted on the Key Management Service (KMS) host—never on the local system. They have a limited time to live and must renew their activation with Microsoft's KMS periodically. Administrators can monitor the status of Windows Vista license activation through the use of a Microsoft Operations Manager (MOM) management pack. When a system doesn't renew its license activation in the specified time frame, it resorts to running in Reduced Functionality Mode (RFM), limiting the functionality of Windows Vista. Organizations can find that laptops stolen with this configuration and that have local drive encryption enabled, such as with BitLocker, have helped deter any would-be data thieves. For more information on Volume Activation with Desktop Deployment, see the Volume Activation Guide in the Microsoft TechCenter at http://technet.microsoft.com/en-us/library/bb490204.aspx.

Working with the Office Migration Planning Manager

Microsoft Office is a core application for most organizations and is why Microsoft integrated it so closely with the BDD 2007 kit. Most organizations will likely deploy Microsoft Office with Windows Vista. The BDD 2007 and related tools includes support for either, including Microsoft Office 2007 inside the Windows Vista image or distributing it as an MSP (Microsoft Package) application. To help administrators accomplish this with ease, Microsoft released several tools for managing Office 2007 deployments, outlined next along with the process for packaging Microsoft Office 2007. More information around Office 2007 deployment in relation to BDD 2007 can be found on Microsoft TechNet site: http://technet.microsoft.com/en-us/library/bb490137.aspx.

Microsoft Office 2007 deployment tools include the following:

- **Office Customization tool**—Selects which Office 2007 applications to install, configures the settings for each of the Office 2007 applications, and creates a MSP file.

- **Office Migration Planning Manager**—Scans systems running Microsoft Office products for analysis to identify potential issues.

- **Office File Conversion tool**—Converts Microsoft Office 97 through 2003 documents to the Microsoft Open XML format (.docx).

- **Office Setup Controller**—Localized routine that manages the Office 2007 installation.

- **Office Local Installation Source**—Adds a compressed (full) copy of the Microsoft Office 2007 setup files to the local system for use during setup and future modification changes.

To configure and package Microsoft Office 2007 as an MSP file, follow these steps:

1. Create a distribution point in the BDD 2007 Deployment Workbench.

2. Copy the Office 2007 DVD to a network share.

3. Apply any service packs or updates to the deployment point.

4. Create the MSP using setup.exe /admin, modify settings (if desired), and save it to the MSP file to a network share. Some examples include the following:

   - Office 2007 installation path
   - Product key

- Specify which Office 2007 applications to include

- Outlook 2007 settings

5. Test the MSP file using the following:

```
Setup.exe /adminfile \\FILESVR1\Office2007\MSP\
office2007_Pro.msp.
```

6. Configure the MSP file to run silently by running `setup.exe /admin` and unchecking the boxes for the Completion Notice and Suppress Modal and setting the display level to None.

7. Test the MSP again.

8. Distribute the MSP as an application with BDD 2007, SMS 2003, or another application deployment program.

Note

BDD 2007 includes support for Microsoft Office 2007 by default, not Office 2003. Guidance around Office 2003 can be obtained from the Upgrading to Microsoft Office 2003 package available at the Microsoft Download Center, www.microsoft.com/downloads.

Summary

The Microsoft Business Desktop Deployment Kit (BDD) 2007 and the Desktop Deployment Center at http://technet.microsoft.com/en-us/desktopdeployment/default.aspx cover everything related to Windows Vista deployments. Understanding the different deployment methods and Requirements, assessing Windows Vista readiness with the Windows Vista Hardware Assessment Tool, and assuring applications will run under Windows Vista using the Application Compatibility Toolkit will prevent a lot of potential issues during the rollout process.

Administrators can seamlessly migrate systems to Windows Vista in addition to user accounts. Migrating user accounts with the User State Migration Tool simplifies the process and assures user's settings, data, and applications are migrated and available for use. This chapter provided guidance for the use of the various deployment tools to automate Windows Vista upgrades, with an emphasis on a more hands-off approach.

PART VII

Windows Vista in an Active Directory Environment

IN THIS PART

CHAPTER 22

Understanding Group Policy Basics to Manage Windows Vista Systems

What Are Group Policy Objects (GPOs)?

Group Policy describes the Microsoft implementation of a methodology of managing computers and users in a centralized fashion in an Active Directory environment. Group Policy Objects (GPOs) are the collections of various application and Registry settings that have been defined by an administrator to enforce a particular behavior on a user or computer object.

This concept was initially introduced back in the Windows NT 4.0 days when an administrator was able to use Policy Enforcement to force a workstation to conform to particular behaviors. This was usually limited to restricting a user's local rights to prevent the user from changing things like the UI or locally installed applications. It was initially a clunky way of doing things, but it set the stage for the introduction of Group Policy Objects in Windows 2000 with the advent of Active Directory (AD). In Windows 2000, administrators were given the capability to easily configure hundreds of common settings in the area of application publishing to security settings to Internet Explorer settings. This was done through a provided editor that utilized ADM files that contained definitions for the user and computer objects to interpret. The drawback to these ADM files was that the format was somewhat cryptic, and it made it difficult for administrators to create their own ADM files for modifying custom applications or to modify applications for which Microsoft had not yet released ADM files. This situation didn't change much with the release of Windows 2003, but it did introduce a new tool called the Group Policy Management console. This tool allowed administrators to more easily view and manage Group Policy Objects as well as to back them up and even port them from one domain to another. It was not until the release of Vista that Microsoft fundamentally changed the way that GPO settings were stored. With Vista came the new ADMX format of files. ADMX is based on XML, or Extensible Markup Language. XML is an open standard for data formatting that is meant to put data into a more human-friendly format. The result is that ADMX files are much easier to create than their ADM predecessors.

Why Administrators Should Use Group Policy Objects

GPOs are designed as a way to globally modify user and computer settings through a controllable and manageable central interface. This is to say, GPOs are meant to replace manual intervention on systems and custom logon scripts.

Take, for example, the implementation of a new web proxy server in an environment. In the old days, you would either go from system to system, logging in as the user and setting the Proxy configuration in Internet Explorer, or if you were adept at scripting, you might write a custom script that would modify the Proxy settings and set it to run in the user's logon script. This situation is very easily handled by GPO. In fact, it can be done with much greater granularity with a GPO. Imagine that in our example there are multiple Proxy servers, and the goal is for users to use the Proxy server that is closest to them. Although this could be accomplished manually, it wouldn't account for users who travel. If a user in the United States was configured to use the Proxy in the U.S., it would result in poor performance if the user were to visit an office in Japan that had a local Proxy server. If the user was well versed in scripting, he or she might be able to write a sub-routine that was "location aware" and modify the Proxy settings when the system was in another location, but that would really be reinventing the wheel. If the administrator used Group Policy, the administrator could create a GPO for each Proxy server and link the GPOs to the sites defined in AD. This would result in systems using the closest Proxy server no matter where they were. The term *linking* in this context refers to tying an Organizational Unit (OU) or a site to a particular OU so that only objects in that site or OU will attempt to use the GPO. This will be explained in further depth later in this chapter.

As you can see from the preceding example, GPOs should be used in situations where an administrator wants to push a setting or configuration to multiple systems and needs the flexibility to limit which systems or users receive the settings.

GPOs are also extremely useful for enforcing the rules of an environment. For example, if a company changed its policy to require computers to be locked after a period of inactivity, this setting could easily be configured via GPO. Although many companies may configure a setting like this when deploying a system, the advantage to doing it by GPO is that no one can "forget" to make the setting. As soon as a computer is joined to the domain, it will inherit the domain-level GPOs and automatically conform the system to your rules.

How to Configure GPOs

GPOs are created in a central manner and are stored on all domain controllers in a forest. GPOs can be accessed via Active Directory Users and Computers:

1. Click Start.
2. Click All Programs.
3. Select Administrative Tools.
4. Pick Active Directory Users and Computers.
5. Expand to an OU.
6. Right-click and choose Properties.
7. Select the Group Policy tab. If you have the GPMC loaded, it will prompt you to open it.

GPOs can also be accessed through the Group Policy Management console:

1. Click Start, Run, type **gpmc.msc**, and then press Enter. If Run is not available from the Start menu, it can be accessed by pressing the Windows and R keys at the same time.

The Group Policy Management Console is preinstalled on Vista.

Introducing the Group Policy Management Console (GPMC)

The release of the GPMC provided huge improvements in the creation and management of GPOs. Prior to the GPMC, an administrator had to open each GPO in the editor and examine all possible settings to determine which settings had been changed from the defaults. In the GPMC, you can view all the unique settings of a given GPO via the following steps:

1. Launch the GPMC (Start, Run, `gpmc.msc`).

2. Expand the Forest container.

3. Expand the Domains container.

4. Expand the Domain Object that holds the GPO you are interested in.

5. Expand Group Policy Objects.

6. Left-click the GPO in question.

7. Click the Settings tab in the right pane.

GPMC will show Generating Report and then the containers that are modified. Click Show All to see all settings contained in the GPO, as shown in Figure 22.1.

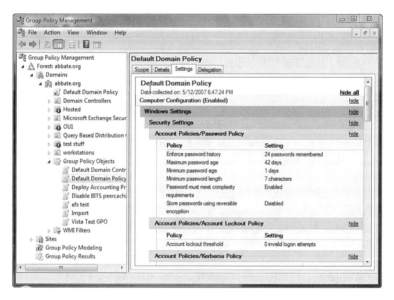

FIGURE 22.1
GPO settings in the Group Policy Management console.

The GPMC is also useful for backing up and restoring GPOs. This should be used whenever a GPO is to be modified. This way, if the GPO causes unwanted issues, an administrator can restore the previous version of the GPO to return systems to their previous configuration. To back up a GPO with the GPMC, follow these steps:

1. Launch the GPMC (Start, Run, **gpmc.msc**).

2. Expand the Forest container.

3. Expand the Domains container.

4. Expand the Domain Object that holds the GPO you are interested in.

5. Expand Group Policy Objects.

6. Right-click the GPO in question and choose Backup.

7. Browse to the location where you want to store the backed up GPO and enter a description. Click Back Up.

8. When the backup is completed, click OK.

To restore a GPO with the GPMC, follow these steps:

1. Launch the GPMC (Start, Run, **gpmc.msc**).

2. Expand the Forest container.

3. Expand the Domains container.

4. Expand the Domain Object that holds the GPO you are interested in.

5. Expand Group Policy Objects.

6. Right-click the GPO in question and choose Restore from Backup.

7. When the wizard launches, click Next.

8. Browse to the location of the backup and click Next.

9. Choose the backup you want to restore (Note: this is where entering a description was helpful) and click Next.

10. Click Finish and the restore will begin.

11. When the restore has completed successfully, click OK.

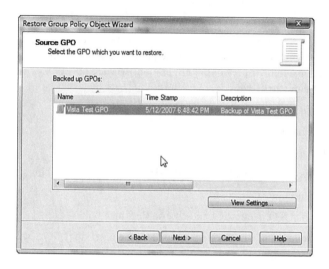

FIGURE 22.2
Selecting the backup to restore.

Creating a New GPO in the GPMC

The GPMC is the logical place to create new GPOs. Generally speaking, the creation of a GPO should coincide with the desire to automate some specific configuration across multiple machines. This means that the person creating the GPO should already know what settings to assign to a given GPO.

To create a new GPO, follow these steps:

1. Launch the GPMC (Start, Run, **gpmc.msc**).

2. Expand the Forest container.

3. Expand the Domain container.

4. Expand the Domain Object that holds the GPO you are interested in.

5. Right-click Group Policy Objects and choose New.

6. Enter the name of the GPO you want to create (use a descriptive name) and click OK.

This will create a new, empty GPO in the management console.

To modify settings within the GPO, you need to use the GPO Editor. Right-clicking the new GPO and choosing Edit will launch the GPO Editor.

Using the GPO Editor

The GPO Editor that is triggered via the GPMC is the same editor originally used since Windows 2000. Not much has changed. The editor expresses the GPO in two sections, Computer and User settings, as shown in Figure 22.3. Although an administrator can set both user and computer settings in the same GPO, it is considered a best practice to limit a given GPO to either User or Computer settings. This is related to the way GPOs are linked and is discussed in more detail later in this chapter.

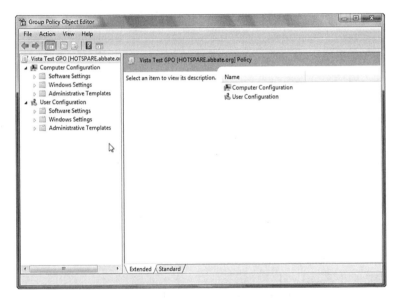

FIGURE 22.3
The Group Policy Object Editor.

The editor allows the administrator to browse through the available configuration settings in a graphic format. For example, you could expand User Configuration, Administrative Templates, System, and Windows HotStart to have the ability to turn off Windows HotStart. Because this is a new GPO setting, you might wonder what Windows HotStart is. By selecting Turn Off Windows HotStart, you will see that an explanation of the setting has appeared to the left of the setting. To save space in the window, you could click the Standard tab at the bottom of the screen. To get the explanation back, click the tab labeled Extended.

What's New in GPOs?

With the release of Vista, Microsoft has added several new areas that can be managed via GPOs and has expanded several existing areas. These areas include the following:

- Antivirus
- Background Intelligent Transfer Service (BITS)
- Client Help
- Deployed Printer Connections
- Device Installation
- Disk Failure Diagnostic
- DVD Video Burning
- Enterprise Quality of Service (QoS)
- Hybrid Hard Disk
- Internet Explorer 7
- Networking: Quarantine
- Networking: Wired Wireless
- Power Management
- Removable Storage
- Security Protection
- Shell Application Management
- Shell First Experience, Logon, and Privileges
- Shell Sharing, Sync, and Roaming
- Shell Visuals
- Tablet PC
- Terminal Services
- Troubleshooting and Diagnostics
- User Account Protection
- Windows Error Reporting

With these new areas available, administrators are able to continue to manage functions and settings on the client workstations to reduce overall administrative efforts.

ADMX Format

Vista brings with it a new format for storing GPO-related information. Whereas in the past, GPOs were built with .adm files that stored the individual configuration objects, Vista uses a new .admx format. The new format allows for language-neutral as well as language-specific resources. This allows the various Group Policy tools to adjust their operating system to the administrator's configured language. The net result of this is that an administrator in the United States can create a GPO and a colleague in France can review the same GPO, but the colleague will see it in French.

The new .admx files are based on XML. This makes it easier for developers to integrate GPO information into their applications.

An observant administrator will notice that the available settings are different when viewed from Vista in contrast to viewing via a Windows 2003 domain controller. This is because Vista is able to see the settings available from the new .admx entries.

Network Location Awareness (NLA)

Network Location Awareness (NLA) is a mechanism that improves the ability of Group Policy to deal with changes in network conditions. NLA allows Group Policy to utilize event notification and resource detection within Vista to become aware of events, such as leaving standby or hibernation or the establishment of a VPN connection. Even an event such as connecting to a wireless network can be detected to trigger processing of GPOs.

Some of the major benefits of NLA include the following:

- **More efficient startup times**—NLA will allow Group Policy to determine the state of the network connection, resulting in a reduction of timeouts while waiting for a connection to a domain controller. NLA will accurately determine whether a network card is enabled or disabled and will use this information to determine whether to try to contact a domain controller to download a GPO.

- **NLA allows a client to apply a policy when a connection to a domain controller is restored**—This is especially helpful in the case of wireless network connections that require user interaction or in the case of Virtual Private Network connections where connection to a domain controller doesn't occur until after the login event has been processed. This same behavior will occur when a client exits hibernation or standby. The benefit here is that if the refresh period of the GPO has expired, the client will immediately attempt to download and process GPOs as soon as connectivity to a domain controller is restored. This will improve overall system protection because there is no delay in processing new settings.

■ **NLA also removes the dependency on ICMP (Ping) for determining available bandwidth when determining whether to process GPOs**—This allows administrators to further protect clients by blocking ICMP in the local firewall without breaking GPO functionality.

How to Manage GPOs

As you can likely tell from this chapter, GPOs are an extremely useful and powerful way to manage workstations in a domain. Like most utilities that are powerful, it is easy to cause problems for yourself if you don't manage the process well. Knowing how GPOs work, where the components are stored, and what you need to do to utilize them are the key pieces to making GPOs work for you.

Where Are GPOs Stored?

For GPOs to be useful across the forest, the GPOs must be available to users and computers. The way in which Active Directory deals with this is to store the GPOs in the SYSVOL volume that is replicated across all domain controllers in the forest. Specifically, the files are stored in `\\Domain\sysvol\domain\policies`.

They will appear in directories with names like {162EBD2C-FAAC-4852-8B28-FB2D4ABA1CD5}, as shown in Figure 22.4. Contained in these directories is a configuration file (`gpt.ini`) as well as subfolders for the Machine and User settings.

New to Vista and Windows 2008 is an additional directory under Policies called PolicyDefinitions. This directory contains the new ADMX files that are used by Vista and Windows 2008. This directory is referenced by new GPOs that contain Vista or Windows 2008 settings.

If the directory for a newly created GPO does not appear on remote DCs within 15–30 minutes, you should suspect that there may be issues with the File Replication Service on one domain controller or more.

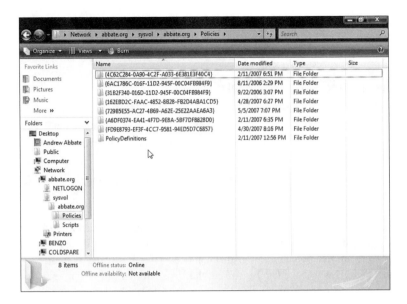

FIGURE 22.4
Group Policy Object directories.

How GPOs Replicate Throughout the Domain

Because GPOs are stored in the SYSVOL volume of domain controllers, they are automatically replicated to all domain controllers in the domain through the File Replication Service (FRS). It is very important that FRS be operating successfully to ensure that all users in the domain are getting consistent settings via GPOs. If a domain controller is having FRS issues, it may not become aware of changes to a given GPO. This will result in some systems not getting the correct version of the GPO. This can be a major issue if GPOs are being used to configure important security settings or to apply patches or hotfixes to workstations.

A very simple way to verify the health of FRS is to place a text file in the SYSVOL directory of a domain controller and check the SYSVOL directory of other domain controllers to ensure that the new file appears within the expected replication intervals.

Keeping an eye on the FRS section of the event viewer of domain controllers is another easy way to become aware of FRS problems. If you want to keep a more watchful eye for potential FRS problems, Microsoft has a tool called

SONAR, available at www.microsoft.com/downloads/details.aspx?FamilyID= 158cb0fb-fe09-477c-8148-25ae02cf15d8&DisplayLang=en that will allow you to keep closer tabs on FRS performance.

How to Link a GPO to an OU

After a GPO has been created, it needs to be linked to an OU or site to actually do anything. Interesting to note is that the User and Computer containers in Active Directory are not actually OUs and thus can't be used as a link point for a GPO.

The concept of linking a GPO is that the GPO is effectively being assigned to objects contained in or under the OU to which it is linked. This is traditionally the largest point of confusion to administrators. As mentioned previously in this chapter, GPOs are separated out into two sections: Computer and User settings. When a GPO with both Computer and User settings is linked to an OU, there are two potential things that can occur. If a user object is in or below the OU where the GPO is linked, the User settings will be applied (assuming the user has permissions to apply the GPO). Similarly, if a computer object is in or under the OU where the GPO is linked, it will attempt to apply the Computer settings (if the computer has permission to apply the GPO).

The common mistake made by administrators is assuming that both User and Computer settings will get applied if *either* the user or computer object is in or under the linked OU. This is an incorrect assumption.

In some situations, it may be very desirable to apply both Computer and User settings when a user logs on to a specific computer. A classic example of this is when a user is logging on to a Terminal Server. It may be useful to apply User settings when the user is on the Terminal Server that wouldn't be desired when the user logs in to their normal workstation. This is where the concept of *loopback processing* comes into play. Loopback processing is a Computer GPO setting that will effectively apply User settings based on the computer object being in a linked OU when the user object isn't. The two options are to append the User settings to existing inherited user GPOs or to replace the existing GPOs.

To link an existing GPO to an OU, perform the following steps:

1. Launch the GPMC (Start, Run, `gpmc.msc`).

2. Expand the Forest container.

3. Expand the Domains container.

4. Browse to the OU to which you plan to link the GPO.

5. Right-click the OU and choose Link and Existing GPO.

6. Choose the GPO you want and click OK.

The domain and OU view in GPMC is an excellent way to quickly tell what GPOs are being applied to what containers, as shown in Figure 22.5.

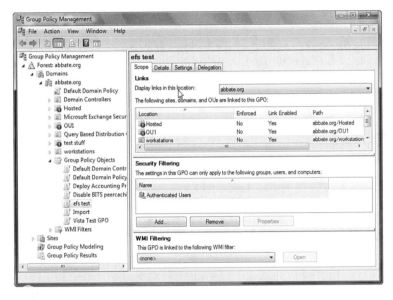

FIGURE 22.5
Viewing OUs to which GPOs are linked.

How to Control Who Can Modify a GPO

After a GPO has been created, an administrator can control who is allowed to edit an existing GPO. This can be helpful in environments where the creation of GPOs is a centralized and controlled event but where a local OU Admin might be empowered to make modifications to existing GPOs. To alter the rights on a GPO to allow for editing, perform the following steps:

1. Launch the GPMC (Start, Run, **gpmc.msc**).

2. Expand the Forest container.

3. Expand the Domains container.

4. Browse to the Group Policy container.

5. Highlight the GPO you want to alter permissions on.

6. In the right pane, click the Delegation tab.

7. Click Add and type the name of the user or group to which you want to delegate rights.

8. Click Check Names and then click OK.

9. In the Permissions drop-down list, choose Edit and click OK.

Now the person or group that was delegated is able to edit the existing GPO but is not able to alter the permissions on it.

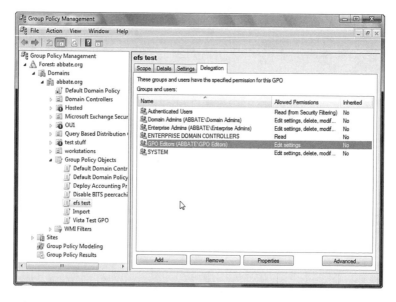

FIGURE 22.6
Viewing security delegations.

How to Limit Who Can Apply a GPO

Typically, the role of GPO administrator is limited to a particular subset of administrators in Active Directory. This minimizes the potential for an administrator to make an unauthorized change that could potentially impact all users in the domain.

A best practice is to separate out the two key roles of Group Policy: creation and application. One group should have the capability to create GPOs but should not have the rights to link them to any containers. Another group should have the capability to link but not create. This creates a situation where no one person has the capability to place new GPOs into production. To delegate these rights, perform the following steps on a domain controller:

1. Click Start.

2. Click All Programs.

3. Click Administrative Tools.

4. Click Active Directory Users and Computers.

5. Click View and then click Advanced Features.

6. Right-click the domain object and select Delegate Control; then click Next.

7. Click Add and type in the name of the group to which you are delegating the capability to link GPOs.

8. Click OK twice and you should see the group you added. Click Next.

9. Check the box for Manage Group Policy Links and click Next.

10. Click Finish.

To control who can create GPOs, follow these steps:

1. Click Start, Run, and type **gpmc.msc**.

2. Expand Forest.

3. Expand Domains.

4. Expand the domain you are managing.

5. Highlight Group Policy Objects.

6. Select the Delegation tab in the right pane.

This shows the groups and users that are currently able to create GPOs in the domain.

To delegate a new group to be able to link GPOs, perform the following additional steps:

1. Click Add.

2. Type the name of the group you want to add and click Check Names.

3. Click OK.

How to Filter a GPO

In many cases, an administrator might want to apply a GPO to most users or computers but exclude specific groups. Although this can be done by controlling where the GPO is applied in the OU structure, sometimes this would require too much granularity in the OU structure. In these cases, you can use GPO filtering to prevent specific groups of objects (users or computers) from applying the GPO. This is called *GPO filtering*.

Imagine, for example, that you create a GPO that will enable a screensaver with a password after 60 seconds of inactivity. Although this might be great for security, it can really bug an executive who is trying to do a PowerPoint presentation that requires a lot of talking. In this situation, it might be worthwhile to filter the presenter from the GPO. To accomplish this task, perform the following steps from a domain controller:

1. Click Start, Run, and type `gpmc.msc`.
2. Expand Forest.
3. Expand Domains.
4. Expand the domain you are managing.
5. Highlight Group Policy Objects.
6. Right-click the GPO in question and click Scope.
7. Add the group you want to filter and change the permissions to Apply GPO—Deny.

Blocking Inheritance

In most OU structures, there is a container for protected objects that in many cases should not have GPOs applied to them. This might include administrator accounts, validated computer systems, or even service accounts. The safest way to protect these accounts from accidental changes via GPO is to place them in an OU that is blocking inheritance. This is to say that even though a GPO might be applied to a container that is above the protected container in the OU hierarchy, the GPO will still be blocked.

To set blocking on an OU, from a domain controller follow these steps:

1. Click Start.
2. Click All Programs.
3. Click Administrative Tools.
4. Chose Active Directory Users and Computers.

5. Click View and then click Advanced Features.

6. Right-click the OU you want to set inheritance blocking on and select Properties.

7. Click the Group Policy tab.

8. Check the box for Block Policy Inheritance and click OK.

Important to note is that if a GPO exists at a higher level in the hierarchy, the blocked inheritance is set to Enforce. This setting will trump the inheritance block and will be applied anyway.

Troubleshooting GPOs

Although GPOs generally work very well in Active Directory environments, occasionally administrators will encounter issues when working with GPOs. If this should occur, there are several client and server side tools that can be used to determine the issue that is preventing a given GPO from applying properly.

Using the Resultant Set of Policies Tool

Resultant Set of Policies (RSoP) is part of the GPMC that provides a GUI interface that enables you to test a policy implementation prior to rolling it out in production and also enables you to view what policies a user or computer is actually receiving. The RSoP allows an administrator to pick a computer and user object and determine which GPOs would get applied. This allows an administrator to model the results without needing access to the user or the user's computer.

Group Policy Modeling Using RSoP

RSoP Planning mode enables you to simulate the deployment of a specified Group Policy, check the results, change, and then test the deployment again. This is very helpful in a lab environment where you can create and test a new set of policies. After RSoP shows that the GPO is correct, you can then use the backup functionality to back up the GPO configuration and import it into production.

To run RSoP in simulation mode, right-click Group Policy Modeling in the forest that will be simulated, and choose Group Policy Modeling Wizard. The wizard allows for inputting the possibility of slow links, loopback configuration, and WMI filters as well as other configuration choices. Each modeling is presented in its own report as a subnode under the Group Policy Modeling mode.

Using RSoP Logging Mode to Discover Applied Policies

RSoP in Logging mode enables you to view what exact policies a user or computer might be receiving. It shows in a readable format what polices are enforced, where conflicts exist, and what different policies are being applied to the user/computer. It can be run either on the local computer or on a remote computer by choosing the proper options in the wizard. To run RSoP in Logging mode, right-click Group Policy Results in the GPMC, and then click the Group Policy Modeling Wizard selection and follow the wizard that appears.

Using GPResult

One of the most common questions in GPO troubleshooting is, "How do I know it even tried to apply my GPO?" This is a very easy thing to test, and it tends to provide a lot of interesting information. Vista workstations have a utility available called GPResult. To run this, open a command prompt, type **gpresult**, and press Enter.

The utility will determine what groups the user and the computer belong to, and it will show you what GPOs it found linked to the OU hierarchy. It will point out GPOs that were skipped because of security filtering, and it will show you which ones were applied. It will even go so far as to tell you what OU your user and computer objects are in. This can be very helpful in determine why a GPO was or was not applied.

Using GPUpdate

Another helpful tool for testing out GPOs is the GPUpdate utility. This will trigger a download and application of GPOs outside of the normal GPO processing schedule.

You can limit the tool to only request updates to user or computer GPOs by using:

```
Gpupdate /target:computer
```

or

```
Gpupdate /target:user
```

You can force the system to immediately apply changes by using

```
Gpupdate /force
```

And you can even use Gpupdate /sync to include a reboot of the system to process GPO settings that occur only on system startup.

Best Practices in Working with GPOs

GPOs can be very powerful when used correctly, and they can also be very dangerous when used incorrectly. Many tricks can be employed to improve overall management and application of GPOs, ranging from ways to make GPOs faster to process to ways to more easily roll back mistakes with GPOs.

Speeding Up GPO Processing

To speed up login and boot times for users, it is recommended that if the entire User Configuration or Computer Configuration section is not being used in a GPO, the unused section should be disabled for the GPO. This expedites the user logon time or the computer boot time because the disabled sections aren't parsed on boot or login.

To disable configuration settings using Active Directory Users and Computers, follow these steps:

1. Right-click a Group Policy.
2. Click Properties.
3. Go to the General tab.
4. Click one of the boxes, either Disable Computer Configuration Settings or Disable User Configuration Settings, whichever section is not being utilized.

To disable configuration settings using the GPMC, follow these steps:

1. Click the Group Policy in GPMC.
2. Click the Details tab.
3. Click the drop-down box at the bottom of the Details tab.
4. Choose Computer Configuration Settings Disabled or User Configuration Settings Disabled, depending on which portion needs to be disabled.

Reusing Basic GPOs

If a Group Policy will be applied to many locations, you should create the policy once, assign the permissions, and then link the policy to the other locations rather than creating the policy multiple times. Linking the policies achieves the following objectives:

- **Creates fewer group policies in SYSVOL**—This allows for quicker domain controller promotion and less replication traffic.

- **A single point of change for the GPO**—If the GPO is changed, the change is applied to all the locations where the GPO is linked.

- **A single point of change for permissions**—When permissions are configured or changed in one location on a linked GPO, the permissions are applied universally to each place where the GPO is linked.

Understanding Inheritance

Group Policy objects are applied in a specific order. Computers and users whose accounts are lower in the Directory tree can inherit policies applied at different levels within the Active Directory tree. Group Policy is applied in the following order throughout the AD tree:

- Local Security Policy is applied first.

- Site GPOs are applied next.

- Domain GPOs are applied next.

- OU GPOs are applied next.

- Nested OU GPOs and on down are applied next until the OU at which the computer or user is a member is reached.

If a setting in a GPO is set to Not Configured in a policy higher up, the existing setting remains. However, if there are conflicts in configuration, the last GPO to be applied prevails. For example, if a conflict exists in a Site GPO and in an OU GPO, the settings configured in the OU GPO will "win."

If multiple GPOs are applied to a specific AD Object, such as a site or OU, they are applied in reverse of the order they are listed. The last GPO is applied first, and therefore if conflicts exist, settings in higher GPOs override those in lower ones. For example, if a Contacts OU has the following three Group Policies applied to it, and they appear in this order (as shown in Figure 22.7) the policies will be applied from the bottom up:

- Contacts Default Group Policy

- Contacts Software Policy

- Contacts Temporary Policy

The Contacts Temporary Policy will be applied first. The Contacts Software Policy will apply next, and finally the Contacts Default Group Policy will be applied. Any settings in the Contacts Default Group Policy will override the settings configured in the two policies below, and the settings in the Contacts Software Policy will override any settings in the Contacts Temporary Policy.

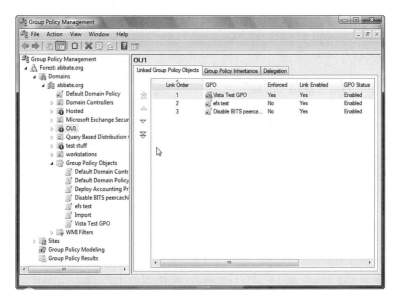

FIGURE 22.7
Group Policy objects are applied in order.

Where to Link GPOs

Administrators will quickly find that it can be very confusing to determine what GPOs are applied to a given user or computer and which aren't. One way to reduce this confusion is to try to eliminate questions of security filtering and policy inheritance overwrite whenever possible. This is to say that in many cases, it's best to push the application of a GPO as far down the hierarchy as is possible. This may result in the same GPO being linked to multiple locations.

Utilizing WMI Filtering

Linking WMI Filters enables you to apply group policies and establish their scopes based on attributes of target computers. You can do this by using the WMI filters to query the WMI settings of the target computers for true/false and apply group policies based on the true/false WMI queries. A "false" on the target computer results in the GPO not being applied. Conversely, a "true" results in the application of the GPO.

Because WMI filters are separate from GPOs, they must be linked to GPOs in the GPO Scope tab to function properly. Only one WMI filter can be applied to each GPO. Additionally, WMI filters will work only on Windows XP and later workstations, not Windows 2000 or before, or non-Microsoft operating systems.

Rolling Back Bad Ideas

Most administrators will experience a bad idea GPO at least once in their career. Sometimes settings that seem innocuous will cause problems, or perhaps an administrator will try to save time and link a GPO that hasn't been fully tested. In these cases it's necessary to quickly revert to an older version of a GPO. Unfortunately, there isn't a native method for rolling back a GPO; however, a few simple administrative tasks can allow for a quick restore to a known good GPO.

The key to being able to quickly revert from a bad GPO is to ensure that GPOs are always backed up and that they are always given a descriptive name.

Let's take as an example a GPO that we'll call Disable BITS Peercaching. It has a simple setting that disables BITS Peercaching. We've followed our first rule and given the GPO a descriptive name. We'll back up this GPO with the following steps:

1. From within GPMC, right-click the GPO and select Back Up.

2. Click Browse and choose the location where you will store your GPOs.

3. Enter a description that explains the last set of changes and the date that it was saved; click Back Up.

4. When the backup is completed, click OK.

Now imagine that an administrator has modified this GPO to include some settings that are incorrect or that are causing problems. It is very possible that the contents of the original GPO have been forgotten. You can revert to the old version of the GPO by doing the following:

1. Select the GPO you want to revert, right-click, and choose Restore from Backup.

2. The Restore Group Policy Object Wizard will launch. Click Next.

3. Click Browse and navigate to the location where the GPOs are saved. Click Next.

4. In this screen, you will see all GPOs that have been backed up with a description and a time stamp. Select the version of the GPO you want to restore and click Next.

> **Note**
>
> You can use the View Settings button when highlighting a backed up GPO to review the settings of that GPO in an XML format. This can be helpful if you just want to see what the old version of the GPO was and not actually restore it.

    5. Review the summary information and click Finish.

    6. When the GPO has successfully restored, click OK.

Because the GPO is restored on the Domain Controller that currently has focus within the Group Policy Management console, it may take a short while for the restored GPO to replicate to all domain controllers in the domain.

Summary

As we've seen, Vista has brought with it many changes to the available GPO settings as well as to the way in which they are stored and managed. We've seen the necessity of carefully managing and maintaining GPOs and have discussed ways to troubleshoot GPOs should any problems occur.

Always remember to carefully delegate who can create GPOs and who can link them. This will make it much less likely that you ever deploy a GPO that can cause problems for your users. Always try to do a peer review of a GPO before it's linked, and always first link it to a test OU to make sure it has no unintended effects.

Keep these things in mind, and GPOs will help you more easily maintain your Vista community.

CHAPTER 23

Expanding on the Use of Group Policies to Better Manage Windows Vista Systems

Available Group Policy Objects (GPOs)

Perhaps the most daunting task when working with GPOs is determining what GPOs should be used and which ones are best left alone. Generally speaking, GPOs should be created only when there is a specific need that can be addressed by a GPO. This is to say, the GPO should be driven by a company decision rather than being implemented because it looks useful.

Some companies fall into the trap of flipping through every possible GPO setting and deciding yes or no on each setting. This is a bad idea and will generally cause more issues than it will fix. The better approach is to ask yourself, "What have I always wished I could set for a common group of computers?" and then see if you can automate that setting with a GPO.

Existing GPOs That Work with Vista

Generally speaking, most GPOs that worked with Windows XP will continue to work with Microsoft Vista. This is because Microsoft wrote Vista to be backward compatible whenever possible. Even with this in mind, it is still a good idea to thoroughly test existing GPOs when first deploying Vista into the environment to make sure the systems are still being conformed to your existing standards. This is especially critical with GPOs that are in place to enforce security settings or to point to update servers for patches or definition files.

New Vista-Specific GPOs

For administrators wanting to familiarize themselves with all the new GPOs available for Vista, Microsoft has posted a spreadsheet detailing the new settings at the following location:

http://go.microsoft.com/fwlink/?linkid=54020

This spreadsheet includes

- Filename containing the GPO
- Scope (user versus machine)
- Policy path (where to find it)
- Policy setting name
- Version of OS supported by the GPO
- Explanation of the GPO
- Reboot requirements (if any)
- Logoff requirements (if any)
- Schema or Domain requirements

With this information, administrators can more easily plan for future GPOs to implement to conform new Vista systems to their corporate standards.

Further Understanding GPOs

Chapter 22, "Understanding Group Policy Basics to Manage Windows Vista Systems," touched on many of the rules and requirements around GPOs and their use in a domain environment. This chapter builds on the information presented there to give administrators a greater understanding of their uses and limitations.

Understanding the Order in Which Group Policies Are Applied

As mentioned previously, GPOs are applied in a specific order. Computers and users whose accounts are lower in the Directory tree can inherit Policies applied at different levels within the Active Directory tree. Group Policy is applied in the following order throughout the AD tree:

- Local Security Policy is applied first.
- Site GPOs are applied next.

- Domain GPOs are applied next.

- Organizational Unit (OU) GPOs are applied next.

- Nested OU GPOs and on down are applied next, until the OU at which the computer or user is a member is reached.

If a setting in a GPO is set to Not Configured in a policy higher up, the existing setting remains. However, if conflicts exist in configuration, the last GPO to be applied prevails. For example, if a conflict exists in a Site GPO and in an OU GPO, the settings configured in the OU GPO will "win."

If multiple GPOs are applied to a specific AD object, such as a site or OU, they are applied in reverse of the order they are listed. The last GPO is applied first, and therefore if conflicts exist, settings in higher GPOs override those in lower ones. For example, if a Contacts OU has the following three Group Policies applied to it and they appear in this order the policies will be applied from the bottom up:

- Contacts Default Group Policy

- Contacts Software Policy

- Contacts Temporary Policy

The Contacts Temporary Policy will be applied first. The Contacts Software Policy will apply next, and finally the Contacts Default Group Policy will be applied. Any settings in the Contacts Default Group Policy will override the settings configured in the two policies below, and the settings in the Contacts Software Policy will override any settings in the Contacts Temporary Policy.

Modifying Group Policy Inheritance

The Block Inheritance, Enforcement, and Link Enabled features allow control over the default inheritance rules.

GPOs can be configured to use the Enforcement feature. This setting does not allow the parent organizational unit to be overridden by the settings of the child OU if conflicts exist. Additionally, it nullifies the effects of Block Policy Inheritance if that functionality is applied on sub-GPOs.

OUs can be set to Block Policy Inheritance. This feature prevents the AD object that has the GPO applied to it from inheriting GPOs from its parent organizational unit, site, or domain (unless the parent GPO had Enforcement enabled as described previously).

To block Policy Inheritance on an OU, perform the following steps:

1. Launch the Group Policy Management console (GPMC) (Start, Run, **gpmc.msc**).

2. Expand the Forest container.

3. Expand the Domains container.

4. Browse to the OU to which you plan to Block Inheritance.

5. Right-click the OU and choose Block Inheritance.

The OU will now display a blue circle with a white exclamation mark to indicate that Policy Inheritance is blocked from this point down in the hierarchy (see Figure 23.1). This is to say, GPOs set above this point will not affect objects below the point of blocking. This behavior can be overwritten by setting a GPO to Enforced.

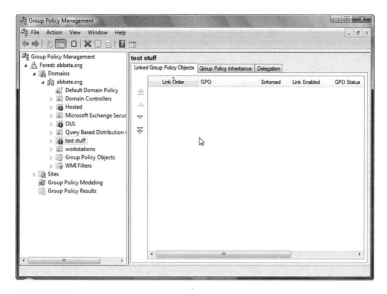

FIGURE 23.1
The OUs that are blocking inheritance display a blue circle with a white exclamation mark.

Finally, the option exists that allows for the disabling of a GPO, also known as the GPO's Link Enabled status. By right-clicking the Group Policy in the Group Policy Management console and unchecking Link Enabled, you can disable the policy and render it unused until the time it is reenabled.

Configuring Group Policy Loopback

Loopback allows Group Policy to be applied to the user logging in based on the location of the computer object, not the location of the user object in AD. Loopback applies a Group Policy based on the computer the user is using, not the user logging in to the computer. An example of a good use of the loopback option concerns Terminal Services. If you need to apply specific permissions to everyone who logs in to a particular Terminal Server, regardless of the user Group Policies, loopback in replace mode will accomplish this objective by ignoring all user GPOs. Loopback also provides a merge mode that merges the GPOs that apply to the user and computer but gives precedence to the computer GPOs, overriding any conflicting user GPOs.

The GPO setting for Group Policy Loopback processing is located under `Computer Configuration / Administrative Templates / System / Group Policy / User Group Policy loopback processing mode`.

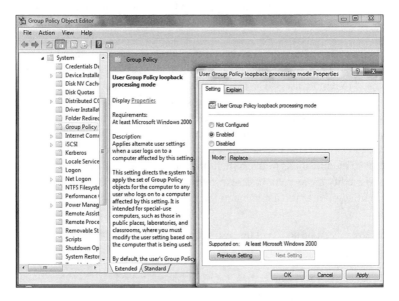

FIGURE 23.2
Selecting Group Policy Loopback mode.

Leveraging Local Policy

Local Policies can be used to enforce many of the same settings that GPOs can enforce. The advantage of the Local Policy is that it is enforced regardless of whether the computer can contact a domain controller. This means that settings can be placed into the initially deployed image and will be in effect from the moment the computer is powered on.

One very useful way to use Local Policy is to essentially reverse the paradigm of GPOs when dealing with security-related settings. For example, suppose that you want to configure Vista workstations so that their users can't run the Registry Editor. In this example, we assume that we'd like the local help desk staff to be able to run the Registry editor. The two ways to do this are the following:

- **Option 1**—Block the capability to run Registry Editor via GPO. Link the GPO to the container holding typical users. Place help desk personnel in another container in Active Directory. Do not link the Registry Editor blocking GPO to those users.

- **Option 2**—Block the capability to run Registry Editor in Local Policy on the deployed Vista image. Create a GPO that enables running the Registry Editor. Link it to a container that holds help desk personnel.

Although at first glance the two options might seem equivalent, they are in fact somewhat different in their scopes. Imagine that Vista systems are being deployed to remote users. The system is built and shipped out to the end user. The user receives the computer and powers it on for the first time. If the user is on the network at this first boot, the GPO will be received and applied properly. If the system is not on the network, the domain GPOs cannot take effect. In Option 1, the remote user would be able to run the Registry Editor and make modifications to the system. In Option 2, the user would not be able to modify the system. In cases where the computer needs to be protected or modified prior to its first logon to the domain, Local Policy is a better option.

Local Policy can be accessed by performing the following steps:

1. Click Start.
2. Click All Programs.
3. Click Administrative Tools.
4. Click Local Security Policy (see Figure 23.3).

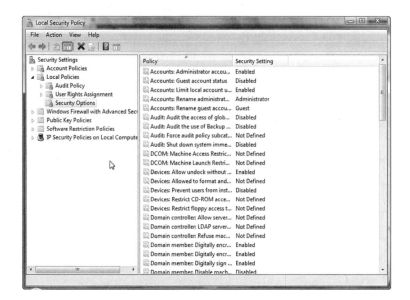

FIGURE 23.3
Viewing Local Security Policy.

Examples of Useful GPOs in Vista

Administrators who are relatively new to GPOs and Vista are likely wondering what GPOs other administrators are commonly configuring in their environments. This section will cover some of the more commonly used GPO settings and will walk you through the process of configuring them.

Example 1—Deployed Printers

One very common use of GPOs is to assign printers to users based on either group membership or the site they log in to. This allows an administrator to ensure that users have access to a local printer that is not only conveniently located, but is enabled for their use. This prevents calls to the help desk for printer assignments and allows users to easily roam from office to office without interruption to their productivity.

How to Configure Deployed Printers

To properly deploy printers via Group Policy, you should perform a few prerequisites. First, printers should be shared from a print server. This is done with the following steps:

1. From a print server, click Start, Settings, Printers and Faxes.

2. Click Add Printer.

3. When the wizard launches, click Next.

4. If you are going to host a networked printer (this is the most common scenario) choose Local Printer Attached to This Computer and click Next.

5. Choose Create a New Port and change the drop-down to read Standard TCP/IP Port. Click Next.

6. When the Printer Port Wizard launches, click Next.

7. Type the IP address of the networked printer (for example, 192.168.10.12). This will populate the Port name field for you. Click Next.

8. When the printer is contacted, click Next.

9. The Printer Port Wizard will display a summary of the port created. Click Finish.

10. In the left pane, choose the manufacturer of the printer. In the right pane, choose the model of printer. Click Next.

11. Type the name of the printer and click Next.

12. Choose Share Name and type the name you want to use for sharing this printer. This is the name that users will see. Click Next.

13. In the Location field, type a description of where the printer is located. This will help in cases where users want to "self-serve" a different printer. Type any necessary comments. Click Next.

14. Choose Yes to print a test page. This will enable you to ensure that the driver and print configuration are correct. Click Next.

15. Review the printer configuration and click Finish.

Now that network printers are available (assuming they didn't already exist) you can configure the Group Policy to deploy printers. From a Vista system, logged in with the rights necessary in the domain to create a GPO, perform the following steps:

1. Click Start, Run, and type `gpmc.msc`.

2. Expand Forest.

3. Expand Domains.

4. Expand the domain in which you will deploy the new GPO.

5. Expand Group Policy Objects.

6. Right-click and choose New.

7. Type a name for the new GPO and click OK.

8. Right-click the new GPO and choose Edit.

9. Expand Computer Configuration.

10. Expand Windows Settings.

11. Right-click Deployed Printers and choose Deploy Printer.

12. Click Browse, navigate to your print server, and click Select.

13. Click the printer you want to deploy and click Select.

14. Click Add to deploy the printer via GPO. You can add more than one printer. Click OK.

15. Close the GPO Editor.

In this example, we are deploying a printer for the accounting department in Building 4 (see Figure 23.4). As such, we will link the GPO to the site "Building 4" and filter the GPO by the accounting group. This will result in only the Accounting users in Building 4 getting this printer deployed.

We will perform this filtering with the following steps:

1. In the GPMC, expand Sites.

2. If your sites aren't present, right-click and choose Show Sites, select all, and click OK.

3. Right-click the site to which you want to link the Deploy Printers GPO and choose Link an Existing GPO.

4. Select the GPO from the list and click OK.

   At this point, systems located on the site to which the GPO is linked will attempt to process the GPO at startup.

5. Click the GPO linked to the site. You will receive a pop-up stating that you have selected a link rather than an actual GPO and that changes made here will affect the actual GPO. Click OK to accept this fact.

6. In the Security Filtering window, in the lower-right pane, you will see Authenticated Users listed. This is by default.

7. Click Authenticated Users and click Remove. Click Yes to confirm.

8. Click Add.

9. Type the name of the group you want to add. In this example, we'll add Accounting. Click Check Names and then click OK.

With this security filtering set, the GPO will apply only to accounting users located in the Building 4 site. Clever administrators can use this methodology to create multiple GPOs to account for all the sites and groups that they manage. In this way users can travel seamlessly between sites and get the printers that are most appropriate for their use.

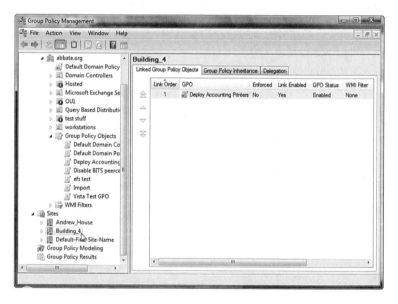

FIGURE 23.4
GPOs linked to Sites.

How to Test Whether a GPO Was Applied Correctly

Although most GPOs can be verified by simply checking the local settings to see if they've been applied, a more systematic method of testing is to query the workstation and see which GPOs it tried to apply.

Vista maintains an application that many administrators may already be familiar with, called `GPResult.exe`. By running `GPResult.exe`, the local system will report several things:

- Computer OU membership
- User OU membership
- Computer site membership
- Computer group memberships
- User group memberships
- Domain name and type
- Domain controller that provided the GPOs
- Applied Group Policies
- Filtered Group Policies

By reviewing this data, you can quickly determine which GPOs were applied and which were filtered. This allows you to quickly troubleshoot GPOs that were not applied. Often this tool will uncover issues with security filtering, inheritance blocking, or replication of GPOs between domain controllers.

Example 2—Standardizing Event Logging on Vista Clients

One of the great things that can be done with GPOs is the conforming of systems to a corporate standard. A good example of this is using a GPO to enforce logging settings on all systems of a particular type. Servers might get one set of settings, domain controllers another, and clients yet another. Setting this via GPO ensures that any system joining the domain will be conformed to the expected standard without anyone having to remember to set them.

How to Configure Event Logging

To deploy a GPO that enforces Event Logging settings, perform the following steps from a Vista system logged in with the necessary rights to create a GPO:

1. Click Start, Run, and type **gpmc.msc**.
2. Expand Forest.
3. Expand Domains.
4. Expand the domain in which you will deploy the new GPO.

   5. Expand Group Policy Objects.

   6. Right-click and choose New.

   7. Type a name for the new GPO and click OK.

   8. Right-click the new GPO and choose Edit.

   9. Expand Computer Configuration.

   10. Expand Administrative templates.

   11. Expand Windows Components.

   12. Expand Event Log Service.

   13. Click Application.

   14. In the right pane, double-click Maximum Log Size.

   15. Select Enabled, enter a Maximum Log Size, and then click OK.

   16. In the right pane, double-click Backup Log Automatically.

   17. Select Enabled and click OK.

   18. In the right pane, double-click Retain Old Events.

   19. Select Enabled and click OK.

   20. Repeat these steps for Security, Setup, and System.

   21. Close the Group Policy Editor.

Now that the settings have been standardized in the GPO, it is necessary to attach the GPO to the objects that should receive these settings. In this example, we'll assume that these settings should be applied to all client workstations but not servers.

In our sample Active Directory is an OU for Managed_Computers, and all workstations have been placed under that container. An observant administrator might wonder why computers were not left in the default Computers container. The reason for this is that the Computers container is not an OU. This means that GPOs can't be linked directly to this container. One could apply the GPO to the domain level and therefore affect all computers but in this case, we only want to affect workstations and not servers or domain controllers. Although one could place the servers in a container where inheritance is blocked, it is simpler and cleaner to put the workstations into another OU, knowing that servers and domain controllers are likely going to receive a different GPO that conforms their Event Log settings.

With the GPO built, it is ready to link to put it into use. In this example, we'll assume that there are OUs below Managed_Computers where local administrators have been delegated full control over their OUs. In our example, we'll also assume that the chief information security officer has stated that it is company policy to retain 50MB event log files and that when the logs fill, they should be backed up and retained. As such, it is necessary to ensure that local administrators cannot prevent these log settings from affecting their computers. This can be accomplished with the following steps:

1. Launch the GPMC (Start, Run, **gpmc.msc**).

2. Expand the Forest container.

3. Expand the Domains container.

4. Browse to the OU to which you plan to link the GPO.

5. Right-click the OU and choose Link an Existing GPO.

6. Choose the GPO you want and click OK.

7. Right-click the newly linked GPO in the right pane and select Enforced.

8. When prompted, click OK to change the Enforced setting.

By setting the GPO to Enforced, the GPO will ignore any Block Policy Inheritance settings on an OU in the hierarchy. Generally speaking, you should only use the Enforced flag in situations where a GPO is being used to directly enforce written IT policies.

Moving Policies Between Domains

In many situations it is useful to be able to take GPOs created in one domain and move them into another. Common scenarios for this would be in the case of a merger/acquisition or even something as simple as taking a GPO that was developed in an isolated task lab and moving it into production. You would initially expect that you'd have to print out the GPO settings and re-create the GPO from scratch with the same settings. Although this is a perfectly acceptable method of doing things, it becomes difficult and time consuming if a GPO contains a significant number of settings. In the case of needing to export or import a large GPO, the simpler solution is to use the import function that allows you to "rewrite" a backed-up GPO to reference objects in your domain. This rewrite is based on a migration table that is configurable by the administrator. Importing a GPO in this manner can be accomplished with the Group Policy Management console with the following steps:

1. Launch the GPMC (Start, Run, **gpmc.msc**).

2. Expand the Forest container.

3. Expand the Domains container and the domain containing the GPO.

4. Browse to the Group Policy Objects container.

5. Right-click the Group Policy Objects container and select Open Migration Table Editor.

6. In the table, input source objects, declare the object type, and enter the destination object (see Figure 23.5).

   For example, you might define groups from one domain and add the equivalent group from another domain as the destination. This would be helpful in GPOs where a group is being modified or granted specific rights on a system.

FIGURE 23.5
Populating the Migration Table Editor.

7. When the migration table is updated, click File, Save.

8. Enter a filename and click Save.

9. Close the editor.

Now that a translation table has been defined, a GPO can be imported. In the source domain, back up the GPO you want to migrate with the following steps:

1. Launch the GPMC (Start, Run, **gpmc.msc**).

2. Expand the Forest container.

3. Expand the Domains container.

4. Expand the Domain Object that holds the GPO you are interested in.

5. Expand Group Policy Objects.

6. Right-click the GPO in question and choose Back Up.

7. Browse to the location where you want to store the backed up GPO and enter a description. Click Back Up.

8. When the backup is completed, click OK.

Copy the backed up GPO to portable media and copy it to the system in the new domain that is running the GPMC.

To import the GPO, perform the following steps from the Group Policy Management console:

1. Launch the GPMC (Start, Run, `gpmc.msc`).

2. Expand the Forest container.

3. Expand the Domain container.

4. Expand the Domain Object that holds the GPO you are interested in.

5. Expand Group Policy Objects.

6. Right-click Group Policy Objects and select New.

7. Enter a name for the GPO that will receive the imported settings. Click OK.

8. Right-click the empty GPO that was created in step 6 and choose Import Settings.

9. The Import Wizard will launch. Click Next.

10. Because the GPO is empty, skip the backup step and click Next.

11. Browse to the location where the backup file from the other domain's GPO is stored. Click OK, then Next.

12. Select the GPO backup and click Next.

13. The Import Wizard will detect security principals and/or UNC (Universal Naming Convention) paths that are foreign. It will walk you through the translations. Click Next.

14. At the Migrating References Wizard, choose to use a migration table. Browse to the previously created migration table and click Next.

15. Review the summary and click Finish.

16. When the import succeeds, click OK.

By mastering the process of mapping security principals and UNC names and such between domains, you can quickly and easily move GPOs back and forth between multiple domains for testing and deployment purposes.

Recommended Practices with Group Policy

If you plan to use GPOs in your environment, you should develop several habits that are useful for reducing the possibilities of negatively impacting the user community when testing and deploying GPOs.

GPO Pilot OU

When linking a GPO in production, it is very helpful to initially limit the scope of who will be affected by it. Although GPOs should always be tested extensively in an isolated lab environment, in many cases a GPO can't be fully tested without access to all the production objects in Active Directory. For example, a GPO might include scripts that map network drives. It might create database connectors or even redirect the user's Documents directory to a file share. Unless all the systems involved were available in the lab, the GPO could not be fully tested. In this case, you will want to apply the GPO to a beta testing group in production first before linking it to a larger group.

The best way to handle this is to create an OU in the production Active Directory where new GPOs will be initially linked and tested. Create dedicated test accounts in addition to test workstations running the operating systems that you support in production. Utilizing Microsoft Virtual PC is an excellent way to deploy multiple operating systems into this testing OU without tying up a lot of resources. After you're comfortable with the results in production, you should then link the GPOs to the OUs they were intended to serve.

Isolating Critical Accounts

Another good habit for administrators is placing critical accounts into an OU that is filtered from receiving Group Policies. This would include accounts such as service accounts and administrative-level accounts. The goal here is to ensure that GPOs can't negatively affect the accounts that would be used to undo the negative effects.

Respecting OU Administrators

Linking a GPO can have far-reaching consequences for users. This is especially true when a GPO is linked near the top of an OU hierarchy or even at the domain level. In these situations, GPOs may affect users in OUs that are controlled by other groups or other administrators.

One of the most common OU structures in Active Directory is loosely based on geography. In these cases, different locations are separated out into OUs, and local administrative staff is delegated control. In these environments, it's critical to properly communicate the implications of GPOs to those other administrators and make sure they are okay with the new GPO.

The simplest way to pass the information to others is in the form of an HTML file. HTML, or Hypertext Markup Language, can be easily viewed from a web browser and is natively supported by the GPMC.

You can export the settings from a GPO into an XML file with the following steps:

1. Launch the GPMC (Start, Run, **gpmc.msc**).

2. Expand the Forest container.

3. Expand the Domains container.

4. Expand the Domain Object that holds the GPO you are interested in.

5. Expand Group Policy Objects.

6. Right-click the GPO you want to export a summary for and choose Save Report.

7. Enter a name for the file and save it in HTML format. (XML is also an option.)

8. Browse to the location where you want to save the file and click Save.

This HTML file can be placed on a commonly accessible web server to act as a quick reference for administrators who want to see what GPOs are currently in place in the environment. Newly proposed GPOs can be placed there as well to give OU administrators a place to look at new settings and give them an opportunity to either authorize or deny the changes before they are placed into production.

Leveraging Other People's Work

As you use GPOs more and more, you will likely make the discovery that your needs are really not that different from other companies', and odds are that most everything you are planning to implement via GPO has been done before by someone else. Rather than always reinventing the wheel, look around to see if the GPO you are considering has already been created by someone else.

A good example is the set of common scenario GPOs that have already been created by Microsoft. Many companies find themselves in need of computers that act as common workstations that might be used by people who aren't necessarily employees. Or perhaps they need a computer on a manufacturing floor that can be used for only one or two specific applications. Rather than researching all the settings necessary to create a kiosk-type machine, you can start with the work that someone else has already done.

Microsoft has published several such GPOs at the following location:

http://technet2.microsoft.com/windowsserver/en/library/
9a758138-d9c0-49bd-ae57-14fb9b6decbe1033.mspx?mfr=true

This page contains descriptions of several common desktop configuration scenarios as well as the GPOs that enforce the settings. Although these scenarios might not be a 100% match for what a particular administrator needs, they nonetheless provide excellent starting points where settings can be tweaked rather than created from scratch.

Summary

This chapter has built on the information presented in Chapter 22 to help administrators further understand how to implement and manage Group Policy Objects in order to make the management of Vista systems easier. It has also offered advice on how to manage users and computers to ensure that GPO manipulation can't accidentally cause problems in the enterprise.

Administrators should take the opportunity to get more familiar and confident with GPOs in a lab environment and use the processes given in this chapter to implement the GPOs into production with minimal impact to the domain.

Index

Numbers and Symbols

A

B

GPOs (Group Policy Objects), 329-330, 567

restoring from, 325-328

Windows Backup, 17, 426

Balanced power plan, 238

base scores, 62

.bat files, 338

batteries

battery status, viewing in Mobility Center, 235

critical battery alarms, 244

low battery alarms, 243-244

BCDEdit.exe utility, 520

BDD (Business Desktop Deployment Kit) 2007

deploying Windows Vista with Systems Management Server

deployment points, 548

Image Capture CDs, 550

image deployment process, 550

overview, 547-548

deploying Windows Vista with Windows Deployment Services

adding images to Windows DS, 545

image deployment process, 546-547

operational modes, 545

overview, 542-543

WDSUTIL utility, 545

Windows DS installation, 543-544

Windows Server 2008, 547

deployment points

configuring, 541-542

creating, 539-540

overview, 539

updating, 542

Deployment Workbench, 530

Distribution Shares, 533-536

Information Center

Components section, 532-533

Documentation section, 531

News section, 532

Management Packs, 529

migrating systems to Windows Vista

Application Compatibility Toolkit (ACT), 553-554

LoadState, 557-558

Office Migration Planning Manager, 559-560

overview, 551-552

ScanState, 555-556

User State Migration Tool (USMT), 555-558

Volume Activation Management tool, 558

Windows Vista Hardware Assessment Tool, 552-553

overview, 527-529

system builds, 536-538

system requirements, 529-530

Big Endian, 247

M

O

S

U

The **Management and Administration** series goes far beyond the basic installation and setup information found in many other resources. These books look at day-to-day administration, best practices, tips, and step-by-step configurations based on real-world examples found in the industry.

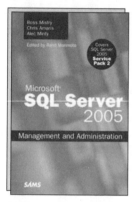

Microsoft® SQL Server 2005 Management and Administration
ISBN: 0672329565

Microsoft® Windows Vista® Management and Administration
ISBN: 0672329611